CHINESE IMPERIAL CITY PLANNING

CHINESE IMPERIAL
CITY PLANNING

NANCY SHATZMAN STEINHARDT

UNIVERSITY OF HAWAII PRESS

HONOLULU

© 1990 University of Hawaii Press

Printed in the United States of America

90 91 92 93 94 95   5 4 3 2 1

Library of Congress Cataloging-in-Publication Data

Steinhardt, Nancy Shatzman.

Chinese imperial city planning / Nancy Shatzman Steinhardt.

p.   cm.

Includes bibliographical references.

ISBN 0-8248-1244-1 (alk. paper)

1.   City planning—China—History.   I.   Title.

NA9265.S8   1990

711'.4'0951—dc20   89-20541

CIP

University of Hawaii Press books are printed

on acid-free paper and meet the guidelines

for permanence and durability of the Council

on Library Resources.

TO PAUL

CONTENTS

PREFACE

THIS book began with questions about one Chinese imperial city. The city was the capital built by Khubilai Khan in China, and the questions ranged from what buildings had stood in that city to why the buildings were arranged as they were. Had there been a preconceived plan, and if so, to what degree of specificity? Who was the planner, and why had this plan been implemented? Was the city plan a traditional one, part of a Chinese urban design system already in place in the thirteenth century, or did this city bear obvious signs of the non-Chinese heritage of its chief resident? Research conducted between 1978 and 1980 into literary documents and physical evidence proved that it was possible to recover the plan of a thirteenth-century Chinese city and to compile a list of its major architectural monuments. In fact, for Khubilai's city it was possible to describe building by building what had stood there. Furthermore, the evidence gave way to the at first surprising determination that the plan of the city was very much a Chinese one, exhibiting no sign of the Mongolian origins of its ruling occupants.

Khubilai's city of Dadu—more specifically, its plan—became the focus of my dissertation. Upon the completion of my thesis in 1981 I began another investigation of Chinese imperial cities, one directed at the evolution of the imperial Chinese plan. To those with knowledge of civilizations other than China, the question of the evolution of form may seem trivial. For the Chinese imperial city plan, however, not only could one make the standard association of nonevolution of form as symbolic of participation in the august Chinese past, but there existed as well an often quoted and occasionally illustrated passage from a classical text that described Wangcheng ("Ruler's City"). This passage has been the starting point, almost without exception, of every discussion of the Chinese city—indeed, a theory of urbanism based on this text was almost universally accepted even before data to prove it were available.

As recently as the 1970s, there did not exist a historical survey in which the plans of all major Chinese imperial cities were reproduced and discussed. By the early 1980s the results of Chinese excavation at a wide range of cities over a thirty-year period had finally become available, and suddenly Chinese and Japanese researchers became interested in Chinese city planning. Five books on the subject appeared after 1980, by Murata Jiro, Dong Jianhong, Wu Liangyong, and two by He Yeju. All of them begin with the classical description of Wangcheng; and one, by He, is devoted to the relationship between the literary passage and the Chinese city.

In 1981, I began without the preconceived notion that Chinese imperial planning occurred in a certain way because a classical text said that it should. To prove this, it was necessary first to survey the full range of available material. I turned, therefore, to the earliest literary, archaeological, and visual evidence of imperial Chinese urbanism and continued through evidence of Beijing, the most recent capital. My research into other Chinese cities quickly showed that the four types of documentary evidence which I had found for Khubilai's city —accounts of native and non-Chinese residents (sometimes with very different impressions of the same thing), officially sponsored publications and publications by scholar-officials of the premodern centuries, scholarly literature from China and Japan, and excavation reports of the capital—also existed to some extent for almost every earlier and later Chinese capital. Furthermore, accompanying some of the literature was a fifth type of evidence: plans.

The reliability of the plans varied as that of the literary sources, but I took them as primary sources nevertheless. The premodern plans were especially interesting for they were evidence of how artists or draftsmen visualized, or were told to visualize, an urban environment. The most noteworthy comparisons arose when a plan published with a premodern written description such as a local or provincial record could be placed alongside the postexcavation plan and description of the same city. The plans proved, for instance, that the two-dimensional drawings of some cities, such as the second and first century B.C. capital Chang'an, had been rendered accurately in size and shape in its earliest known versions of the first millennium A.D.; and other cities, from later times with more accurate means of measuring, notably the city at Kaifeng in the tenth to twelfth centuries, had only once in the last thousand years been somewhat accurately described in plan. As for the site of Wangcheng, excavators' plans proved that the first millennium B.C. city built there did not correspond in any specific way to the text. More significant, plans of excavated cities made it clear that indeed all Chinese imperial city plans share numerous features, but the notion of a single nonevolutionary planning system in China is far too simplistic. This book presents an explanation of a multifaceted evolutionary process of Chinese imperial city planning. It also explains why one finds great discrepancies between textual descriptions, accompanying and later plans, and archaeologically confirmed plans.

Research for this book began during my last year as a Junior Fellow at Harvard University. Without that year of support, I probably would never have initiated such a wide-ranging study. Between 1983 and 1985 I taught courses on the Chinese city at Bryn Mawr College and the University of Pennsylvania. During approximately the same time period I gave talks about Chinese imperial planning at Columbia, Cornell, Harvard, MIT, Penn, Princeton, Stanford, SUNY–Binghamton, and the University of Washington. Thus I had opportunities to direct my research to students who had little or no background in urban planning or Chinese studies and also to colleagues whose expertise ranged from art history, to archaeology, to city planning, to sinology. This book addresses both groups. The introduction is intended both as an explanation of the fundamental issues of imperial planning in pre-modern China and as general background information necessary for students to begin research on Chinese cities. The chronological discussion of cities in the chapters that follow is, in contrast to the introduction, based upon my reading of primary sources, scholarly discussions of them, and actual plans.

Research in China in 1983 was made possible by a summer stipend from the National Endowment for the Humanities; during academic year 1984–1985 I was aided by a postdoctoral fellowship from the American Council of Learned Societies. Photograph purchases and other illustration costs were defrayed by a grant from the Research Foundation, University of Pennsylvania.

I have discussed this manuscript with teachers, colleagues, and friends for the last five years and have benefited from each encounter. I would particularly like to thank Chan Hok-lam, Chang Kwang-chih, Albert Dien, Huang Yunsheng, Ronald Knapp, Barbara Miller Lane, Jonathan Lane, Susan Naquin, David Phillips, and Denis Twitchett for reading (and in several cases rereading) sections of the manuscript at various stages and for advice, comments, criticism, and encouragement. I would also like to thank Fu Xinian, Guo Husheng, Hou Renzhi, Liu Kaiji, Frederick Mote, Nathan Sivin, Tanaka Tan, and Xu Pingfang for important discussions or correspondence about Chinese urbanism. For advice about the focus and potential audience for this book I thank Renata Holod, Victor Mair, Judith Smith, and Michael Tomlan.

At least half of the photographs published here have gone through serious transformations in order to be used. Whether their original versions were published during the war years of the 1930s and 1940s in China or Japan, or in the post-1949 era in China, many began as casual sketches on poor-quality paper. The painstaking work of H. Fred Schoch and John Taggart of the University Museum, University of Pennsylvania, and of the staff at the University of Hawaii Press, to all of whom I owe tremendous thanks, brought the illustrations to the forms in which they appear here. In some cases I have decided that a graphically inferior plan was interesting or important enough for what it illustrated to warrant publication, and I take full responsibility for that decision. The map of China and several of the maps of the primary capital sites through history were drawn by Huang Yunsheng.

Strong support for this book by the University of Hawaii Press was apparent from the beginning. In particular I thank editors Patricia Crosby and Eileen D'Araujo for their commitment to the manuscript and the final product. I also thank copy editor Don Yoder.

Finally, I thank Paul, our children, and my parents, without whose goodwill and enthusiasm this book would still not be finished.

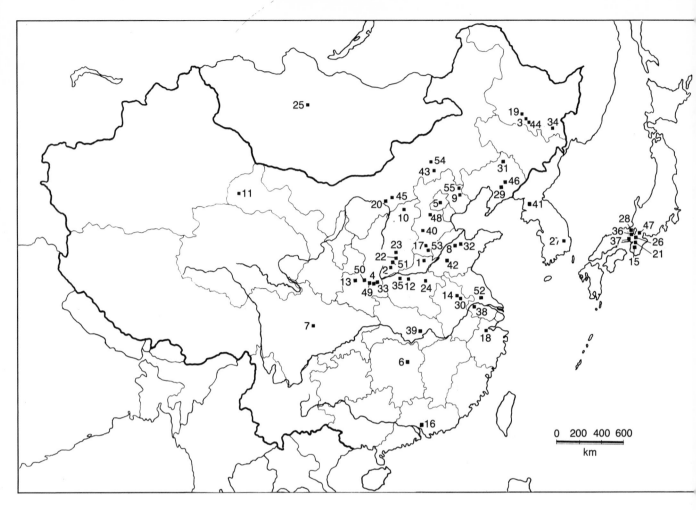

1. Anyang	15. Fujiwara-kyō	29. Liaoyang	43. Shangdu
2. Anyi	16. Guangzhou	30. Linhao	44. Shangjing (Jin)
3. Baicheng	17. Handan	31. Linhuang	45. Shengle
4. Banpo	18. Hangzhou	32. Linzi	46. Shenyang
5. Beijing	19. Harbin	33. Lishan	47. Shigaraki
6. Changsha	20. Heicheng (Khara-Khoto)	34. Longquan Fu	48. Xiadu
7. Chengdu	21. Heijo-kyō (Nara)	35. Luoyang	49. Xi'an
8. Chengziyai	22. Houma	36. Nagaoka-kyō	50. Xianyang
9. Dading Fu	23. Jiang	37. Naniwa-kyō	51. Xintian
10. Datong	24. Kaifeng	38. Nanjing	52. Yangzhou
11. Dunhuang	25. Khara-Khorum	39. Panlongcheng	53. Ye
12. Erlitou	26. Kuni-kyō	40. Pingshan	54. Yingchang Lu
13. Fengchu	27. Kyongju	41. Pyongyang	55. Zhongjing (Liao)
14. Fengyang	28. Kyōto	42. Qufu	

Map of cities and sites

I

INTRODUCTION

ONE of the immediate directives of the newly founded government of the People's Republic of China in the autumn of 1949 was the redesign of Beijing, the site of a capital for most of the last thousand years of Chinese imperial history. Specifically targeted for overhaul were the city's age-old focus—the 250 acres known as the Forbidden City (Figure 1) and the 4.5-kilometer approach northward to it from the south gate of the outer city wall—and former imperial spots scattered throughout the city (Figure 2). After some debate, the new city planners agreed that an international symbol of China like the Forbidden City could not simply be torn down. Yet neither, they decided, would it be appropriate to honor past regimes by leaving unaltered their imperial monuments. Thus was conceived one of the most dramatic architectural transformations of this century: palace square to people's square, a three-dimensional manifestation of "letting the past serve the present" (Figures 3 and 4).

Although never so tersely stated, the past's service of the present was a central issue in the planning of each of the five dynastic capitals built between the tenth and seventeenth centuries whose ruins are today covered by the metropolis Beijing. Indeed, the search for a spatial arrangement that would symbolize state goals, satisfy but not compromise the needs of the leader, and recognize the ties of a particular regime to its past was not exclusively a goal of Beijing's most famous ruler-planners Khubilai Khan (1215–1294), Emperor Yongle (1360–1424), or Chairman Mao (1893–1976). The ideal capital city plan had been a profound concern of each empire builder and his descendants on Chinese soil; it was an issue discussed and debated by the Chinese government in every age.

Through the centuries very specific and even peculiar imperial whims have been satisfied by capital city plans in China. Still, what has traditionally

Figure 1. Aerial view of Forbidden City, Beijing, in the twentieth century. [Yan Chongnian, *Zhongguo lidai ducheng gongyuan,* front plate]

been viewed as a most impressive feature of the Chinese capital plan is its homage to the past and deference to the imperial planning tradition that has come before it. This bond is so strong that, in spite of the true evolution of the city plan and variations in design that are explained in this book, all Chinese royal cities of the last four thousand years do share certain architectural features regardless of when they were built, their locations, or the nationalities of their patrons.

Yet, for almost as long as imperial city buildings, some of their locations, and certain spaces within

the city have been standardized and prescribed, the arrangement of the largest city spaces that encompass them has varied. The number of uniform features is so great, and their similar architectural detail even over the course of thousands of years is at times so striking, that the different possibilities resulting in two-dimensional plans have either gone unnoticed or have been dismissed as inconsequential. In fact, three fundamentally different designs were created for imperial cities in China by the first millennium B.C., and each is traceable for more than another thousand years of Chinese urban plan-

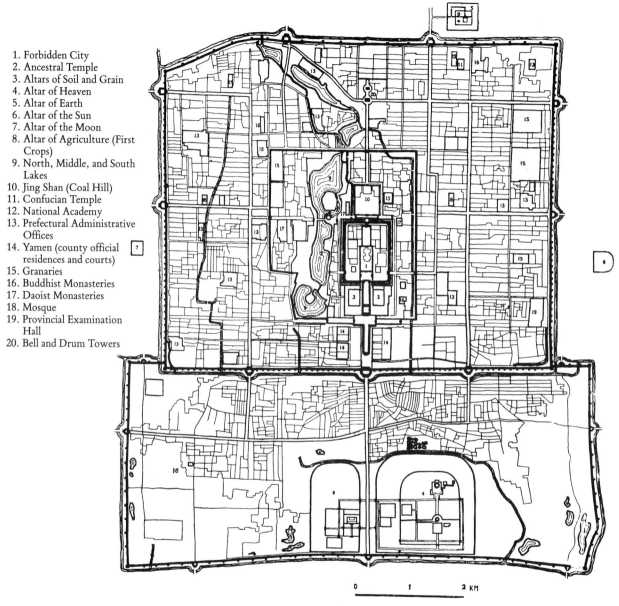

1. Forbidden City
2. Ancestral Temple
3. Altars of Soil and Grain
4. Altar of Heaven
5. Altar of Earth
6. Altar of the Sun
7. Altar of the Moon
8. Altar of Agriculture (First Crops)
9. North, Middle, and South Lakes
10. Jing Shan (Coal Hill)
11. Confucian Temple
12. National Academy
13. Prefectural Administrative Offices
14. Yamen (county official residences and courts)
15. Granaries
16. Buddhist Monasteries
17. Daoist Monasteries
18. Mosque
19. Provincial Examination Hall
20. Bell and Drum Towers

Figure 2. Plan of Beijing from the seventeenth through the nineteenth centuries showing imperial and administrative buildings. [*Zhongguo jianzhu jianshi*, fig. 6–12]

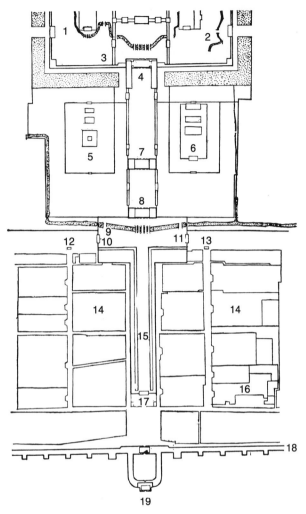

1. West Hua Gate
2. East Hua Gate
3. Forbidden City
4. Wu Gate
5. Altars of Soil and Grain
6. Ancestral Temple
7. Duan Gate
8. Chengtian Gate
9. Imperial-City Wall
10. Chang'an Right Gate
11. Chang'an Left Gate
12. West Gongsheng Gate
13. East Gongsheng Gate
14. Official Bureaus
15. Qianbulang ("Thousand-Pace Corridor")
16. Hospital
17. Da Ming (Qing) Gate
18. Inner-City Wall
19. Zhengyang Gate

Figure 3. Beijing palace-place—focus of the imperial city beginning in the fifteenth century. [Hou and Wu, *Wenwu* no. 9 (1977), p. 7]

ning. These schemes and their significance will be explored beginning in Chapter 2, after the shared characteristics and architectural components of the city, major urban sites, and key terminology for the study of Chinese city planning are described.

The elements that comprise every Chinese imperial city, and make it recognizable, are not necessarily exclusive to China. Beijing in the fifteenth century or imperial Chang'an in the eighth had palaces, royal monasteries, mausoleums, shrines, altars, parks, government offices, granaries, workshops, treasuries, and libraries, as did Rome, St. Petersburg, Constantinople, and Isfahan in their imperial ages. Yet in China the buildings and their locations within the city were preestablished by age-old traditions set forth in revered literature or documents of the classical age.

The reason every Chinese capital including the present one of Beijing is so closely tied to the scheme of earlier rulers' cities can be explained by the particular Chinese context of the two words imperial and planning. In China as elsewhere the ruler's power and authority were unchallenged, but in China, in addition, an emperor's reign was always compared to the exemplary models of rulership of former emperors and even preimperial dynasts. The form of the capital city and its architecture were just two of the many means the emperor used to display his legitimized position as both ruler and guardian of tradition. The alteration of an accepted design was therefore considered a challenge to the imperial past. The imperial city was such a powerful symbol of rule that a nonnative conqueror would always choose to implement a Chinese design instead of plans more reminiscent of his homeland.

The Chinese ruler was more than an absolute authority. He was the Son of Heaven, an intermediary between human labors and heavenly favor. His virtue and proper performance ensured the sta-

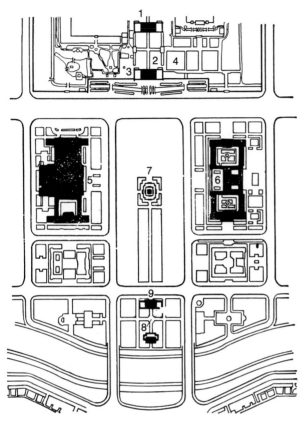

1. Duan Gate
2. Tian'an Gate (former Chengtian Gate)
3. Sun Yat-sen Park
4. Workers' Cultural Palace
5. Great Hall of the People
6. Museum of the Chinese

Revolution, Museum of Chinese History
7. Monument to the People's Heroes
8. Former site of Zhengyang Gate
9. Mausoleum of Chairman Mao

Figure 4. Tian'an Men Square, Beijing, 1958–1980s—focus of the capital of the People's Republic of China. [Hou and Wu, *Wenwu* no. 9 (1977), p. 11]

bility of the state and guaranteed a pacified world. Although an artisan or engineer was needed to draw the plan, it was only through imperial participation that the city could be constructed. Before laying the foundation for a new city, heaven had to be consulted. The site and date of groundbreaking had to be confirmed by heaven in advance. The city's architecture was often named for auspicious heavenly bodies or lucky numbers.[1]

Planning in a premodern Chinese context meant more than simply the abstract notion that a city scheme was conceived in its entirety from its inception—remarkable though it is that planning was conducted this way over the course of four thousand years of one nation's history. In traditional China, planning also meant that a plan was drawn. The earliest known Chinese site plan is from the first millennium B.C., but literary descriptions of cities suggest that they were conceived as two-dimensional plans even earlier.

The importance of the plans cannot be overemphasized. First of all, they are tangible and specific evidence of the shape and interior spaces of cities. (Size and orientation are not specified on the plans until modern times.) Second, variant plans made in later premodern centuries of earlier cities allow for discriminating comparisons between plans and written records. Plans based on excavation at city sites provide yet another level of comparative accuracy.

In China the imperial city is more than the ruler's capital. It is an institution. It is an articulated concept for which a design is drawn and about which ideology—namely purpose and meaning—has been written, accepted, and transmitted through the ages. All this took place long before most imperial cities as we know them today were built.

CHARACTERISTICS

A steadfast commitment to the supremacy of an imperial plan established in the remote past underlies all later imperial planning in China. As a consequence, all of the fundamental planning principles should also be uniform. Most of the characteristics of Chinese imperial planning can be seen in Figure 2, the plan of seventeenth-century Beijing.

The fundamental feature of the Chinese imperial city is four-sided enclosure. Every Chinese imperial city is encased by four outer walls which meet at right angles to form a rectangle. Within the walls are at least one and sometimes two or more sets of walls that define smaller rectangular enclosures. Inside the smaller enclosures palatial sectors are elevated. Until the fourteenth century the material of outer enclosures was most often pounded earth. In later times outer walls were sometimes faced with brick. Smaller enclosures were generally constructed with plaster walls or pillared arcades. The most extensive enclosure of all, the Great Wall of China, was built of pounded earth beginning in the first millennium B.C.

Outer and inner city walls were pierced by gates (Figure 5), the second characteristic of the Chinese imperial city. Often, but not always, three gates were found at each outer wall face for a total of twelve. Ideally, gates of opposite city walls were equidistant from the adjoining wall corners. Inner cities of the imperial capital generally had no more than one gate at each side. One central gate always was placed at a south city wall. Most city wall gates were built for entrance or exit by a land route, usually a major urban thoroughfare, but some imperial cities had sluice gates as well.

Another feature of Chinese imperial city outer

Figure 5. City walls of Xi'an (Ming dynasty). [Steinhardt photograph]

walls was the defensive projection, which took the form of a lookout tower or a protective battlement. Lookout towers were built at the four corners of a city and atop city gates, where troops could be quartered (Figures 6 and 7; see also Figure 5). The two types of battlements most common in Chinese imperial cities were *wengcheng* and *mamian*. *Wengcheng* were additional walls built in front of gates. They projected in front of and up to outer wall gates, with their own openings for access to the city (see Figure 6). *Mamian*, literally "horse faces," alternately known as *yangma*, were simply additional fortified perimeter space that curved around the outer city wall at intervals, providing no access to the city interior. The use of *mamian* in medieval China is confirmed by an illustration in the eleventh-century military treatise *Wujing zongyao* (Collection of important military techniques) (Figure 8). Both defensive *wengcheng* and *mamian* were also used at nonimperial Chinese cities.

The plan of imperial Beijing in Figure 2 shows that major north–south and east–west streets crossed the city at right angles. Often the city roads and avenues ran from a northern to a corresponding southern gate, or from an eastern to a western one, giving way to a design feature that can be called clearly articulated and directed space. The principal north–south thoroughfare ran along a line that passed through the central northern and southern gates of each city wall. Parallel to the gate-initiated streets in both directions were smaller avenues, and parallel to them were *xiang* and *hutong*, east–west and north–south oriented lanes and alleys. The unambiguous articulation of north–south and east–west space was such that even the city's smallest regions were encased by walls or streets that ran perpendicular to one another. Seen from above, the

Figure 6. Heyi Gate with *wengcheng*, western outer wall of Dadu, Yuan period, now destroyed. ["Yuan Dadu de kancha," *Kaogu* no. 1 (1972), pl. 8]

Figure 7. Corner watchtower of imperial Beijing. [Courtesy of University of Pennsylvania slide collection, slide no. 153P3795 I/INN(B)]

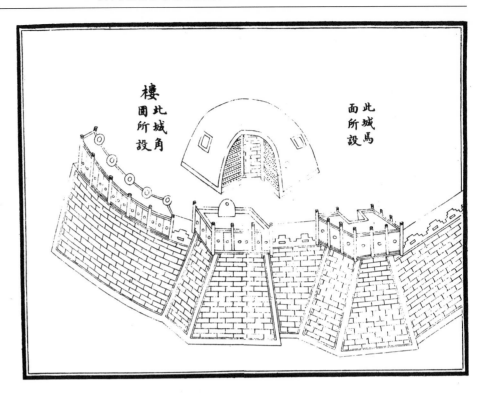

樓
圍此
所城
設角

此城
面馬
所設

Figure 8. *Mamian (yang-ma)*. [After Zeng, *Wujing zongyao* (ca. 1040), *Siku quanshu zhenben chuji* no. 167, pp. 8a–b]

city of Beijing appeared as a checkerboard in maps drawn during the reign of the Qianlong emperor (r. 1736–1796) (Figure 9), and the image is still apparent in a twentieth-century photograph of Xi'an, formerly an imperial city (Figure 10). Orientation of the streets, like the walls, was according to the four cardinal directions—symbolically the clearly demarcated boundaries of the Chinese empire.

The four-sided Chinese city is a physical manifestation of the traditional belief in a square-shaped universe, bounded by walls, with the Son of Heaven at its center. Tradition associates each of the four world quarters and the center with a symbolic animal, color, metal, season (excluding the center in this case), and a host of other phenomena.[2] South, for instance, is the direction of summer, fire, the bird (often a phoenix), and the color

vermilion.[3] South is the cardinal direction the emperor faced when seated in his hall of audience, and thus most of the imperial buildings of an imperial city have a southern exposure. Continuing around the square, east is the quadrant of spring, wood, and the azure dragon; north is winter, water, and the black tortoise; west is autumn, metal, and the white tiger. Autumn and white are associated with death in Chinese culture, fall being the season of decay that, after the freezing of winter, will give way to new life and renewal in the spring. Thus tombs are often constructed north or west of the capital, the quadrants of death and decay. The names of imperial city structures also reflect attitudes toward cosmological alignment. At many Chinese imperial cities the palace of the crown prince or another hall is named Taiji, a reference to the polar star, and the Forbidden City of

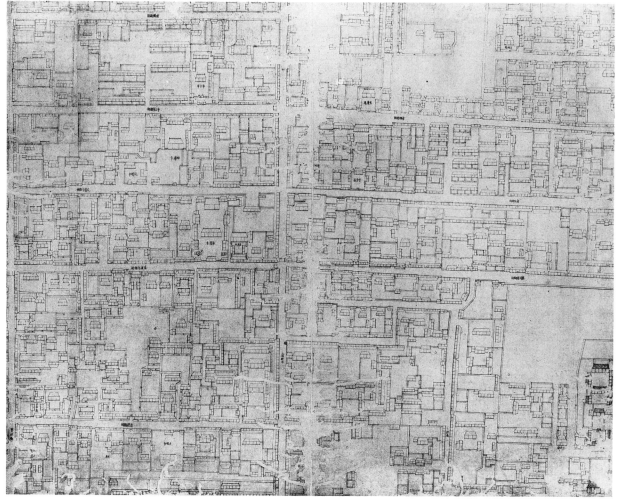

Figure 9. Plan of Beijing in the eighteenth century showing orientation to cardinal directions of streets, lanes, and alleys. [Imanishi, *"Genryūkyō-jō zenzu,"* folio 2, p. 5]

Beijing is known as Zijin Cheng, the Polar Forbidden City.

Four-sided enclosure of the city and cardinal orientation of its major routes lent themselves to the further enclosure of virtually every city sector according to the four cardinal directions. Bounded regions of the city made census taking and population control possible even in the late first millen-

nium B.C. By the time of the seventh through ninth centuries a sophisticated system of one hundred eight walled wards was in place in the capital Chang'an (Figure 11). Just a century later the ward system would be a weak reflection of its former self, but the practice of dividing the city into governmentally controlled spaces that were inhabited predominantly by peoples of one occupational, reli-

Figure 10. Aerial view of Xi'an in the twentieth century. [Photo collection of the late E. A. Gutkind, printed with the permission of the late G. Gutkind]

gious, or ethnic group persisted in Beijing into the twentieth century.

Easy access to a good water supply also is essential to the plan of every Chinese imperial city. In addition to choosing a site near an abundant water source, the Chinese capital was usually surrounded by a moat, and human-directed waterways were channeled into the city. The Three Lakes of Beijing (see Figure 2, no. 9) are an example of an artificial water source dug in the twelfth century that was preserved by each subsequent dynasty.

Vast size may also be considered characteristic of the Chinese imperial city. Until Beijing in the fifteenth century, most Chinese capitals were the largest cities in the world during their times of flourishing. Beijing shown in Figure 2 encompassed an area of 62 square kilometers. In the seventh century the outer wall of the capital Chang'an spanned a distance of 36.7 kilometers. In the Warring States period (481–ca. 256 B.C.) the capital of just one state, Yan, was about 32 square kilometers.

Related to the size of the Chinese imperial city is another feature: its population. Until the fourteenth or fifteenth century most primary Chinese capitals had the largest urban populations in the world. Means of assessing the population of traditional Chinese cities vary from strict reading of local records to educated interpolations of them, and opinions differ about the validity of counting resident military in urban population figures. It is generally agreed, however, that both Chang'an in the eighth century and Beijing at the end of the sixteenth had populations of one million. The tenth through thirteenth century Song dynasty capitals at modern-day Kaifeng and Hangzhou had populations of well over one million; even the early Chinese capitals of Chang'an in the last centuries B.C. and Luoyang in the first and second centuries A.D. had at least three hundred thousand people.[4]

One reason for the huge concentration of people in Chinese capitals was the common imperial practice of relocating masses of the population. If historical texts can be trusted, then at times hundreds of thousands of people were transferred to new capital cities. The lower echelons of society functioned as builders of new imperial projects, the upper classes were state servants, and those in the middle served as merchants, artisans, and commercial agents for the newly transplanted urban population.

Another characteristic of the Chinese imperial

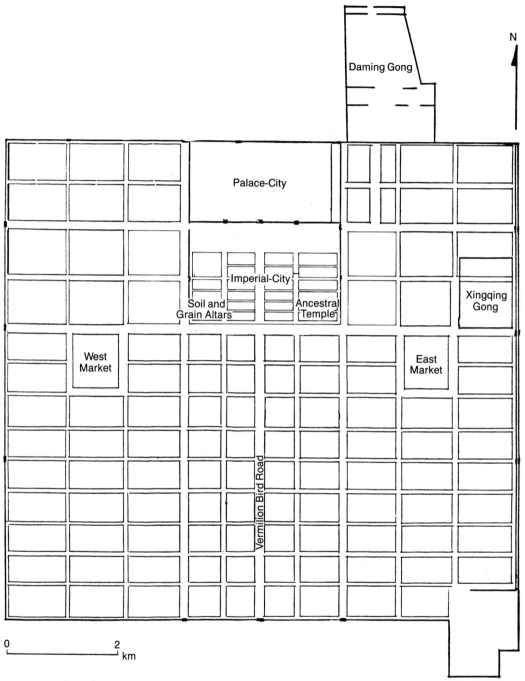

Figure II. Plan of Sui Daxing–Tang Chang'an showing its one hundred and eight wards. [Hou and Wu, *Wenwu* no. 9 (1977), p. 2]

Figure 12. *The Diviner Inspects [a Site] for a Dwelling.* [Sun Jianai, *Shu jing tu shuo, juan* 32/2b]

ditionally been concerns for imperial city builders are the location of protective mountains (or in their absence an artificial hill) to the capital's north and water to the south.

The final characteristic of Chinese imperial city planning has not always been possible to implement, but it should be mentioned. Ideally the Chinese imperial city was planned in entirety from its inception and was constructed beginning with the outer wall. At times building inside the outer wall occurred before the enclosure was complete, but the size and shape of the wall, and thus the enormous size of imperial cities in China, were rarely accidental.

Eleven features thus characterize imperial city planning in China: four-sided enclosure, gates, defensive projections, clearly articulated and directed space, orientation and alignment, the ward system, accessibility of water, vast size, huge population, siting, and building order.

COMPONENTS

The two-word designation "imperial city" calls to mind imperial Rome, St. Petersburg, Constantinople, Isfahan, Fatehpur Sikri, and premodern Beijing. The image is one of monumental architecture replete with signs and symbols of the monarch: one or more palaces, imperial cathedrals or other institutions of kingly faith, mausoleums, and structures of particular cultural significance, be they shrines, altars, or memorials. An imperial city also had its sectors of pleasure and privacy, arenas or gardens, for instance, and all the supporting structures necessary to maintain imperial life such as kitchens, granaries, workshops, treasuries, and libraries.

The Chinese imperial city is part of this group in name, and it shares many of the manmade forms that give an imperial city its image. Foremost among them are the ruler's palace, the architecture of the state religion (in the Chinese city, places for

city may be called siting. Siting describes the belief that natural phenomena—mountains, wind, water —must be harmoniously interrelated at a site in order to ensure auspicious human existence. The practice of divination for the purpose of determining a positive balance of natural forces before selecting a site is often called *fengshui* or *kanyu,* both sometimes translated as Chinese geomancy.[5] References to the process by which a site was chosen are found in early Chinese written and illustrative records (Figure 12). Aspects of siting that have tra-

imperial ceremonies directed toward heaven), and royal tombs. Yet two important factors distinguish the Chinese imperial city from the others listed above. First, each of the cities except Beijing is associated with a specific period in a country's history, whereas Chinese sites and their architectural components have endured for millennia. Second, in China the locations of imperial buildings were standard. In fact, the positions of imperial structures are more standardized than the city plans.

A Chinese city cannot be imperial without a palace. In China the word *gong,* usually translated as "palace," refers to a group of palatial halls enclosed by a four-sided wall or covered arcade and interrelated by courtyards and adjoining covered ways or corridors. Palace complexes in premodern China often have three main buildings as their focus. The buildings are oriented toward the cardinal direction south and are located on the major north–south line of the city that encompasses them on at least three sides. Sometimes only the front and back of the three halls are actual structures, each wider in the east–west dimension, and the middle building is replaced by an adjoining covered way. The resulting shape of the three halls, or two halls and corridor, resembles the Chinese character *gong* (a different character than the above-mentioned palace complex), and the architectural arrangement is therefore referred to as a *gong* plan. A *gong* scheme can be seen just above no. 1 in Figure 2.[6]

Two different types of halls are found within the palace precinct of every Chinese imperial city. One is for holding court, imperial audiences, or state ceremonies. The second is a private, residential chamber. In the Chinese city the more public imperial halls are referred to as *chao,* literally "court," often translated as hall of audience. *Chao* stand south (or in front according to Chinese descriptive terminology) of *qin,* the private or residential halls. An imperial city of the magnitude of Beijing in the seventeenth century had more than one of each type

of building. There the southern group of three halls forming a *gong* plan were all ceremonial, and the three halls which formed a *gong* scheme behind them were residential. Later the three back halls became ceremonial as well, and residences were moved east and west of the main north–south imperial line.

Since early imperial times working and residential space for government officials was maintained inside the city walls. Initially the official bureaus and the homes of their employees were in the vicinity of the palace compound, and proximity to the emperor was a sign of rank. By the late sixth century, however, the offices of government were enclosed within their own walled city, called *huang-cheng*—the administrative-city or, more literally, the imperial-city. The imperial-city was distinct from the walled enclosure *gongcheng,* the palace-city, which accommodated only the residential and private halls of the emperor and his immediate relatives. From here on the two walled regions *gong-cheng* and *huangcheng* will be translated by the hyphenated terms "palace-city" and "imperial-city" (or administrative-city), respectively.

A large open palace-place (see Figure 2 near nos. 2, 3, and 14) has been a standard component of the Chinese imperial city since the first millennium A.D. The focus on the palace-place as the city center is sharpened by a several-mile-long approach to it from due south, a road which is then continued as the major north–south axis through the city. The approach to the palace-place, called the imperial-way *(yudao),* usually has three lanes, one for passage toward the throne, one for passage away from the throne, and a central lane for imperial passage. Palace-place and imperial-way combine in premodern Chinese cities to form a T—clearly visible at the approach to the imperial-city in sixteenth-century Beijing. (See Figure 3 and Figure 2 between nos. 14.)

Beyond the palace-city were altars for imperial

sacrifices. Even though the Chinese emperor was not a devotee of a religion in the Western sense, he did look to the heavens for blessings, and the Chinese people looked to him as their intermediary between heavenly favor and human labors. Therefore, at set times each year the emperor went out from the palace-city to suburban altars to perform sacrifices and to pray to heaven on behalf of earthly concerns. In the first millennium B.C. only altars to the imperial ancestors and to soil and grain were built at the imperial city. By the fifteenth century the number of imperial sacrificial spots in the Chinese capital had more than tripled. The altars themselves were often exposed to the heavens, but they were always built inside of walled compounds. The altars of imperial Beijing, shown in Figure 2, are described below.

The Altars of Soil and Grain (She Tan and Ji Tan) (Figure 2, no. 3) were twin altars on the west side of the imperial city, sometimes located directly opposite the Ancestral Temple. On the Soil Altar were placed five colors of earth: vermilion, azure, black, and white at positions corresponding to the four directions, and yellow earth at the center spilled onto the four sides. The Grain Altar was covered only with yellow earth.

Altar of Heaven (Tian Tan) is the common name for a group of three structures that still stand at what was the far south, east of the main axis of seventeenth-century Beijing (Figure 2, no. 4; see also Figure 153). In the sixteenth century the horseshoe-shaped Tian Tan complex included numerous buildings for the emperor's presacrificial preparation and for the storage of ceremonial objects, in addition to the one exposed altar and two covered structures that stand today. By that time sacrifices to heaven had supplanted all other imperial devotion, even sacrifices to the imperial ancestors.[7]

The Altar of Agriculture (Nengye Tan), alternately known as the Altar of the First Crops (Xiannong Tan) (Figure 2, no. 8), was located opposite the Altar of Heaven. Initially this altar was intended for ceremonies honoring the first crops of the year; in 1532 the emperor added twin altars to heaven and earth and an altar for the worship of the planet Jupiter at the same site.

Other altars of the Chinese imperial city were erected to the earth (Di Tan; Figure 2, no. 5), the sun (Ri Tan; Figure 2, no. 6), the moon (Yue Tan; Figure 2, no. 7), and silkworms (Xiancan Tan), the latter built in the sixteenth century on an island in the West Park (Three Lakes) (Figure 2, no. 9) where the empress performed the rite of cocoon washing.

Different from the exposed suburban altars was the Ancestral Temple (Tai Miao or Zong Miao). It was the main building of an architectural complex entered by the ruler to pay homage to the founder of the dynasty, his wife, and other imperial ancestors, whose names were entered on tablets in the temple. The Ancestral Temple stood to the east of the main axis of the imperial city, left of the audience hall as one faced south (Figure 2, no. 2).

Beginning in the fifth century, temples and great monasteries to Buddhism and Daoism could be seen in Chinese imperial cities. In later centuries religious edifices for less popular foreign faiths were also erected. Often the emperor or his wives and concubines practiced several religions, so neither permanent imperial religious monuments nor standard locations for them were established at the capital. Buddhist temple complexes were called *si* and Daoist monasteries *guan* or *gong* (the same character used for palace complex).

Three temples (*miao*) dedicated to native Chinese heroes were also constant features of the imperial city landscape. The most important was the temple to Confucius. First built in the capital of the state of Lü (today Qufu in Shandong province) immediately following the death of the sage in the fifth century B.C., in later centuries Confucian temples were built in all major Chinese cities. The main hall of a Confucian temple, Dacheng Hall, housed a tablet inscribed with Confucius' name, rather than his statue (Figure 13). Tablets honoring other Confucian disciples could be placed in the same temple complex, or independent temples or temple complexes to the disciples could be built.

Balancing the Confucian, or civil official's, temple in the Chinese capital was a temple dedicated to the military god Guandi and by extension to military officials. The main Guandi Temple in China is in Yuncheng, Shanxi province (Figure 14). A third temple found in every Chinese capital, and in other cities of import, was the City-God Temple (Chenghuang Miao).[8] Thus the Chinese word *miao* can refer to a temple dedicated to a historical or popular legendary figure or to a local god.

Three ritual buildings mentioned in early texts about Chinese imperial cities may be considered components of the planned capital, even though they were not always constructed. Like dynastic altars, the ritual spaces were the sites of imperial ceremonies, but they served other purposes also. Descriptions of the three ritual spaces, and records of their locations in the imperial city, are ambiguous.

The most frequently mentioned imperial ritual space is the Ming Tang, literally "bright hall." It was an ideally conceived multistory structure whose architectural components were circular or square in plan. Ming Tang were built at Chinese cities and in the provinces in the last centuries B.C. and the first centuries A.D. and occasionally at later times. Initially the Ming Tang was the site of imperial sacrifices, but in time it came to share the space and functions of two other ritual structures.

A ritual space with which the Ming Tang may have shared a location if not an actual structure was known as Bi Yong, literally "jade-ring moat." Bi Yong is referred to in most of the classical Chinese texts that describe the Ming Tang. It is believed to have been a circular, moat-surrounded building.

Among its functions was the education of candidates for imperial service. This purpose was taken over in later Chinese capitals by the National Academy (Guozi Jian) (Figure 2, no. 12). Another later imperial city building pertinent to official education was the Imperial Library.

A third ritual space in the Chinese imperial city was the Ling Tai, a platform for observation of the heavens. The role of the Ling Tai, where the em-

Figure 13. Honorific tablet to Confucius, Dacheng Hall, Confucian Temple, Tainan, Taiwan. [Steinhardt photograph]

Figure 14. Guandi Temple, Yuncheng, Shanxi (Qing dynasty). [Beijing Tourist Bureau brochure]

peror ascended for the ceremonial regulation of the calendar, was probably superseded in later times by astronomical observatories. The later observatories were also imperially sponsored building projects.

Reconstructions of the three ritual spaces were proposed and debated at the Chinese court for two thousand years. An important reconstruction by Wang Shiren is based on his belief that a composite ritual hall, one in which the functions of Ming Tang, Bi Yong, and Ling Tai were housed under one roof, was located in the southern suburbs of the imperial city Chang'an at the beginning of the first century A.D. (Figure 15).[9]

The last structure planned inside the walls of the Chinese imperial city was the freestanding tower. One and often two types of the multistoried structures stood on the main north–south axis of imperial Beijing and certain earlier Chinese capitals (Figure 2, no. 20; Figure 16). The towers housed either a bell or a drum, and their functions were those of urban timekeeping devices. The bell or drum was

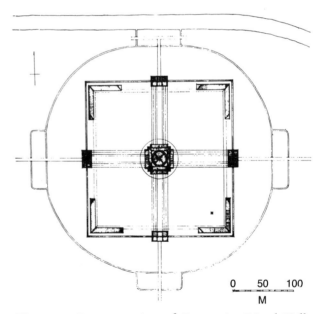

Figure 15. Reconstruction of Composite Ritual Hall, early first century A.D. [Yang Hongxun, *Jianzhu kaoguxue lunwen ji*, p. 198]

Figure 16. Bell Tower of Xi'an (Ming dynasty). [China Tourist Bureau brochure]

sounded at regular intervals during the day and night.[10]

Imperial gardens and parks could be found inside any of the capital's walls and occasionally beyond them. Chinese emperors of the last centuries B.C. maintained game reserves, both for hunting and for the confinement of exotic animals. Planned gardens and parkland for imperial pleasure were also part of the Chinese imperial city. Beginning in the first millennium B.C., an imperial garden was almost always located directly north of or adjacent to the palace area.

Chinese imperial cities always had designated market areas where nonimperial urban dwellers could shop. The locations and number of these market districts varied from city to city.[11] Although the primary purpose of the Chinese capital was administrative, and separate market towns flourished across the country, often the imperial city was the location of some of the nation's most active commercial districts. Both goods produced in the capital and imported products were available for purchase.

The last component of the Chinese imperial city, the royal necropolis, lay beyond its outer wall. Except for the Mongolian rulers of China, whose graves are at unmarked sites in Mongolia, or final dynastic rulers whose bodies were not accorded imperial burial by the new dynasty, every Chinese ruler built a tomb near his imperial city but outside the walls.[12] The earliest known royal cemetery survives at Xibeigang, where rulers of the mid-second millennium B.C. capital at Anyang were interred. The plans of imperial tombs after Xibeigang are somewhat standard, consisting of a long approach to the burial precinct, a subterranean multichamber grave, and, by the end of the first millennium B.C., a mound covering the subterranean portion and an enclosure around the whole area (Figure 17). Underground tombs were built of brick and stone,

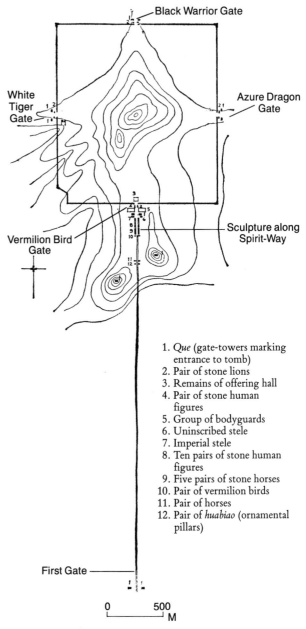

1. *Que* (gate-towers marking entrance to tomb)
2. Pair of stone lions
3. Remains of offering hall
4. Pair of stone human figures
5. Group of bodyguards
6. Uninscribed stele
7. Imperial stele
8. Ten pairs of stone human figures
9. Five pairs of stone horses
10. Pair of vermilion birds
11. Pair of horses
12. Pair of *huabiao* (ornamental pillars)

0   500
          M

Figure 17. Plan of Qianling, tomb of Emperor Gaozong (d. 683) and Empress Wu (d. 705), outskirts of Xi'an, Shaanxi. [Liu Dunzhen, *Zhongguo gudai jianzhu shi*, 1st edition, p. 145]

permanent materials that presented a dramatic contrast to the timber construction of the Chinese capital. The architectural principles of imperial cities of the dead, however, were borrowed from those of the living.

SITES

Each component of the Chinese imperial city—the palace compound, government buildings, the imperial-way and palace-place combination, dynastic altars, the Ancestral Temple, temples to Confucius, Guandi, and the City-God, the ritual spaces that included the Ming Tang, Bi Yong, and Ling Tai,

towers, gardens and parks, markets, and the royal tombs—was planned (if not actually constructed) for the main sites of imperial Chinese urbanism. Four primary sites and five occasional ones have been the locations of China's most important imperial cities. All but one have been continuously occupied, even during the centuries when they did not serve as capitals.[13] The first four cities are Xi'an, Beijing, Luoyang, and Nanjing; Kaifeng, Hangzhou, Datong, Chengdu, and Ye are the others.

Some of the earliest remains of urban settlement have been uncovered in the vicinity of modern Xi'an at the contemporary village Banpo, where foundations and pottery suggest it was inhabited in

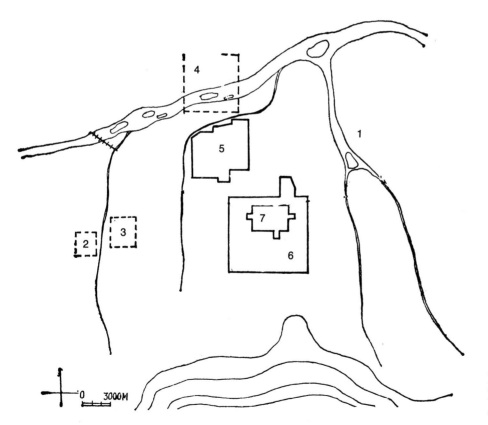

1. Banpo
2. Feng
3. Hao
4. Xianyang
5. Han Chang'an
6. Sui-Tang Chang'an
7. Ming Xi'an

Figure 18. Xi'an through history. [Dong, *Zhongguo chengshi*, p. 16]

the fifth millennium B.C. (Figure 18, no. 1). The first capital cities, Feng and Hao, were built by the Zhou kings Wen and Wu, respectively, at the beginning of the first millennium B.C. There is some disagreement about the exact locations of Feng and Hao, but they have been tentatively identified by archaeologists at the places indicated in Figure 18. Texts relate that after occupation during King Wen's reign at Feng (Figure 18, no. 2), Hao was the main Chinese capital for about three hundred and fifty years (Figure 18, no. 3) until the primary capital was moved eastward to Luoyang. The next important period in the history of Xi'an was the time of the First Emperor and unifier of China, Shi Huangdi (r. 246–209 B.C.) of the Qin dynasty (ca. 255–206 B.C.). A few remains of his palaces survive in the vicinity of Xianyang, north of the Wei River (Figure 18, no. 4), but he is best known for his tomb complex, located near Lintong, where thousands of lifesize funerary figurines have been excavated. Chang'an, south of the Wei River (Figure 18, no. 5), was the primary Chinese capital for the next two hundred years, from which time survives the foundation of the composite ritual hall mentioned above.

The city of Chang'an in the eighth century (Figure 18, no. 6) was not only the largest but probably also the most cosmopolitan city in the world. Extending farther north–south and nearly the full east–west distance of Xi'an today, excavation at the former imperial city has yielded evidence of secular and religious architecture of the Tang dynasty (618–906). Chang'an was never the site of the primary Chinese capital after the tenth century, but a wall was built around the city in the Ming dynasty (1368–1644). (See Figure 18, no. 7.)

Urban settlement in the vicinity of Beijing has a history almost as long as Chang'an's, but the important period for the imperial city occurred only after the fall of the Tang dynasty. Prior to then, beginning in the second millennium B.C., a city there was called Ji. It became a larger and more important town in North China, which it remained through the second century A.D. In the tenth century the site was designated the southernmost capital, Nanjing (Figure 19, no. 1), of the non-Chinese dynasty Liao (947–1125). The Liao city was enlarged by the succeeding non-Chinese dynasty Jin (1115–1234) (Figure 19, no. 2), for whom it was the central capital of an empire that extended as far south as Henan province. The Jin were conquered by the Mongols, whose primary capital Dadu (Figure 19, no. 3) was built in China beginning in 1267 by Khubilai Khan. That city, the Cambalac (Khan-baliq) described by Marco Polo, was the predecessor to Beijing (Figure 19, no. 4).

Imperial construction in the vicinity of Luoyang may be traceable to the first half of the second millennium B.C., from which time what may well have been palaces of Shang kings have been uncovered near Erlitou (Figure 20, no. 1). Luoyang was the imperial capital of the Eastern Zhou kings beginning about 770 B.C. (Figure 20, no. 2). At that time it was called Luoyi, the character *yi* being a word for walled city. Luoyang remained an imperial city site through the period of China's first unification and the subsequent Western Han dynasty (206 B.C.–A.D. 8). It became the primary capital again in A.D. 25 (Figure 20, no. 3). When the Eastern Han fell in 220, China split into three kingdoms and eventually fragmented into more kingdoms and states. During the three hundred and seventy years of disunity, Luoyang was the site of several important imperial capitals, from which time Buddhist architecture still survives. All of these capitals occupied part of the former capital of the Eastern Han (Figure 20, no. 4). The city called Luoyang was moved to a new site when it became a capital of the Sui (589–618) and the Tang (Figure 20, no. 5). After the mid-tenth century the city's

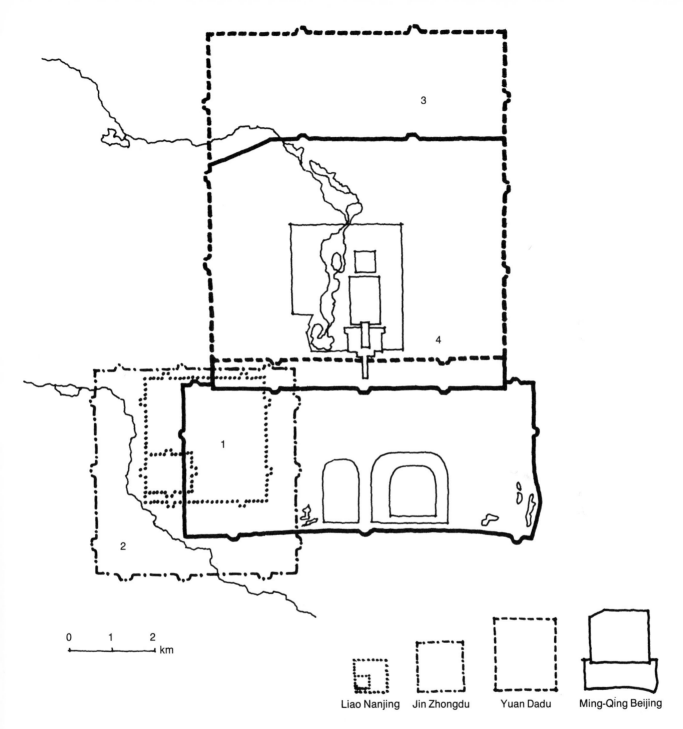

Figure 19. Beijing through history. [Drawn by Huang Yunsheng]

Liao Nanjing   Jin Zhongdu   Yuan Dadu   Ming-Qing Beijing

0   1   2   km

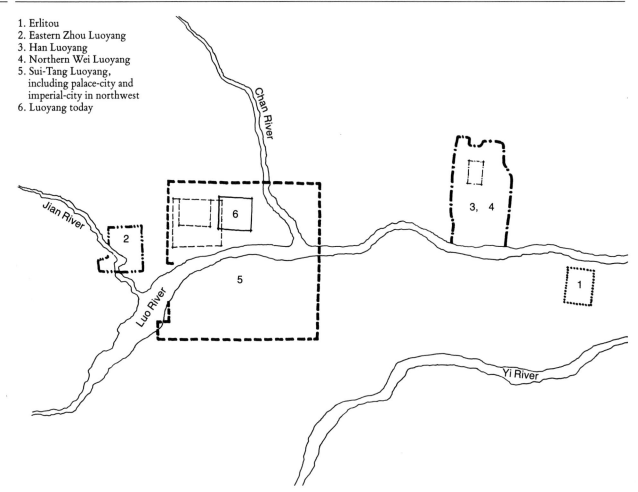

1. Erlitou
2. Eastern Zhou Luoyang
3. Han Luoyang
4. Northern Wei Luoyang
5. Sui-Tang Luoyang,
   including palace-city and
   imperial-city in northwest
6. Luoyang today

Figure 20. Luoyang through history. [Drawn by Huang Yunsheng]

importance waned. It was the western capital of the Northern Song dynasty (960–1126) but never again achieved imperial status. Figure 20, no. 6, is the present location of the city Luoyang.

Nanjing has also yielded excavated remains from Neolithic times, including those of the Beiyinyangying culture of about 3000 B.C. In the first millennium B.C. the vicinity of Nanjing was known as Jinling and then as Moling, a county administrative town. Under the Han, a city there was called Dan-

yang. It was the capital of the Wu kingdom (one of the Three Kingdoms) in the third century A.D. and the capital of subsequent dynasties between 280 and 589, when it was known as Jianye or Jiankang (Figure 21, no. 1). From 937 to 975 Nanjing was the site of the capital of the Southern Tang, one of several dynasties vying for control of China (Figure 21, no. 2). It became the primary Chinese capital again after the fall of the Yuan government in 1368, from which time buildings and portions of the outer city

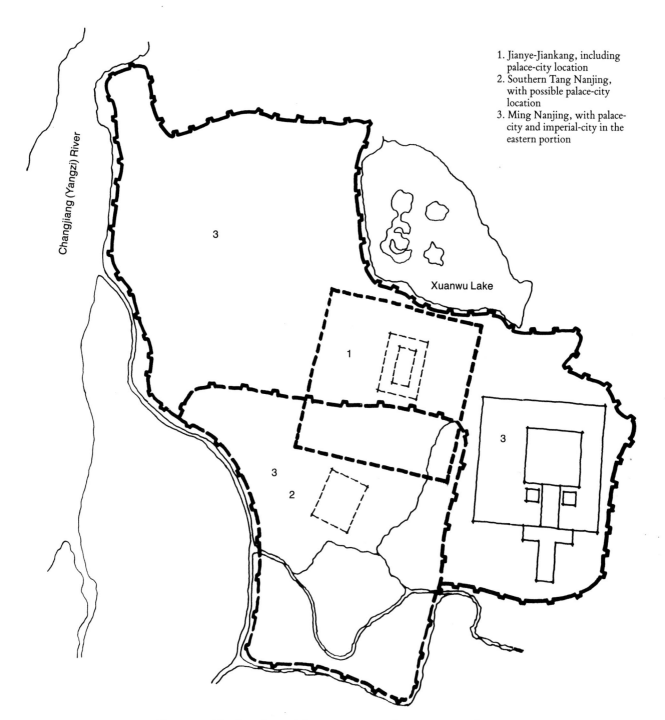

1. Jianye-Jiankang, including palace-city location
2. Southern Tang Nanjing, with possible palace-city location
3. Ming Nanjing, with palace-city and imperial-city in the eastern portion

Changjiang (Yangzi) River

Xuanwu Lake

Figure 21. Nanjing through history. [Drawn by Huang Yunsheng]

wall remain (Figure 21, no. 3). Even though its status was reduced to secondary capital in the fifteenth century, Nanjing has remained one of China's largest and most influential cities.

Tradition tells that it was in the vicinity of modern Kaifeng that Fu Xi, first of the legendary emperors, built his capital at Chen. The state of Wei had a capital at Kaifeng in the fourth and third centuries B.C. (Figure 22, no. 1). At the end of the sixth century the site was known as Bianzhou, then as Kaifeng, and from the tenth century onward as Bianzhou, Bianjing, or Bianliang, when it became the eastern and primary capital of the Song dynasty (Figure 22, no. 2). During the Jin dynasty, which succeeded the Song in North China, Bianliang was the southern of five capitals. It was also an auxiliary capital in the Ming dynasty (Figure 22, no. 3). The most important period for the imperial history of the city was the Northern Song dynasty.

Hangzhou, first walled in the Sui dynasty, is the newest of China's imperial cities (Figure 23, no. 1). It was the principal capital of the Southern Song for about one hundred twenty-five years, beginning in the second quarter of the twelfth century (Figure 23, no. 2). At that time the city was called Lin'an. What remained at Hangzhou in the late thirteenth century was immortalized in Marco Polo's description of the world, in which Lin'an is referred to as Quinsai.

Datong was the site of main capitals of non-native Chinese dynasties. It was the first capital established in China proper by the Turkic people who came to be known as the Northern Wei. Their city Pingcheng had been used as an auxiliary capital since 313, when the main Northern Wei stronghold was located to the north in the present Inner Mongolian Autonomous Region. During the last forty years of the fifth century, Pingcheng, walled in 422, was the site of fervent Buddhist cave construction, including the Yun'gang Caves. At that time it was also the primary Northern Wei capital. Datong's status was elevated again in the mid-eleventh century, when it became the western capital of the Liao dynasty, from which period Buddhist timber architecture survives. The city remained the western capital of the Jin until the takeover of North China by the Mongols in the first half of the thirteenth century. Neither the extent of the Northern Wei nor the Liao–Jin outer walls has been fully determined.

Like most cities that served as imperial capitals, Chengdu has a history traceable to the Spring and Autumn period (770–475 B.C.). Chengdu was an important city, although not a capital, during the Han dynasty, but immediately afterward became the capital of Shu-Han (220–263), one of the Three

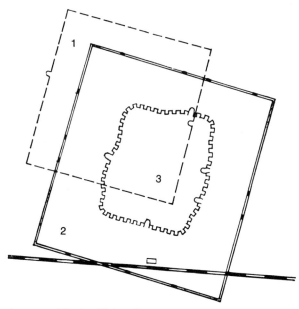

1. --- Warring States city
2. === Northern Song Bianliang
3. ⌐⌐⌐ Kaifeng in the Ming and after

Figure 22. Kaifeng through history. [Yan Chongnian, *Zhongguo lidai ducheng gongyuan*, p. 105]

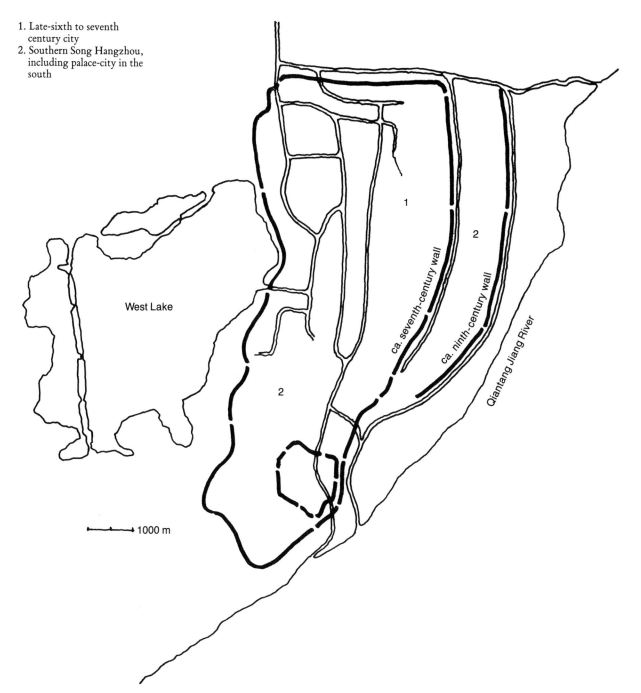

1. Late-sixth to seventh century city
2. Southern Song Hangzhou, including palace-city in the south

West Lake

ca. seventh-century wall

ca. ninth-century wall

Qiantang Jiang River

1000 m

Figure 23. Hangzhou through history. [Drawn by Huang Yunsheng]

Kingdoms. Chengdu's only other time as an imperial city was in the tenth century when it was capital of the state of Shu.

Ye began as a capital of Qi in the Spring and Autumn period and remained an administrative center through the Han dynasty. In the first decade of the third century it became the power base of the military leader Cao Cao (155–220). Ye was one of five capitals of the Wei state in the third century; it was the main capital of Eastern Wei and Northern Qi in the sixth century. After the late-sixth-century unification of China, Ye was never again an imperial city.

Why did the Chinese return again and again to the same sites for imperial cities? One practical reason has been a site's defensibility. A second pragmatic reason was the presence of essential natural features such as an abundant water supply, accessibility by land and water routes, and sufficient land to support a local farming population. Once a city had been established, the natural framework could be repeated even if the old plan and specific site were amended. Third, and perhaps most significant, a past history of imperialism conferred both legitimacy and an aura of rule. Even if the site's former walls and buildings were all but destroyed, the new dynasty, even a non-Chinese regime, could enhance its own ruling potential by building a new city near the old one.

TERMINOLOGY

The earliest Chinese references to a city are found on oracle bone or bronze vessel inscriptions from the second millennium B.C. Among them is the pictograph for city wall, a square with two or four gates (Figure 24).

The three words *cheng, du,* and *jing* are the most common Chinese terms that are either translated into English as "city" or are used as the second syllable in the Chinese name of imperial cities. In his annotated translation of *Zuo zhuan,* a commentary on the annals of the Spring and Autumn period probably written in the late first millennium B.C., James Legge writes that at the time of the text, *cheng,* as a verb, meant "walling a city."[14] Later, in imperial China, *cheng* referred to a walled administrative city.[15] In common parlance, however, *cheng* is translated as "city wall" or simply "wall."[16]

When referring to the outermost enclosure of a city, the terms *dacheng* ("great wall") or *waicheng* ("outer or outside wall") are used. In post-sixteenth-century Beijing, *waicheng* had a more specific meaning. It referred to the newly walled area built due south of the original outer city wall (see Figure 2). From that time on, the northern enclosure of Beijing was designated *neicheng,* literally "inner city." This use of *neicheng* is rare, however, for much more often the Chinese *neicheng* or other

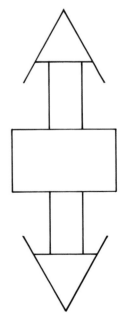

Figure 24. Chinese pictograph for "walled city."

Chinese words translated into English as "inner city" refer to a walled enclosure within *dacheng*.

The common references to the walled areas inside of *dacheng* at a Chinese imperial city have already been mentioned. Yet both premodern and contemporary writing about Chinese cities offer alternatives. *Huangcheng,* for instance, which has been used here to refer to the administrative-city or more literally the imperial-city, can be called *licheng* ("inside-city"). The innermost enclosure *gongcheng* may be labeled *danei* ("great inner") or *zicheng* ("smaller city"). An alternative name for the outermost wall, *luocheng* ("spread-out city"), can also be found.

During the second half of the first millennium B.C., *cheng* referred only to the inner enclosure of a city, the place where ceremonial or administrative buildings were located. At that time, *guo* was used to designate the outer walled city, what has here been called *dacheng* or *waicheng*.[17] Another term in use in the Shang and Zhou periods was *yi,* a reference to a small town with as few as ten households.

Just as *cheng* is the most common second syllable in the name of a walled city, *du* is one of two terms used frequently as the second syllable for the capital itself. *Du* has been defined as a "walled town having an ancestral temple with the spirit-tablets of former rulers."[18] In other words, *du* is an imperial city, for which, as noted earlier, one of the main components is an ancestral temple. Well-known Chinese cities with *du* as the second syllable of their names are Dadu, the "great capital" of Khubilai Khan begun in 1267, and Zhongdu, the "central capital" of the Jin dynasty begun in the early 1150s at what is today part of Beijing. Some cities better known by other names have alternative designations that employ the character *du.* Luoyang from the late sixth to ninth centuries was known as Dongdu, the "eastern capital"; Kaifeng was the eastern capital Dongdu during the Northern Song

dynasty (960–1126) when Luoyang was the western capital; and Fengyang in Anhui province was the central capital, Zhongdu, in the late fourteenth century.

Jing is the second term used as the second syllable of an imperially designated city. Like *du,* the syllable *jing* often follows a directional indicator. The northern and southern capitals, Beijing and Nanjing, respectively, are the most widely known city names in which this character is included.[19]

It should already be clear that the name of a capital could change during its multimillennial history. The most common name change would occur as a result of the redesignation of imperial city status. Often five cities were awarded capital status. The five would be determined by special considerations such as the birthplace of the dynastic founder, center of his greatest military support, or the political stability of a region. Even though some of the same cities were primary capitals during one dynasty and auxiliary capitals in earlier and later times, no single city maintained the same status or directional designation during the course of all the dynasties. We have already seen, for instance, that in Tang times Luoyang was the eastern capital, but under the Song the city at Kaifeng was called Dongdu.[20]

Other terms that follow capital names are indications of administrative divisions of the Chinese countryside. Like the words that refer to specific city walls, the references to provinces, prefectures, counties, and districts changed with time—sometimes, but not always, because of amendments in the system of local government administration. In the Warring States period when China was not unified under one ruler, states called *guo* were governed by kings from walled enclosures within the *guo.* At that time the country was divided into *jun* (military commanderies). These government districts in turn supervised smaller military divisions of the country called *xian* (district). The term *xian* is still in use today, now referring to a county subject to its own administration but also answerable to higher government offices. In the Song dynasty, the *zhou* ("prefecture") was roughly the equivalent of what had in earlier times been *jun*. Song "prefectures" situated in very important cities were called *fu* ("superior prefectures"). Song China was also divided into much larger regions known as *lu* ("circuits"). During the Qing dynasty (1644–1911) similar divisions were known as *sheng*. Today Chinese local government is divided into *sheng* (provinces), *diqu* (regions roughly the equivalent of what formerly were *zhou* or *fu*), *xian* (counties), *zhen* (towns), and *xiang* (townships), each of which has its own administrative offices.

A city can be the location of more than one government office from the national to city level. In imperial times, too, a city might have housed offices of both *fu* and *xian* government. Moreover the status of a city and the administrative jurisdiction could change from dynasty to dynasty. Thus at different times in its history, the city Suzhou, for instance, was the center of Suzhou Fu and Suzhou Xian.

China may be the only civilization for which so many characteristics, components, sites, and terms of imperial city planning can be so rigidly defined. The Chinese imperial city may, in fact, be alone in the applicability of these four topics over such a long period of history and for so many cities. The pages that follow will show how well these criteria may be used to understand the truly unique phenomenon of Chinese imperial city planning.

2

BEGINNINGS

When we speak of transferring the capital, changing
the metropolis,
We are following the tracks of Pan Geng.[1]

LITERARY RECORD

UNTIL this century it was said with some confidence that the earliest records of Chinese imperial
cities were literary. Using the texts of China's classical age, notably the *Shu jing* (Book of documents), *Shi jing* (Book of songs), *(Lüshi) Chun Qiu*
(Spring and Autumn annals), *Zuo zhuan* (Commentary of Zuo), *Shi ji* (Records of the historian),
and *Zhou li* (Rituals of Zhou), it was possible both
to compile a list of rulers and their cities of the second and even the third millennium B.C. and to find
details about how those cities should have looked.[2]

From the *Spring and Autumn Annals* and their
commentaries, for instance, one learns that Fu Xi
(2852–2737 B.C.),[3] first of the legendary rulers, had
his capital at Chen, which one could determine to
have been located at Kaifeng. Fu Xi's successor
Shen Nong (2737–2697 B.C.) had his first capital at
the same spot, but later moved it to Qufu in modern-day Shandong province. Only one of the three
subsequent legendary kings had his capital at a site
used by a ruling predecessor. The better known of
the succeeding legendary rulers, Yao and Shun, had
their capitals in modern Pingyang prefecture of
Shanxi province, but at two different locations. So
did Yu, founder of the so-called Xia dynasty.[4] If
one can generalize from these terse references to
rulers and their cities during the third millennium
B.C., then one might say that from the beginning
each Chinese ruler established his capital at a new
site—often in the vicinity of a predecessor's imperial city but rarely on top of it.

Using the same texts the list of rulers and capitals
could be extended through the second millennium
B.C., that is, through the years of the Xia dynasty

and the succeeding Shang. The Shang, texts say, had seven different imperial city sites, located in Henan, Shandong, and Anhui provinces.[5]

The rulers and sites of first millennium B.C. China had also long been studied through the literature of the period. Most of the first millennium B.C. in China—from approximately 1100 until about 255 B.C., the Zhou dynasty—is named for a group of people who conquered the Shang after many years of warfare. The Zhou is divided into two periods, named Western and Eastern after the locations of their two primary capitals near modern Xi'an and Luoyang, respectively. The Western Zhou used two sites in the vicinity of Xi'an for capital cities. Feng (Figure 18, no. 2), the earlier Western Zhou capital, was a ruler's city even before the accession of Zhou. The second capital, Hao (Figure 18, no. 3), was located across the river from Feng. The Eastern Zhou capital near Luoyang became the primary Zhou capital in about 771 B.C., after the fall of the western portion of Zhou territory. The site had been a ruler's city since the twelfth century B.C. Thus by the end of the second millennium B.C. the initial Chinese pattern of changing the location of the capital almost as frequently as the transfer of power was replaced by a more permanent capital system.

Textual records also inform us that the Later Zhou dynasty was divided into two periods. The earlier part is known as the Spring and Autumn period, and its history is documented in the *Spring and Autumn Annals* and the *Zuo zhuan*. The later phase, which begins in about 481 B.C., is known as the Warring States period. As its name indicates, the fifth, fourth, and third centuries B.C. were an age of at times hundreds of contending states. Each state had a ruler and a capital. The names of these cities and their lords are recorded in the *Zhan Guo ce* (Discourses of the Warring States).

Literature of China's classical age records much more than simply events and places. Reading the early texts it is clear that an ideology of capital city building had already been formulated. The earliest of the relevant texts, the *Shu jing,* written during Zhou times, says that upon the founding of the capital Luoyang, the ruler's brother-in-law, the Duke of Zhou (d. 1105 B.C.), said: "May the King come and assume the responsibility for the work of God on High and himself serve (in this capacity) at the center of the land. I, say that, having constructed this great city and ruling from there, he shall be a counterpart to August Heaven. He shall scrupulously sacrifice to the upper and lower (spirits), and from there govern as the central pivot." Later in the same text the Duke of Zhou counsels his ruler: "I say, if you rule from this central place, the myriad states will all enjoy peace and you, the King, will achieve complete success."[6]

The Duke of Zhou, highest-ranking Chinese official in the twelfth century B.C., is pictured in the early twentieth century illustrated version of the *Shu jing* (Figure 25). In "Building a City in the Eastern State," we find the Duke of Zhou in the center of construction activity, standing as would the emperor at the heart of his imperial city. The *Shu jing* also describes the process of divination that precedes imperial city building. In Figure 26, the Zhou diviner of the capital uses a compass to determine the auspicious characteristics of the topography. Thus the ruler's association with heaven, his central position, and the necessity of heavenly satisfaction through divination—the ideology, in other words, of imperial city building—are articulated in the classical text and explicitly illustrated in later documents.

Another passage from the *Shu jing* justifies the transfer of royal cities:[7]

Our king Zu Yi came and fixed on Geng for his capital. He did so from a deep concern for our people, because he would not have them all die where they cannot help one another to preserve their lives. I have consulted the tortoise shell[8] and obtained the reply: "This is no place for us." When the former kings had any important business they gave reverent heed to the commands of Heaven. In a case like this especially they did not indulge the wish for constant repose; they did not abide ever in the same city. Up to this time the capital has been in five regions. If we do not fol-

low the example of these old times, we shall be refusing to acknowledge that Heaven is making an end of our dynasty here. . . . Heaven will perpetuate its decree in our favor in this new city. The great inheritance of the former kings will be continued and renewed.[9]

From the *Shi jing* comes a description of the process by which a royal capital came to be built—and another statement about the correspondence between imperial construction and heaven:

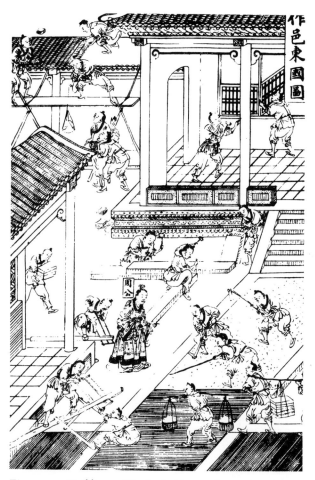

Figure 25. *Building a City in the Eastern State.* [Sun Jianai, *Shu jing tu shuo, juan* 33/2a]

Figure 26. *Divining the Capital at the Jian and Chan Rivers.* [Sun Jianai, *Shu jing tu shuo, juan* 33/6a]

The Ding-star is in the middle of the sky,
We begin to build the palace at Chu.
Orientating them by the rays of the sun
We set to work on the houses at Chu. . . .[10]

The plain of Zhou was very fertile,
Its celery and sowthistle sweet as rice-cakes.
"Here we will make a start; here take counsel,
Here notch our tortoise."
It says, "Stop," it says, "Halt.
Build houses here."
So he halted, so he stopped,
And left and right
He drew the boundaries of big plots and little,
He opened up the ground, he counted the acres
From west to east;
Everywhere he took his task in hand.
Then he summoned his Master of Works,
Then he summoned his Master of Lands
And made them build houses.
Dead straight was the plumb-line,
The planks were lashed to hold the earth;
They made the Hall of Ancestors, very venerable.
They tilted in the earth with a rattling,
They pounded it with a dull thud,
They beat the walls with a loud clang,
They pared and chiselled them with a faint *ping, ping;*
The hundred cubits all rose;
The drummers could not hold out.
They raised the outer gate;
The outer gate soared high.
They raised the inner gate;
The inner gate was very strong.
They raised the great earth-mound,
Whence excursions of war might start.
And in the time that followed they did not abate
    their sacrifices,
Did not let fall their high renown;
The oak forests were laid low,
Roads were opened up.[11]

In addition to the specifics of construction, the first poem from the *Shi jing* refers to master craftsmen, the Masters of Works and Lands, and tools—the plumb line, planks, and pounders. It also tells us that city construction was initiated by the drawing of boundaries. The walls and platforms were made of beaten earth, walls were pierced by gates, and halls were supported by timber pillars. In the second ode, the reference to the Ding-star may be interpreted two ways. Either building commences upon the appearance of a certain auspicious heavenly sign; or the palace buildings are oriented to this sign. According to Arthur Waley's note to his translation, the star is from the constellation Pegasus. The third line of this poem unambiguously declares a relationship between celestial orientation and human affairs.

The *Shi jing* has also been used as a source of knowledge about early Zhou capitals. The poem "Wen Wang you sheng" records the first Zhou ruler Wen Wang's use of Feng as his capital and his successor Wu Wang's use of Hao:

> Wen Wang made a city in Feng. . . . The wall he built was moated. . . . He did not alter his [predecessors'] plans, He came and was filial. The walls of Feng were where the four quarters came together; The royal ruler was their support; . . . The one who examined the oracle was the king; He took his residence in the Hao capital; The tortoise directed it, Wu Wang completed it; Wu Wang was splendid.[12]

The divination process, enclosure of the city by a moat, and the use of a past ruler's city plan—all part of imperial building ideology—are thus described here. So is the centrality of the imperial city.

According to the *Shi ji,* a chronicle of Chinese history which includes biographies of famous men from earliest times through the year 206 B.C., a capital was established at a different site by the next Zhou ruler, Cheng Wang. Initially Cheng Wang had chosen the old site Feng for his imperial city, but he subsequently decided to reside in Luoyi, where the Duke of Zhou was put in charge of imperial building. This event is illustrated in Figure 25.

The Zhou capital at Luoyi has received more attention in early Chinese literature than any other imperial city. A portion of the late second millennium B.C. Luoyi was known as Wangcheng (literally, "ruler's city"). Wangcheng is described in the *Kaogong ji* (Record of trades) section of the *Zhou li*. The *Kaogong ji* is believed to be a late first millennium B.C. addition to the *Zhou li,* a replacement for a lost portion from earlier Zhou times. What the *Kaogong ji* describes, however, is believed to be pre-Han, possibly even referring to practices of the Shang.[13]

The famous passage from the *Kaogong ji* that describes the laying out of King Cheng's city Luoyi, built under the supervision of the Duke of Zhou, reads:

> The *jiangren*[14] builds the state, leveling the ground with the water by using a plumb-line. He lays out posts, taking the plumb-line (to ensure the posts' verticality), and using their shadows as the determinators of a mid-point. He examines the shadows of the rising and setting sun and makes a circle which includes the mid-points of the two shadows.
>
> The *jiangren* constructs the state capitals. He makes a square nine *li* on each side; each side has three gates. Within the capital are nine north-south and nine east-west streets. The north-south streets are nine carriage tracks in width. On the left (as one faces south, or, to the east) is the Ancestral Temple, and to the right (west) are the Altars of Soil and Grain. In the front is the Hall of Audience and behind the markets.[15]

The majority of books that focus on Chinese city planning begin with the second paragraph of this quotation.[16] The attention this passage has received is understandable, for in these few lines are included the fundamental principles and specific components of every Chinese imperial city. The passage, in summary, states that: (1) The preparation of the site, including a reconciliation with natural forces, is first; (2) a midpoint is determined for the geometrically planned city; (3) the ruler's city is constructed anew, a total concept from its inception, with the boundaries determined before any individual structures are built; (4) the city boundaries are walls and their shape is a square; (5) each side wall is pierced by three gates; (6) major arteries cross the city perpendicular to one another; (7) certain spots are designated as essential to the Chinese imperial city—an Ancestral Temple on the east, Altars of Soil and Grain on the west, the Hall of Audience in front (that is, to the south), and markets behind (or north of it).

Like other passages from classical texts, this one has been illustrated. Figures 27 and 28 show fifteenth- and seventeenth-century drawings of the ruler of Zhou's city. In both schemes a feature of imperial planning is drawn that was not specified in the *Kaogong ji* passage but was inherent to Chinese planning from earliest times. It is the palace-city, situated in the center of the outer wall and bounded by its own enclosure. This wall is the one manmade feature that impedes the otherwise perfect checkerboard arrangement of city streets.

The two illustrations of Wangcheng present the palace-city buildings differently. In Figure 27, from the early-fifteenth-century encyclopedia *Yongle dadian,* twelve buildings, each a palace hall or residential chamber, are shown behind the front (south) courtyard. Behind them should be the markets. The later illustration from *Sanli tu* (Illustrated three ritual classics) shows no individual buildings in the

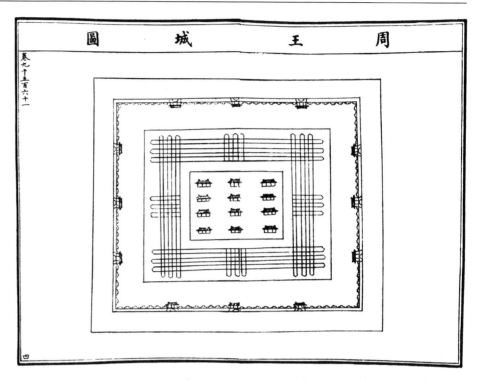

Figure 27. Wangcheng.
[*Henan zhi* as preserved in
Yongle dadian, juan 9561]

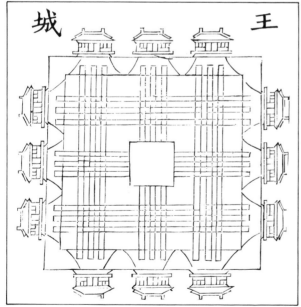

Figure 28. Wangcheng. [Nalan, *Sanli tu,* pt. 1, *juan* 4/2b]

palace-city. A twentieth-century drawing of Wang-cheng, however, provides details of what the interior should look like (Figure 29). In addition to the Ancestral Temple and Soil and Grain Altars, the private, or sleeping, chambers *(qin)* are directly north of the Hall of Audience *(chao)* and markets are at the far north. The private chambers are not referred to in the passage from the *Kaogong ji,* but elsewhere in the text is the stipulation *"qianchao, houqin"* ("in front, Hall of Audience; behind, private chambers"), which in actual city building would take precedence over the "audience hall in front, market in back" order of arrangement. As mentioned in Chapter 1, markets may be found in almost any part of a Chinese imperial city, even beyond the outer wall. The location of commercial districts is an example of the pragmatism that is necessarily a part of all imperial planning. The smells of the markets, more than a classical dictum,

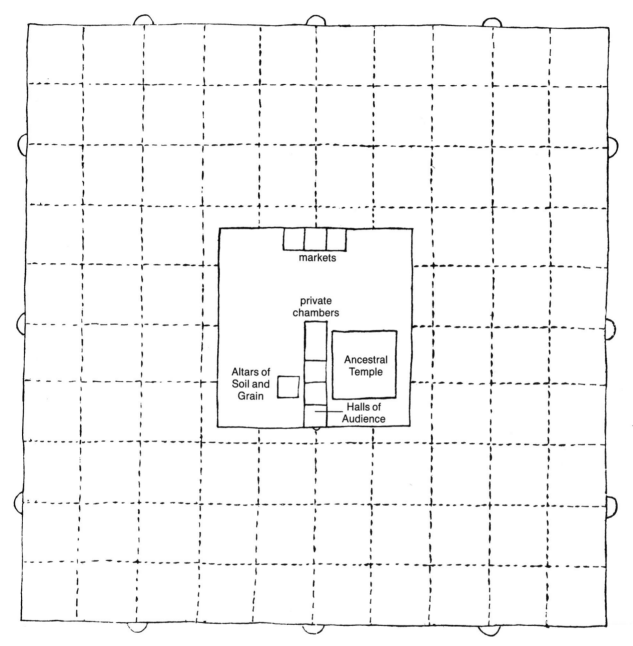

markets

private
chambers

Altars of
Soil and
Grain

Ancestral
Temple

Halls of
Audience

Figure 29. Wangcheng. [Yao Jiazao, *Zhongguo jianzhu shi*, fig. 92]

may have set their locations far from the city center. Another feature of Chinese imperial cities suggested by later drawings of Wangcheng is the division of the city into wards. They may be imagined between the dotted street lines in Figure 29.

Finally, the enigmatic components of the Chinese imperial city, Ming Tang and Bi Yong, are described in early classical literature. Chapter 14 of the Han dynasty *Li ji* (Record of rituals), for instance, is devoted to the Ming Tang. The Bi Yong is mentioned in "Wen Wang yu sheng," partially quoted above, from the *Shi jing*.[17]

ARCHAEOLOGICAL RECORD

Beginning about 1950, and to a lesser extent a few decades earlier, the reliance on texts for descriptions of Chinese imperial cities was demoted to secondary status as scholars in China and the West realized that excavated material constituted the best proof of the imperial urban history of ancient China. In just the last thirty-five years archaeological excavation in the People's Republic has brought forth visual evidence of Chinese ceremonial and daily life from Neolithic times through recent centuries. Excavation has also shown what certain interior spaces in premodern China looked like, for the excavation of tombs has produced stone, earthen, and brick facsimiles of wooden building parts. Digging into tombs has also yielded several two-thousand-year-old site plans. The unearthing of cities, however, has been more difficult because the primary locations of urban development in traditional China are, with few exceptions, the places of burgeoning metropolises today. Nevertheless, using literary records as guides, archaeologists have been able to locate and study some monuments and a few larger walled enclosures from China's earliest capitals. Chance finds have also added to the evidence about the earliest imperial cities. The following sections survey what is now known about Neolithic settlements and second and first millennia B.C. rulers' cities up to the time of the Han dynasty. Based primarily on archaeological evidence, the discussion indicates the extent to which excavation has confirmed what in prearchaeological days had been assumed about Chinese imperial urbanism.

Pre-Shang Settlements and Shang Cities

A Neolithic settlement representing what was probably typical of North China five or six thousand years ago was found at modern-day Banpo, just east of Xi'an (Figure 30; see also Figure 18, no. 1). The forty-five dwellings and more than two hundred tombs unearthed there between 1954 and 1957 were arranged in a 50,000-square-meter area that also included a kiln and one very large building. This oversized structure was located at the center of the north–south oriented village. Excavators suggest that the hall was inhabited by the oldest and youngest people of the village and, moreover, that it was a communal gathering place.[18] A cemetery stood north of the village. One observes, then, the orientation of buildings to cardinal directions, the central location of the main hall, and the placement of the cemetery to the north—all general characteristics of premodern Chinese imperial urbanism discussed in Chapter 1. Individual structures also revealed the general features of later Chinese buildings, such as four-sided enclosure and a timber frame.

Excavation of other sites from Neolithic China proves that sophisticated principles of urban planning were in operation long before the *Kaogong ji* or earlier texts were written. The most profound declaration of Chinese urbanism is the walled city, of which the Neolithic settlement at Chengziyai in Shandong province is one early example.[19] The Chengziyai wall was built with layer upon layer of

Figure 30. Remains of Neolithic village at Banpo, Shaanxi (ca. 3000 B.C.). [Steinhardt photograph]

pounded earth, a technique called *hangtu* that would be universal in Chinese wall construction for thousands of years. The existence of the wall suggests that even in China's Neolithic age an enclosed sector was considered distinct from the rest of the countryside.

Five Shang sites will be examined here. Two are chosen because they were almost undoubtedly royal capitals. The other three show the implementation of building principles that govern all later Chinese cities. Together the five indicate that the scheme and certain components of Chinese imperial cities predate the earliest surviving texts by more than a millennium.

The earliest of the five sites is at Erlitou. Located south of the Yellow River, Erlitou is about 25 kilometers east of Luoyang, one of the primary sites of Chinese imperial building (Figure 20, no. 1).[20] The 1.5 by 2.5 kilometer site has been considered a possible repository of pre-Shang, or Xia, culture—

proof of which would be the first evidence of historical Xia civilization.[21]

No outer city wall has been uncovered at Erlitou, but within the nearly 4-square-kilometer site were at least two palace compounds. One was squarish, approximately 108 meters east to west by 100 meters north to south, with a thus far unexplained jut at the southeast corner (Figure 31).[22] The second palace compound's enclosure was a more perfect rectangle (Figure 32).[23] In both schemes a pillar-supported, south-oriented hall stood in the north. Remains of another Shang city were uncovered less than 10 kilometers northeast of Erlitou.[24]

The second Shang capital, Ao, where the tenth ruler Zhong Ding moved, has been identified as the Shang site excavated at the contemporary city Zhengzhou, about 100 kilometers east of Erlitou. The Zhengzhou site has yielded the most extensive evidence to date of a second millennium B.C. walled city. Its outer wall extended 6,960 meters and was

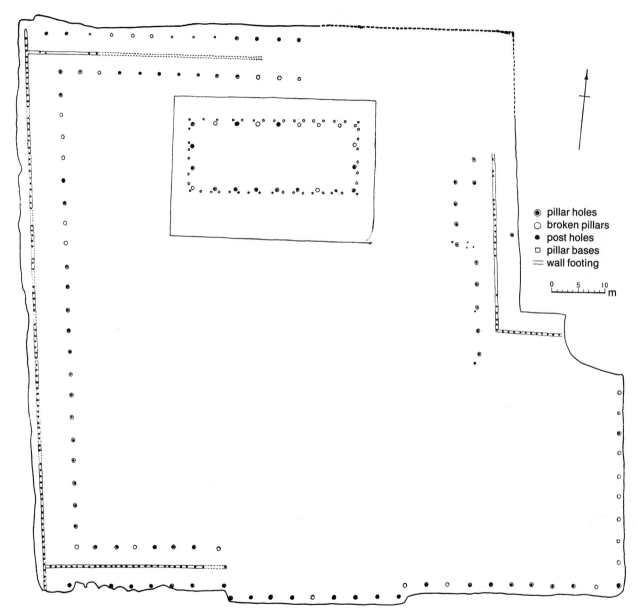

Figure 31. Plan of Palace 1 at Erlitou (second millennium B.C.). ["Henan Yanshi Erlitou Zao Shang gongdian,"
Kaogu no. 4 (1974), p. 235]

pillar holes
broken pillars
post holes
pillar bases
wall footing

0   5   10
            m

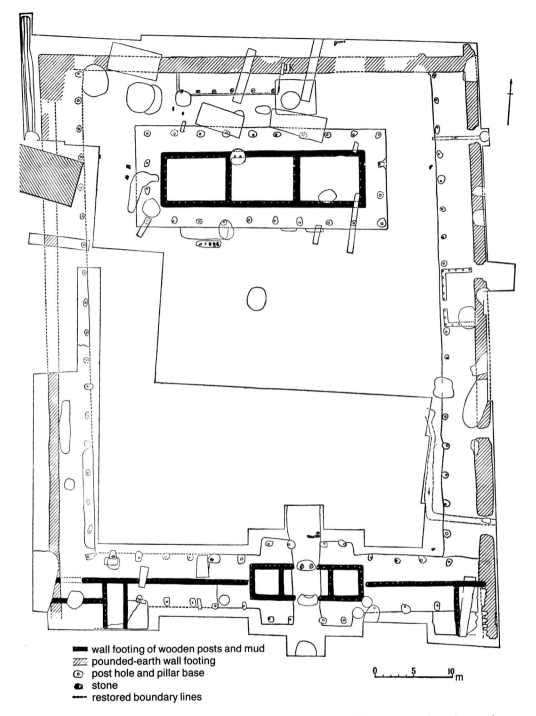

wall footing of wooden posts and mud
pounded-earth wall footing
post hole and pillar base
stone
restored boundary lines

0   5   10
m

Figure 32. Plan of Palace 2 at Erlitou (early Shang period). ["Henan Yanshi Erlitou erhao gongdian," *Kaogu* no. 3 (1983), p. 207]

made with the *hangtu* technique—slanting layers of earth firmly pounded on either side of wooden planks, after which earth was poured between them. The plan of the Zhengzhou site published in 1954 shows that the Shang capital was nearly square, oriented to the south, and had a gate at each face (Figure 33). Within the city wall, palace-style residences were raised on earthen mounds, also pounded firm by the *hangtu* technique. Tombs have been excavated at several locations beyond the outer city wall, including the northwest. Among the most important objects uncovered at Zhengzhou were bronze vessels that have aided in the designation of a mid-Shang date for the site.[25]

Excavations at two other Shang sites provide evidence, in microcosm, for the principles of imperial urbanism believed to have been implemented at the cities of which they were parts. The earlier of these was uncovered at Panlongcheng in Hubei province. Much smaller than the Zhengzhou site, Panlongcheng is believed to have been the ruling center of a high official or prince. Its 290 by 260 meter outer *hangtu* wall may have been surrounded by a moat. Ten meters from the north wall edge was a large

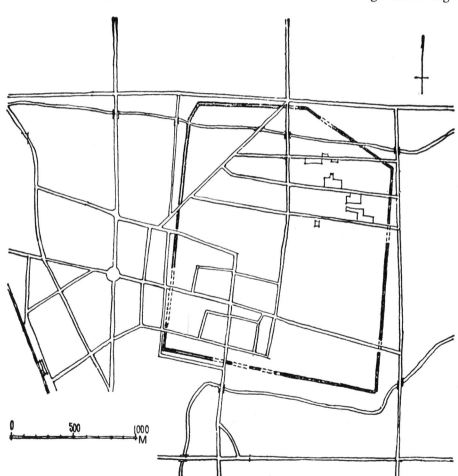

Figure 33. Plan of outer wall of Zhengzhou (middle Shang period). [Tao Fu, *Jianzhu lishi yu lilun* 3–4 (1982–1983), p. 28]

0   500   1000
                          M

pounded-earth foundation, six times wider in the east–west dimension than north–south. Three halls stood on it, one of which, built on a 40 by 12 meter platform, is shown in plan in Figure 34.[26] Although the hall is called residential by the archaeologists, it seems possible that the three elevated together may have been rather the restricted ceremonial space of the larger complex from which more than fifty buildings have been uncovered.

The site of the last Shang capital, Yin, at modern Anyang in Henan province, was determined and excavated during the Republican period of this century. Continued digging at Anyang intensely between 1928 and 1937, and to a lesser extent afterward, has made it possible to know in great detail how the last Shang imperial city looked. Referred to since the Han dynasty as Yinxu ("remains of Yin"), Yin was an extremely organized urban center. The true extent of Yin cannot be determined because an outer wall has never been found, but certainly two areas dominated its core: the largely administrative and residential sector, known as Xiaotun, and a huge royal cemetery called Xibeigang (Figure 35).[27] The plan shown in Figure 35 indicates that the palace-temple area was roughly in the center of the urban network and the royal cemetery was to the northwest. Graves of commoners were spread through the entire area, in many cases near the residences of the interred. Bronze vessels were important manufactured items at Yin, and indeed bronze workshops have been uncovered everywhere. No specific market area has been located. The administrative-ceremonial center, Xiaotun, was divided into three sections. Of these, the central sector (from north to south) had the most impressive palatial-style buildings.

Kwang-chih Chang has defined the Shang city as a wall-enclosed area that contained an aristocratic center within which were aristocratic and ceremonial buildings; beyond were specialized industries such as bronze foundries and farming villages.[28] Other characteristics of the ancient city, as defined

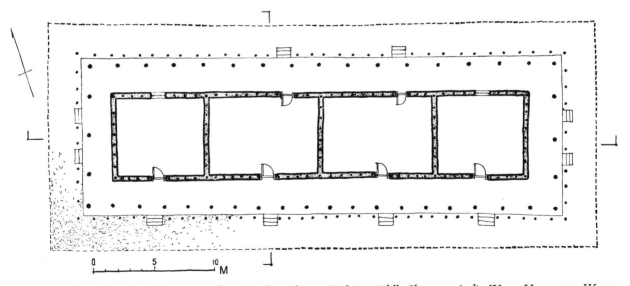

Figure 34. Plan of residential structure from Panlongcheng, Hubei (middle Shang period). [Yang Hongxun, *Wenwu* no. 2 (1976), p. 23]

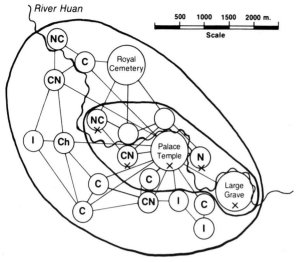

Figure 35. Structural model of the Anyang urban network during the Shang period. [Kwang-chih Chang, *Shang Civilization*, p. 30; published with permission of Yale University Press]

by Chang, are its location on a level plain near a waterway and hills, enclosure on four sides by walls made by the *hangtu* technique, the same method used in building platforms, and orientation to the cardinal directions.[29] Excavation at Erlitou and Panlongcheng confirms the orientation of administrative or ceremonial structures to the cardinal directions; four-sided enclosure; and the forerunners of a bay system. Anyang and Zhengzhou further confirm that cities of the dead, certainly of the imperial dead, were part of the greater city of the living and attest as well to the vast size of imperial cities in second millennium B.C. China. Also proved by archaeological evidence is the existence of a palace-city, or at least its antecedent in the palatial-ceremonial sector of greater cities.

Zhou Capitals

Zhou conquered Shang in north central China near the beginning of the twelfth century B.C. After the conquest some Shang cities continued to flourish.

In addition, new cities were built throughout the larger territory of Zhou occupation. Still a bronze-using culture, the early Zhou were centered in the Yellow River basin, especially in Shaanxi province. The year 771 B.C. marks the beginning of the Eastern Zhou, when the power center was shifted to the Luoyang region in western Henan.

Traditional histories of China and the Chinese city begin the discussion of the Western Zhou with the capitals built by Wen Wang at Feng and by Wu Wang at Hao fifteen years later. The histories make reference to the ode from the *Shi jing* quoted above. Yet thirty-five years of excavation in the vicinity of Xi'an have yielded only the roughest sketch map of Fengyi and Haojing, whose proposed locations are shown in Figure 18. In the case of these two Zhou imperial cities history has worked against the archaeologist: Both cities were destroyed even by the time of the First Emperor of Qin, who, according to the *Shi ji*, had only "heard of the likes of Feng and Hao."[30] A century later, at the time of Emperor Wudi of Han (r. 140–86 B.C.), in all probability Kunming Pond was dug on the former capital sites. Two thousand years of moving water and human habitation in the vicinity of pre-modern Xi'an have further complicated archaeological exploration. After some excavation at what were believed to have been the sites of the first Zhou capitals, and after reading of relevant classical texts, two archaeologists, Wang Shimin and Hu Qianying, published in 1958 and 1963, respectively, opinions about the locations of Kunming Pond, the Feng and Hao rivers, and Hao and Biao ponds.[31]

One building complex uncovered at Fengchu, some 130 kilometers west of Xi'an in Shaanxi province, seems to represent the architectural principles of Early Zhou construction. It has been studied and theoretically reconstructed as a gate and two halls enclosed by an arcade of rooms (Figures 36 and 37).[32] The buildings, elevated on platforms approached from the south, faced south and were ori-

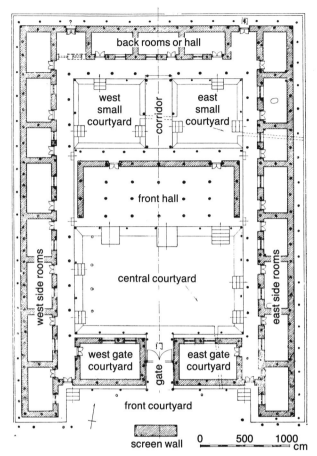

back rooms or hall

west small courtyard — corridor — east small courtyard

• front hall •

west side rooms — central courtyard — east side rooms

west gate courtyard — gate — east gate courtyard

front courtyard

screen wall 0   500   1000 cm

Figure 36. Plan of architectural complex at Fengchu, Shaanxi (predynastic Zhou?). [Yang Hongxun, *Wenwu* no. 3 (1981), p. 24]

ented just 10 degrees west of due north. If the front, or south, hall was for ceremonial purposes or for holding audience, and the building behind it served more private purposes, then this architectural scheme exemplifies the planning principles of the imperial sectors of the Chinese city in microcosm.

Eastern Zhou Capitals

Until archaeological finds push the date backward, it can be argued that the most important period in

the history of Chinese urbanism was the Eastern Zhou. Remains of cities from this period that are specifically referred to in texts have been excavated. The earliest known site plan is also from the Eastern Zhou.

More than one hundred cities were built, conquered, settled, or resettled by contending rulers who rose and fell between the movement of the primary capital to Luoyang in 771 B.C. and the fall of the Zhou and other surviving states to the Qin unifier of China in 256 B.C. Warfare was almost constant between the states *(guo),* which were governed by cities during the Eastern Zhou. During the earlier half of the Eastern Zhou—the Spring and Autumn period (771–481 B.C.)—battles were generally small in scale, never exceeding eight hundred chariots and twelve thousand men. Warfare was accompanied by elaborate ritual. By 481 B.C., when the last entry is made in the Lü state annals (Spring and Autumn annals), only twenty-two contending states were left. They continued the fight for control of China by longer and greater battles during the fittingly named Warring States period (403–221 B.C.). Indeed, one of the two characteristics of Eastern Zhou cities always named in scholarly literature is their dual function as military and administrative centers.[33] The second characteristic is the use of inner and outer walls, probably in place in Chinese urban schemes before the Eastern Zhou, but which by this time also served as double walls of defense for those quartered within the inner set.

What is amazing about the Eastern Zhou capitals is that only three different plans are found among the twenty or so cities that have been excavated.[34] Only in a civilization like China's, with such a strong trust in the supremacy of the institutions of former times, one of which was the imperial city, and with such faith in the power of these institutions to produce models of legitimate rulership, could this be the case, especially when one considers China's size and diverse geographic regions.

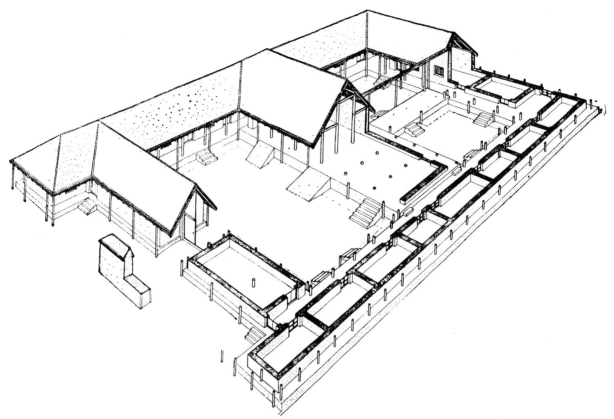

Figure 37. Theoretical reconstruction of architectural complex at Fengchu. [Yang Hongxun, *Wenwu* no. 3 (1981), p. 25]

The first of the three imperial urban schemes is the one prescribed in the *Kaogong ji* section of the *Zhou li*. Ironically, excavated evidence from the site of this city known as Wangcheng, at modern Luoyang, does not conform closely to the literary specifications. Since Luoyang was nevertheless the site of a primary and long-lived Zhou capital, its appearance based on limited excavations there will be described before proceeding to the more obvious evidence of the three first millennium B.C. imperial urban plans.

The plan of Zhou Luoyang published in 1959 is still the most authoritative available (Figure 38). The site of course had an urban history prior to the transfer of the main Zhou capital there in 770, for it was where the Duke of Zhou had built his brother-in-law's city in around the year 1100 B.C., and even earlier remains in the vicinity have been discovered. Inscriptions on later bronze vessels record two distinct walled areas, Chengzhou and Wangcheng, whose locations are believed to correspond roughly to the sites of the "old city" of the Han–Wei in the eastern suburbs of modern Luoyang and the area east of the Jian River and west of the Sui–Tang city, respectively (see Figure 20). At the beginning of the Eastern Zhou period, however, Wangcheng had been occupied continuously by twelve Zhou rulers from Ping Wang (r. 770–

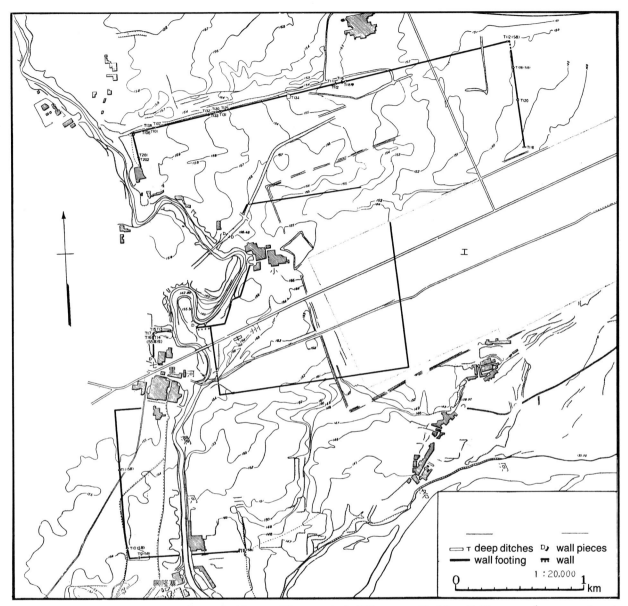

Figure 38. Remains at Luoyang from the Eastern Zhou period. ["Luoyang Jianbing," *Kaogu xuebao* no. 2 (1959), between pp. 16 and 17]

719) through Jin Wang (r. 544–520). Only in the last decade of the sixth century B.C. did the split between Chengzhou and Wangcheng occur.[35]

According to the excavation report, the outer wall of Wangcheng was roughly square. Its northern face, whose foundation has been completely uncovered, was 2,890 meters long and about 5 meters in width. Other surviving wall portions are indicated in Figure 38. The majority of rammed-earth building platforms were found in the south and central areas of the enclosure, suggesting the location of a ceremonial center there. (The inner wall shown in Figure 38 is of the later Han capital of Henan Xian, and there is no indication that it was built on the ruins of an earlier wall.) Remains of kilns and industrial areas confirm the existence of an economic support system for the imperial city.

Evidence of cities planned in accordance with the

description of Wangcheng comes from outside the vicinity of the Eastern Zhou capital. One example is Lüdu, part of which is today Qufu in Shandong province, a site which in the Western Zhou had been the capital of the Lü state. The plan of Lüdu that resulted from the Japanese excavation in the late 1930s and early 1940s shows a city center and enclosing outer wall (Figure 39). The central portion consisted of a man-made mound on which stood an ancestral temple, probably the same location as the later Lingguang Hall. The 10-meter raised area was approximately 500 by 550 meters and was located about 400 meters northeast of the northeast corner of the current city Qufu, only about one-quarter the size of the ancient outer wall. Excavation by Komai and Sekino in the early 1940s yielded enough late Zhou material on or in the vicinity of the central mound to satisfy the

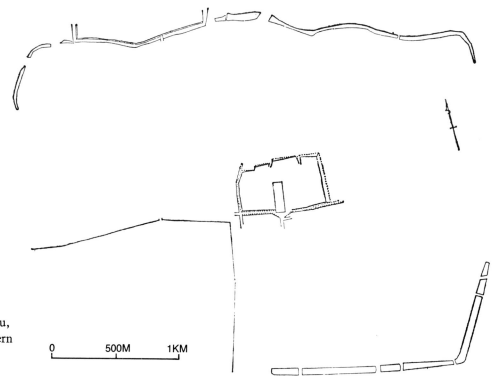

Figure 39. Plan of Lüdu, Shandong, in the Eastern Zhou period. [Komai, *Chūgoku tojō,* p. 25]

0   500M   1KM

excavators that it had been the site of palatial architecture during the Warring States period; with this evidence they cautiously posited that a palace-city stood there even during Spring and Autumn times. A palace-city wall was not excavated, but one is suggested by the position of the Zhou ancestral temple. Recent Chinese study of Lüdu also indicates that the ancestral temple was in the center of a walled enclosure; although it was repaired in the Han dynasty when Lingguang Hall was erected, its perimeter is the same as that of the Eastern Zhou wall.[36] The new evidence from China records the dimensions of Qufu as approximately 3.5 kilometers east to west by 2.5 kilometers north to south, with eleven outer wall gates from which emerged major urban arteries. A tomb area was to the city's northwest.

A second Warring States city whose plan corresponded to that of the idealized Wangcheng was found at Anyi, a capital of the Wei state, in southwestern Shanxi (Figure 40).[37] Like Lüdu's wall, the outer wall at Anyi was more rectangular than square: It measured approximately 4,500 meters north to south and 2,100 meters east to west. Neither of the Warring States examples of the Wangcheng scheme is oriented due north–south. Both cities were surrounded by moats.

The Jin state capital in southern Shanxi province may also have been built according to the *Kaogong ji* plan. It consisted of separate inner and outer walled enclosures, approximately 1,100 square meters and possibly 3,000 square meters, respectively. The southeastern, southwestern, and southern portions of both walls are now beneath the Guai River, but the plan as it has been reconstructed from the remains indicates that a palace-city was roughly centralized, closer to the eastern outer wall than to the western one.[38]

The second imperial urban pattern of the first millennium B.C. is represented by Jiang, another capital of the Jin state in Shanxi.[39] Its plan is distin

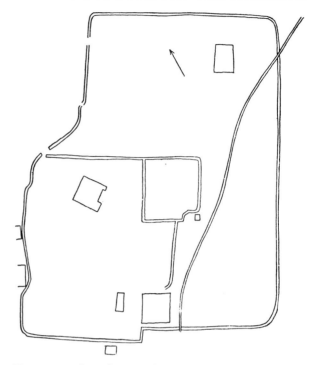

Figure 40. Plan of Anyi, Shanxi, in the Warring States period. [Tao and Ye, *Wenwu* no. 4/5 (1962), p. 61]

guished by the location of the palace-city in the north center of the outer city and by the sharing of a common northern wall portion by the two areas (Figure 41). Possibly existing from the Spring and Autumn period, the inner city of the Jin capital was approximately 1 kilometer square; the fairly straight outer wall extended more than 8,480 meters, its southern boundary slightly longer than the northern. The outer wall was surrounded by water. Within the city remains more than 1 kilometer of a street that began at the north wall of the outer city and ran southward through the inner city and beyond.

The third imperial city type is much more in evidence during the Warring States period. It can be called the double city. The double city consists of two walled enclosures which may or may not have

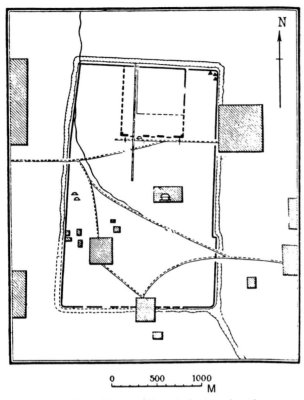

Figure 41. Plan of Jiang, Shanxi, during the Zhou period. [Chang Wenzhai, *Kaogu* no. 10 (1963), p. 544]

the same initial building dates, but which stand at the same time. Most often the two areas of the double city share either an entire wall face or two ends of wall faces that form a corner and interlocking component to that corner. Usually only one of the walled regions contains a palace-city, in which case the palace-city may be located in the center or north center of its outer wall, corresponding to the first two imperial city types.

The capital of the Yan state, Xiadu, near Yi Xian, Hebei province, has long been the subject of archaeological and scholarly interest (Figure 42).[40] At Xiadu the eastern city was built earlier than the western and seems to have been the focus of more

urban activity. Palaces, residences, bronze, iron, and ceramic workshops, and cemeteries filled the eastern portion, itself divided into small northern and larger southern areas. The large pounded-earth platforms uncovered in the northern enclosure of the eastern area identify it as a palace-city, positioned as the palace-city of Jiang. Adjacent to the main palaces, in the northwest, where one has come to expect them, were tombs. Water flowed between the eastern and western cities, and a portion of moat has been uncovered outside the eastern wall.

Handan, capital of the state of Zhao in Hebei, flourished later than Xiadu, from 386 to 228 B.C. The foundation of its western city wall was intact at the time of excavation (Figure 43, lower left). It measured about 1,400 meters on each side. The surviving eastern city wall was approximately one-half that size in width but the same length. Another wall portion was found north of the eastern city. Near the center of the western city a row of four large platforms, presumably palace halls, stood in a north–south line. Squarish platforms were similarly arranged in the eastern city, suggesting that at Handan the two walled enclosures had separate ceremonial centers, even during a period of coexistence. Recent excavation has shown occupation of the site to have been much more widespread than was believed in 1940 when the first excavation report was published. It is currently thought that the double city plus northern extension comprised one of two cities that flourished at Handan in the Warring States period. (A second, larger city to the northeast, not shown in Figure 43, was called Wanglangcheng.) Handan might, therefore, be referred to as a double city, one of whose portions consisted of three adjoining walled regions.[41]

A more complex urban site has been uncovered during the last twenty years near modern Houma in Shanxi province. Within an approximately 4-by-

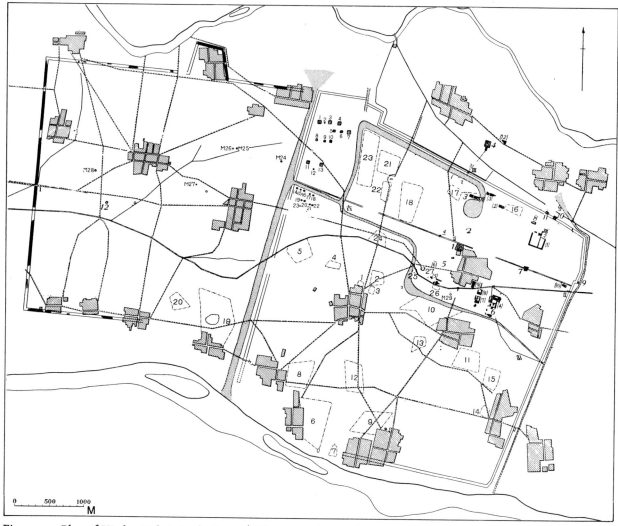

Figure 42. Plan of Xiadu, Hebei, in the Eastern Zhou period. ["Hebei Yi Xian Yan Xiadu gucheng," *Kaogu xuebao* no. 1 (1965), p. 84]

2-kilometer site, four large and more smaller walled enclosures have been excavated (Figure 44). Many of them have been linked with Eastern Zhou cities mentioned in the *Zuo zhuan*. The two labeled Old City of Taishen and Old City of Niucun in Figure 44 resemble the most typical double-city configura-tion of two adjacent cities sharing one wall face. Evidence from Houma is best used, however, to illustrate the continued rebuilding or return to a site by different rulers for imperial purposes.[42]

Linzi, capital of the state of Qi, may be consid-ered a double city also. Its walls joined at the cor-

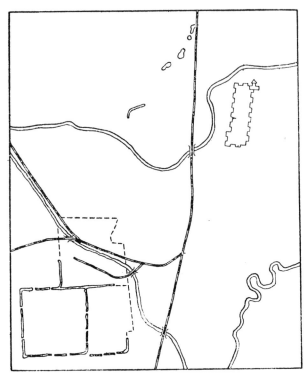

Figure 43. Plan of Handan, Hebei, in the Warring States period. ["Hebei Handan," *Kaogu* no. 2 (1980), p. 142]

usually a four-sided one.[44] From the Han dynasty on, however, no imperial city was to be built with fewer than two walled areas. Single walls, perhaps even in the first millennium B.C., defined only cities of less than imperial status.

Almost fifty years of excavation of Eastern Zhou cities thus proves that three different plans coexisted for imperial cities. In other words, the idealized urban plan of Wangcheng, immortalized for two thousand years as the genesis of all Chinese imperial planning, is but one of three city types. Although it alone is described in a classical text, all three imperial schemes would continue as the established designs of Chinese rulers and rulers seeking to emulate Chinese city building standards for over a millennium more.

One final fundamental aspect of Chinese urbanism is established by the time of the Eastern Zhou. It is the site plan. The drawing of the imperial necropolis found in the tomb of King Cuo, ruler of the Zhongshan kingdom (today in Hebei province), who reigned at the end of the fourth century B.C., is presently the earliest Chinese site plan (Figure 46).[45] The arrangement of five tombs on the 94 by 48 by 1 centimeter plate recalls the four enclosed rooms in the plan of the building complex from Panlongcheng (see Figure 34). Both the funerary and residential schemes show the principles of imperial city architecture manifest in microcosm. More important, the plan from the Warring States period proves that even before the end of the first millennium B.C. the Chinese conceived of their space as a predetermined design that corresponds to a perfect geometrical form.

Qin Xianyang

The unification of the states occurred in the year 221 B.C., two-thirds of the way through the short-lived Qin dynasty (255–206 B.C.). The unifier of the remaining six states along with his own, Qin,

ners rather than side by side (Figure 45). Located in Shandong, Linzi was also excavated by Japanese archaeologists.[43] Unlike the other three double cities discussed here, however, at Linzi the southwestern enclosure contained the palace-city. Near the center of Linzi's palace-city was a mound approached by two sets of three stairs. One of the larger and more complex Warring States cities uncovered to date, Linzi had more than 14,000 meters of outer walls with a total of eleven gates. Ten major roads ran through the urban area, which also had an underground sewage system.

Among the other Eastern Zhou cities that have been excavated and studied, one might isolate a fourth type—namely, the city with only one wall,

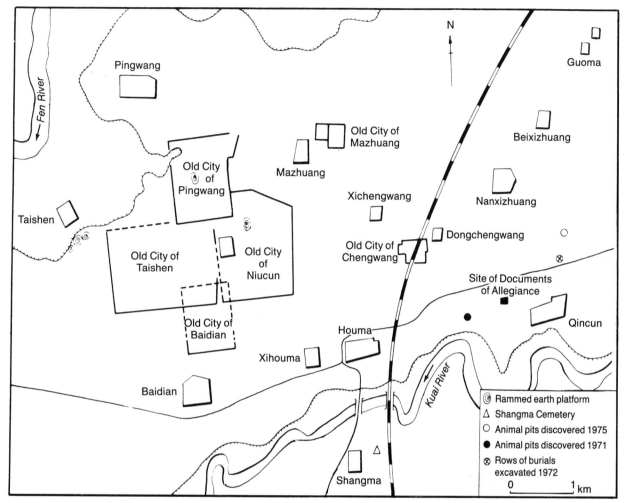

Figure 44. Plan of walled enclosures at Houma, Shanxi, in the Eastern Zhou period. [Li Xueqin, *Eastern Zhou and Qin Civilizations*, p. 42; published with permission of Yale University Press]

was the fourth ruler Prince Zheng, better known by his later title, First Emperor, Shi Huangdi (r. 221–209 B.C.). This man founded an imperial system whose fundamental principles would endure for more than two thousand years. Among Qin Shi Huangdi's contributions to the Chinese system were the division of the empire into commanderies, further divided into districts, unified weights and measures, a standard currency, a common written language, and a central government based at his capital city Xianyang, in the Wei River valley in Shaanxi province, near the sites of the early Western Zhou capitals Feng and Hao (see Figure 18, no. 4). The First Emperor also commissioned three hundred thousand men to join the walls protecting the northern frontier into a single Great Wall of

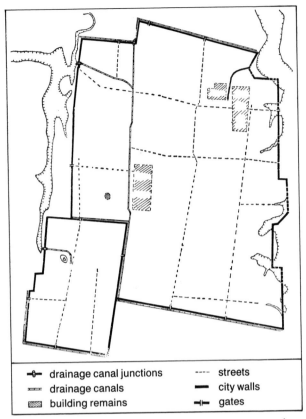

—●— drainage canal junctions	---- streets
═══ drainage canals	—— city walls
▨ building remains	—‖— gates

Figure 45. Plan of Linzi, Shandong, in the Eastern Zhou period. [Zhang and Zhu, *Kaogu* no. 9 (1988), p. 785]

pounded earth, extending 5,000 kilometers from present-day Gansu province in the west to Liaoning in the northeast. Called a megalomaniac by some, a tyrant by others, during his short reign Shi Huang-di exhausted the empire's resources to build a summer resort, Shanglin Yuan, parks, and a most impressive subterranean tomb complex at Lishan which contained a lifesize terra-cotta army of thousands.[46]

Although the First Emperor's contributions to Chinese civilization, specifically to its imperial self-image and ideology, are often called innovative, or at least distinguishable from what had come before

them, his imperial capital and its palaces are more easily seen as continuations, or perhaps climaxes, of urban and palatial architectural developments of the Zhou.[47]

Shi Huangdi's imperial city Xianyang has not been fully excavated, but some details about it are known. The site had been the capital of the Qin state for over two hundred years before the time of the First Emperor, and ruins uncovered beneath the Qin city were from a Warring States palace complex. Excavators' reconstruction of the Xianyang outer wall indicates that its shape was close to a square (Figure 47).[48] Within that wall, in addition to the palaces surviving from Qin rule prior to the First Emperor's unification of China, palaces imitating those of the six defeated states plus one representing the Qin were erected anew.

Across the Wei River from the palaces of Xianyang, the First Emperor commenced the building of the palace complex called Epang, whose front hall was said to have been 50 *zhang* (1 *zhang* = about 3.3 meters) by 50 *bu* (1 *bu* = about 5 *chi*, or Chinese feet).[49] This bilevel structure, it was said, could accommodate ten thousand men in the upper story and had a 5-*zhang* flagpole rising from the lower story.[50] Access between Epang Palace and the rest of Xianyang was possible via a two-story cov-

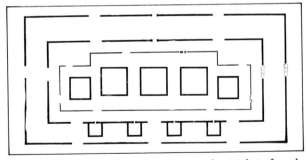

Figure 46. Plan of Zhongshan necropolis, Hebei, fourth century B.C. ["Hebei Sheng Pinghang Xian," *Wenwu* no. 1 (1979), p. 23]

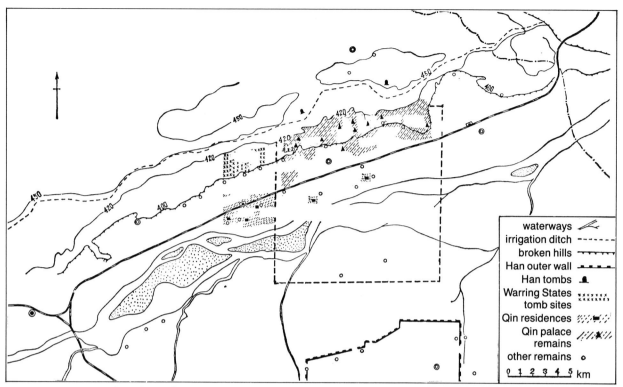

Figure 47. Suggested outline of Xianyang outer city wall, Shaanxi, third century B.C. ["Qindu Xianyang diyihao gongdian," *Wenwu* no. 11 (1976), p. 12]

ered way across the Wei River, likened in Chinese texts to the Milky Way. As Alexander Soper notes, although the Chinese text may be inclined to hyperbole and the downfall of the First Emperor may be attributed to his excessive ways, still the palatial architecture of Xianyang set the standard for much of Chinese imperial architecture to follow.[51]

Shi Huangdi's concern for the physical appearance of the Qin imperial city was derived from his ideology of palace building. In justification of his grand expansion plan of 212 B.C., the First Emperor said: "I have heard of Wen Wang of Zhou's capital city at Feng and of Wu Wang's capital of Hao. The likes of Feng and Hao are the imperial cities of emperors. Therefore I shall build my dynastic palace in the parkland south of the Wei River. This palace will have the capacity to entertain one hundred thousand men who will come by cart to drink wine and on horseback to warm their hands by the fire. One thousand men will sing and ten thousand will harmonize. Thus shall we receive the army of heaven."[52] The ideology of the Qin state, as the grandeur of its imperial city, was perpetuated long after the First Emperor's short reign.

Shi Huangdi died before Epang Palace could be completed. What did stand at the time of his death was destroyed in a fire which is said to have burned for three months.

3

FIRST

GREAT EMPIRE

Just look at the layout of the city walls—
On every side there opened three gates,
Each with a three-lane roadway level and straight.
Running parallel were chariot tracks, twelve in
    number,
Streets and thoroughfares crossed back and forth.
The residential plots and wards followed regular
    lines,
The tiled roofs were even and smooth.
The high-class residences of the Northern Watch-
    tower
Opened directly to the road.
They selected the most adept craftsmen to apply their
    skills,
And expected their dwellings never to crumble or
    collapse.
The timbers were garbed in pongee and brocade;
The ground was painted vermeil and purple.
The imperial arms of the Arsenal
Were placed in racks and crossbow frames. . . .
They greatly expanded the Nine Markets,
Joined by encircling walls, girdled by gates.
From the flag pavilion, five stories high,
Officials looked down to inspect the countless shop
    rows . . .
Precious wares arriving from all quarters,
Gathered like birds, amassed like fish scales.
Sellers earned double profit,
But buyers were never lacking. . . .
The palaces and lodges of the capital commanderies
    and kingdoms
Were one hundred forty-five in number. . . .
The encircling walls stretched continuously
Four hundred *li* and more. . . .[1]

THE fall of the Qin to a man of common origins,
Liu Bang, ushered into China a dynasty of long
duration. The two hundred years of the earlier part
of the dynasty, the Western Han (206 B.C.–A.D. 8),

allowed an initially strong government to develop a lasting cultural and literary heritage and to build a sprawling walled capital. A brief interruption in Han rule occurred from A.D. 9 to 23, when a usurper named Wang Mang took the throne. His control of China was quickly undermined by resistance to his policies and rebellion. By the time power returned to the Han ruling family, Chang'an, their imperial city for over two hundred years, lay in ruins. The Han emperor therefore decided to transfer the capital eastward to Luoyang, near the site of the former Eastern Zhou imperial city. Thus was Eastern Han rule initiated.

Compared to the capitals of the Shang and Zhou, Han Chang'an and Luoyang are tangible. Literary records of the cities written during the Han dynasty or shortly afterward survive. Notable among these are the *fu*, rhapsodic descriptions of both capitals (and subsequent ones) compiled by Xiao Tong (501–531) in the *Wen xuan* (Literary selections); and *Sanfuhuang tu,* which has been quoted in Chapter 2. With a preface by Miao Changyan, who calls himself a Chang'an resident, *Sanfuhuang tu* is believed to have been composed several centuries later than the period it describes. In addition, influential men of the Early Han are immortalized in the biographies of Sima Tan and Sima Qian's historical record, *Shi ji*. Ban Gu's *Qian Han shu* (History of the Former Han) covers the period 209 B.C. to A.D. 25. Information pertaining to imperial cities is also found in Fan Ye's (398–445) *Hou Han shu* (History of the Later Han). Names of Han city planners are also preserved.[2] As well, maps of the Han capital Chang'an survive from the Song dynasty and those of Luoyang survive from Yuan times.[3] Furthermore, Chang'an was a subject of great interest for Chinese, Japanese, and Western scholars during the 1930s and 1940s.[4] Finally, Han remains from both Chang'an and Luoyang have been extensively excavated.[5]

WESTERN HAN CHANG'AN

The imperial city of the Han during the last two centuries B.C. was located about 2 kilometers south of the Wei River, southeast of Xianyang and not far from the ruins of Epang Palace. The capital was begun even before the first Han ruler Gaozu (r. 206–194 B.C.) had returned from his pacification of the empire. Perhaps because the expanse of imperial domains and power was not anticipated, or perhaps simply because palatial residences were not immediately necessary, the minister in charge of building the new city began in the emperor's absence with only two palaces—Changle and Weiyang. In this respect Chang'an is different from the idealized capital of the King of Zhou described in the *Kaogong ji,* for which the text dictates that construction of the outer city wall should precede the building of the rest of the city.

Changle Palace was built on the ruins of a former Qin "detached" pleasure palace called Xingle Gong. The palace complex was enclosed by an irregularly shaped wall about 10 kilometers in length. The shape was probably the result of building on former ruins, for Weiyang Palace, 2,150 by 2,250 meters, was of regular shape. Pounded-earth building foundations and an 11-meter section of the western enclosing wall of Weiyang Palace still stand. The distance between the Changle and Weiyang palaces was approximately 1 *li*, and in that space Han Gaozu built an arsenal, 880 by 320 meters, which contained seven storage sections. In addition, warehouses were erected under the Han founder. Initially Changle was the palace complex where the emperor held court, but later it became the residence of the empress dowager. This change indicates that the multiple functionality of post-and-lintel construction was part of China's earliest building history. Weiyang Palace subsequently became the place where court was convened.

Details about these two palace complexes abound. Recent excavation has shown that Changle Palace was surrounded by a huge wall, more than 10,000 meters in length. In other words, it occupied an area of over 6 square kilometers—nearly one-sixth the area of the entire capital. The squarish wall of Weiyang Palace was not much smaller: It extended almost 9,000 meters, and its 5-square-kilometer area occupied one-seventh the entire space of Chang'an.[6]

Some fifty years before the most recent archaeological publications about the Western Han capital, both Chinese and Westerners visited and investigated the remains of Weiyang Palace. Carl W. Bishop described what he saw:

> Immediately west of the city proper and separated from it by the much eroded remains of two parallel earthen walls of no great size which ran north and south about a hundred feet apart, we came upon the old palace-enclosure of the Han emperors. The surface here also was somewhat undulating in character. . . .
>
> Here . . . we saw a long mound in several superimposed stages, with its major axis extending due north and south and perhaps coinciding with that of the palace-city itself. This mound, our Chinese companions told us, had been the foundation-platform of the . . . celebrated Wei Yang Kung [Weiyang Gong]. . . .
>
> We found the ground-plan of this interesting construction that of a long rectangle, with corners surprisingly well-defined considering its age. The total length was 450 yards, its breadth 145 yards, and it was built in five stages, of which the highest, near the northern end, rose some 50 feet above the surrounding fields. It had been constructed of successive layers of *terre pisé* like those forming the rampart that we had just been examining, and was now thinly covered with grass save for patches of cultivation here and there. . . .
>
> Exactly at the centre of the southern end of the rectangle we found traces of an approach or gradual ascent of some kind, apparently a ramp (A), about 100 feet in width east by west. It extended north, sloping gently upward the while, for some 70 feet, to the level of the top of the lowest terrace (B). . . . The surface of the latter, aside from the ramp, was practically level and extended for 156 yards until it came to the second stage (C), marked by a sharp rise or step of 2 feet. From this point north, a slight upwards slope brought us to another abrupt rise of 2 feet marking the beginning of the third terrace (D). The ground thence continued rising gently until, 95 yards farther north, it reached the edge of the fourth stage (E). This was a steep earthen bank some 10 feet high; from its southern face there projected a somewhat lower platform of earth (F), now much eroded but apparently once rectangular in form; its ends were in exact alignment with the borders of the (unpaved) avenue of approach, which we had been able to trace, intermittently, up to this point.
>
> The mound culminated in a long narrow terrace (G) about 12 yards wide north and south and extending east by west for some 65 yards; its fairly level top stood about 6 feet higher than the preceding stage. Here, at the apex of the mound, was a commemorative stela encased in brickwork (H), erected in the year 1695.[7]

Bishop's drawing of what he described is shown in Figure 48.

A more recent discussion of Weiyang Gong that does not take into account excavation in the People's Republic of China was published in 1972.[8] Using sources like *Sanfuhuang tu* and "Xijing fu" the author, Ye Dasong, drew a detailed picture of the forty-three structures of Weiyang Gong, plus ponds, stables, and platforms (Figure 49). Weiyang Palace, as much as any early imperial city complex, has continuously captured the mind and imagination of the Chinese. It has also been the subject of Chinese painting (Figure 50).

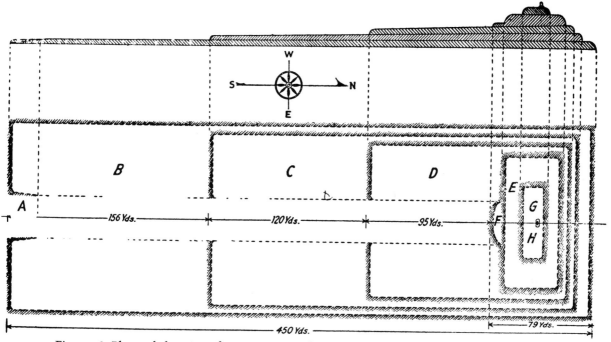

Figure 48. Plan and elevation of Weiyang Gong foundation. [Bishop, *Antiquity* 13 (1938), p. 76]

From excavation more is now known about the Weiyang and Changle palace compounds. Gates provided access to the four walls of both complexes, and two gates of each palace compound wall had *que,* or gate-towers. Ceramic models and rubbings from Han relief sculpture suggest what these gates may have looked like (Figure 51). Turning back to texts, one learns that *que* marked the eastern gate of Weiyang Gong, through which feudal lords came to court, and the north gate, entered by officials for such functions as the presentation of memorials to the throne. It is also recorded that rock from Longshou Mountain, north of Chang'an in Shaanxi province, was used for the foundation of Weiyang Gong main hall, which archaeologists report was 350 meters north to south by 200 meters east to west.

It was not until the reign of the second Han emperor, Huidi (r. 194–187 B.C.), that the outer wall of Chang'an was constructed. Digging suggests that the wall was begun at the northwest corner and that building continued around in a counterclockwise direction (Figure 52).[9] In perimeter the Chang'an wall measured 25,900 meters—divided as 7,200, 4,900, 7,600, and 6,200 meters on the north, west, south, and east sides, respectively. The wall was made of yellow rammed earth and stood more than 12 meters high. Its thickness was 12 to 16 meters, narrowing gradually toward the top. Han Huidi brought men from a radius of 600 *li* to work on the wall, which took five years to complete. Surrounding the city was a moat. As in the prescription for the King of Zhou's city, each wall had three gates.

The irregular wall shape is the most noticeable feature of the plan of Chang'an in Western Han

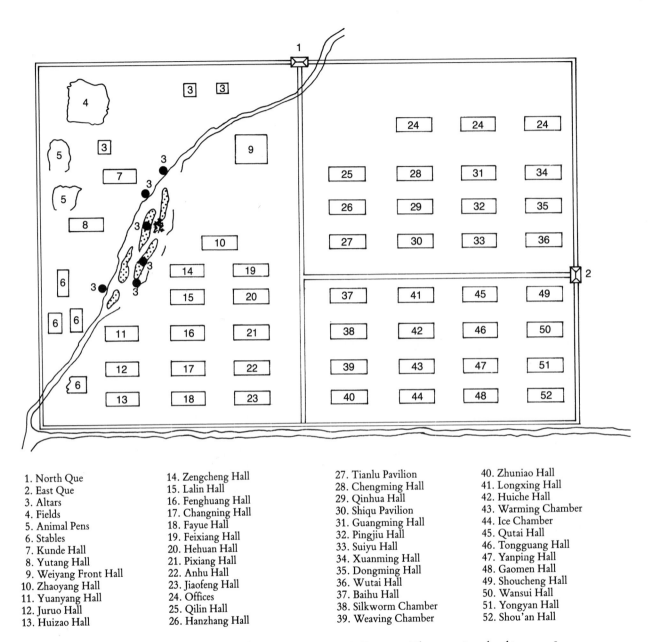

Figure 49. Theoretical plan of Weiyang Gong. [Ye Dasong, *Zhongguo jianzhu shi,* p. 422]

1. North Que
2. East Que
3. Altars
4. Fields
5. Animal Pens
6. Stables
7. Kunde Hall
8. Yutang Hall
9. Weiyang Front Hall
10. Zhaoyang Hall
11. Yuanyang Hall
12. Juruo Hall
13. Huizao Hall

14. Zengcheng Hall
15. Lalin Hall
16. Fenghuang Hall
17. Changning Hall
18. Fayue Hall
19. Feixiang Hall
20. Hehuan Hall
21. Pixiang Hall
22. Anhu Hall
23. Jiaofeng Hall
24. Offices
25. Qilin Hall
26. Hanzhang Hall

27. Tianlu Pavilion
28. Chengming Hall
29. Qinhua Hall
30. Shiqu Pavilion
31. Guangming Hall
32. Pingjiu Hall
33. Suiyu Hall
34. Xuanming Hall
35. Dongming Hall
36. Wutai Hall
37. Baihu Hall
38. Silkworm Chamber
39. Weaving Chamber

40. Zhuniao Hall
41. Longxing Hall
42. Huiche Hall
43. Warming Chamber
44. Ice Chamber
45. Qutai Hall
46. Tongguang Hall
47. Yanping Hall
48. Gaomen Hall
49. Shoucheng Hall
50. Wansui Hall
51. Yongyan Hall
52. Shou'an Hall

Figure 50. Zhao Boqu (Song), *Shaoyang Hall, Weiyang Gong.* [Published with permission of the National Palace Museum, Taipei]

Figure 51. Rubbing of *Que* showing the vermilion bird, from relief sculpture from tomb, Chengdu, Sichuan, Han dynasty. [*Han tuo,* p. 113]

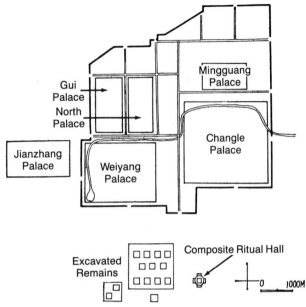

Figure 52. Plan of Western Han Chang'an, Shaanxi, second–first centuries B.C. [Dong, *Zhongguo chengshi jianshe shi,* p. 17]

times. There are two common explanations for the unusual form: that the flow of water necessitated the bend of the northwestern corner and that the line of the south wall was due to the location of Changle and Weiyang palaces, already in place before the wall construction. The Western Han capital would not be the last city where preexistent structures would force otherwise straight city walls to become irregular.

The configuration of the Chang'an outer wall was known long before excavation of the city in the 1950s, and a comparison between the earliest and most recent plans of the capital is remarkable. The oldest known plan of Western Han Chang'an was made by the Song dynasty official Lü Dafang (1027–1097), who, together with Liu Jingyang, was commissioned to make accompanying maps for

the local record of Chang'an, *Chang'an zhi,* which was edited by Song Minqiu (1019–1079) (Figure 53). Although the palaces and gates of the city published in the eleventh century do not correspond exactly to those shown in Figure 52—the most accurate postexcavation plan of Chang'an—the two sharp bends in the northern wall between the westernmost end and the straight northern wall position at its east are noticeably similar. The complete outer wall line that survives in Li Haowen's *Chang'an zhi tu* (Illustrated record of Chang'an) (Figure 54), based on the plans of Lü Dafang and Liu Jingyang, shows approximately the same north wall and the correct southern wall shape, although not of accurate proportions. The fourteenth-century plan further indicates the jut southward in the south wall, to accommodate An Gate, and its true

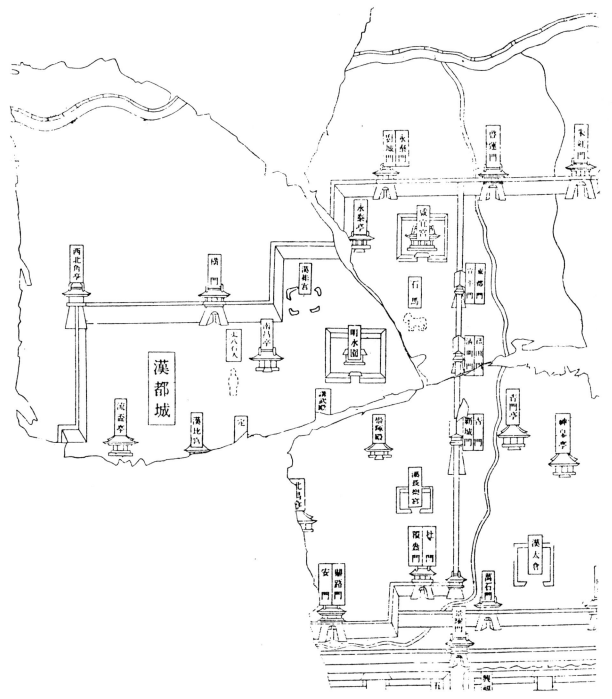

Figure 53. Plan of Western Han Chang'an. [Song Minqiu, *Chang'an zhi;* according to Xiang, "Qian Han gongdian jianzhu dui zhengju de yingxiang," fig. 1]

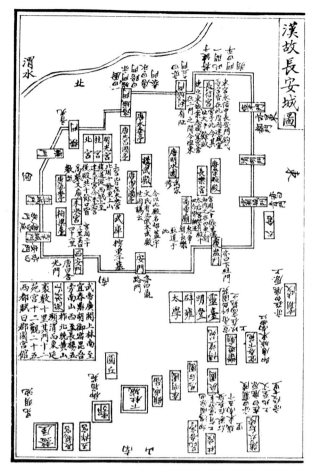

Figure 54. Plan of Western Han Chang'an. [Li Haowen, *Chang'an zhi tu, Jingdiao Tang congshu,* no. 24, *juan* 1/5]

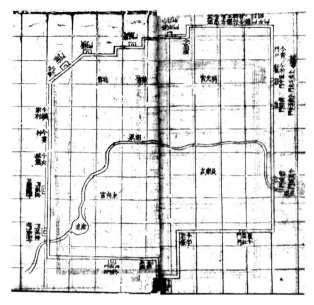

Figure 55. Plan of Western Han Chang'an. [*Chang'an Xian zhi* (1813), *juan* 3/3b–4a]

south border, which extends farther north on the east side of An Gate than on the west in order to accommodate the positions of the Changle and Weiyang palace complexes, respectively. The city plan published in *Chang'an Xian zhi* (Record of Chang'an district) has the same boundaries (Figure 55), as does Yang Shoujing's plan of Chang'an in Western Han times published in the late-nineteenth-century work *Shui jing zhu tu* (Illustrated commentary on the *Water Classic*) (Figure 56).

The most interesting plan of Western Han Chang'an drawn without the benefit of archaeology was published by Yao Jiazao in 1933 (Figure 57). The general city outline, the names and positions of palace compounds, and the number of gates on Yao's plan correspond to those in other renderings (and to actuality). The positions of the palaces and the streets around them, however, are in accordance with the preconceived notion that in a Chinese imperial city major thoroughfares form a grid, running without interruption from north to south or east to west. This idea, of course, comes from the description of the King of Zhou's city in the *Kaogong ji,* and for that reason, combined with the three gates on each outer wall face, a plan like Figure 57 came to be drawn. The true urban design inside the walls of the first Han capital was very different, but the plan is evidence of the overgeneralized assumptions made about Chinese impe-

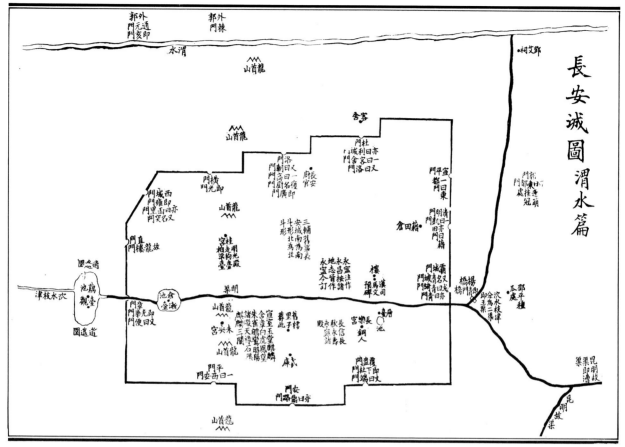

Figure 56. Plan of Western Han Chang'an. [Yang Shoujing, *Shui jing zhu tu,* Taipei repr., pp. 630–631]

rial cities based on the description of Wangcheng in the classical text.

The mapping of palace boundaries of the Han capital in preexcavation days was never so successful as the borders of cities. In no map, for instance, was the irregular shape of the Qin detached palace Changle Gong shown. Often palace lines were not even drawn, but when they were sketched, as in Yao Jiazao's version of Chang'an shown in Figure 57, or in the more famous plans published by Xu Song (1781–1848) in his mid-nineteenth-century publication *Tang liangjing chengfang kao* (Research

on the city districts of the two Tang capitals) (Figure 58), building enclosures always fit into neat geometric compartments. The sizes of palace compounds could also be inaccurate—as seen, for example, in Bi Yuan's drawing of the Han capital published in *Guanzhong tengji tuzhi* (Illustrated research on famous ruins of the Guanzhong area) (Figure 59), in which Changle Palace appears much smaller than Weiyang Palace.

This last fact is surprising, for dimensions of the two palaces and the outer city are provided in early texts such as *Sanfuhuang tu* and the official Han his-

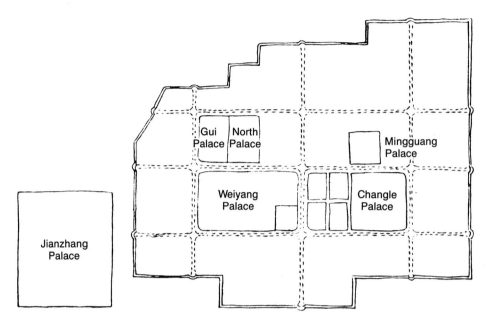

Figure 57. Plan of Western Han Chang'an. [Yao Jiazao, *Zhongguo jianzhu shi*, fig. 102]

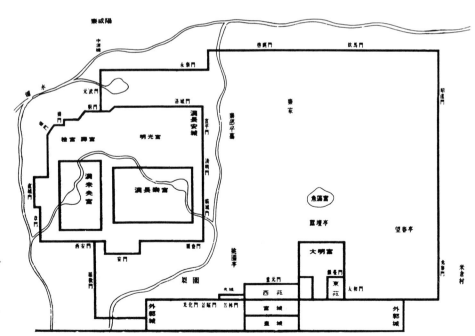

Figure 58. *Plan of the Three Parklands of the Western Capital*, Chang'an. [Xu Song, *Tang liangjing chengfang kao*]

tories. The measurements of both palaces and the outer wall obtained during the excavation of the Western Han site have impressively confirmed the texts. The 25,900-meter outer wall, for instance, would have been nearly 63 Han *li*.[10] The measurement 62 *li* is recorded in *Han jiu yi* (Ancient ceremonies of the Han); 63 *li* is the figure given in the *Shi ji* and in *Xu Han shu;* and *Sanfuhuang tu* records 65 *li* for the outer wall perimeter.[11]

One statement about the outer wall of Han Chang'an reported in both the *Shi ji* and *Sanfuhuang tu* is controversial. The shape of the city, clearly disturbing even in Han times, is explained as built to conform with the Northern and Southern Dipper

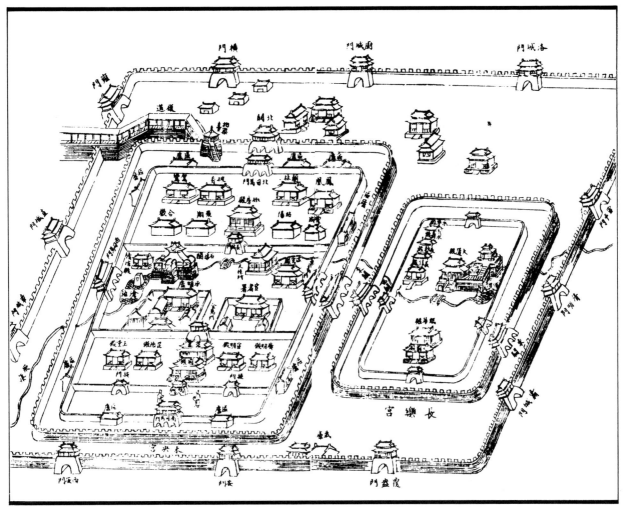

Figure 59. *Changle and Weiyang Palaces of the Han.* [Bi, *Guanzhong tengji tukao, Xi'an Fu,* pp. 23b–24a]

constellations. The northern half of Western Han Chang'an was said to follow the Great Dipper; the southern half was alleged to follow the Little Dipper. In an attempt to verify the statement, Paul Wheatley published a plan of the Han imperial city with the constellations Ursa Major and Ursa Minor superimposed on it.[12] Yet Wheatley admits that evidence cannot support the idea, and Wang Zhongshu comments that the theory is farfetched.[13] That the Chinese sought the favor of the heavens for their imperial cities and that city buildings were named after solar bodies have long been recognized. Astrological associations cannot, however, explain the shape of the outer wall of Chang'an. Rather, simple facts explain its unusual form. Unlike the King of Zhou's ideal city model, Western Han Chang'an was not planned from inception, and thus its walls were constructed after the interior palace compounds. The reuse of old Qin palaces, the construction of new imperial buildings but not an outer wall under the first Han emperor, and the flow of water all combined to produce the highly irregular and geometrically imperfect shape.

Building at the Western Han capital continued after the construction of its outer wall. The next important period occurred under Emperor Wudi (r. 140–86 B.C.). During those years three additional palace complexes—Minghuang, Gui, and Bei—were erected inside the outer city wall, and Jianzhang Gong was built outside the wall, west of the city. Shanglin Park was enlarged and Kunming Pond was dug during these years also.

Noticeable in a recent plan such as Figure 52 are Chang'an's twelve outer wall gates and the long, straight boulevards that cross the city, often emerging directly from outer wall gates. Four of the gates—the two south gates of the western city wall, the east gate of the south wall, and the south gate of the east wall—were close to the southern city palaces, thus preventing easy access into the city but rather quickly leading to the Weiyang or Changle palace compounds. From each of the other eight gates, however, a major boulevard led to the city, the longest going northward 5,500 meters from the center gate of the south wall to the northernmost main city boulevard, near the north wall of Chang'an. The long avenues were approximately 45 meters wide. Contrary to expectations about the city based on the prescription of Wangcheng (which gave rise to Figure 57), however, no main street extended the full distance from any pair of north to south or east to west gates.

The eight gate-boulevards were further divided by drainage ditches into three parallel lanes. Passage on the central and widest lane, approximately 20 meters across, was restricted to imperial use. The two side lanes, which were used by others, measured 12 meters. Based on what we know of later Chinese imperial cities, which frequently have triple-lane main boulevards, it is likely that the outer lanes were each one-way.

Although the sizes of walls, gates, and boulevards may impress us as we view this second and first century B.C. capital today, residents seem to have taken these features almost for granted, remarking more on the activity in the city, especially at the marketplaces. A resident of the first Han capital described it to a friend in the early first century A.D. after the new imperial city at Luoyang had been established:

They erected a metal fortress a myriad spans long,
Dredged the surrounding moat to form a gaping
    chasm,
Cleared broad avenues three lanes wide,
Placed twelve gates for passage in and out.
Within, the city was pierced by roads and streets,
With ward gates and portals nearly a thousand.

In the nine markets they set up bazaars,
Their wares separated by type, their shop rows dis-
    tinctly divided.
There was not room for people to turn their heads,
Or for chariots to wheel about.
People crammed into the city, spilled into the sub-
    urbs,
Everywhere streaming into the hundreds of shops.
Red dust gathered in all directions;
Smoke blended with the clouds.
Thus, the people being both numerous and rich,
There was pleasure and gaiety without end.
The men and women of the capital
Were the most distinctive of the five regions.
Men of pleasure compared with dukes and marquises;
Shopgirls were dressed more lavishly than ladies Ji or
    Jiang.
The stalwarts from the villages,
The leaders of the knights-errant, . . .
Joined in bands, gathered in groups,
Raced and galloped within their midst.[14]

The wards and markets of Han Chang'an have aroused the interest of later scholars also. Although they have not been shown in any plan, for it has not been possible to determine their boundaries, Chang'an was divided into one hundred sixty wall-enclosed sectors called *li* or *lüli*, ("wards"). Each ward had a supervisor *(lizheng)* and was further divided into twenty *bao.* Each ward had four guarded gates, one on each side. The ward population within resided in courtyard-style houses of the type that survive in clay in Han tombs. The purpose of the division and subdivison of the capital— and indeed of all China into 1,587 *xian* and numerous smaller cities and towns—was strict control of the urban residents. Even in Chang'an next-door neighbors who were assigned to two different *bao* were responsible for keeping their eyes on each

other and reporting misconduct to their ward administrators.[15] As Miyazaki Ichisada points out, the persistent watch at all levels of Han society worked against the autonomy of the Han city.[16] At the same time, however, the surveillance within the wards gave way to an augmented role for the marketplace.

The market was the one space in the Han imperial city where the population could wander freely, tell stories, hear gossip, drink tea, play games, witness an execution, and, of course, shop. It is no wonder that the first-century resident was so impressed by what took place there. Of the nine Chang'an markets, the main east and west markets were in the northwest corner of the city and seven more were outside the capital walls. The location of markets is another distinction between Chang'an of the Han period and the idealized Wangcheng—a difference that would persist in most later Chinese imperial cities also. The markets of Western Han Chang'an occupied a total area of 4 *li*.[17]

Population figures are available for the Western Han imperial city in the early texts, but there is some variation. According to Wang Zhongshu, several tens of households are said to have resided in each ward.[18] *Qian Han shu* (History of the Former Han dynasty) records more than 80,000 households, or 246,200 people in the Western Han capital.[19] Miyazaki has calculated the total population of China in Western Han times at just less than 60 million.[20]

What was perhaps the primary purpose of the first Han capital is apparent in the latest version of its plan (Figure 52): Chang'an was a city of palaces. With dimensions for only Changle, Weiyang, and Gui palaces, Wang Zhongshu has still been able to calculate that fully one-half the area of the city was devoted to palatial compounds, the first two palaces alone occupying one-third of the city.[21] It has already been noted that four of the twelve city gates were exclusively for entry and exit to and from palaces. One knows that aristocrats as well as merchants and artisans resided within Chang'an's walls, but many of the latter two groups, and probably most farmers, must have lived outside them. Even if the city was initially planned to have only two palace compounds, by the time of Han Wudi, Western Han Chang'an, like Qin Xianyang, was essentially a group of palaces surrounded by a wall —a complex which functioned primarily as a residence and fortification for the ruling family. Capitals with so much area devoted to the emperor would end with the transfer of the Han capital at the beginning of the first century A.D. At the Eastern Han capital, Luoyang, both the number of palace compounds and the portion of the greater city they would occupy would be greatly reduced.

Royal tombs and ritual structures comprised the imperial portions of Western Han Chang'an beyond its outer wall. The remains of what are believed to have been a composite ritual structure where the functions of Ming Tang, Bi Yong, and Ling Tai were performed were excavated in the southern suburbs of the Han capital in the 1950s. A reconstructed plan of the ceremonial complex shows a circle enclosing a square enclosing a circle enclosing a square (see Figure 15). According to Chinese cosmology, the two perfect shapes represent man (the square) and the heavens (the circle). Although reconstruction of the site and its main building is not universally accepted, there is little doubt that such a ceremonial space or spaces stood at Chang'an even before the time of the usurper of the Han throne, Wang Mang (r. A.D. 9–23), who is thought to have had this particular group of buildings constructed, and at earlier Chinese imperial cities and other sites in the provinces.[22] The physical existence of the ritual hall complex at the Western Han capital is proof of the desired relationship between the emperor and heaven.

EASTERN HAN LUOYANG

Gaozu [founder of the Han] . . .
continued to use the Qin palaces and chambers,
And relied on its storehouses and arsenals.
For building Luoyang by the ancient standards,
Our sovereign had no time.
Thus, an architect from the west constructed the
      palace.
His eyes being accustomed to Ebang [Epang],
The plan and model, far exceeding the norm,
Were neither a meet measure nor a proper scale.
Gaozu reduced it and reduced it again,
Yet it still surpassed the Zhou halls.
Those who saw it deemed it narrow and vulgar,
The emperor himself ridiculed it as too opulent and
      uncomfortable. . . .
Emperor Wen as well was frugal in his person,
And his rule achieved the blessings of ascendent
      peace.[23]

Luoyang, site of the second Han capital, has been described as austere in comparison with the former primary capital to its west, an analogy which would resurge seven hundred years later when the Tang capitals Luoyang and Chang'an were compared. Although larger in population than Han Chang'an (with one-half million of China's 57.7 million people in the first century A.D.), Luoyang, built by Emperor Gaozu on a site that had also been used by the Qin,[24] was in area only one-third Chang'an's size. Luoyang was also smaller than contemporary Rome, but larger than Alexandria.[25] Perhaps the size of the city, modest by Chinese standards, may be attributed more to the building of its outer wall at a very early stage in the city's history, under the first emperor of the restored

Han, Guangwu (r. A.D. 25–58), than to the reputed frugality of the dynastic founder and alleged original city builder, Emperor Gaozu. The outer wall of Han Luoyang was only 13,000 meters (about 30 Han *li*) in perimeter.

Much closer to a perfect geometrical form than Chang'an, Luoyang's north–south measurement was roughly one-and-a-half times its east–west length. Its dimensions—9 *li* 100 *bu* by 6 *li* 11 *bu*—have given it the nickname "9:6 city,"[26] a reference to its longitudinal/latitudinal proportions that would continue to be used in literary allusions to the fifth and sixth century city. Still, Luoyang was not exactly rectangular, and two of its yellow rammed-earthen walls were particularly crooked (Figure 60). Portions remain of the east, west, and north walls, which were originally 3,900, 3,400, and 2,700 meters, respectively. The south wall has been washed away by the change in course of the Luo River, but it is estimated that the south wall measured about 2,460 meters, joining the south ends of the east and west walls at points approximately 300 meters south of their present surviving portions.

Like Chang'an and the ideal city of Wangcheng described in the *Kaogong ji*, Luoyang had twelve gates. They were neither evenly distributed around the four walls, however, nor spaced at regular intervals. As Figure 60 shows, the east and west walls had three gates, but only two pierced the north wall, whereas the south wall had four. Remains of all the gates from the three measurable walls were discovered in an archaeological survey of the city in 1962. The positions of the four south gates shown in Figure 60 were determined by the locations of major north–south thoroughfares of the city.

Eastern Han Luoyang had five main north–south boulevards. There were also five major avenues running east to west in the city, the longest extend-

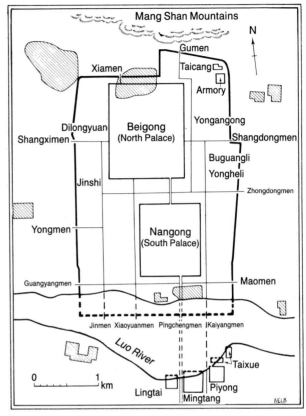

Figure 60. Plan of Luoyang, Henan, in the Eastern Han, first to second centuries A.D. [Wang Zhongshu, *Han Civilization*, p. 45; published with permission of Yale University Press]

ing 2,800 meters. Twenty-four street segments traversed the city in all, a fact confirmed by texts; the average width of a street was 40 meters, but some were only 20 meters wide. All major thoroughfares were laid out in the same way as at the Western Han capital, beginning at gates of the outer city wall and divided into three lanes (the center lane reserved for imperial passage), in this case by walls.

Like Western Han Chang'an, Eastern Han Luoyang had two main palaces. At Luoyang, however, they were north and south of each other, rather than in east and west positions like Changle and Weiyang Gong. Both palace complexes of the Eastern Han capital predated the reestablishment of Han rule after the Wang Mang interregnum. They were greatly expanded after Luoyang became the primary capital site, but no additional palace complexes were constructed. Together their area occupied one-third the space of the walled city.[27]

The smaller South Palace was the main architectural concern of the first Eastern Han emperor. Under the second ruler Mingdi (r. A.D. 58–76), the North Palace was enlarged between the years 60 and 65. A covered passageway from approximately the north center of the South Palace to east of the south center of the North Palace connected the two walled enclosures so that the emperor could change his location in secrecy. Textual evidence has led Hans Bielenstein to suggest that the two palace complexes were adjacent to the northern and southern outer walls of the city, but excavation has not confirmed these positions.[28] From texts one has the impression that the main hall of the North Palace, Deyang Hall, may be likened to the halls of the Qin palace compound Epang. It is claimed, for instance, that more than ten thousand men could be entertained there.[29]

Although there were two residences, it seems that one palace area was always preferred. The South Palace was the predominant imperial residence between the years 25 and 64; the North Palace occupied that position after Mingdi's improvements in 65 until 125 and again from 147 to 189; and the palaces were used alternately by successive emperors during the years 125 to 146. Between 190 and 196 a fire that destroyed all the Luoyang imperial city buildings forced the emperor to return to Chang'an. In general, the North Palace seems to have been more popular because of its landscaping, which included lakes and gardens.[30]

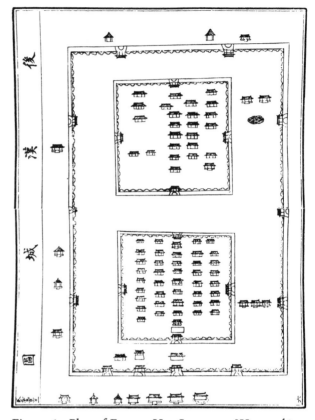

Figure 61. Plan of Eastern Han Luoyang. [*Henan zhi,* as preserved in *Yongle dadian, juan* 9561/6a–b]

Besides the two main palace sectors there were other smaller enclosed imperial residential areas and parks inside the Eastern Han capital walls. Most official bureaus were in the southeast, and a granary and arsenal stood in the north. High-ranking officials were allowed to reside within the city. Han Luoyang had three main markets: the gold market northwest of the South Palace inside the city walls and the horse and south markets beyond the outer wall. Parks were also outside the walls. So were imperial tombs, mostly in the northwest of the city, but several in the southeast or east.[31] A Ming Tang, Bi Yong, Ling Tai, and Imperial Academy were in the southern suburbs. Remains of the Ling Tai have been uncovered.[32]

A plan of the Eastern Han capital from *Henan zhi* (Record of Henan province), compiled in 1075 and reissued in the Yuan period, shows the city as it was believed to have stood in the first centuries A.D. (Figure 61). In the plan are the outer wall and gates, two main palatial compounds, official bureaus, granary, armory, and pond, all of which are shown in Figure 60,[33] as well as other halls recorded in the literature which have not been uncovered during excavation. In the *Henan zhi* plan, the architectural arrangement within the walls of Eastern Han Luoyang appears so rigidly planned and symmetrical, and the illusion of order so overpowering, that one hardly notices the uneven distribution of city gates, the imbalance of halls on the east and west sides of the North Palace area, or the buildings to the east of the palatial axis (or lack of those buildings to its west). Even though Eastern Han Luoyang departed from the idealized scheme of Wangcheng in so fundamental a way as the presence of two palatial areas, in the fourteenth-century illustration the Eastern Han capital was as ideal as every Chinese imperial city plan should be. In fact, when shown alongside the plan of Wangcheng published in *Henan zhi* as it survives in the *Yongle dadian* (see Figure 27),[34] the geometricization of plans combines with the lack of scale to make the two cities appear fairly similar.

Although the prescription for the King of Zhou's city cannot be considered a model for the double-palace capital of the Eastern Han, the publication of such a perfect plan of Eastern Han Luoyang together with Wangcheng in *Henan zhi* nevertheless perpetuated the myth of an ideal city like the King of Zhou's for the time after both cities had been destroyed. The plan of Chang'an in Han times, of course, can be considered no better a model scheme for the later Han imperial city than Wangcheng. Not only are the two Han capitals different from each other, they are also distinct from all Chinese imperial cities that would come after them. Imperial planning in Han times is best understood as a transitional stage during which the multipalace system in use at Qin Xianyang, itself the inheritor of many capitals of many rulers, contracts to only two palace-cities by the beginning of the first century A.D. Every Chinese imperial city after the Han period would have only one palace-city, and even at double cities the power of rule would be confined to one palatial enclosure.

4

PERIOD

OF DISUNION:

A.D. 220–589

THE collapse of the Eastern Han to generals and local families after A.D. 189 ushered into China nearly four hundred years of disunity. At first there were only three main territorial divisions, separated roughly by natural boundaries. This age of warfare, heroic deeds, and invasions by northern tribes, known as the Three Kingdoms period, lasted from the year 220 through most of the third century. The entire time span between the fall of the Han and the reunification of China in A.D. 589 is sometimes called the Six Dynasties period, named after the dynasties which ruled from capitals at present-day Nanjing. The fourth, fifth, and sixth centuries are alternatively referred to as the period of Northern and Southern Dynasties.

The imperial cities of the Three Kingdoms period were Chengdu, capital of Shu (or Shu-Han) in Sichuan province; Ye, capital of Wei in Henan province; and Jianye, capital of the Wu kingdom in Jiangsu. Chengdu had been a garrison town in Han times and has remained an important Chinese city ever since, but it would never again enjoy primary capital status. Ye's age of flourishing was between the fall of Han and rise of the Tang, after which it shrank in size and significance to no more than the ruins that now stand at the old city site. The capital of Wu, on the other hand, had thrived as Jinling and Moling since the late millennia B.C. and as Danyang under the Han, would experience a great period of flourishing during the centuries of disunion, and would continue as an auxiliary and even a primary capital, Nanjing, the name by which the city is best known today. Meanwhile, Luoyang was not abandoned during the years of contention. After just one generation of rule at Ye, Luoyang was established as the center of Wei power in the 220s. The fraction of the Eastern Han city used then would be inherited for the Jin power base in 265. The Eastern Han walled area would be rebuilt as the main capital of the Northern Wei in 493. Two other capitals were used by the Northern Wei before their move south to Luoyang at the end of the fifth century. They were Shengle, located north of China proper in what is today the Inner Mongolian Autonomous Region, and Pingcheng, near modern Datong. Yet more capitals rose and fell during the third, fourth, fifth, and sixth centuries as imperial seats of the contending dynasties and states.[1]

Of the tens of sites established as imperial cities in the four centuries of disunion, five are especially pertinent to the history of premodern imperial planning—either because surviving early maps and texts describe them, because they have been excavated, or both. A survey of the various capitals at these five sites shows that only three different city plans were implemented. They are the same three designs which dominate imperial city building during the Eastern Zhou period of the first millennium B.C.[2] What is more, no new or variant urban plan was introduced during these centuries or subsequently in the history of premodern Chinese imperial planning.

JIANYE AND ITS SUCCESSORS

The Wu kingdom's capital Jianye had a four-sided outer wall with a palace-city in the center (Figure 62). Its plan—and those of subsequent cities that would be built on its ruins for the next three hundred and fifty years—had as a source the idealized version of Wangcheng, although like Lüdu in the first millennium B.C. there is no text for the city which traces its inspiration to the *Kaogong ji*.

The outer wall of Jianye, capital from 229 until the fall of the Wu kingdom in 280, was 20 *li* 19 *bu* in perimeter. East and a little south of its center was a walled palace-city whose main compound was called Taichu Gong. Taichu Gong's main palace hall was Shenlong Hall. In 267 a second palace compound, Zhaoming Gong, was built east of Taichu

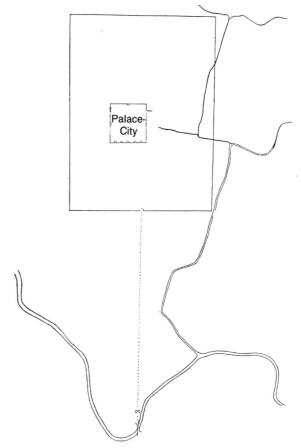

Figure 62. Plan of Jianye, Jiangsu, capital of the Wu kingdom (222–280). [Zhu Xie, *Jinling guji tukao*, between pp. 104 and 105]

Gong. By that time a wall approximately 120 *zhang* on each side with a total of five wall gates enclosed the former palace complex.[3]

Two other features of Jianye shown in Figure 62 should be noted. First, it was a city well supplied with water, for several rivers ran through its eastern half. Second, a long approach emanated from Zhuque (Vermilion Bird) Gate, 5 *li* south of the outer wall, and continued to the wall's south center gate. The gate was named for the bird associated with the direction, and by the fourth century this approach would be known as Vermilion Bird Road. A plan of Jianye published in *Jiangning Fu zhi* (Record of Jiangning prefecture) shows both of these features (Figure 63). In Figure 63 the squarish enclosure is the Jianye outer wall, and the palace-city and five gates are placed within it. Taichu Gong is the central vertical rectangle above the five gates. The confluence of waters around the city is emphasized in this map. Mountains too are prominent, especially in the north, the auspicious direction for them according to *fengshui*. The enclosure southeast of the palace-city is the Han walled city Danyang.

Jianye seems to have been a gay and prosperous city whose people were not so restricted in move-ment as had been the ward residents of northern Chinese imperial cities of the Han:

The city gates are clogged and jammed. . . .
[People] go out walking in pearl-studded slippers,
Move in groups of a thousand or a hundred.
In wards and lanes they feast and drink,
Lifting flying goblets, raising empty cups.
They are able to lift city gates, hoist heavy cauldrons;
They box and shoot, play pitch-ball and
                draughts. . . .
They are joyful and merry;
Nothing is lacking for rejoicing and feasting.
The capital is so prosperous,
People from the four quarters come here to pay their
                respects.

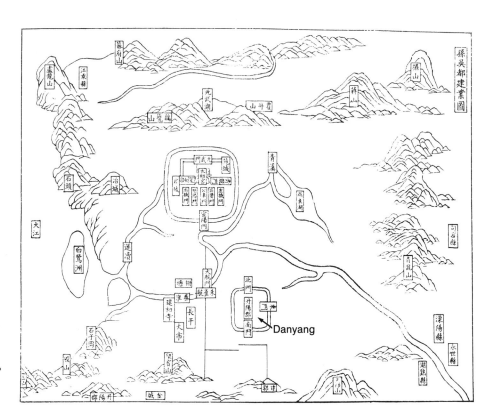

Figure 63. Plan of Jianye. [*Jiangning Fu zhi,* Qing dynasty; photograph taken from Louis Gaillard, *Nankin,* between pp. 44 and 45]

Sailing by water, traveling by land . . .
Singing while they row, their wheels always turning,
They continue all day from dawn till dusk.

They open the market and admit people from far and
    wide;
Thronging crowds clog the gates like a river in
    flood. . . .
Chaotically congested, they are massed and crowded
    together.[4]

In 280, Wu fell to troops of the dynasty known as Western Jin, which had already overtaken portions of North China, and in 282 the capital was divided into northern and southern districts, the northern retaining the name Jianye and the southern using the former city name Moling. The Western Jin lost some of North China to the Xiongnu in 316, and the following year they established their capital at the old Wu imperial city which had been renamed Jiankang in 313. By that time the former palaces had been destroyed, so a new palace-city was constructed. It encompassed some of the Wu remains that were targeted for restoration, including the Back (North) Gardens. The old *5-li* road that approached the palace-city through the outer wall's south center gate was also retained, but it took on the name *yudao* ("imperial-way"), thus initiating the implementation of the approach that would be associated with Chinese imperial city architecture for the next millennium and a half. The position of the imperial-way caused the new palace-city to be off-center to the east (Figure 64). The much enlarged palace-city contained thirty-five hundred rooms *(jian)*—more literally, bays. An Ancestral Temple and Soil and Grain altars were built at Jiankang by its founder Emperor Yuandi (r. 317–323).

The most noticeable contrast between Jianye and Jiankang was the double wall that enclosed the later

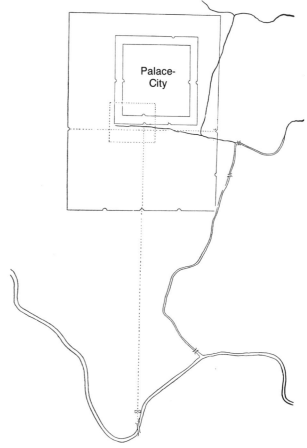

Figure 64. Plan of Jiankang, Jiangsu, of Eastern Jin (317–420). [Zhu Xie, *Jinling guji tukao,* between pp. 104 and 105]

palace-city. The second inner wall is not fully indicated on the map of the Eastern Jin capital published in *Jiangning Fu zhi* (Figure 65), but it did exist. The Qing period plan shows the entire outer city wall, now with sharp corners and more interior buildings, and only the southern half of the second palace-city wall. Figure 64 presents the walls, gates, and some city measurements based on a study of literary sources by scholar-official Zhu Xie earlier this century.[5]

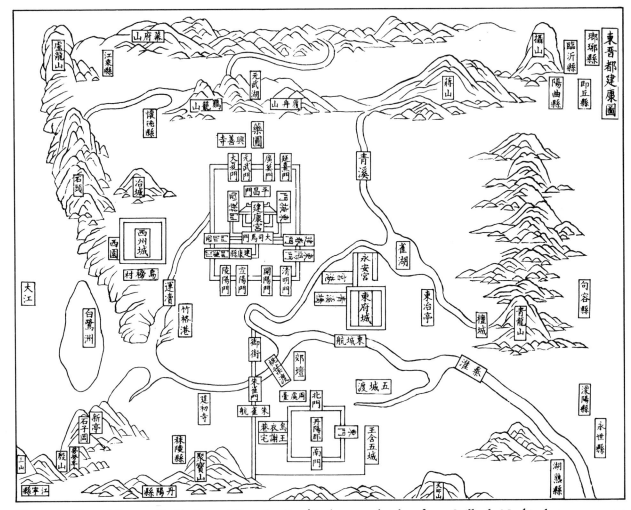

Figure 65. Plan of Eastern Jin Jiankang. [*Jiangning Fu zhi;* photograph taken from Gaillard, *Nankin,* between pp. 50 and 51]

The Eastern Jin palace-city measured about 2 *li* square, with slightly longer north and south walls. Its southern face was 2 *li* from the outer city wall. In the year 378, six thousand workers spent seven months building thirty-five hundred bays of new palace buildings. Less than fifty years later, the Eastern Jin city fell to the Song.

The Song (420–479) inherited the Eastern Jin imperial city. Some building occurred in 443, but the main changes during Song rule involved the names of city gates. The plan of Song Jiankang was essentially unchanged from that of the Eastern Jin capital.[6] In 480, just after the accession of (Southern) Qi, six of the Eastern Jin–Song city gates were rebuilt and portions of the city wall were replaced. Only twenty-two years later Liang succeeded Qi as the ruling dynasty at Jiankang.

Liang added gate-towers to the double-wall enclosure of the Jiankang palace-city. In 511 the most noticeable Liang change to the city was implemented by the addition of a third palace-city wall, added inside the inner of the former two palace-city enclosures (Figure 66). Like their Qi predecessors, the Liang were ardent Buddhists, and many monasteries were built at Jiankang during their rule. One was Tongtai Monastery, for which a north palace-city gate was added to provide direct imperial access to it. Gates were also built at the south, east, and west faces of the third palace-city wall. Still, the Liang city was basically the same as the Qi and Song versions of Jiankang.

In 557, Chen, last of the Six Dynasties, replaced Liang.[7] The only evident change in the Chen imperial plan was the loss of Datong Men, outermost of the three palace-city wall gates that had provided access to Tongtai Monastery. Some rebuilding of Liang structures occurred, including the construction of three high towers of "fragrant wood" in 584. Just five years later the dynasty of slightly more than thirty years' duration fell to Sui, who with the conquest of South China completed the reunification of the country in 589. The first Sui emperor ordered the systematic and total destruction of all traces of the beautiful Six Dynasties city.

One other plan of Jiankang is worthy of attention (Figure 67). Published at the end of the Yuan period in *Zhizheng Jinling xinji* (New record of Jinling from the *zhizheng* reign [1341–1368]), Figure 67 shows much the same configuration of Jiankang that appears in Figure 65. Both illustrate rectangular cities whose four-sided palace-cities are surrounded by water and bordered by northern moun-

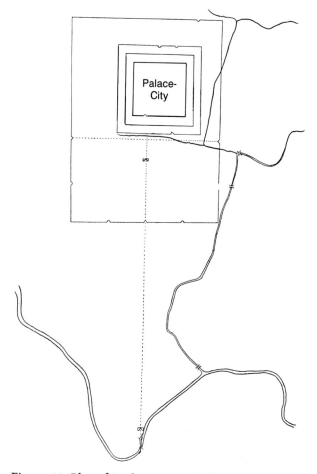

Figure 66. Plan of Jiankang, capital of Liang (502–557). [Zhu Xie, *Jinling guji tukao*, between pp. 104 and 105]

tains. What is different about the two plans is the emphasis. In the Yuan-period scheme, the focus is so exclusively directed to the palace-city and outer city walls that little else is noticeable. Although the palace-city is not centered in relation to the whole, centrality is still the dominant visual message in the comparatively uncluttered plan. In the Qing plan, by contrast, the imperial-way is much less noticeable. After the discussion of Yuan imperial cities

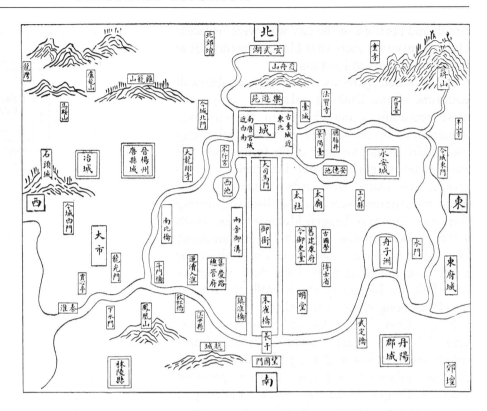

Figure 67. Plan of Jian-
kang. [*Zhizheng Jinling
xinzhi;* photograph taken
from Zhu Xie, *Jinling guji
tukao,* between pp. 104
and 105]

and plans in Chapter 7, it will be clear why the
zhizheng period map was made as it was.

PINGCHENG

Pingcheng, located outside of Datong, was the second imperial city, the first in China proper, established by the Tuoba invaders—the one of the so-
called Five Kingdoms and Sixteen States to have a
long and influential history in China. Pingcheng,
rather than the earlier Tuoba capital at Shengle, is
discussed next because one piece of evidence suggests that its plan, like the contemporary southern
Chinese capitals, may have been built in imitation
of the idealized Wangcheng scheme.

The history of the Pingcheng site can be traced
to the Han dynasty when it was a *xian* capital. In

313, when Shengle was the primary Tuoba capital,
the old Han site underwent repair. At about the
same time it was designated the southern capital.
Tuoba power continued to increase. In 386 the
ruler called himself emperor, according to Chinese
custom. This first Wei emperor, Taizu, decided to
move his primary capital south into China, and
probably with that goal in mind he visited the old
Wei capital Ye in northern Henan province during
the first moon of the year 398. Half a year later
Emperor Taizu journeyed westward from Ye to
Pingcheng; establishing it as his primary capital, he
built palaces, an ancestral temple, soil and grain
altars, and an astronomical hall. Emperor Taizu
died at Pingcheng, and his successor Emperor
Taizong was crowned in Tianwen Hall in 409.
More halls and towers rose at the new Northern

Wei capital in the 410s and, according to the official Wei history, *Wei shu,* numerous banquets were held in the halls of the Western Palace, which probably adjoined a West Garden.[8] The same official record offers evidence about the amazing speed at which buildings of the capital rose and fell. Yong'an and Anle halls, for instance, were constructed in the third moon of 492 along with a palace complex and two other halls. Destroyed in the ninth moon of the same year, they were rebuilt for a large banquet later the same month.[9]

During most of the first two imperial reigns at Pingcheng only the palace-city was walled. In 422, just a few years before Emperor Taizong's death, the 32-*li* outer city wall was constructed. Later, work continued on the palace-city.

Neither the shape nor the exact location of Pingcheng has been satisfactorily determined. Excavation in 1939 in the vicinity of the Datong railroad station, north of the Ming–Qing walled city, yielded 4 to 5 meters of wall and a mound that probably supported the double gate-towers of the main south gate. The report of that team suggested the location of Pingcheng to have been about 2 kilometers north of the later walled city, but excavation during the 1970s has extended the scope of confirmed Northern Wei remains to areas to the south and southeast.[10]

The sole surviving plan of Pingcheng is from the Qing dynasty illustrated geographical study known as *Shui jing zhu tu* (Illustrated commentary on the *Water Classic*) (Figure 68), source of the plan of Han Chang'an in Figure 56. Since its printing this map has been associated with the city and therefore must be considered. The plan shows the palace-city in the center of the outer wall. The configuration of the palace-city, with arc-shaped northern and southern faces, immediately raises doubt about the plan. Even without archaeological or literary confirmation that the plan is fictitious, one must conclude that it is an

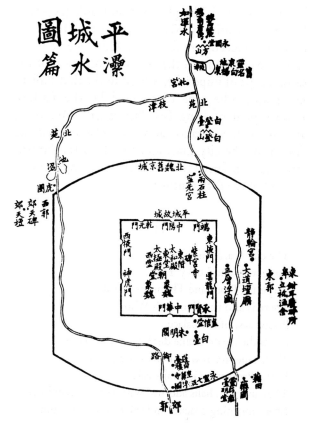

Figure 68. Plan of Pingcheng, Shanxi, in the Northern Wei, fourth century. [Yang Shoujing, *Shui jing zhu tu* (Qing dynasty edition), p. 77b]

idealization inspired by the *Kaogong ji* prescription for the Chinese imperial city.

Murata Jiro and other Japanese archaeologists who studied northern Chinese cities from the Northern and Southern Dynasties period have also been skeptical about the *Shui jing zhu tu* illustration. They argue that the plan of the city visited by Emperor Taizu six months before the establishment of the Northern Wei capital at Pingcheng should have been more influential in shaping the newly designated imperial city than an idealization from a literary source.[11] The plan of Cao Cao's (155–220) Ye, subsequently the Wei capital in the third century, was indeed very different. That scheme is the earliest example from the period of disunion of the second type of imperial city built in the first millennium B.C.—the type represented by the Eastern Zhou capital of Jiang (see Figure 41). Moreover, after its implementation at Ye this plan became the design for the city Luoyang, to which the Northern Wei transferred their capital from Pingcheng at the end of the fifth century.

YE

The city wards include:
Longevity and Lucky Yang,
Perpetual Peace and Thoughts Loyal.
There is also the Consort's Ward
Placed east of the palace.
From their gates come distinguished persons;
Their lanes teem with nobles and peers.
In the Protector General's palace
They dwell in halls adorned with latticed windows.
Every morning coaches and riders in massive numbers
Congregate within its midst.
They have built guest lodges all around the city districts,
Decorated the places where visitors gather,
And beautified the gates and doors of sumptuous towers; . . .
They cover the walls with thatch, plaster the chambers;
The rooms and verandahs are intricately joined.
Engraving knives never cease their carving; . . .

Elaborating on the old Three Markets, merchants have started up shops;
Tucked along the level thoroughfares, they radiate in all directions.

They arrange the serried stalls for an orderly display,
Place walls and gates as "collar and girdle."
They have alleviated fluctuations in supply and demand;
At high noon, everyone converges on the marketplace.
They erect flag pavilions spiring tall and lofty,
Boast extravagantly of the grandeur of the things to be seen.
In the hundreds of shop rows carts strike hub to hub,
And follow in a continuous line, ten thousand strong.[12]

If these descriptive passages from Zuo Si's (Taichong's) *fu* are accurate, Ye in the third century, like Han Chang'an and other Chinese imperial cities before it, was a thriving commercial center as well as an imperial seat of power. Like other Chinese imperial cities, it also experienced several hundred years of urban history before becoming a capital, having been established as a military commandery in the first decades of Western Han rule. By the end of the Han, Ye was under the control of a military leader and his sons, surnamed Yuan, from whom Cao Cao captured it in 204. When Cao Cao died in 220, his son Cao Pi made himself emperor of the Wei dynasty. Ye was only one of Cao Pi's capitals. The other was Luoyang. Less than a decade after Cao Pi assumed the Wei throne he transferred his main capital to Luoyang. Even so, the plan of the short-lived capital Ye is very important.

Several plans of the city have been published. The earliest, from *Shui jing zhu tu* (Figure 69), shows the outer wall and provides gate and building names. It generally agrees with more recent plans, but it does not deal with the controversial issue of where in the north of the outer city the palace-city was located. Figure 70, the plan currently used in China, clearly shows that Cao Cao's capital at Ye had a palace-city in the north center, a position that corresponded to the location of the palace area of Jiang in Eastern Zhou times (see Figure 41).[13] The main hall of the palace-city was named Wenchang. Extending as far south as the palace-city, but to its east, was a ward for imperial relatives; occupying the corresponding area to the west was a park containing an arsenal, a stable, and, in the northwest, three brick altars known as San Tai, two of which survive today. A broad street running the entire 7-*li* width of Ye separated these areas from the rest of the imperial-city which housed residences of the general population and some offices. Another street covered the 5-*li* length of the city, emerging from a gate at the northeast corner of the palace-city and ending at a gate in the south wall. The last main thoroughfares of Ye extended from south of the palace-city to gates at the south center of the outer wall. They may be compared to the 2-*li* imperial-way at Eastern Jin Jiankang (see Figure 64), which ran from the south wall of the palace-city through the south center outer wall gate and then beyond for another 5 *li*.

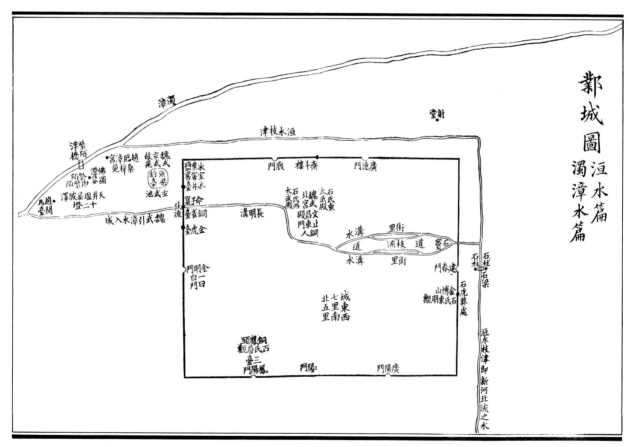

Figure 69. Plan of Ye, Hebei, in the Wei kingdom, beginning of third century. [Yang Shoujing, *Shui jing zhu tu*, Taipei repr., pp. 626–627]

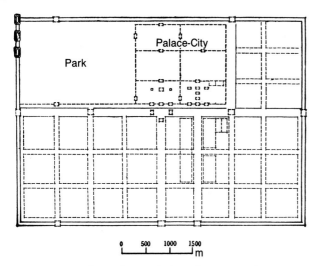

Figure 70. Plan of Ye of the Three Kingdoms. [He Yeju, "*Kaogong ji*," p. 17]

The location of architecture in the Cao–Wei capital Ye is known largely through two literary sources. The *Yezhong ji* (Record of Ye), probably written in the Jin period, must be studied together with "Yedu fu" (Ye capital rhapsody) by Zuo Si, contained in the *Wen xuan*. Zuo writes:

> Inside the city
> Streets and crossroads converge like wheel spokes;
> Vermillion watchtowers are attached to the corners.
> Stone bridges and soaring spans
> Lead out over the Zhang Canal.
> They have dredged conduit ditches to flank the roads;
> Planted rows of green pagoda trees to shade the avenues.
> Like the Canglang, the waters are cleansing;
> And the boulevards are better than a covered walkway.
> Bustling busily are the caps and canopies;
> Swarming and thronging are crowds of people.
> White-haired men do not carry heavy burdens;
> Pedestrians yield the road.

Here they establish offices, apportion duties;
And each official lives at his command, dwells at his post.
The city is jammed with bureaus and headquarters,
Scattered with wards and gates.[14]

The wards of Ye are sketched in Figure 70. This plan also indicates that the palace quarters were closer to the eastern outer wall than to the western one. The Back Palace (*hou gong*), Cao Cao's own residence, was located behind the Hall of Audience in accord with classical tradition. Both building complexes were west of the east north wall gate. The residences of imperial relatives occupied a smaller area, according to this reconstruction of the city, than did the park.

THE 9:6 CITY

During the years of contention, Luoyang was never abandoned. After the fall of the Eastern Han it was reestablished as the capital of the Wei kingdom by Cao Cao's successor. Destroyed and rebuilt many times during the Six Dynasties period, its initial outer wall under the Northern Wei, the final dynasty to rule at Luoyang during the years of disunity (from 493 to 534), was the same wall that had been used by the Han and during intervening years (Figure 71; see also Figure 60). The only addition to this city wall in Northern Wei times was a thirteenth gate, located in the far north of the western side. The interior of Luoyang, however, underwent extensive revision in the third and especially at the end of the fifth centuries.[15]

When the Wei capital was moved to the former Han capital of Luoyang in 220, the old north palace was restored. Parts of the Han south palace were also restored by the work of tens of thousands of laborers under the second Wei ruler Mingdi (r. 227–240). In addition, Mingdi built three altars, in imitation of the San Tai of Ye, beyond the north-west corner of Luoyang. These altars were the predecessors to Jinyong Cheng—a fortified area to which the Wei retreated in 265 when they were overtaken by Jin (or Western Jin, as the dynasty which lasted until 317 is generally known). The total area of the approximately 13-meter-thick walls that surrounded Jinyong Cheng was about 1,080 by 250 meters. The three enclosures were connected on the interior north and south walls by gates. Their exterior walls had fortifications every 60 to 70 meters. An idealized and erroneous plan of Jinyong Cheng published in the *Henan zhi* shows it

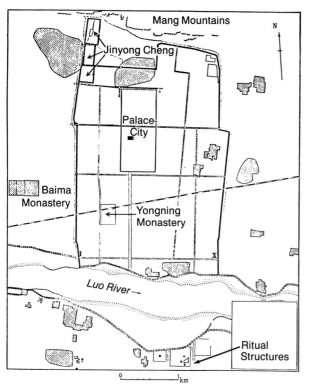

Figure 71. Plan of Northern Wei Luoyang showing Jinyong Cheng, fourth to fifth centuries. ["Han–Wei Luoyang Cheng chubu kancha," *Kaogu* no. 4 (1973), p. 199]

as a city of three palaces, rather than the three-walled city it was (Figure 72).[16]

The Western Jin probably maintained the Wei walls, gates, and gate names,[17] but upon their accession to the throne they did raise a new suburban altar in the south of the city. By the time of the second Jin ruler at Luoyang, however, the dynasty was rapidly weakening. In 303 the city was attacked and by 317 Western Jin rule at Luoyang had ended. Approximately one hundred eighty years later a new plan for the city of Luoyang was initiated by the Northern Wei, who moved their capital south from Pingcheng. It was to be the last city built on the old Han site.

Two extremely significant changes occurred in the Luoyang plan during the forty years of Northern Wei rule. One, within the city walls, was the substitution of one palace-city for the former north and south palace complexes of the Han (see Figure 71). The second was the extension of what had formerly been a vertically rectangular plan—proportioned according to the golden ratio with a length of approximately 9 *li* north to south and a width of about 6 *li*—into a similarly proportioned city but with the longer dimension running east to west. Based on one or both of the schemes, the city retained the nickname "9:6 city."

The new palace-city was larger than the Han north palace compound. Its walls enclosed an area 1,400 meters north to south by 600 meters east to west. Because there was only one palatial sector it was possible to build longer, continuous north-south and east–west avenues. In all, four main arteries extended in both directions. One avenue ran the entire north–south distance of Luoyang with only one bend, from the eastern north gate to one of the south gates. Two straight streets joined eastern and western city gates, the northern uninterrupted even by the palace-city walls. This passage-way, the broadest in Luoyang, was 50 meters wide

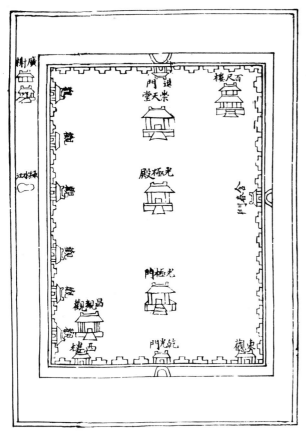

Figure 72. Plan of Jinyong Cheng. [*Henan zhi,* as preserved in *Yongle dadian, juan* 9561; Taipei repr., 1974, 3d plan]

at places (the other main streets measured from 12 to 42 meters) and divided the palace-city into the audience area in the south and the residential quarters in the north (as specified in the classical passage "audience hall in front, private chambers in back"). Similarly the east–west avenue just south of the Northern Wei palace-city separated the imperial palaces and parks to the north from the official bureaus, monasteries, aristocratic residences, and imperial altars to the south. The Ancestral Temple and Altars of Soil and Grain, not indicated in Figure 71 because their exact locations have not been confirmed by excavation, were located east and west, respectively, of the city's widest north–south boulevard, which ran from the south gate of the palace-city to the second gate from the west of the southern city wall. The 42-meter-wide thoroughfare, Bronze Camel Avenue, bore the name of the two markets just south of the palace-city. A four-ward great market was located in the west center of the city, and a small market one-fourth that size stood in the east. Their positions contradicted the *Kaogong ji* specification that the markets should be in the imperial city's north. A Ming Tang, a Ling Tai, and a National Academy, each occupying a double-sized ward, were south of the center of Luoyang's original outer wall.

Until 1978, the 9:6 aspect of the Luoyang plan was a subject of major debate among scholars of Chinese city planning.[18] The measurements of the city shown in Figure 71 were the ones published during successive excavations at Luoyang in the mid-1950s, early 1960s, and 1972.[19] These dimensions have been used to confirm that the city was 9 *li* north to south and 6 *li* east to west. Yet the 9:6 scheme contradicts the important description of the Northern Wei capital provided in about 547 by Yang Xuanzhi's text *Luoyang qielan ji* (A record of Buddhist monasteries of Luoyang) and in official histories of dynasties that established capitals there. The crux of the problem is the following passage:

The metropolitan area of Luoyang measures from east to west twenty *li* and from south to north fifteen *li*. The total number of households is slightly more than 109,000. Excluding the space occupied by temples, palaces, and government offices, the rest of the area is divided into wards *(li)*. Each ward is a square [each side of which] measures 300 *bu*. Each ward has four gates. At each gate there are two wardens, four sub-officials, and eight guards. There are altogether 220 wards.[20]

Three questions are raised here: Where were the wards? Why are two hundred twenty mentioned here and three hundred twenty or three hundred twenty-three specified in the *Wei shu* (History of Wei)?[21] And was the city 9:6 or was it really 15:20?

In 1978 archaeologist Su Bai published a plan of what he believed the appearance of Northern Wei Luoyang to have been after A.D. 501, when, according to the *Wei shu,* an outer city wall was begun with the labor of fifty-five thousand men (Figure 73).[22] The boundaries of the outer wall were restricted at the north by the Mang Mountains and at the south by the Luo River, so that the north–south dimensions of Northern Wei Luoyang could have extended only 1 *li* north and 5 *li* south beyond the Han wall, which in post-501 writings was referred to as *neicheng,* the inner city. The potential for urban expansion was much greater eastward and westward, and Su believes the Luoyang outer city to have grown nearly 7 *li* in each direction.

The outer city of the Northern Wei capital should have been divided into two hundred twenty square-shaped wards, each 300 paces square. These precincts were enclosed by walls and had one gate at each wall face. Passage through the gates was strictly supervised by wardens. Opened at dawn and shut at dusk, the ward gates still functioned as they had at Han Chang'an—to control the population, which, according to *Luoyang qielan ji,* numbered just over 109,000 households at the beginning of the sixth century.[23]

Research since 1978 on Chinese cities has produced several new plans of the three-walled, post-501 Northern Wei capital at Luoyang. Some show ward divisions only in the outer city; others show no wards at all.[24] Certainly the wards should have spread through at least the second and outer enclosures, if not through the palace-city, as they are pictured in Figure 73.

What was contained in the regularly shaped Luoyang wards, and why it was necessary for the city to grow so dramatically in such a short time, is well documented. Luoyang more than most other Chinese imperial cities can be called a Buddhist city; as such, it housed an unprecedented number of monasteries. Yang Xuanzhi relates that between 307 and 313, during Jin rule, only forty-two temples or monasteries stood at Luoyang. Under the Northern Wei, the city contained 1,367 Buddhist structures,[25] most of which did not survive the end of Northern Wei rule. Monastery property occupied more than one-third of the city area, with as many as three thousand clergy associated with a single monastery.[26] Of the long, long list of religious spaces mentioned in Yang Xuanzhi's text, Yongning Si, located southwest within the city walls, and Baima Si, west and slightly north of Yongning Si but outside the city walls, were two of the most important. Both are shown in Figure 71.[27] Many of the monasteries had earlier been private residences and were given to the church by devout citizens.

The forty-one-year history of Northern Wei Luoyang is a period of special interest for imperial planning in China because the Buddhist capital was built by non-Chinese rulers. The circumstances epitomize the confrontation between China and the two key forces of the times—"barbarians" (the standard Chinese name for non-Chinese peoples) and Buddhism. The establishment by the Tuoba–Wei builders of Pingcheng of a capital in southern Henan province, at the site of a former Han imperial city, seems to mark a turning point in their sinification. The major vehicle for this sinification was the Buddhist faith, as foreign to Chinese soil as its Northern Wei patrons. Yet acceptance of the one encouraged mutual acceptance of the other. Imperial patronage as a means of sinification, a process observed in the construction of Buddhist caves and sculpture at Yun'gang (outside of Pingcheng)

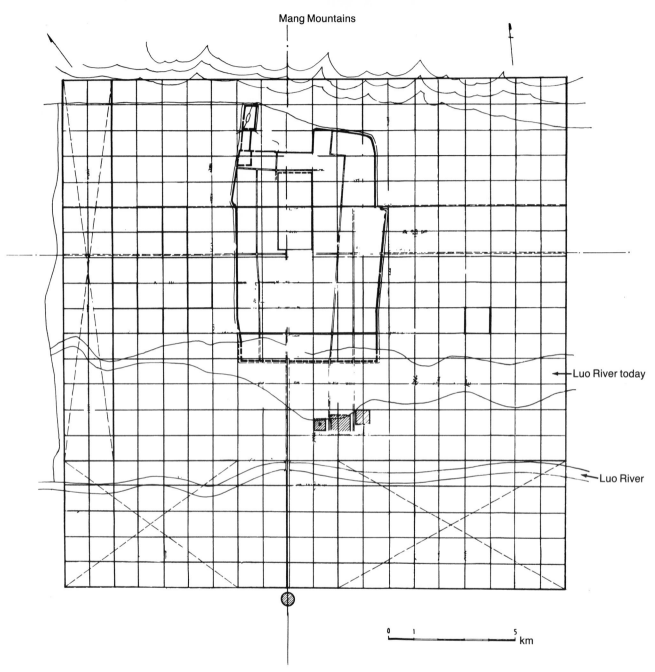

Mang Mountains

Luo River today

Luo River

0 1   5
└─────────┘ km

Figure 73. Plan of Northern Wei Luoyang showing probable post-501 boundaries. [He Yeju, *Zhongguo gudai chengshi guihua shi luncong,* between pp. 186 and 187]

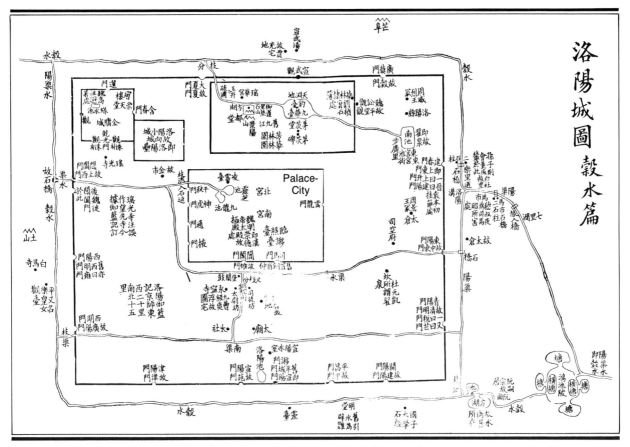

Figure 74. Plan of Northern Wei Luoyang. [Yang Shoujing, *Shui jing zhu tu,* Taipei repr., pp. 628–629]

in the 460s,[28] occurred in the construction of the later Northern Wei capital Luoyang also.

Viewing Luoyang as it appears in Figure 71, one is inclined, even in this study which diminishes the role of Wangcheng in Chinese imperial planning, to see the city as a version of the *Kaogong ji* idealized scheme and thus as a harbinger of late imperial city plans such as Beijing. The plan of Luoyang published in Yang Shoujing's *Shui jing zhu tu* (Figure 74) shows its palace-city to have been more centrally located, as does, as one might expect, the

Henan zhi plan (Figure 75). The issue here is not overidealization of plans. The postexcavation plans of Northern Wei Luoyang do not convincingly confirm that the palace-city was in the exact center of its second wall or that it was in a north central position. At Luoyang there was at least enough room between the northern palace-city and outer north walls for a park. The position of the Luoyang palace-city will be questioned again in the next chapter, when we investigate Japanese imperial cities based on Chinese designs.

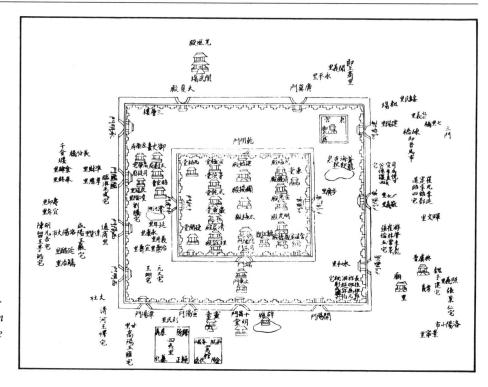

Figure 75. Plan of Northern Wei Luoyang. [*Henan zhi,* as preserved in *Yongle dadian, juan* 9561; Taipei repr., 1974, 4th plan]

BACK TO YE

The plan for Eastern Wei (534–550) Ye, to which a puppet emperor was taken from Luoyang after its burning in 534,[29] was an elongated replica of the city directly north of it designed for Cao Cao in the third century (Figure 76). The positions of the two cities led to the names northern and southern for them. Initially the old city had been used as the Eastern Wei capital, but in 536 tens of thousands of men built a new city. Materials for it came from dismantled buildings of Luoyang. In 539 the new city was completed. Its appearance and the use of old building parts suggest that Luoyang was its model—and perhaps, therefore, that the plan of Luoyang had its palace-city in the north center also.

The perimeter of the new city is believed to have been 6 *li* by 8 *li* 10 *bu*—several *li* more than the 25 *li* recorded in *Bei Qi shu* (History of the Northern Qi).[30] Even with the larger perimeter, Eastern Wei Ye would have been just smaller than Luoyang but close enough to a 9:6 city to further suggest the 493 version of Luoyang without its wards as the model for the later capital. Major north–south and east–west arteries provided access across the city from wall to wall. Between the main thoroughfares were wards. Behind the palace-city was a garden, and it is believed that gates in the north wall provided access to what remained of third-century Ye. Murata Jiro has made a study of literary sources to determine the names and histories of the halls and gates of Ye.[31]

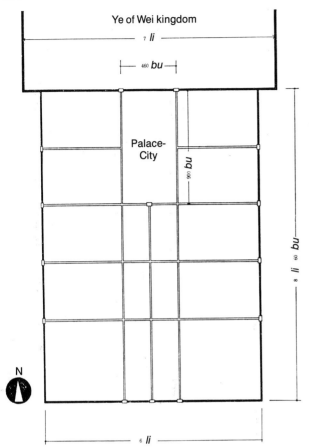

Figure 76. Plan of Ye of the Eastern Wei (534–550) and Northern Qi (536–577), showing Wei kingdom Ye directly north. [Murata, *Chūgoku no teito*, p. 227; published with permission of Sōgeisha Press]

DOUBLE CITIES

Two other imperial cities established during the age of disunion, although unrelated to each other, were versions of the third imperial plan known in China since the first millennium B.C.: the double city. The earlier is the capital of the third of the Three Kingdoms, Shu, sometimes known as Shu-Han, at Chengdu in Sichuan province. Its two cities are described by Zuo Si in "Shudu fu" (Shu capital rhapsody) of the *Wen xuan:*

> A metal fortress and stone walls
> Enclose and encircle the central district.
> Both majestic and lofty,
> It truly is the Consummate Capital.
> They constructed eighteen passage gates,
> Laid out broad avenues two lanes wide,
> Built new palaces on a bright summit,
> Erected hostels just like those of Received Brilliance
>   [a guard hostelry at Han Chang'an],
> Attached long galleries to Yangcheng [Gate],
> Set belvederes and terrace halls soaring into the
>   clouds.
> They opened high porches to look down on the hills;
> They arranged ornate windows to gaze at the
>   rivers. . . .
> Next we come to the Lesser City,
> Which adjoins it on the west.
> The hub of markets and shops,
> The pool of a myriad merchants,
> Its shop rows stand a hundred layers deep,
> With thousands of stalls nestled neatly together.[32]

The history of the site can be traced more than one thousand years before the Shu capital to the ninth century B.C. Later, in the Warring States period, it was the capital of the state of Shu, one of the states eventually conquered by the First Emperor in the third century B.C. Under Qin rule, two enclosed cities which shared one wall face were constructed by Zhang Yi. They were known as Greater City *(dacheng)* and Lesser City *(shaocheng)* with the alternate names *tai-, zi-,* or *gui-cheng* and *xiaocheng,* respectively.[33] Lesser City was located to the west. Their walls were probably 12 Han *li* in perimeter and measured 7 *zhang* in height. No ref-

Figure 77. Relief of city streets of Chengdu from tomb tile, Chengdu, Eastern Han period. [Published with permission of Chinese Cultural Center, San Francisco]

erence to a double city is indicated in what must be one of the earliest plans of Chengdu found in the form of relief sculpture from a Han tomb, in which the plan of the city is a square with central north–south and east–west thoroughfares (Figure 77). In the Tang dynasty a larger wall known as *luocheng* was built around the double-walled city, giving rise to the appearance suggested by Figure 78. When Marco Polo visited Chengdu in the 1270s it was still a three-walled city.[34] The city walls were rebuilt or repaired at the time of the early Ming dynasty.

The appearance of Chengdu during its brief history as an imperial city in the third century, however, remains ambiguous. Literary evidence suggests that almost a kilometer separated the two

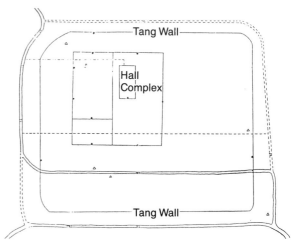

Figure 78. Plan of Chengdu showing Tang dynasty walls. [Wang Wencai, *Sichuan shiyuan xuebao* (1981), p. 63]

walled enclosures,[35] but this feature is indicated neither in Figure 78 nor in the plan of the city published in *Shui jing zhu tu* (Figure 79). Two features, however, are not controversial: that there were two separate walled areas at what is today Chengdu from the Warring States period through at least the third century and that under Shu rule one of the city areas had palaces while the other was primarily commercial in function.

The second double city of the period of disunity was a Han garrison town that was turned into a double city by the addition of a second walled enclosure in the fourth century. The city was Shengle, situated about 12 kilometers north of Hohhot in the Inner Mongolian Autonomous Region. Shengle was the first city used by the Tuoba–Wei, who occupied the site in 259. After 313, when the city was walled, it is referred to in the *Wei shu* as Beidu ("northern capital") (Figure 80). About 1,200 meters of the southeastern corner of the Northern Wei city walls, which probably shared a border with the earlier Han town, survive.[36]

The importance of the period of disunion in the history of imperial planning in China cannot be overemphasized. Even though aspects of the plan of

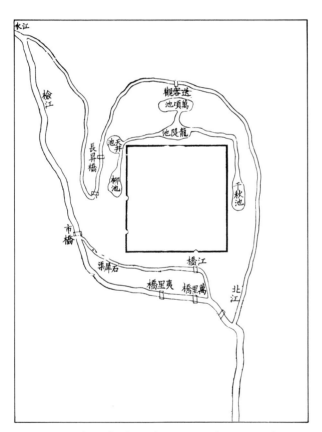

Figure 79. Plan of Chengdu. [Yang Shoujing, *Shui jing zhu tu,* Taipei repr., p. 639]

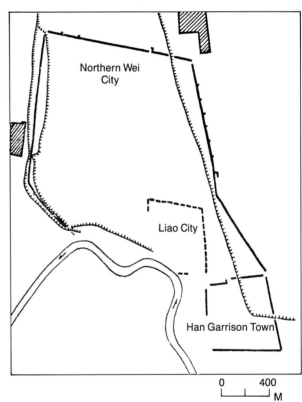

Figure 80. Plan of Shengle, Inner Mongolian Autonomous Region, showing Han, Northern Wei, and Liao walls. [Su, *Wenwu* no. 11 (1977), p. 38]

Northern Wei Pingcheng or Luoyang are subject to debate, it is certain that in the third or fourth centuries each of the three imperial city schemes implemented in the last period of disunity, the Eastern Zhou, reemerged.

The three plans show that post-Han imperial planning was governed by more rules than had existed in the past. Four features of the schemes were to profoundly influence all later Chinese imperial planning. First, the ideal square shape of the outer city wall has given way to a rectangular configuration, usually longer in the north–south than in the east–west dimension.[37] Second, the inner of two concentric walled enclosures contains the single palace-city. Third, a major artery approaches the palace-city main south gate from farther south than the main south outer wall gate, through which it passes. And fourth, the ward system has become more rigid—indeed, the plan of an imperial city that shows wards often resembles a checkerboard.[38]

5

SUI-TANG

DYNASTIES

THE reunification of China in the 580s by the man who became the first emperor of a new dynasty, Wendi of Sui (r. 589–618), initiated a long period of growth, prosperity, and optimism. Although the Sui itself endured only two reigns, the succeeding Tang dynasty built an empire based on the Sui model which would last for nearly three hundred years.

The new empire was vast in size and vision. The Tang dynasty had relations with empires of Asia and Africa, receiving through their envoys not only goods but knowledge. Chinese rulers of the time came to enjoy the art and music of foreign lands, employing teachers from abroad to perform in their court and to train courtiers and servants in exotic arts. Moreover, the Chinese saw in their cities merchants and travelers from all parts of the world and purchased foreign goods in the city markets.[1] Chinese people came into contact with new religious philosophies through monks who brought to the Chinese court and to local monasteries new forms of Buddhism from the West across Central Asia or through practitioners of faiths of Persia and Central Asia residing in Chinese cities. By the end of the eighth century the taste for foreign exotica and religion, especially the new forms of Buddhism, and aspects of China's governmental structure had been transmitted eastward to Japan and northward to seminomadic peoples. A century later, when the Tang dynasty fell, certain of its institutions, among them city planning, and their symbolic associations with strong Chinese-style rulership survived beyond China's borders.

The breeding ground for cosmopolitanism and an international spirit, the place where the most foreigners could be seen, the most exotic goods purchased, and the greatest number of faiths propagated, was the capital city Chang'an. By the seventh century Chang'an was the largest city in the world, boasting a population of one million. In the eighth century it was the most important city in East Asia.[2]

DAXING AND CHANG'AN

Chang'an had been the site of the Western Han capital some seven hundred years earlier. Sui Wendi began his imperial city Daxing (to be known as Chang'an again in the Tang dynasty) in 582 at a new site approximately 10 kilometers (21 *li*) southeast of the former Han city (see Figure 18). The official beginning of the city is recorded as a night in the sixth moon of 582, when the new emperor decided upon a new site. Whether or not the real motive was the haunted associations between what remained of former palaces of the Northern Zhou (557–581), the last dynasty to rule at Chang'an, and their murdered eight-year-old emperor and accessory officials, the following morning a diviner submitted a memorial which, using astrology and divination as justifications, predicted the move of the capital. In an imperial edict issued later the same month, the old Han site was deemed inappropriate because neither astrology nor divination had been used in its determination. Thereupon the new site at the foot of Longshou (Dragon Head) Mountain was selected.[3] To balance the geomantic forces of this mountain in the north, Qujiang Pond was dug southeast of the city. Within six months, by 8 February 583, Daxing was completed.

Wendi built his city outward, beginning with the palace-city, then adding the imperial-city, and finally completing the outer wall. The city was nevertheless extraordinarily well planned and symmetrical (Figure 11). The rectangular outer wall was 36.7 kilometers in perimeter (84 square kilometers). Its construction was of the pounded-earth technique and measured an average of 9 to 12 meters in thickness, although at points its breadth was only 3 to 5 meters. Positioned in the north center of the city was the palace-city comprised of three palace complexes—Yiting, Taiji, and the Eastern Palace, from west to east—occupying a total area of 2,820 meters east to west by 1,492.1 meters north to south. Due south of the palace-city and of the same east–west dimension was the imperial-city, measuring 1,843.6 meters north to south. In it were government offices and monasteries, the Ancestral Temple on the east, and the Altars of Soil and Grain on the west.

The strict adherence to a grid pattern for the streets and the almost perfect symmetry of the city were emphasized by the streets' lengths: Twenty-five of them, fourteen longitudinal and eleven latitudinal, ran the entire distance of the outer wall. Only the palace-city and imperial-city impeded their courses. The widest street in Daxing divided the two cities. This 220-meter-wide avenue which extended from the northern east wall gate to the corresponding gate of the west wall,[4] where the Chinese emperor announced amnesties, was also a place from which imperial troops could watch for disturbances and if necessary take action. Other especially wide streets ran north–south between gates of the outer city wall; the main central north–south artery of the city, Vermilion Bird Road, 150 to 155 meters wide, began at the south gate of the palace-city and continued to the main south gate of the outer wall. Each of the major streets had two drainage canals dividing it into three lanes.[5]

The horizontal dividers of the city have been associated with the hexagram *qian* of the *Yi jing* (Book of changes). This first of sixty-four hexagrams, according to the classical text, is a series of six unbroken lines said to symbolize great fortune. These lines occur at every other of the fourteen east–west streets, beginning with the north city boundary, including the streets south of the palace-

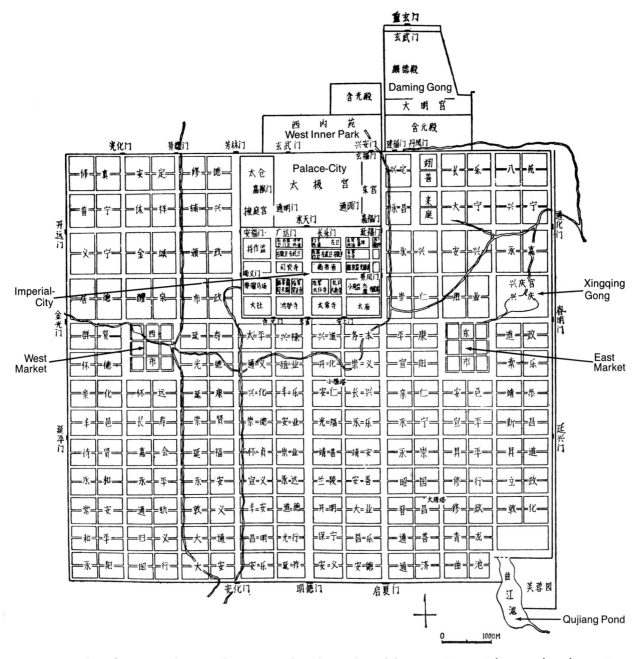

Figure 81. Plan of Daxing–Chang'an showing wards and partial ward divisions. [Dong, *Zhongguo chengshi,* p. 28]

city and imperial-city, and every third main street thereafter; the final line is the south city border. According to this interpretation, first found in Chinese sources in 813, the palaces, for instance, were built at the second line because "the dragon is perceived as an open space; it is advantageous to visit a great man."[6]

The imperial-city was also divided by streets into a gridlike configuration, making it a small-scale replica of the great outer city. In addition to the three central north–south boulevards which ran through it, seven avenues crossed the imperial-city from east to west.

Much like Northern Wei Luoyang after 501, four-sided wards enclosed by walls were bordered by major and minor streets throughout the city, except in the imperial sectors. Each ward had main east–west and north–south streets which bisected each other at four gates, one on each side (Figure 81). Also in the manner of earlier capitals, the wards were strictly supervised—their primary function was still population control. Unlike the two hundred twenty Northern Wei Luoyang wards, however, not all of Chang'an's one hundred ten wall-enclosed sectors (one hundred eight wards and two markets) were the same size: Those closest to Vermilion Bird Road were the smallest, and the wards in the northern part of the city were larger than wards in the south. Certain wards were designated for specific purposes, for instance a craft or commerce; others attracted residents from one foreign land or practitioners of an exotic religion. These divisions were intensified by the increasing foreign population in Tang times.

Finally, the city had two symmetrically located markets, one in the east and the other in the west. Each occupied an area equivalent to two wards, the west market being slightly larger than the east. By the eighth century the less crowded Wannian district in the eastern half of Chang'an catered to the wealthier citizens; the ethnic population, including foreign merchants, tended to live and shop in the Chang'an district on the western side of the city. The Chang'an markets functioned both as shopping areas for the metropolitan population and as the hub of imperial-sanctioned purchasing, selling, and price fixing.[7] The city as it has just been described, plus an imperial park to the northeast outside the city wall, was built almost in its entirety during the lifetime of Sui Wendi.

Among the impressive documentation about the layout of the city and its structures in Sui times are the names of planners, supervisors, and engineers.[8] One name always mentioned is Vice-Inspector General Yuwen Kai, whose family had originally come to China from farther west in Asia. Yuwen was responsible for Anji Bridge, the Grand Canal connecting northern and southern Chinese cities, and the model of a Ming Tang—indeed, his name is sometimes associated with Daxing to the point of eclipsing the many others who were instrumental in its plan and execution, including some of higher rank and involvement at earlier stages. Among those who played important roles in the design of the new Sui capital were Gao Jiong, Liu Long, and Helou Zigan, in supervisory positions, and Yan Pi, He Chou, and Yang Suo, who served as architect-engineers.

Yuwen Kai played an especially prominent role in the service of Wendi's son and successor, Yangdi, who four months after his father's death began a new capital at Luoyang. Although similarities in the two cities may be attributed to Yuwen's contributions to both city designs, one cannot ignore the evidence of the past which suggests that once an imperial plan had proved successful in China it was readily accepted as the norm for successive generations.

LUOYANG

The new city Luoyang to which Wendi's son, Yangdi, ordered inhabitants in 605 was situated 40 *li* west of the Zhou dynasty capital (Figure 20, no. 4).[9] Completed in fewer than two years, the eastern capital was smaller than Daxing but in many ways similar to it. Like the outer wall of the earlier Sui capital, Luoyang's wall was essentially square: 6.138 kilometers on its north side, 6.778 on the west, 7.270 on the south, and 7.312 on the east (Figure 82). These dimensions, gathered during excavation of the capital, correspond roughly to those specified in the *Henan zhi* (Record of Henan), in which the north wall is said to have been the shortest, followed in length by the west, south,

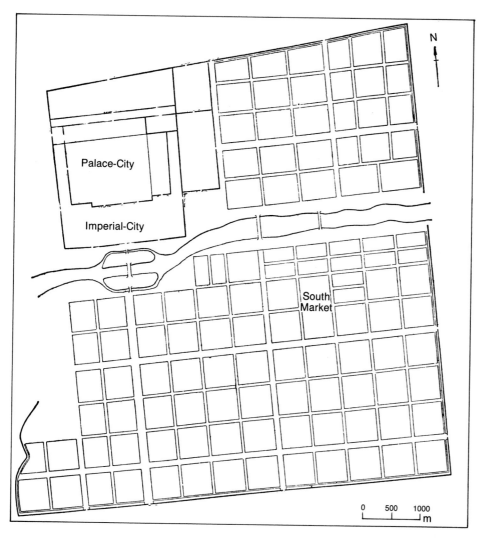

Figure 82. Plan of Sui–Tang Luoyang, seventh to tenth centuries. [Su, *Kao-gu* no. 6 (1978), p. 419]

and east wall faces, respectively, the latter two being nearly the same size.[10] Sui–Tang Luoyang had twelve outer wall gates: four at the north wall, three at the east and south, but only two on the west. The outer city area was divided by major north–south and east–west avenues, ten in either direction, into 134 four-sided wards. Important differences between the two Sui–Tang capital cities were the locations of a major waterway at the eastern capital and the site of the imperial-city and palace-city.

One recalls that the earlier Luoyang capitals of the Han, Wei, Jin, and Northern Wei had been north of the Luo River, extending perhaps to the north bank of the waterway, which in the first to fourth centuries was probably somewhat farther south than its present position. The Sui capital was divided in two by this waterway, giving rise to a city plan unprecedented in the history of Chinese imperial planning. Perhaps the new arrangement evolved in response to the need for a larger area than had been anticipated and the desirability of water at a centralized location.

The second unique feature—the northwestern position of the inner walled cities—may not have been planned. Rather than place them in this unusual location, Yuwen Kai probably intended to replicate for Yangdi the grand imperial scheme employed during the reign of the first Sui emperor at Daxing. After building commenced, however, it was decided to leave ancient tombs undisturbed in what should have been the western half of the city and to nevertheless include the abundant water supply within the city's boundary.

The imperial areas, too, were different from what had been built at Chang'an. The separate sectors of palace-city and imperial-city and their distinctions as the residential and administrative sectors of the capital were maintained at the Tang eastern capital, as was the northern position of the

palace-city. However, recent archaeological investigations have determined that, unlike the arrangement at Chang'an, at Luoyang the palace-city was enclosed on all but its north side by the imperial-city and that parkland stood north of the palace-city between it and the outer city's north wall.

Interestingly, the two imperial sectors appear as separate entities, north and south of each other, in plans by Xu Song (1781–1848) published the year of his death in *Tang liangjing chengfang kao* (Research on the city districts of the two Tang capitals) (Figure 83). Xu's highly idealized scheme is along the lines of published idealizations of earlier Chinese cities. More surprising is an alternative plan presented in *Henan zhi* (Figure 84), in which the palace-city is surrounded on four sides by the imperial-city. One wonders what sources were used in the Yuan provincial record of Henan, why the *Henan zhi* plan seems to have been unknown or disregarded by Xu, and what led to enclosure of the

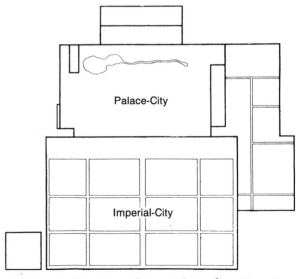

Figure 83. Palace-city and imperial-city from Tang Luoyang. [Xu Song, *Tang liangjing chengfang kao,* Taipei repr., 1974, 9th plan]

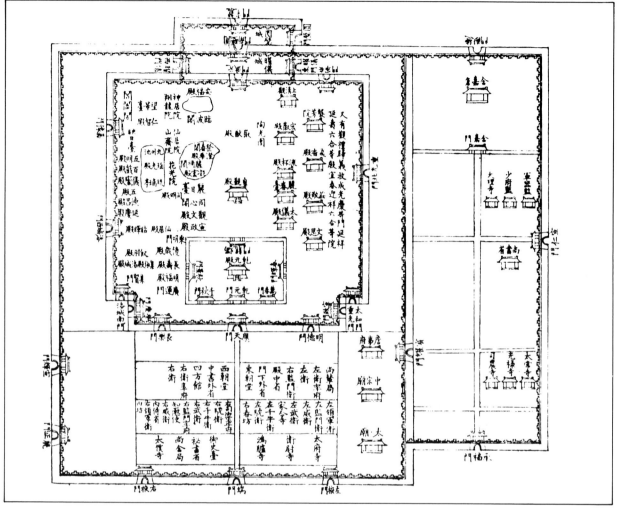

Figure 84. Luoyang in Tang times. [*Henan zhi,* as preserved in *Yongle dadian, juan* 9561]

north palace-city face in the *Henan zhi* version. Perhaps encasement of the palace-city on four sides was in deference to the position of the palace-city in the idealized Wangcheng scheme, illustrated together in the same text. About one feature of both Sui–Tang capitals all the plans are definite. It is the distinction between palace-city and imperial-city. This aspect of the imperial scheme, probably inherited

from the latest version of Northern Wei Luoyang, would remain standard in Chinese imperial city design for the following fourteen hundred years.

Although the frequently published plans of both Chang'an and Luoyang are called "Sui–Tang," it is certain that even Chinese cities were not static over the centuries. Religious centers, popular neighborhoods, and palace buildings changed between the

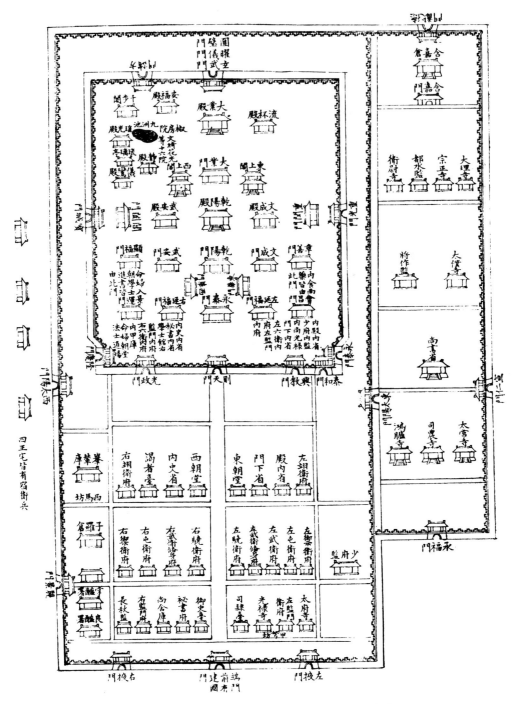

Figure 85. Luoyang in Sui times. [*Henan zhi,* as preserved in *Yongle dadian, juan* 9561]

years 589 and 906. The maps in *Henan zhi* provide evidence of the architectural changes at Luoyang during the Tang dynasty. Even in these highly stylized plans it is apparent that in the seventh century, when the primary Tang capital was returned to Chang'an, structures in the southern imperial sector that had existed at the main capital of Yangdi in Sui times (Figure 85) stood no longer. Several changes at the Tang city Luoyang are apparent in Figure 84: the addition of a road in the enclosed eastern palace sector which led southward from the gate of the northernmost building compound; the concentration of buildings on the eastern side of the new road; two new halls in front and behind a hall that had stood in apparent isolation in the southeastern portion of the Sui city; and perhaps a change in official bureaus.[11] Sui hall names, as well, were changed under the Tang.[12] Except for its stint as primary Tang capital during the reign of Empress Wu (r. 684–705)—who, legend tells, found the stench of executions she had ordered during her usurpation of the throne unbearable—Luoyang was the secondary capital, smaller and more austere than Chang'an, as it had been under the Han.

BUILDINGS OF THE TANG CAPITAL

Palaces were added at the primary capital, Chang'an, after the initiation of Tang rule. Owing to literary documentation, excavation, and reconstruction of some of these palaces, we know more about the imperial architecture of this seventh through ninth century capital than any other Chinese capital except Beijing. The most intensive building period at Chang'an was in the early decades of the seventh century. Initially, former Sui halls in all three complexes of the palace-city were replaced by new structures. Then, in 634, an additional palace area was begun northeast of the outer city wall in the trapezoidal-shaped region which had been an imperial park under Sui Wendi. In 635

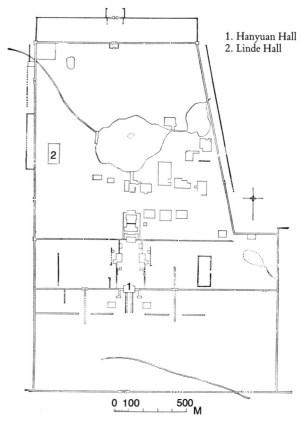

1. Hanyuan Hall
2. Linde Hall

0 100   500 M

Figure 86. Plan of Daming Gong, Tang Chang'an. [Liu Dunzhen, *Zhongguo gudai jianzhu shi,* 1st edition, p. 108]

this area was named Daming Gong, and from 663 until the 880s when it was burned, it was, with few exceptions, the main imperial residence (Figure 86).

Remains of more than thirty structures have been excavated within the pounded-earth outer walls whose perimeter stretched 7,628 meters. Excavations confirm the positions of two palace complexes to have been much as they were drawn in the map published by Xu Song which predates excavation by a century (Figure 87).

The arrangement of the Daming Gong halls was similar to that of most Chinese architectural complexes: Main halls stood along a strict north–south

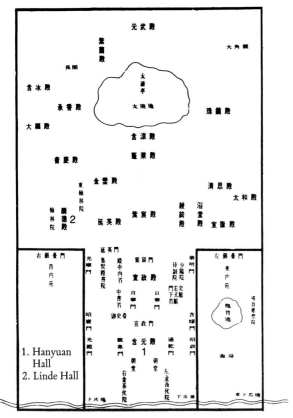

元武殿
紫蘭殿
大角觀
池閣
含冰殿
承香殿
太液亭
太液池
珠鏡殿
大福殿
含涼殿
蓬莱殿
會慶殿
金鑾殿
東翰林院
清思殿
太和殿
翰林院 麟德殿 2
延英殿
紫宸殿
結綺殿
浴堂殿 宣徽殿

1. Hanyuan
   Hall
2. Linde Hall

右銀臺門
西內苑
延英殿
紫宸門
少陽院
明義門
左銀臺門
東內苑
光順門
殿中內省
待制院
龍首池
昭慶門
宣政殿
月華門
日華門
門下史館
含耀門
光範門
宣政門
含元殿 1
通乾門
明福門
御場
朝堂
朝堂
右金吾仗院
左金吾仗院
下馬橋
下馬橋
東下馬橋

Figure 87. Plan of Daming Gong. [Xu Song, *Tang liang-jing chengfang kao,* Taipei repr., 1974, 5th plan]

line. At Daming Gong the inverted U-shaped ceremonial hall, Hanyuan, was elevated in the south center, facing south, with three more private imperial chambers due north of it (Figure 86, no. 1; Figure 87, no. 1). Other hall complexes of less significance stood on secondary east–west axes. Such was the case of Linde Hall complex (Figure 86, no. 2; Figure 87, no. 2), where the emperor feasted high officials. Main gates pierced the north and south centers of the wall which enclosed Daming Gong. All halls were part of multistructural complexes, and all were surrounded by pillared arcades or walls, some of which had corner towers.[13]

In the eighth century another palace complex was erected in Chang'an by Emperor Xuanzong (Minghuang; r. 713–756). Called Xingqing Gong, it was built east of the imperial-city near Chunming Gate of the eastern city wall. Soon afterward, Xingqing Gong became a residence for elderly princes or consorts. Both the Xingqing and Daming palace complexes are shown on the oldest known Chinese city plan, the fragmentary stele of Tang Chang'an (Figure 88) carved in 1080, almost two hundred years after the fall of the Tang.

In spite of the many foreigners and the exotic faiths practiced in Chang'an, the Buddhist presence was strong. The numbers—one hundred thirty Buddhist monasteries and forty Daoist monasteries—may seem small in comparison to the 1,367 religious buildings or building complexes at Northern Wei Luoyang,[14] but several of the Chang'an monasteries were vast establishments occupying entire city blocks. Like palaces and rulers, monasteries prospered or declined with the fortunes of the religion. One monastery whose history spanned the Sui and Tang dynasties was Qinglong Si, located in Xinchang ward in the southeastern section of the capital.[15]

Imperial tomb construction flourished in the seventh and eighth centuries in the northwestern suburbs of Chang'an. Although the excavation of emperor and empress tombs is still awaited, site plans from local records have shown for centuries who was interred and where they were laid to rest (Figures 89 and 90). Excavated evidence and resulting site plans of the mausoleums have confirmed information in the old drawings. For example, one of the best-known imperial tombs is Qianling, resting place of the third Tang emperor Gaozong (r. 650–683) and his wife Wu Zetian (d. 705), the infamous Empress Wu. Figure 89 shows an aboveground mound approached from the south by a spirit-way *(shendao)* and surrounded by a roughly

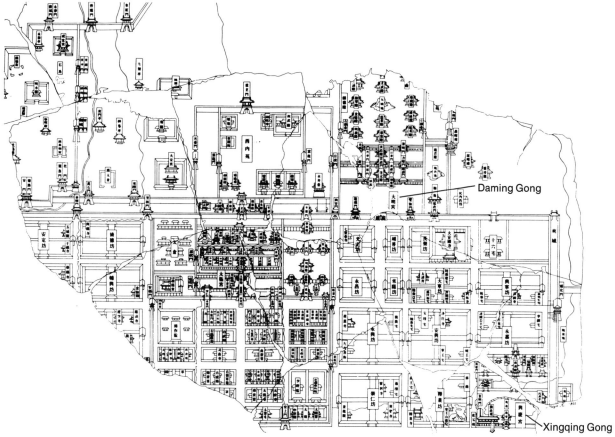

Daming Gong

Xingqing Gong

Figure 88. Plan of Tang Chang'an preserved on stone stele of 1080. [Courtesy of Institute of Humanistic Studies, Kyōto University]

square-shaped wall with a gate at each side center. The same features appear in the postexcavation plan (see Figure 17). *Shendao* is the funerary equivalent of *yudao* for imperial cities, and the surrounding wall (no longer extant) was the counterpart to the outer wall of Chang'an. Somewhat in the manner of the imperial apartments of an imperial city, perhaps, Qianling was surrounded by satellite tombs of imperial relatives. At the underground entry of one of the satellite tombs shown in Figure 89, that of Crown Prince Yide, are the gate-towers of the

city of Chang'an (Figure 91). The equation between the underground architectural and painting program and the city of the living prince, Chang'an, has been visualized by Fu Xinian (Figure 92).[16] Fu's research also suggests a direct correspondence between the plan of Crown Prince Yide's tomb and the apartments of the Chang'an Eastern Palace, residence of the crown prince. In Figures 93 and 94, both groups of three halls are arranged according to the *gong* scheme. That the Chinese tomb is intended to recreate the former liv-

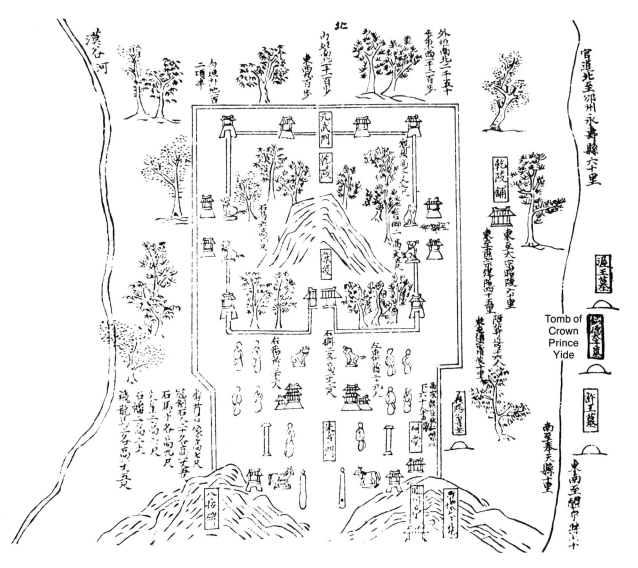

Figure 89. Plan of Qianling, imperial necropolis of Emperor Gaozong (d. 683) and Empress Wu (d. 705), and satellite tombs, Shaanxi. [Li Haowen, *Chang'an zhi tu, Siku quanshu,* ser. 9, vol. 162, *juan zhong* / 5a–b]

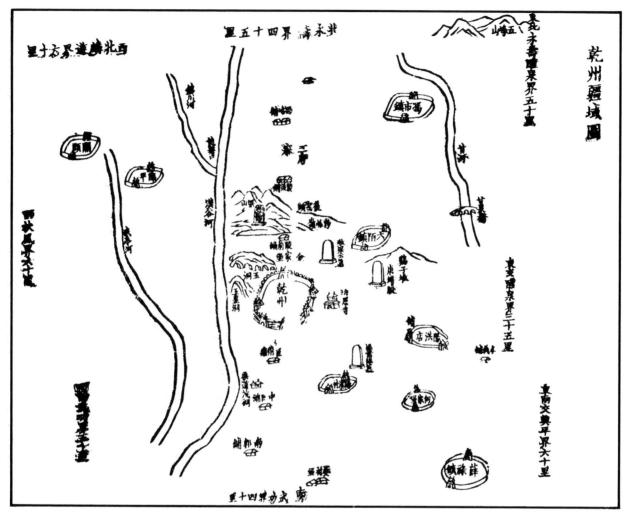

Figure 90. Plan of Qianling and satellite tombs. [*Shaanxi tongzhi, juan* 6, p. 82 (Taipei repr. [*Shaanxi tongzhi xu tong-zhi*], vol. 1, p. 191)]

Figure 91. Gate-towers of Chang'an from tomb of Crown Prince Yide (ca. 706), Shaanxi. [*Han-Tang bihua*, pl. 86]

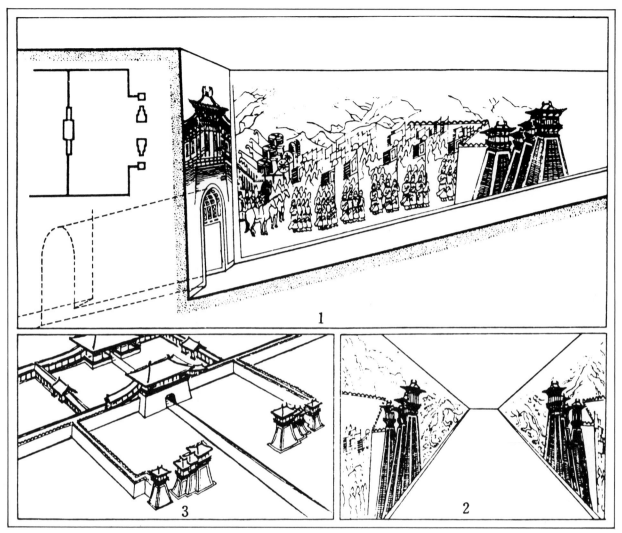

Figure 92. Visualization of gate-towers of Chang'an in the Tang dynasty based on wall paintings in Figure 91. [Fu, *Wenwu yu kaogu lunji,* p. 333]

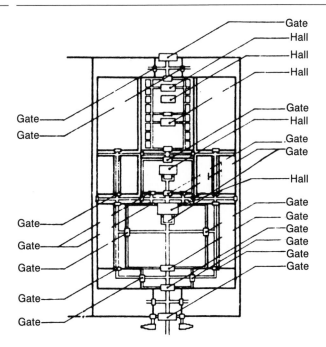

Figure 93. Plan of Eastern Palace, residence of crown prince, at Tang palace-city. [Fu, *Wenwu yu kaogu lunji*, p. 340]

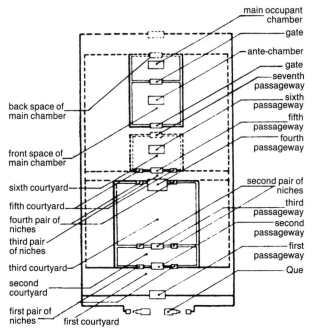

Figure 94. Plan of tomb of Tang Crown Prince Yide. [Fu, *Wenwu yu kaogu lunji*, p. 340]

ing world of the interred, of course, is a long-held belief, but Fu's research articulates the closest correspondence to date between the architecture of these two worlds. The position of royal tombs northwest of the capital was probably in accordance with age-old associations of west and north with autumn and winter, the seasons of natural decay and death.

CHANG'AN PLAN ABROAD

It is no surprise that the plan of the most magnificent Sui–Tang city would be manifest in the second Chinese capital Luoyang. During the Tang dynasty, Chang'an and its plan also became famous beyond

China's borders, where the scheme was intentionally replicated. Less than one hundred years after the construction of the new Sui capital Daxing, the Chinese city plan was implemented eastward across the sea in Japan. In the eighth century a city modeled after Chang'an was built on the Asian mainland beyond China's northeastern boundary.

This plan was adopted in Japan, no doubt, because of the availability of Chinese cultural types and the readiness of the Japanese to implement them during the seventh and eighth centuries. Besides the merchant and missionary envoys who carried goods and faiths across the sea from China were official Japanese ambassadors and messengers to the Tang court who returned home with tales of the glories of Tang, as well as craftsmen and handbooks from the Asian mainland. Unquestionably the strongest Asian nation at the time, China was thus the obvious place toward which a less powerful or newly formed state would turn for imperial guidance—China offered symbolically potent models for capital city design, bureaucratic organization, governmental institutions, and even a state-sponsored religion, Buddhism, whose non-Chinese origins had been all but lost in the sinification process. For city building in particular, the visual impact of urban China from the outermost walls to the individual palatial component must have overwhelmed the foreign eye. Whether or not they were aware of the associated symbolism of a heavenly sanctioned world order, the plan of the Tang Chinese city and its architectural program could fulfill the political aspirations of non-Chinese rulers. Ironically, survivals in replica beyond China's borders have accounted for some of our knowledge of what has not endured on Chinese soil.

Case of Japan

Between the mid-seventh century and the end of the eighth century, seven imperial cities were built in Japan. Although the number sounds high when compared with the two primary and several auxiliary capitals in use in the huge country of China at the same time, for the Japanese the establishment of a city in conjunction with a palace, and the use of both for even tens of years, was a new concept that was no doubt inspired by the Chinese system. At least from the time of Empress Suiko (r. 592–628) and her regent Prince Shōtoku (572–621), Japanese rulers had conducted their government in palaces. Famous among them was Prince Shōtoku's Ikaruga Palace, later to be incorporated into the monastery Hōryū-ji, and Asuka Palace, used in the mid-seventh century by Empress Kōgyoku (r. 642–645).

Up to this time, each new ruler had built his or her palace anew, sometimes constructing more than one palatial residence, and posthumous occupation of the palace by another ruler was taboo.[17]

So far, excavation has shown that seventh-century Japanese palaces conformed to a roughly uniform plan (Figure 95). Farthest south was the Chō-shū-den (Imperial Assembly Hall), which opened onto a courtyard flanked by two buildings that faced it. Next was the administrative section of the palace, called Chōdō-in, consisting usually of twelve official bureaus that formed a U which opened to the north. Third was the Daigoku-den (Great Hall of Council), which included one or more buildings also arranged around a courtyard. Farthest north was the Dairi (Great Inner), the imperial residence. It is obvious that a "court in front, private chambers in back" system was implemented here.

The point at which the Japanese palace was combined with a larger city is presently believed to have been after 645. The presumed location was Naniwa, just outside of modern Osaka.[18] The Japanese history *Nihon shoki (Nihongi),* composed in 720, has an entry for the year 679 which refers to an outer city wall, *luocheng.* (The Japanese chronicle is written in Chinese characters.) Based on its Chinese meaning, *luocheng* should have been a second wall surrounding a city beyond the palace area. Even though remains of this wall have never been uncovered, Japanese scholars generally accept its existence.[19] Furthermore, an entry for the year 683 in the *Nihon shoki* suggests the adoption of a multiple-capital system,[20] probably inspired by the Chinese model.

Reconstructions of Naniwa-kyō[21] show it to have greatly resembled the plan of the Fujiwara capital, Fujiwara-kyō, whose reconstruction is more fully confirmed by excavation (Figure 96).

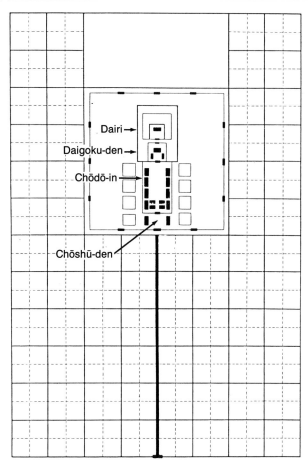

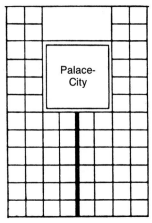

Figure 96. Fujiwara-kyō in the late 690s. [Ueda, *Tojō*, p. 103; published with permission of Shakai Shisōsha]

Figure 95. Japanese palace plan of the seventh century. [Ueda, *Tojō*, p. 130; published with permission of Shakai Shisōsha]

Fujiwara-kyō was a perfectly rectangular city: 3,086 meters north to south by 2,118 meters east to west. Its boundaries were determined by four pre-existing streets, Lower, Middle, Yamada, and Great Horizontal roads. A square palace area, whose buildings and their arrangement were the same as those shown in Figure 95, stood in the north center, south of a garden that bordered the north wall.[22] The city south of the palace area was first of all divided into east and west, or left and right, sectors by a main north–south street that ran from the south center of the Fujiwara Palace area to the south center of its outer boundary; the rest of the city was further divided by twelve streets running east to west and seven (including the main thoroughfare) going north to south. This division was to become customary in Japanese cities through the eighth century, as would be the names *jō* for the east–west divisions and *bō* for the north–south divisions. City addresses could be designated and spaces measured by *jō* number, beginning with first *jō* at the north down to twelfth *jō* at the south, and *bō* number, the latter measured outward left or right from the main central north–south thoroughfare. In other words, Fujiwara Palace stood on a four *jō* by four *bō* plot, two *jō* from the north city boundary, and covered the third through the seventh *jō* and the first and second *bō* left and right. Like wards of a Chinese capital, the four-sided enclosures bounded by *jō* and *bō* were divided by bisecting north–south and east–west cross streets. One such sector of four parts was also called *jō* (a different character than that for an east–west thoroughfare). Markets have not been uncovered during excavation at the Fujiwara capital. Nor has it been determined whether or not an outer wall enclosed the city, for no wall remains have been found. Yet similarities between Fujiwara-kyō, Tang capitals, and other Japanese capitals suggest that the possibility of an outer wall should not be ruled out.

Before the end of the first decade of the eighth century the transfer of the Japanese capital was discussed at court. The move occurred in 710, and the site of the new capital, called Heijō-kyō, was modern Nara, less than 20 kilometers north of Fujiwara-kyō.[23] The new walled city measured 4.9 kilometers north to south by 4.3 kilometers east to west. Within the wall were *jō* (precincts, same as the Chinese character *fang*) defined by seven streets running north to south and eight going east to west (Figure 97). Unlike the square precincts of the Fujiwara capital, at Heijō-kyō three north–south streets and three east–west avenues subdivided the *jō* into sixteen units known as plots. A main road named Suzaku (Vermilion Bird) Road—the same name as the main north–south avenue through Chang'an—bisected Heijō-kyō. Whereas at Chang'an the two city districts were named Wannian and Chang'an, at Heijō-kyō they were labeled according to the Japanese sys-

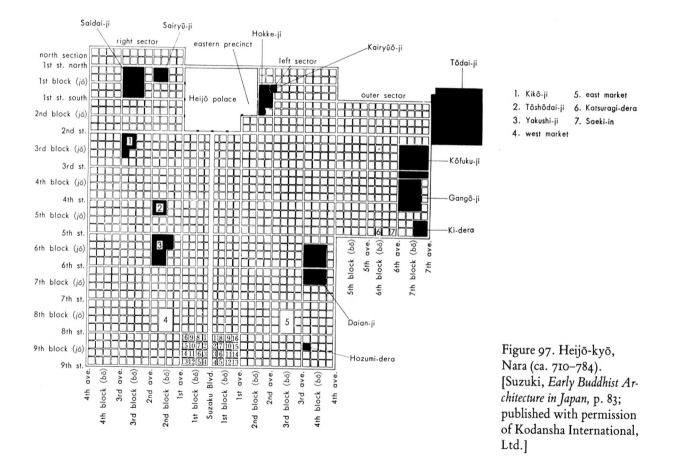

1. Kikō-ji
2. Tōshōdai-ji
3. Yakushi-ji
4. west market
5. east market
6. Katsuragi-dera
7. Saeki-in

Figure 97. Heijō-kyō, Nara (ca. 710–784). [Suzuki, *Early Buddhist Architecture in Japan*, p. 83; published with permission of Kodansha International, Ltd.]

tem in use at Fujiwara-kyō as simply left and right sectors. East of the left sector at Heijō-kyō (left being designated according to the Chinese system as the side of the ruler as he faced south) was the outer sector, an area 2.2 kilometers north to south by 1.6 kilometers east to west. An additional one-by-three-block sector was located north of the right city district. Similar to Chang'an, Heijō-kyō had east and west markets, here located farther south than at the Chinese capital, and great monasteries stood in the northeast and northwest of the Japanese capital. Since ceremonies of the Chinese state were not practiced in Japan, neither an ancestral temple nor soil and grain altars were erected.

The imperial portion of the Heijō capital was in the center north. This area, which combined the functions of the Tang palace-city and imperial-city, was due south of the north city wall. Its buildings were those of the pre-eighth-century Japanese palace-administrative complex shown in Figure 95, but in name and structure such buildings as Vermilion Bird Gate, the south central entrance to the capital, were Tang in style.[24] Initially a square-shaped region 960 meters on each side, a 240 by 720 meter sector was later added to the palace area's east.

During the more than seven decades of Japanese rule at Heijō-kyō, imperial cities were also constructed elsewhere in Japan. Excavation and reconstructed plans of the eighth-century cities Kuni-kyō and Nagaoka-kyō show that both of them, especially Nagaoka-kyō, had much in common with the Fujiwara and Heijō capitals and their ultimate imperial Chinese models.[25] Nagaoka-kyō (Figure 98), where the capital was transferred during the second half of 784 with the aid of three hundred thousand workers, was a more perfect scheme than Heijō-kyō. At Nagaoka-kyō the palace-city bordered the northern boundary, was approached by Vermilion Bird Road from the south, and had the

same number of precincts in the left and right city sectors. Except for a small group that faced the north wall, all precincts were of uniform size. Geography and history gave rise to the unusual configuration of the earlier Kuni-kyō (Figure 99), built under Emperor Shōmu (r. 724–748). The left sector of Kuni-kyō was a 4,770 by 530 meter rectangle, with the palace area of the entire capital at its north center. The east market of the capital was placed due south of the palace near the southern city boundary. Separated from the left sector by mountainous terrain was the right sector of Kuni-kyō, approximately the same size, with the same number of precincts, and a west market positioned symmetrically to the left sector's eastern market, but no palace. A river ran through the Kuni capital. Kuni-kyō is an example of the implementation of a standard and idealized scheme on imperfect terrain. The resulting configuration, a city cut in two by a river, with palace area in the north but not at the city center, may be compared to the Sui–Tang plan of Luoyang (see Figure 82).

Why so many transfers of the capital occurred during the eighth century in Japan is in part explained by internal factions at court, both in the imperial family and among powerful aristocrats. Strife at court was common in China, as well, yet only once between the founding of the Tang dynasty and the 880s, during the reign of Emperor Xuanzong (713–756), did the court leave Chang'an or Luoyang. The value of a single imperial location —and the power it commanded as a hub of imperial rule—was not realized in Japan until the end of the eighth century. The last eighth-century Japanese capital was Heian-kyō, where the court moved from the Nagaoka capital in 794. The plan of the new city would be a perfect implementation of what had become the Japanese ideal. The site remained the primary imperial residence for the rest of premodern Japanese history.

Palace-City

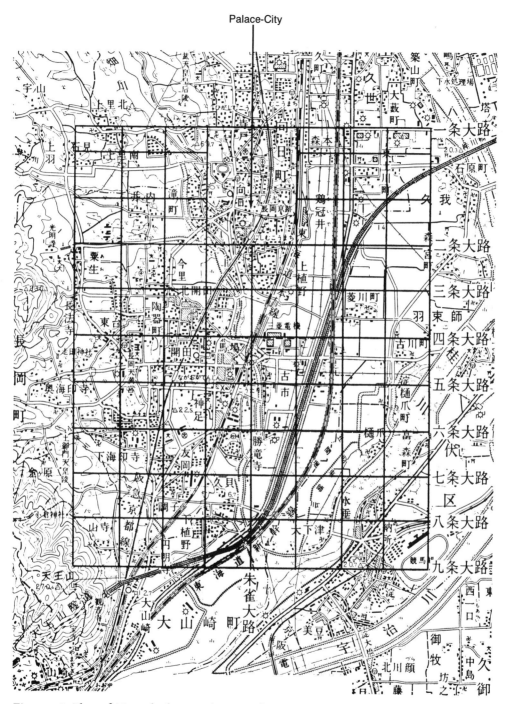

Figure 98. Plan of Nagaoka-kyō in the seventh century superimposed on the modern city. [Ueda, *Tojō*, p. 239; published with permission of Shakai Shisōsha]

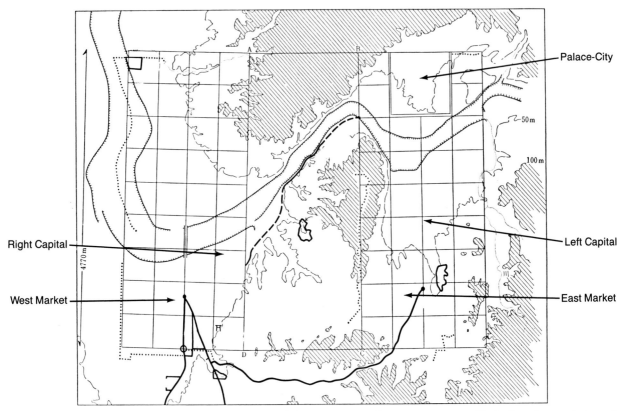

Figure 99. Reconstructed plan of Kuni-kyō in the eighth century. [Ueda, *Tojō*, p. 202; published with permission of Shakai Shisōsha]

Heian-kyō, modern Kyōto, was a walled city 4,509 meters east to west by 5,241 meters north to south (Figure 100).[26] Its nine main east–west streets (*jō*) were numbered from north to south, and the distance between the first and second was two-and-a-half times the distance between streets numbered two to nine. The four main north–south thoroughfares east and west of central Vermilion Bird Road were given individual names. The palace area extended north to south between *jō* one and two, ending at the northern terminus of Vermilion Bird Road. As at Heijō-kyō, the precincts between *jō* and north–south avenues were divided by cross streets into sixteen sections. The locations of markets and great monasteries at Heian-kyō were east and west in the southern portion of the city.

In sum, then, there were several similarities between the Japanese imperial cities and their Tang counterparts. A question worth raising, however, is the possibility of pre-Tang Chinese sources for the imperial Japanese city plans. Might Northern Wei Luoyang or sixth-century Ye have influenced the plans of Japanese capitals like Fujiwara-kyō? It is true that only at pre-Sui Chinese capitals can the buildings that will become palace-city and imperial-city be found within a single enclosure, as in Japan.

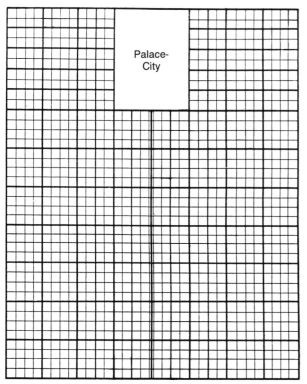

Figure 100. Heian-kyō (ca. 794–1185). [Ueda, *Tojō*, p. 250; published with permission of Shakai Shisōsha]

Japanese scholars have debated the issue of pre-Tang urban influences on Japanese cities built in Chinese styles, and the importance of this issue merits a brief discussion here.

Eight factors should be considered in comparing the cities Daxing–Chang'an (Figure 11), Sui–Tang Luoyang (Figure 82), Northern Wei Luoyang (Figures 71 and 73), Eastern Wei Ye (Figure 76), Fujiwara-kyō (Figure 96), Heijō-kyō (Figure 97), and Heian-kyō (Figure 100): (1) the dimensions and shape of the outer city; (2) the presence of an outer wall; (3) the location of the palace area, both in relation to an outer wall and to a back garden; (4) bilateral symmetry of the plan, including the division of the two halves by a major north–south thoroughfare known as Vermilion Bird Road; (5) the location of markets; (6) the ward system; (7) the distinction between palace-city and imperial-city; and (8) the presence of a palace complex named Taiji.[28]

Regarding the first point of comparison, one recalls that in the early literary discussion of Northern Wei Luoyang, *Luoyang qielan ji*, the nickname "9:6 city" was attached to it. The longer north–south dimension is more similar to the length/width proportions of Fujiwara-kyō, Heijō-kyō, Heian-kyō, the other seventh-century Japanese capitals, and Ye of the mid-sixth century than to those of the Sui–Tang cities Chang'an or Luoyang. The questionable aspect of the comparison is the use of only the original enclosures of Northern Wei Luoyang, before its wards were built, with the relatively final versions of the other cities. The post-501 Northern Wei capital more closely resembled the Sui–Tang capitals than it did the eighth-century Japanese cities. Given its short imperial history and out-of-the-way location, it is difficult to assign great influence outside of China to the plan of Eastern Wei Ye; and the earlier third-century Ye scheme is not the vertical rectangle being sought as

Yet the Northern Wei capitals were long destroyed by the time even the earliest Japanese "permanent" capital was built—and, probably more significant, it seems that an axiom in building a Chinese-style capital in Japan was that the imagery of the current design must manifest some likeness of Tang-style power. Although pre-Tang art forms traveled from China to Japan, often by way of Korea, in the sixth and early seventh centuries, China itself was largely unseen by Japanese eyes. During the Nara period, however, officials and missionaries crossed the sea directly between China and Japan, a practice that continued into the ninth century, first century of the Heian period in Japan.[27] Still, both Chinese and

a source but more squarish in shape, like the plans of the later Chinese cities. The explanation preferred here is that although the four preexisting roads determined the outer shape of Fujiwara-kyō, its plan was made in imitation of a Tang Chinese design. If the exterior shapes of subsequent Japanese capitals were constructed in imitation of Fujiwara-kyō, their designers may have believed that Fujiwara-kyō was already modeled after a Chinese scheme.

As for the second point, all Chinese imperial cities and most other cities had outer walls, often constructed before the buildings of the city. Since outer city walls stand at no Japanese city discussed here, enclosures are seldom associated with Japanese urban schemes. Yet archaeological evidence has confirmed that the outer regions of the Heijō and Heian capitals were indeed walled. Similar evidence suggests an outer wall to have been built at Fujiwara-kyō also.

We turn now to the third point of comparison: location of the palace area. Except for Sui–Tang Luoyang, and possibly Kuni-kyō, whose special geographic considerations have already been mentioned, all the other cities under consideration in this chapter had a palace area in the north center. Each Chinese city, as well as Heijō-kyō and, it seems, Fujiwara-kyō, had an imperial park or garden north of the palace. At Fujiwara-kyō, Heijō-kyō, and Northern Wei Luoyang, however, the parkland was within the outer city boundary; at Chang'an it was outside of it; and at Heian-kyō the park was south of the imperial sectors. Kishi Toshio considers these differences crucial evidence for his theory that Northern Wei Luoyang—and not a Sui–Tang city—was the source of the Fujiwara-kyō plan.[29] One must consider, however, how rigorous imitation must be in order to conclude that it has occurred. That is, building without experience in a Chinese imperial city, and possi-

bly from orders rather than plans, one wonders if the builders of the Japanese capitals were not simply given a directive such as "the park goes north of the palaces," instead of "the park goes north of the palaces, within (or beyond) the northern boundary of the city." Had Japanese builders been instructed to locate the back garden beyond the city bounds, it seems logical that if the topography had allowed it, the garden would have been there. More likely, building instructions were not so specific and the location of the park on one side of the northern city wall or the other should not be primary evidence in determining whether a specific Chinese city was the source for the Japanese imperial capitals.

The fourth point concerns the issue of bilateral symmetry. The division of the imperial city into east and west sectors by a major north–south thoroughfare between the main south gate of the palace area and the south center of the outer city wall must always be regarded as a primary characteristic of an ideal Sui–Tang plan or copies of it. At Heijō-kyō and Heian-kyō, at least, and at the Sui–Tang cities, the thoroughfare was named in honor of the red bird, the one of the *sishen* associated with the south. One recalls that an imperial way with the same name had been built at Jiankang, but at Northern Wei Luoyang the main southern approach to the palace-city was Bronze Camel Avenue, named for the adjacent markets. Other features of bilateral symmetry in the Chang'an, Heijō-kyō, and Heian-kyō plans are the situations of east and west monasteries and markets.

Regarding the fifth point, the location of markets at the Japanese imperial cities has thus far been confirmed both at Heijō-kyō and Heian-kyō, where they stood east and west of Vermilion Bird Road— at Heijō-kyō near the second and third *bō* of the eighth *jō* and at Heian-kyō in the first and second *bō* of the eighth *jō*. At Chang'an the symmetrically positioned markets are indicated on almost every plan; although a third market was originally intended in the southern portion of the city, it was never built. Because of the special geography of Sui–Tang Luoyang, its one main market, known as the south market, was located east of the palace area. Like earlier Chinese imperial cities, the Northern Wei capital at Luoyang had more than two markets, located variously inside and outside the capital. Market location indicates two things about these cities: First, as utilitarian spaces for the populace their positions are more subject to the pragmatic or functional pressures that can override form than are other spots in the Chinese capital; second, therefore, the close relationship between market locations at Chang'an and the Japanese capitals should be considered important evidence for the serious implementation of the Sui–Tang plan in the early-eighth-century Japanese capital.

We turn now to the sixth point: the ward system. In comparing the implementation of the ward system at Chinese and Japanese imperial cities, the shape of the wards and the number of subunits within them are important criteria, for every Chinese capital since Han times was planned with some system of internal subdivision in mind. The wards of all the cities considered in this section were four-sided and had at least one major access point at each side. However, at Northern Wei Luoyang and each of the Japanese imperial cities (except the northernmost regions of Heijō-kyō and Nagaoka-kyō) wards were square and uniformly sized, whereas at Sui–Tang Chang'an and Luoyang, wards were rectangular and of varied dimensions. Bilaterally symmetrical wards of Chang'an had the same dimensions. Kishi has used ward shape as significant evidence for his theory of the Northern Wei origins of the Japanese imperial plan. Yet an important distinction between the wards at both Luoyang capitals and the ward system of Chang'an, Heijō-kyō, and Heian-kyō can be made. At Northern Wei and

Tang Luoyang, and at Fujiwara-kyō, only two streets, one in either direction, divided the ward. At the other cities, including Chang'an, six main thoroughfares ran through the wards, three in each direction, giving way to sixteen internal divisions (Figures 101 and 102).

The seventh criterion concerns the single palace area as opposed to individually enclosed palace-city and imperial-city. In Kishi's comparison of Northern Wei Luoyang and the Japanese imperial cities, he considers only the original two walls of Northern Wei Luoyang. Yet one cannot ignore the fact that within the pre-501 Luoyang outer city were government offices located in the inner enclosure of Japanese capitals. In other words, it may have been the intention from the beginning for an additional wall to enclose the Northern Wei capital. A better explanation of why the Japanese cities did not differentiate between palace-city and imperial-city has been put forth by Wang Zhongshu.[30] Wang points out that the Japanese palace-city, which contained the palatial and administrative structures of a capi-

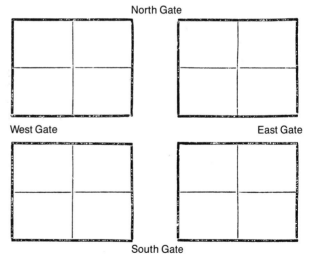

Figure 101. Plan of a typical ward at Tang Chang'an. [Su, *Kaogu* no. 6 (1978), p. 410]

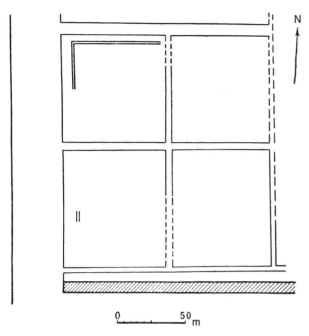

0 |_____| 50 m

Figure 102. Plan of Mingjiao ward at Tang Luoyang.
[Chen Jiuheng, *Kaogu* no. 6 (1978), p. 371]

tal, predated the construction of Naniwa-kyō. Although the Japanese city builders maintained their native single enclosure even after a second wall which separated administrative from palatial functions had become standard in China, Wang still believes that for comparative purposes the Japanese palace-city should be regarded as a palace-imperial-city. Given the monumental change from short-lived to permanent capitals that occurred at this time, perhaps Japanese planners decided to leave unaltered the palatial-bureaucratic building scheme that had worked for them in the past and chose simply to position it in the north center according to Chinese imperial plans of the time.

The eighth point involves the presence of a palace complex named Taiji. Comparisons have been made between the Taiji Hall which stood among the palace buildings at Chinese capitals such as Northern Wei Luoyang and Tang Chang'an and Daigoku-den (Japanese pronounciation of Taiji Dian) of the Japanese palace area. The problem here is that in China *taiji* is associated with the North Star and the building complex was a palatial residence. In Japan, Daigoku-den was the Great Hall of Council, an administrative building. On the other hand, with all the available names for halls, it may be more than coincidence that the same named hall appeared in more than one Chinese imperial city and in every Japanese one.

A final comparative point may be noted. The only features that marred the perfectly geometrical shape of Chang'an's outer wall in the pre–Daming Gong era were Qujiang Pond (dug, it has been suggested, for geomantic purposes) and a garden in the southeast corner of the capital. Remains of a pond extending beyond the city boundaries have also been uncovered in the southeastern corner of Heijō-kyō.[31]

North of the Great Wall

Two well-documented examples of the implementation of the ideal Tang city plan are found northeast of China. One was the eighth-century city at Longquan Fu, built as Shangjing, the upper capital, of the Bohai kingdom. The Bohai were an amalgam of Tungusic tribes plus a Korean (Koguryŏ) elite, who, under the leader Ta Zurong, moved into the area of the Mudan River in present Jilin and Heilongjiang in the last years of the seventh century. Heavily influenced and at times a tribute state of the Tang dynasty, the Bohai kingdom endured until 926. During their period of flourishing they governed according to five capitals, fifteen *fu*, sixty-two *zhou*, and more than one hundred thirty *xian* in emulation of the Chinese system. The capital Shangjing—constructed in 755, used for more than thirty years, and then reestablished as the primary imperial residence from 794 until the collapse of the regime—was clearly patterned after the Sui–Tang Chang'an plan (Figure 103).[32]

The outer wall of Shangjing measured 5.5 kilometers across its northern face and 5 kilometers at the south. The east and west walls were about 3.5 kilometers.[33] The foundation of the wall was made of large stones. The wall itself measured 7 to 10 meters at the base, and its upper portions of pounded earth were 2 to 3 meters wide at the top. Three gates pierced the north and south sides and two, the eastern and western sides. Major streets ran north–south and east–west across the city, dividing it into wards. The broadest street, the equivalent of Vermilion Bird Road, was 88 meters wide. It divided Shangjing into east and west sectors. Shangjing also had east and west markets (not shown in Figure 103). As of 1980, ten monasteries had been uncovered within the city walls.

The imperial-city and palace-city regions of Shangjing were an outer enclosure known as *neicheng* which measured 1,060 by 1,180 meters and a 620 by 720 meter palace-city at its north center. The arrangement was similar to Luoyang's, where the palace-city was also enclosed on at least three sides by the imperial-city. Directly east of the palace-city was a garden about 1.5 kilometers in perimeter. North of the imperial-city was a walled region that extended beyond the northern boundary of the outer wall. The precedent of Sui–Tang imperial planning suggests that it was a park. Inside the palace-city seven structures faced south along a north–south line (Figure 104).

Exactly seven structures define the axis of imperial palaces at Anhag, palace-city of Pyongyang, capital of the Koguryŏ kingdom in Korea before 668, when it fell to Silla (Figure 105). Similar to Japanese capitals of the next century, the enclosed Korean palace-city was surrounded by only one outer wall. The influence of Chinese planning—

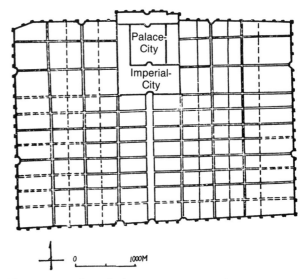

Figure 103. Plan of Shangjing, capital of the Bohai at Longquan Fu, Heilongjiang (ca. 755–926). [Dong, *Zhongguo chengshi*, p. 37]

and the Tang model in particular—is evident in the detached eastern palace, residence of the crown prince in China, and the pond in the southeast, patterned, it would seem, after Qujiang Pond.[34]

Late Evidence of the Tang Plan

More than five hundred years after the establishment of the Bohai or Koguryŏ capitals, the Mongols built an administrative town at Yingchang Lu ("circuit"), today in the Inner Mongolian Autonomous Region. Its plan represents the latest known implementation of the Sui–Tang scheme.

Constructed in 1271 (as Yingchang Fu, which it remained for twenty years), this residence of the Prince of Lü was a rectangular city: 650 meters north–south by 600 meters (Figure 106).[35] A 10-meter-wide east–west avenue cut across the city, and a 20-meter equivalent of Vermilion Bird Road bisected its southern portion. The palace area, enclosed by the east–west thoroughfare in the cen-

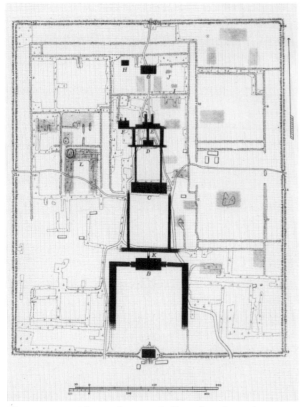

Figure 104. Plan of main halls of Bohai Shangjing palace-city. [Harada and Komai, *Tung-ching-ch'eng,* fold-out map 3]

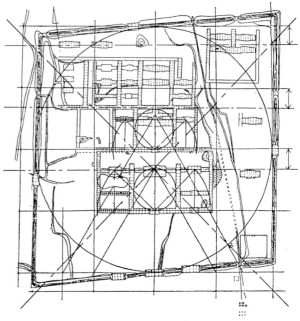

Figure 105. Plan of palace-city of Anhag, Pyongyang, North Korea. [Nagashima, *Naniwa-kyū seki no kenkyū* 7 (1981), p. 260]

ter of the northern half of Yingchang Lu, consisted of two main halls with a pavilion between them, arranged according to the *gong* scheme. Other buildings of the palace-city were symmetrically placed east and west of the central axis, and more government offices stood to the east, south of the main east–west street. Although Yingchang Lu was not a precise replica of a Tang city, the similarities to one are apparent in the concentration of imperial architecture in the north and in the locations of the two widest city thoroughfares. Moreover, the arrangement of Yingchang Lu is so differ-

ent from any other post-Tang imperial city or walled town built under Mongolian rule of China that it is best interpreted as a late survival of a once most popular imperial scheme—suggesting the possibility of the post-Tang use of this plan at additional nonimperial locations. Yingchang Lu flourished for just a hundred years; it was abandoned after the death of the last Mongolian emperor there in 1370.

Earlier this century, before the wealth of excavated material available today was known, theories were put forth to explain the ideal Tang plan, represented by Sui–Tang Chang'an, and specifically to explain why its palace area stood in the north center of the city. Naba Toshisada and Chen Yinke traced the evolution of the plan as far back as the first Wei capital at Ye and suggested that non-Chinese rulers must have preferred this presumably non-Chinese plan. Chen Yinke further suggested that Northern Wei Pingcheng should also have had such a plan.[36] These two scholars and Mori Shikazō took note of economic and geographic factors, such as water supply, that might have given rise to the

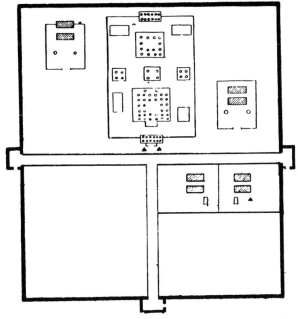

Figure 106. Plan of Yingchang Lu, Inner Mongolian Autonomous Region, Yuan period. [Li Yiyou, *Kaogu* 10 (1961), p. 531]

Sui–Tang scheme.[37] Komai Kazuchika contends that the imperial sectors were located in the north due to an association of the position with the North Star, suggesting thereby an explanation for the name Taiji for palace compounds at Chang'an and other Chinese cities.[38] The most original explanation for the Sui–Tang plan, however, was put forth centuries earlier, in *Chang'an zhi.* Its authors wrote that Sui Wendi's dislike of the populace was so great that he enclosed himself within a city of palatial buildings and used the imperial-city as a further barrier between him and the masses.[39]

To understand the design of Sui–Tang imperial cities, one needs no further explanation than its place in the evolution of transmitted plans that began in the second millennium B.C. One feature often associated with the Sui–Tang model city, however, did originate in the Northern Wei plan of Luoyang, too short-lived, perhaps, to receive proper credit: the division between palace-city and imperial-city. The sector of selfish imperial prerogative, as *Chang'an zhi* viewed it, would nevertheless be implemented in all future imperial Chinese cities. Its position was soon to be altered, however, giving way to a plan in which the tripartite division would be used in conjunction with the idealized scheme of ancient Zhou kings. This plan will be discussed in Chapter 7.

AT CHINA'S BORDERS

ALONG China's northern fringe and north of China proper a group of very different cities were established after the fall of the Tang by non-Chinese rulers who set up dynasties in Chinese fashion. It was not the first time that non-Chinese leaders had conquered territories along China's northern and western frontiers. Yet the disintegration of the Tang gave way to the longest continuous period of rule by conquest dynasties that China would experience, culminating with the occupation of all China by the Mongolian empire.

In the first half of the tenth century, during which time native rulers vied for control of China from former imperial city sites, the threat of foreign domination was posed by the seminomadic people known in English as the Khitan (Qidan). In 926, eight Khitan tribes who banded together under the leadership of a tribal chieftain, called Abaoji in Chinese, destroyed the remains of the Bohai state. In 946 they claimed the throne of China. The next year the Khitan formally established the Liao dynasty, which maintained control of much of North China and areas beyond its northern borders for almost two hundred years.

By the end of the first quarter of the twelfth century the territory under Liao rule plus an additional portion of North China had fallen to another group of originally seminomadic people, this time of Tungusic origins from northern Korea and former Manchuria, known as the Jurchen (or Jurched; Nüzhen in Chinese). The Jurchen leader, Aguda, allied himself with the Song in order to eradicate the Liao. After gaining control of Liao territory, Aguda quickly broke his pact with the Song and added North China as far south as the Yangzi River to his empire. The Jurchen dynasty endured for just over a century, falling to the Mongols in 1234.

The small faction of Liao that survived the Jin conquest became known as the Western Liao, alternatively known as the Khara-Khitay. For five generations, between 1124 and 1211, these descendants of the Liao ruling clan maintained control of a small empire in Central Asia whose capital was Balāsāghūn, a still unexcavated site between Gansu province of China and the Amu Darya River. Later in the thirteenth century the Mongols destroyed the Western Liao, Jurchen, Song, and most of the other Asian empires.

The Khitan administered their dynasty through five capitals, following the system which had been used by the seminomadic Bohai kingdom, itself based on the multicapital system of Tang China.[1] Each of the Liao capitals was the administrative center of an imperial "circuit," which was subdivided according to the Chinese system into smaller administrative districts of *fu, zhou,* and *xian.*[2]

The Jurchen adopted the Liao five-capital system, for similar to their non-Chinese predecessors, both the Khitan and Jurchen dynasties found it necessary to adapt to certain sedentary ways in order to maintain control of a civilization like China's. Four of the Jin capitals actually stood on or by Liao ruins, following a long-standing Chinese tradition of building the new dynastic capital at or near an already legitimate imperial site. The fifth and southernmost Jin capital was at the former Song Chinese imperial city Bianliang (Kaifeng). A final contemporary imperial city influenced by Chinese planning was Khara-Khoto (Heicheng)—near the present border between Gansu, the Ningxia Hui Autonomous Region, and the Inner Mongolian Autonomous Region—capital of the Xixia (Tanguts) in the twelfth and thirteenth centuries.

The sites and something of the architecture of the Liao, Jin, and Tangut capitals are known. Of these, reliable plans exist only for three Liao, three Jin, and the Tangut imperial cities.

LIAO IMPERIAL CITIES

The earliest Liao capital was also the farthest north. Known as Shangjing ("upper" or "supreme capital"), it was located at a former Bohai capital site amid the nomadic pastureland of the predynastic Khitan. In 918, thirty years before the creation of the Liao empire, a city wall was built at Linhuang, today in the Inner Mongolian Autonomous Region. This symbol of urbanism marked the beginning of Liao accommodation to the sophisticated ways of the Chinese.

After the new empire was established, the walls of Shangjing came to serve a second important purpose. Before the end of the tenth century the upper capital was a double city (Figure 107). The north city, known as Huangcheng, was squarish, each side measuring between 1,470 and 1,580 meters. Its three surviving walls, and presumably the south wall, also, had one gate each. (The south wall has been partially destroyed by water.) The Huangcheng walls were punctuated by both *wengcheng* and *mamian* fortifications, positioned at intervals of approximately ninety paces. The smaller adjoining south city shared the same east–west wall length as the north city but measured only between 1,000 and 1,150 meters north to south.[3] Much of the southern boundary is gone. The three southern wall sides were lower than those of Huangcheng and much less fortified. The south city was known as Hancheng.

The term Han, name of the early Chinese dynasty, has the added meaning of "Chinese"— with special reference to the people of North China. Northern Chinese of course constituted the majority of the Chinese population of Shangjing. For the Liao, Hancheng referred to the city area restricted to non-Liao residents, many of whom served the Liao as artisans.[4] The reduced fortifica-

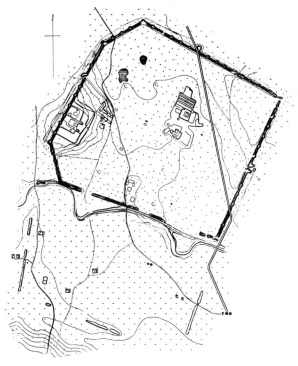

Figure 107. Plan of Shangjing, first Liao capital at Lin-huang Fu, Inner Mongolian Autonomous Region (918–ca. 1125). [Tamura, *Chūgoku seifuku,* vol. 1, p. 320; published with permission of Tōyōshi kenkyū kai]

tion of the non-Liao city gave the clear message that the chief concern of the northern walled enclosure, Huangcheng, was protection of its non-Chinese imperial rulers and their relatives.

Such obvious evidence of function has not been apparent in the designs of double cities of the first millennium B.C. The fourth century A.D. capital Shengle had multiple walls simply because of adjacent earlier and later construction. Beginning in the tenth century, however, the double city served the specific purpose of segregating the ruling dynasty and its race from nonnative subjects. Such double cities would be the predominant plan type for Liao

and Jin capital builders north of China's old Tang border. Five hundred years later the Manchu rulers of China's last dynasty would follow a similar practice by referring to the sixteenth-century extension of Beijing, where most of the non-Manchu population lived, as Hancheng. Ironically, although the ward system of Tang and pre-Tang Chinese imperial cities was no longer rigidly implemented, Hancheng under the Liao offered an alternative enclosure scheme for a similarly restrictive purpose.

Architecture of the Liao upper capital suited the double-city scheme. Like other aspects of dynastic Liao civilization, building represented a blending of native and sedentary tendencies—models for sedentarism being primarily acquired from the Tang and Bohai. At Shangjing the architecture of imperial Huangcheng included permanent governmental and religious structures, but the Khitan themselves resided in tents. Within Hancheng, on the other hand, the residential architecture was more exclusively Chinese in style. Yet the city walls, inspired by Chinese tradition, afforded enough privacy so that it was not obvious from the outside what kinds of residences stood where or the extent to which native residential taste was maintained by the rulers. Even after the double-city plan was abandoned in Mongolian times in favor of more typically Chinese designs, non-Chinese conquering rulers continued to reside in tents within Chinese-style walled cities.

The most important buildings of the northern city Huangcheng were three great halls, presumably arranged along a straight line.[5] They were elevated near the center of the city. The rest of Huangcheng beyond this area, which seems to have been equivalent to a Chinese palace-city, was divided into two *xian,* much in the manner of the Tang capital Chang'an. Three sides of Huangcheng were enclosed by a moat. Seven *xian* comprised the southern city, the economic center of Shangjing.

Only one of the seven Hancheng districts had exclusively Chinese inhabitants. This hub of Liao imperial rule was connected by road to the old Bohai capital at Longquan Fu, to the Song capital Bianliang, to Korea, and to Jurchen territory.

The Liao took their second capital in 919. Settlers, predominantly Bohai, were brought to the capital near modern Liaoyang, in Liaoning, in 927, still twenty years before the official establishment of the dynasty. The site had a long pre-Khitan history dating to its inclusion in the state of Yan in the Warring States period. After the collapse of the Western Jin at the beginning of the fourth century the territory had been taken by the Korean Koguryŏ kingdom, eventually falling to the Tang in 669. The Liaoning site was designated Dongjing, ("eastern capital") in 938.

Liao Dongjing too was a double city. Its two parts were known as Bencheng ("native city") and Hancheng, or Waicheng ("outer city"), *wai* having the double meaning of "outer" and "foreign." Little excavation has occurred at the Liao eastern capital, and no plan of it is known. Yet, based on what is recorded in the *Liao shi* and the plans of other Liao capitals, especially its predecessor Shangjing, it is believed that the two walled areas were roughly north and south of each other and that Hancheng was the southern city. The total exterior perimeter was a wall 30 *li* long and 3 *zhang* high. This fortified wall had eight gates and four corner towers. Enclosed by a 3-*zhang*-high wall of its own, in the north of Bencheng was a palace-city. Two markets were located north and south of each other in Hancheng. This non-Liao section of the eastern capital was occupied predominantly by people of Bohai ancestry. The total population of the eastern capital exceeded 40,600, the majority of whom were non-Khitan, suggesting perhaps that Hancheng was the larger of the two walled portions.[6]

The official establishment of the Liao dynasty by the man called Emperor Taizu coincided with the conquest of the Chinese city Yuzhou—the southern Liao capital known as Nanjing, or Yanjing. Located at a site that had been a Chinese settlement or garrison town since the Spring and Autumn period, the Liao southern capital reflected the strong Chinese influences around it. In fact, one account of the times relates that all the residents of Nanjing wore Chinese clothes.[7]

No early plans of the cities whose ruins comprise the earliest layers of civilization under Beijing survive. Based on detailed descriptions, however, it has been possible to make reconstruction drawings of both Nanjing and the locations of some of its buildings (Figures 108 and 109). Records relate that the Liao capital within China proper was different from the other four capitals and was essentially a Chinese-style imperial city. Liao Nanjing was a multiwalled city consisting of an enclosed imperial area. Inside this imperial space was a palace sector in the southwest corner. The perimeter of the outer city wall was probably 27 *li*.[8] The location of the inner enclosure was probably determined by three Chinese halls which stood at the site when Taizu arrived in 938. They had been built or rebuilt during the brief period between the fall of the Tang and the Liao conquest.[9] Of these halls, the main one was a banquet hall named Yuanhe Dian, which probably had a central position. The names of more than twenty other buildings from Liao Nanjing are known from stone stelae or literary sources. Those whose positions within the imperial-city can be identified are shown in Figure 109.

Evidence of Liao rule in China is still visible at the former southern capital. Noteworthy is the octagonal pagoda of Tianning Monastery.[10] The pagodas of Beijing and the predominance of Buddhist architecture among Liao remains at their other capitals are evidence of both the Liao devo-

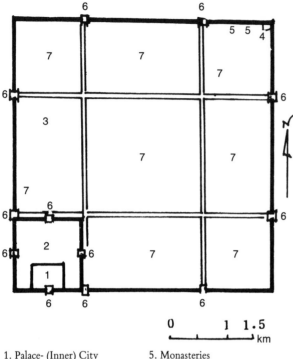

1. Palace- (Inner) City   5. Monasteries
2. Imperial-City   6. Gates
3. Liang Hall   7. Outer City
4. Corner Tower

Figure 108. Proposed reconstruction of the Liao southern capital, Nanjing, at modern Beijing, tenth to eleventh centuries. [Ye Jiazao, *Zhongguo jianzhu shi,* vol. 2, p. 455]

tion to Buddhism and patronage of it by the imperial Khitan.

The concentric-walled scheme of contemporary Chinese imperial planning was not implemented at the last two Liao capitals, although the buildings of both cities were unquestionably influenced by China.[11] The fourth capital, Zhongjing, the central capital, in what is today Pingquan Xian, Hebei province, was, according to the Japanese archaeological survey, a double city with a third walled enclosure to the west (Figure 110). It was built in the first decade of the eleventh century primarily by

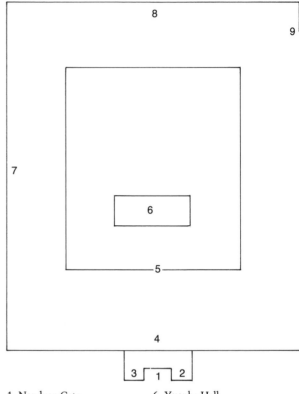

1. Nanduan Gate   6. Yuanhe Hall
2. Left Side Gate   7. Xianxi Gate
3. Right Side Gate   8. Zibei Gate
4. Wufeng Tower   9. Yanjiao Gate
5. Yuanhe Gate

Figure 109. Proposed reconstruction of buildings of palace-city of Liao Nanjing. [Zhu Qiqian, *Wenzhe jikan* 6, no. 1 (1939), p. 59]

workers resettled from North China. After two years of construction the site was established as Dading Fu, a name which survived through the Jin dynasty. The two main cities, north and south of each other, were known as Huangcheng and Hancheng, respectively. The perimeter of the wall that encompassed them has been recorded as 1,400 meters east to west by 2,000 meters north to south, with a height of between 5 and 9 meters. Joining the west side of the south city was a wall

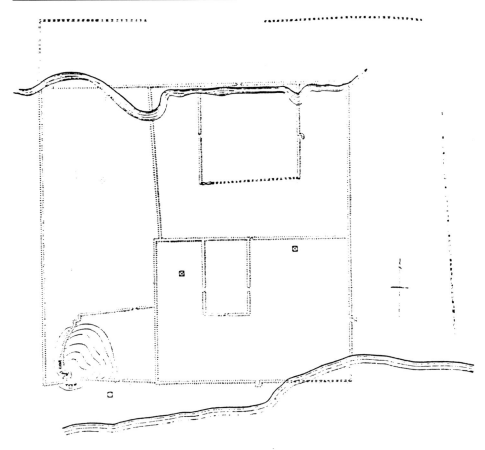

Figure 110. Plan of Liao central capital Zhongjing, Hebei, eleventh to twelfth centuries. [Tamura, *Chūgoku seifuku,* vol. 1, p. 336; published with permission of Tōyōshi kenkyū kai]

that ran about 870 meters east to west and extended to or onto a natural hill.[12]

At Zhongjing, unlike Shangjing, each of the main walled enclosures had its own palace-city, located in both cases in the north center (see Figure 110). The positions of the palace-cities may well have been inspired by the Tang model, as were the names of certain architectural components. The south gate of the northern city was Vermilion Summer Gate, an appellation whose symbolism corresponded to that of Vermilion Bird Gate. This gate was the southern terminus of a 4-*li* equivalent of an imperial-way that led directly to the south entry of the palace-city.

Remains of thirteen-story octagonal pagodas and other Buddhist art have been uncovered at the Liao central capital. Names of Liao halls are also known, but no ruins have been specifically identified. Rather, most of what was excavated at the site of Zhongjing is believed to be from the Jin or later periods. It is known that the south gates of both city walls were on the same axis and, moreover, that an Ancestral Temple and halls to the civil and military officials of China stood symmetrical to one another in the north city. The Liao central capital has been called a humble version of the Song capital Bianliang,[13] a claim that is impossible to substantiate.

The last Liao capital, Xijing, was a Liao strong-hold in the 930s, but it was not established as the western capital until late in 1044. The site near modern Datong is in the vicinity of the Northern Wei imperial city Pingcheng. Records tell that its outer wall was 20 *li* in perimeter with a gate at each side. There is no evidence about the number of walled enclosures at the western capital. Datong in Liao and Jin times is most famous for the grand Buddhist monasteries Huayan Si and Shanhua Si.[14]

JIN IMPERIAL CITIES

By the end of the first quarter of the twelfth century the Liao empire and the northern regions of the contemporary Chinese Song dynasty fell to another group of seminomadic tribes: the Jur-chen.[15] Results of imperial urbanism by the Jurchen are comparable to the Liao and Bohai capital build-ing practices: All three groups ruled from five cit-ies. Moreover, the Jurchen dynasty, called Jin in Chinese, used several Liao sites. Perhaps because cities were among the spoils of Jin conquest of Liao and Song, the process of imperial Jin urbanization was more rapid than it had been for the Liao. All five Jin capitals were established during their initial thirty years of rule.

The first Jin capital was begun under the second ruler, Wuqimai (r. 1123–1135). Known as Shangjing (upper capital) and during the Qing dynasty as Bai-cheng (White City), the capital stood in the Sun-gari River valley about 30 kilometers southeast of Harbin, now in Heilongjiang. Soviet and Japanese excavations at the site in the 1920s and 1930s yielded numerous Jin objects and resulted in a city plan (Figure 111). However, scholarly debate per-sisted during those decades and later about building order and the age of specific parts of the capital.[16]

Figure 111 clearly shows that Shangjing in Jin times, like Liao imperial centers that predated it,

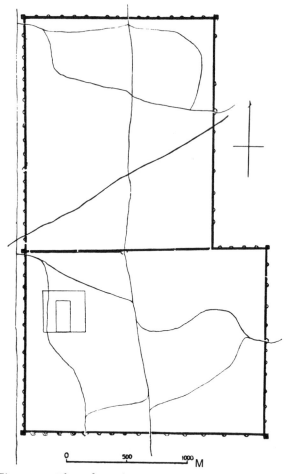

Figure 111. Plan of Jin Shangjing, Heilongjiang, twelfth century. [Sonoda, *Kōkogaku zasshi* 29 (1939), p. 413]

was a double city. The combined outer wall perim-eter was 10,945 meters. A heavily fortified mud-earth wall of the north city measured 1,900 by more than 1,550 meters, and the south city walls were about 1,500 by more than 2,000 meters. Also following Liao precedent, the north city is believed to have been Hancheng, and the south city, with palace enclosure about 137 meters from the west wall, is thought to have been the walled palace-city of the imperial Jin.

Both Sonoda and Murata Jiro believe that the south city was built earlier than the northern one and that the north city walls were constructed shortly afterward when the city expanded.[17] The specific building dates of the walls, even if the order were reversed, is not established. A reference in the *Jin shi* (History of Jin) states that Lu Yanlun "built" walls at Shangjing in 1124. Yet from that time until 1138 the name "Shangjing" was used in the official history to refer to the Liao upper capital, which would not be destroyed by the Jin until 1153. Even since the time of Wuqimai's predecessor Aguda (r. 1115–1123), however, thousands of people from all walks of life, including "470 imperial clansmen, erudites and students of the imperial academy, eunuchs, medical doctors, artisans, prostitutes, imperial gardeners, artisans of Imperial Constructions, actors and actresses, astronomers, and musicians," had been relocated to Shangjing.[18] Thus even if walls were not constructed, some urban building did occur in the 1120s. One record states that the first Jin capital was built in imitation of the Song capital Bianliang but on a much reduced scale.[19]

Excavation has not confirmed this statement, but it has shown that within the Jin imperial enclosure of Shangjing, an area of approximately 600 meters north to south by 546 meters east to west, the main halls were arranged along a strong north–south axis (Figures 112 and 113). Six platforms were uncovered along this line. Several have been associated with hall names mentioned in the *Jin shi*. Sonoda believes, for instance, that the second platform was the foundation of Qianyuan Hall, which was built in 1125 and became known as Huangji Hall in 1138.[20] He further suggests that the third platform may have been the foundation of the middle gate (*zhongmen*) and that the fourth and fifth combined as Qingyuan Hall and a back residential chamber according to the "court in front, private chambers

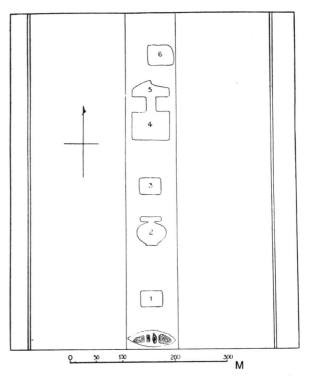

Figure 112. Plan of palace-city at Jin Shangjing. [Sonoda, *Kōkogaku zasshi* 29 (1939), p. 426]

in back" principle for imperial Chinese construction. Both of these and the last hall were probably rebuilt by Jin Emperor Shizong (r. 1161–1190), who returned to Shangjing, by then a former capital site, for one of his *xinggong,* or "traveling palaces," a temporary residence during imperial travels.

The six halls facing south and standing along a single north–south line within the confines of a palace-city recall the arrangement of main halls of the palace-cities of the Bohai upper capital at Longquan Fu (see Figure 104) and the Koguryŏ capital at Pyongyang (see Figure 105). That plans of the palace-cities of the first capital of the still seminomadic Jin and the earlier non-Chinese capitals were less complex than the building pattern at Daming Gong from Tang Chang'an—or the Japanese pal-

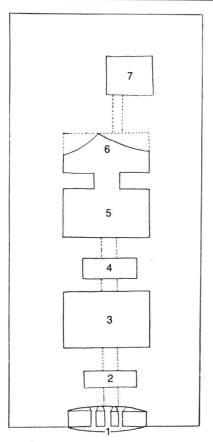

Figure 113. Idealized reconstruction of Jin Shangjing palace-city. [Sonoda, *Kōkogaku zasshi* 29 (1939), p. 437]

ace-city areas of capitals built according to Chinese models or the arrangement of buildings from the contemporary Song capital—is not surprising. The plans still reflect the implementation of a Chinese building scheme but for the limited needs of a semi-nomadic imperial architectural setting. The palace-city structures of the Liao southern capital, built within the Chinese sphere, were, by contrast, arranged according to a more complex and more Chinese program (see Figure 109) in which the main hall was centered by four gates, with an additional magnificent south gate at its approach.

The second and only other Jin capital used during the reign of Wuqimai was the western capital. The city was established in 1125 at modern Datong, the same site used by the Liao for their western capital. Predominantly Buddhist architecture, much of it rebuilt at former Liao monasteries, survives from the period of Jin rule.

The Jin also took the former Liao eastern capital for their eastern imperial city, establishing it formally in 1144. During the second moon of that year new palace buildings rose. The names of two of them, plus two gates' names, have been preserved.[21] Five months later an Ancestral Temple was built at Liaoyang Fu. Only pagodas are believed to remain from this Liao–Jin capital.[22]

In 1153 the Jin ruler Hailing Wang established three more capitals. Two were at old Liao sites that had been laid to waste by the Jin. Their names were redesignated in deference to the southward movement of the center of Jin power. The former Liao central capital became the Jin northern capital,[23] and the old Liao north capital, considered too far north for Jin purposes, was destroyed. The southern capital of Liao became the Jin central capital, and the southern Jin capital would be the splendid Song imperial city Bianliang.

More plans and much more information can be found about the central capital Zhongdu, located in what is today Beijing on a site that included the Liao southern capital within its boundaries (Figure 114), than about any other Jin imperial city. Zhongdu was designed by Lu Yanlun, chief planner for Jin Shangjing, with the assistance of Liang Han-chen and Kong Yanzhou. Eight hundred thousand men and four hundred thousand troops aided in the construction.[24]

Zhongdu was probably a double-walled city with a third enclosure around its palace area. The three walls were concentric (Figure 115).[25] The outer wall measured more than 25 *li* (14 kilometers) in perime-

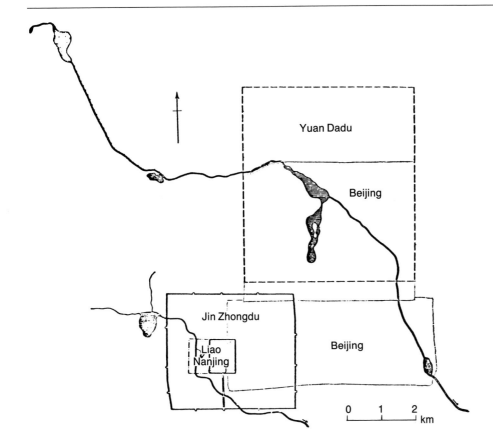

Figure 114. Plan of Liao Nanjing, Jin Zhongdu, and Yuan Dadu superimposed on Ming–Qing Beijing. [Hou, *Wenwu* no. 5 (1973), p. 3, fig. 1]

ter and had twelve gates, three on each side. The next walled enclosure, measuring 9 *li* and 30 *bu*,[26] included the enclosed palace compound. The south gate of each of the walls stood along the major north–south axis of the city where important imperial structures and an imperial-way were built.

Zhu Qiqian's study of Zhongdu published in the 1930s, based on textual descriptions, identified many of the imperial buildings.[27] As shown in Figure 116 (nos. 1 and 2), Wen and Wu (Civil and Military) towers were located symmetrically east and west of the imperial-way in front of the imperial-city south gate. East and west gates (Figure 116, nos. 3 and 4) stood on either side of this gate,

Yingtian Men (Figure 116, no. 5), named Tongtian prior to 1165. The main palace-city building complex was formed around Da'an Hall, raised on a pounded-earth platform and surrounded by a covered corridor pierced by eight gates (Figure 116, no. 9). Da'an Hall was where imperial gifts were received. To its northeast was the Eastern Palace complex (Figure 116, no. 14), the same name as the dwelling of the crown prince at Sui–Tang Chang'an. North of the Eastern Palace was Shoukang Gong, residence of Hailing Wang's mother, the empress dowager (Figure 116, no. 15). Due west was the Secretariat (Figure 116, no. 16), an administrative structure that would have been within the

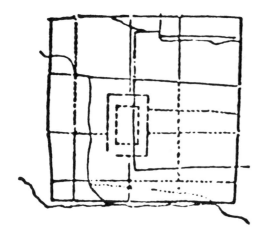

Figure 115. Plan of Jin central capital Zhongdu, at modern Beijing, twelfth century to 1234. [Hou and Wu, *Wenwu* no. 9 (1977), p. 4]

second enclosure of a tri-walled Chinese imperial city. Renzheng Hall was located at no. 17. In all, thirty-six hall names were identified by Zhu Qiqian. Twice that number of tower and pavilion names survive. Zhongdu also had ponds, gardens, and parks, including Tongyue Park (Figure 116, no. 18) of the palace-city. The most magnificent of these was Qionghua Island, built in 1179. Hailing Wang built an Ancestral Temple at his central capital in 1153. Altars of Soil and Grain were erected by his successor in 1167.

A map of Zhongdu published in the fourteenth-century encyclopedia *Shilin guangji* offers rare pictorial evidence about the non-Chinese imperial city (Figure 117). In the lower central rectangular area of the upper third of Figure 117 are two conical-topped structures. These are tents standing amid the tree-studded enclosures of the northern section of the city. The fourteenth-century plan of Zhongdu, in other words, proves that the nomads-turned-emperors did reside in steppe-style architecture within the confines of the Chinese walled imperial

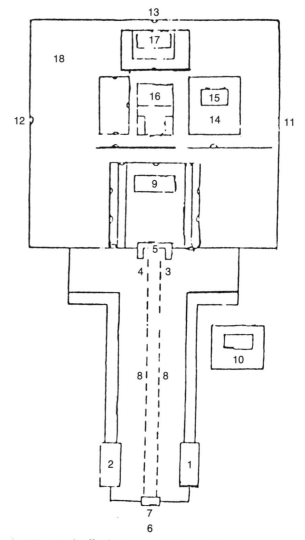

1. Wen (Civil Officials) Tower
2. Wu (Military Officials) Tower
3. East Gate
4. West Gate
5. Yingtian (Tongtian) Gate
6. Longjin Bridge
7. Xuanyang Gate
8. Qianbulang ("Thousand-Pace Corridor")
9. Da'an Hall
10. Ancestral Temple
11. Xuanhua Gate
12. Yuhua Gate
13. Gongcheng Gate
14. Eastern Palace Complex
15. Shoukang Palace
16. Secretariat
17. Renzheng Hall
18. Tongyue Park

Figure 116. Plan of palace-city of Jin Zhongdu. [Zhu Qiqian, *Wenwu cankao ziliao* no. 7 (1955), p. 69]

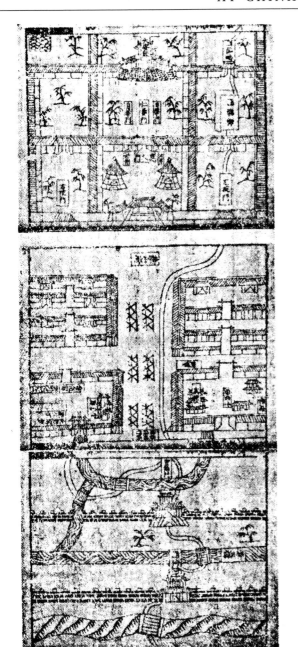

Figure 117. Drawing of Zhongdu palace-city. [*Shilin guangji,* 1330s; photograph taken from Zhu Qiqian, *Wenwu cankao ziliao* no. 7 (1955), p. 68]

city. South of the tent area is, one assumes, the palace-city.

Contrasting the tent architecture of the predynastic Jurchen period was the palace architecture of the central capital. Fu Xinian, the archaeologist who drew Figures 92 and 94 based on excavated evidence from the tomb of Tang Crown Prince Yide, has presented an equally impressive theory to help visualize the Jin central capital. This time his information is drawn from images on the western wall of the main hall of Yanshan Monastery, Shanxi province, whose pictorial program was completed by 1167 and repaired several times between the fourteenth and seventeenth centuries (Figure 118). Fu has drawn a plan of the building complex portrayed in the mural (Figure 119), which he believes corresponds closely to the plan of the main palace complexes of Zhongdu as they are described by Fan Chengda of the Song dynasty in the same text used by Zhu Qiqian for Figure 116.[28] In Figure 120, the first hall of the front *gong* group of buildings is Da'an Hall (Figure 116, no. 9), the enclosed area to its east is Shoukang Palace (Figure 116, no. 15), and the front hall of the back *gong* scheme is Renzheng Hall (Figure 116, no. 17).

Documentary evidence about Jin Zhongdu points to links with the main capital of the conquered Northern Song. It is told that in preparation for the construction of their central capital the Jin consulted diagrams of the former Bianliang and, further, that screens, doors, and walls were brought north for use at the Jin city.[29] That this decision was made the same year Bianliang was designated the Jin southern capital implies that nominally the Jin had to identify a capital site as far south in China as possible, but in actuality the center of their power and their grandest imperial city must have been Zhongdu. More will be said about similarities between the Song and Jin plans in the next chapter.

Figure 118. Line drawing of paintings from western wall of Yanshan Monastery main hall (ca. 1167). [Fu, *Jianzhu lishi yanjiu* 1 (1982), between pp. 130 and 131]

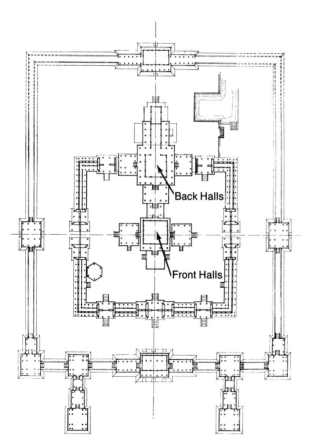

Figure 119. Reconstructed plan of Figure 118. [Fu, *Jianzhu lishi yanjiu* 1 (1982), p. 132]

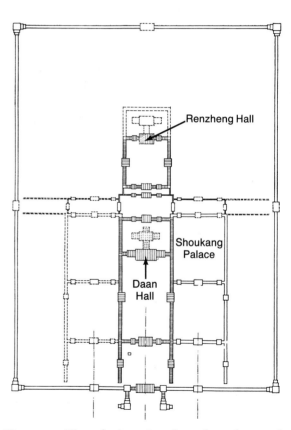

Figure 120. Plan of palace-city of Jin Zhongdu according to *Lanben lu,* Song dynasty. [Fu, *Jianzhu lishi yanjiu* 1 (1982), p. 133]

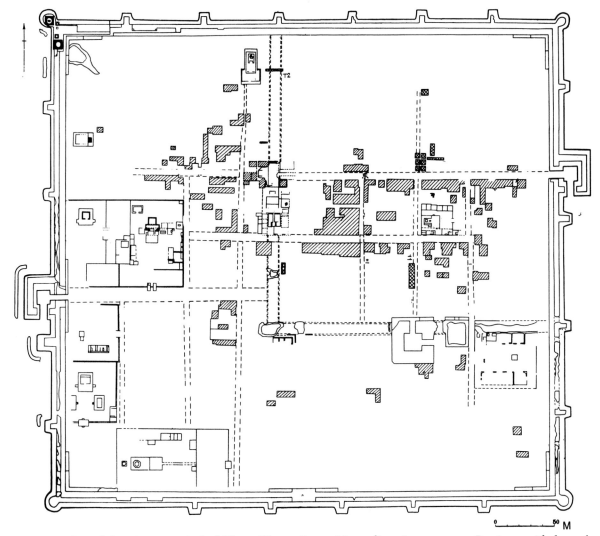

Figure 121. Plan of the Tangut capital of Khara-Khoto, Inner Mongolian Autonomous Region, mid-eleventh century to 1227. [Guo and Li, *Wenwu* no. 7 (1987), p. 2]

What the Jin left in Bianliang is uncertain. No palace halls from then or its earlier imperial building period survive today, and although it is presumed that the old Song palaces were reused for imperial Jin purposes, no excavation beneath the much newer architecture of Kaifeng has been

undertaken. It is also believed that whatever the Jin used or built did not compare to the magnificent capital of Song times.

Thus the Jin actually had six imperial centers during their approximately one hundred twenty year rule of North China. Four had been former

Liao imperial sites; one was the Northern Song capital; and the first Shangjing, their initial experiment with the urbanism of a sedentary Chinese-style empire, soon became too far north of their center of power to retain its status, thereupon being demoted to a *xinggong*.[30]

KHARA-KHOTO

The final imperial city discussed in this chapter is in the Inner Mongolian Autonomous Region. It represents the far reaches of the Chinese imperial plan as a symbolic medium through which non-Chinese rulers established Chinese-style states. Known as Khara-Khoto (literally "black city," Heicheng in Chinese) and as Edzin-gol, the city's recorded history in Chinese sources can be traced from the Han dynasty through the approximately two hundred years from the mid-eleventh century when it became the Tangut (Xixia) capital until its fall to the Mongols in 1227. The Tanguts were a people of Tibetan origin who had initially used the city as a garrison town. Non-Chinese groups, including Uygurs and some Chinese, were among the Tanguts' subjects.[31]

Several building periods have been uncovered at Khara-Khoto. The Tangut capital is believed to have consisted of an enclosed area within a walled city. The outer wall ran about 421 meters east to west by 374 meters north to south (Figure 121).[32] It was heavily fortified: Square-sectioned *wengcheng* were built beyond its west and east wall gates (on the east at a road that ran through the inner city), and *mamian* were located at its corners and at intervals of less than 100 meters along a wall whose thickness ranged from 11 meters at the base to 3 meters at the top. Long, nearly straight major streets ran north–south and east–west through the capital, especially in the inner city, enclosing many Buddhist monasteries. Shop remains were uncovered at three locations, and many residences of two to three rooms were found throughout the city. The wall structure, the fortifications, the street patterns, the existence of inner and outer cities—all suggest the influence of Chinese imperial urbanism. Nevertheless, Khara-Khoto is also reminiscent of the plan of ninth to tenth-century Bukhara.[33]

The fall of the Jin, Tanguts, and most of the rest of Asia to the Mongols in the thirteenth century marked the termination of the double city in China and at its northern borders. Perhaps the two-walled divisions never again had such an obvious purpose as had been the case under Liao and Jin rule. A more likely reason for the implementation of different city schemes beginning with the rule of China by the Mongols, however, is the application of a more studied approach to imperial city building and the purposeful selection of certain Chinese designs.

7

FROM BIANLIANG

TO DADU

THE disintegration of the Tang empire gave way to a fifty-three-year period known in Chinese history as the Five Dynasties (907–960). During these decades, while the Liao consolidated their forces to the north, fifteen rulers of five dynasties tried to maintain control of thrones in North China. The would-be emperors based themselves at Nanjing, Chengdu, Chang'an, Luoyang, and the former Tang garrison town Bianzhou, in Henan province. According to historical records, the imperial quarters of these cities were located on the grounds of earlier palaces, most of which were rebuilt or restored. Meanwhile, ten kingdoms were established in South China at cities that included Yangzhou, Hangzhou, Fuzhou, Guangzhou, and Changsha. The southwestern and especially the coastal cities would remain crucial entrepôts in the flourishing trade that was to characterize China during the Song dynasty (960–1276).

IMPERIAL CITIES OF THE SONG

Northern Song Bianliang

Among the capital cities of dynasties and kingdoms of North and South China was Bianzhou, where the first Song emperor set up his eastern capital in 960.[1] Bianzhou—also known as Bianliang and in the Song as Bianjing, part of modern Kaifeng—was built by the Tang in 781 as a small walled military town. In 907 it was transformed into an auxiliary capital with a palace-city about 2.76 kilometers in perimeter located in the northwest part of the city. These walls measured 20 *li,* roughly 11.4 kilometers, and had ten gates. (Two more gates were added under the Song.)[2] During the Five Dynasties period, under Later Zhou rule (951–960), the walled city was too small and part of the population had to move outside of it. In 956 a wall was built to protect the suburban inhabitants. This wall measured just under 27 kilometers and would eventually be expanded another kilometer or so. It had twenty-one gates. Thus even before Song times Bianliang was a triple-walled city.

Between the mid-tenth century and the fall of the Northern Song to the Jurchen in 1127, the capital became an international center of commerce. One of the earliest projects of the Song government was to extend the Grand Canal to their new capital which was situated on the Bian River and linked to the Yellow River. Trade between North China and points south was so vigorous that what occurred in the Northern Song metropolis may be called an economic revolution—indeed, the results have led some to name twelfth-century Chinese society "early modern."[3]

Like Tang Chang'an, the Northern Song imperial city was divided into *xian* which were further divided into *fang,* or wards. Yet the intercity divisions no longer regulated the population. Even by the end of the Tang dynasty the ward system and its strict control of the metropolitan markets had weakened,[4] and in Song times every variety of commercial and social activity poured out into the streets. Reduced government control over commerce, marketing, and agriculture, and the increased ease of transport by water, led to the growth of a society with more money, more credit, wholesalers, middlemen, stock options, specialization of the labor force, and more investment than China had ever witnessed.[5]

The impact of the strong economy on Bianliang was immediate. Population growth was almost exponential. Between 976 and 984, one hundred eighty thousand households were registered in the city. A century later there were fifty thousand more; two decades later, another thirty thousand. The population of the Song capital, including military quartered there, has been estimated as high as 1.7 million.[6] With an area less than one-half that of

the Tang capital, and more than one-and-a-half times the population, the people of the economic boomtown quickly poured beyond the outer city walls. The faubourgs of the city, to use Edward Kracke's term, sprawled in every direction.[7] No known plan of Bianliang shows them.

Many plans of the three-walled city do exist. Each is to some extent different, probably because this city did not become a great capital at a specific moment like its famous predecessor Chang'an. Built from the inside outward, in contrast to the stipulations of the *Kaogong ji,* and walled for the third time in response to natural urban sprawl, a highly irregular outer wall shape must have resulted.

The earliest modern plan of the Northern Song capital was published in Shanghai by Yao Jiazao in 1933 (Figure 122). Drawn according to Yao's reading of the Song text *Dongjing menghua lu* (Record of dreaming of *hua* in the eastern capital), the walled palace-city stands northwest within the imperial-city, and the irregular outer wall spans

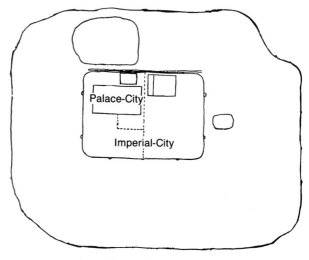

Figure 122. Plan of Northern Song Bianliang, Henan (960–1126). [Yao Jiazao, *Zhongguo jianzhu shi,* fig. 96]

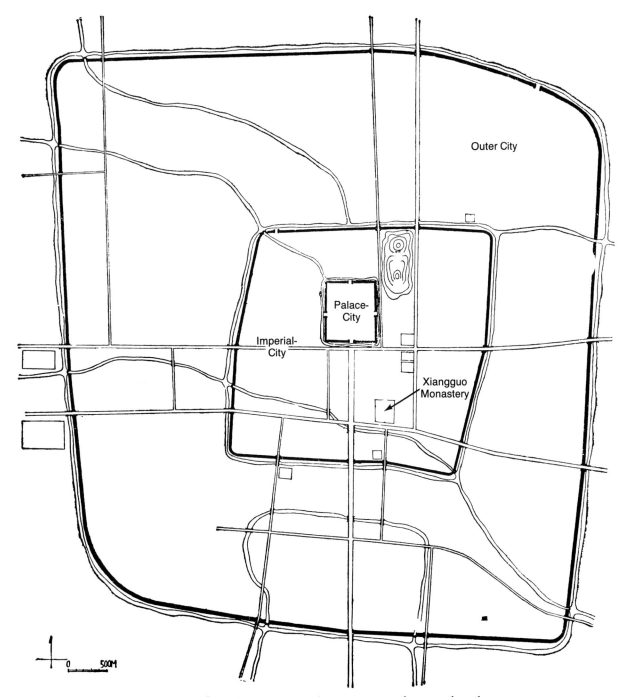

Outer City

Palace-City

Imperial-City

Xiangguo Monastery

0   500M

Figure 123. Plan of Northern Song Bianliang. [Dong, *Zhongguo chengshi*, p. 43]

more than twice the perimeter of the imperial-city which it surrounds. More recent plans of the tenth to twelfth-century capital vary from Yao's, but several recognize, if to a lesser extent, the irregular shape of Bianliang's outer boundary (Figures 123 and 124). A second feature of the three Bianliang plans, the location of the palace-city, not only varies from scheme to scheme, but Figures 123 and 124 indicate disagreement with the northwest position specified in *Dongjing menghua lu* and *Song huiyao jigao* (Rules and regulations of the Song),[8] the latter also compiled in the Song dynasty. Most often, the palace-city is within, perhaps just slightly northwest of, the imperial-city center or due north of the

imperial-city (the case in Figure 124). Other plans, including some published by authors who cite *Song huiyao jigao,* are similarly misleading. One plan of the 1980s, for instance, shows Bianliang as a city of three nearly perfectly rectangular walls.[9] Arthur Wright, whose plan of Bianliang recognized the northwestern position of the palace-city, made the error of showing the capital with a perfectly square outer wall.[10] An even more problematical plan was published in 1977 by Hou Renzhi and Wu Liangyong (Figure 125). In it Bianliang is presented as a square city with truncated corners, in the center of which stood the palace and surrounding imperial-city.

Only one explanation for such variation, especially in the direction of perfect geometricity for what population patterns necessitated to have been an irregular outer wall, seems plausible. The truncated corners of the 1977 plan (Figure 125) are a clue to its source—and probably to the origins of other plans of the Northern Song capital. The source is

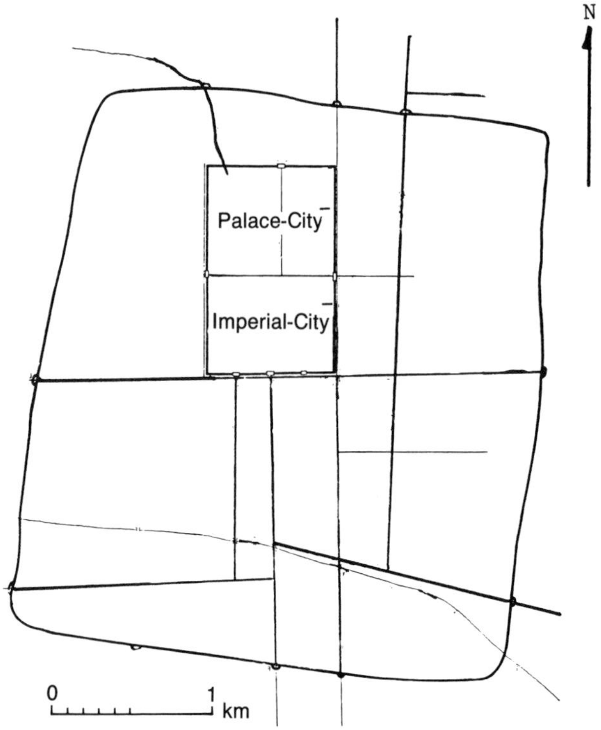

N

Palace-City

Imperial-City

0   1 km

Figure 124. Plan of Northern Song Bianliang. [After Mei Yuanyou, in Murata, *Chūgoku no teito,* p. 124; published with permission of Sōgeisha Press]

Palace-City

Imperial-City

Imperial-Way

Figure 125. Plan of Northern Song Bianliang. [Hou and Wu, *Wenwu* no. 9 (1977), p. 3]

the earliest plan of Bianliang, drawn during the decade of the 1330s when China was under Mongolian rule. The early date of the plan (Figure 126) must have enhanced its authenticity, but a stronger reason for its widespread influence exists. The source of Figure 126 is, of course, Wangcheng (see Figures 27 and 28). Why the Wangcheng design gave rise to Figure 126 and other idealized and even fictitious renderings of Chinese imperial cities will be explained later in this chapter.

Besides its three walls, another notable feature of Bianliang was the long and wide approach from the outer city south gate through gates of the imperial-city and palace-city (Figure 127). This three-lane imperial-way had its origins, as we have seen, during the period of Northern and Southern Dynasties. Bianliang also had its share of monasteries. One of the grandest, Xiangguo Si, shown in Figure 123, was located east of the imperial-way as one approached the regal sectors.[11] Although remnants of Song religious architecture survive at Kaifeng

even today, monastery building was not as important in the Song capital as it had been at earlier Chinese imperial cities. The Northern Song capital also maintained imperial altars, and occasionally Song emperors performed the Ming Tang rituals outside the imperial city.[12] In general, however, the city is best described as "secularly urban." This label is shown nowhere more descriptively than in Zhang Zeduan's famous twelfth-century painting of the spring Qingming festival (Figure 128).[13]

One feature of the Song city was by all accounts marvelous. It was *genyue,* a landscaped artificial

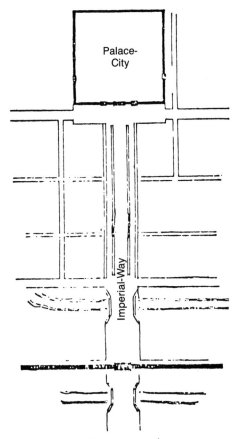

Figure 127. Plan of T-shaped approach to Bianliang palace-city. [Hou and Wu, *Wenwu* no. 9 (1977), p. 3]

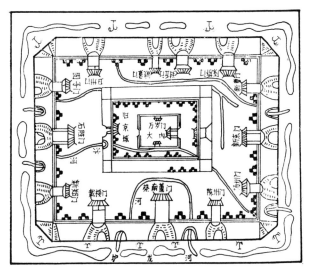

Figure 126. Idealized plan of Bianliang. [*Shilin guangji,* 1330s; photograph taken from Dong, *Zhongguo chengshi,* p. 42]

Figure 128. Zhang Zeduan, *Qingming shanghe tu* (detail), twelfth century, Beijing, Palace Museum. [Zhang Anzhi, *Qingming shanghe tu,* pp. 8–9]

mountain. The stone for this mountain entered the capital only a decade before the fall of the Song government in North China. It is told that stone more than 20 *zhang* in height was borne by boat from Lingbi prefecture, in present Anhui province, to Bianliang. A city gate-tower was destroyed so the stone could be moved inside the city walls. Even then, it was possible only to carry the stone into the imperial garden. Emperor Huizong (r. 1101–1126) wrote an inscription at the site.[14]

Bianliang to Zhongdu

Stone of the same name, *genyue,* was used in the construction of a ritual-pleasure island at the Jin central capital Zhongdu during the twelfth century. If the *genyue* of the Jin island Qionghua was the same stone with which the Song artificial mountain had been built, then it must have been moved together with the screens, doors, and walls

from the Northern Song capital that were transported northward for use at Zhongdu in 1152 and 1153.[15] In fact, dismantling and removal of what remained of Song imperial halls after the Jin conquest may account for the much reduced size of the former Bianliang when it served as the Jin southern capital.

A second feature of the Jin central capital plan has a more obvious connection with Bianliang and earlier Chinese capitals. It is the imperial-way, bordered by government offices of the imperial-city, plus palace-place, combining into the T-shaped approach to the palace-city (Figure 129). Like the 200-meter-wide approach to the palace area at Song Bianliang, the imperial-way at Jin Zhongdu was three-laned. Trees lined the canals that divided the lanes. At least since the Song dynasty, the approach went by the alternate name *qianbulang,* literally "thousand-pace corridor," although the lengths of

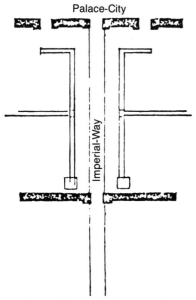

Figure 129. Plan of T-shaped approach to Zhongdu palace-city. [Hou and Wu, *Wenwu* no. 9 (1977), p. 4]

the approaches at both cities exceeded a thousand steps.

The function of the palace-place—if one did exist in the wide space between palace-city and imperial-city at Tang Chang'an—changed by the Song period. The transformation was a reflection of the greater freedom of movement permitted the population in Song cities in comparison to previous dynasties. At festivals, for instance, the population of Bianliang was allowed to gather just south of the palace-city.[16] No comparable data are available about celebrations at Jin Zhongdu, but it is certain that the residents of Chang'an never came so close nor in such great numbers to the large area between palace-city and imperial-city.

The third and most obvious similarity between the plans of Zhongdu (see Figure 115) and the Song capital was the concentric position of outer and inner city walls (even if the Bianliang palace-city and imperial-city shared a wall face). Indeed, Zhongdu was the Jin imperial city most likely to have had a Chinese plan as its model—and if so, that plan should have been Bianliang. More will be said about the Chinese model at the end of the chapter.

Lin'an

Upon the fall of North China to the Jin in 1126, a descendant of the Song emperor and several thousand members of the former Song household regrouped in South China. Eventually this remnant of the Song chose the city Lin'an, today Hangzhou, in Zhejiang province, for their new capital. Perhaps because of the numerous and detailed contemporary descriptions of thirteenth to fourteenth-century Hangzhou, including the longest chapter of Marco Polo's travel account, or perhaps because it has long been considered one of China's most beautiful cities, the site chosen by the Song has been a research subject for several of Europe's great twentieth-century sinologists, including Arthur C. Moule, Étienne Balazs, and Jacques Gernet.[17] No new archaeological evidence about the Southern Song (1127–1279) imperial city has appeared since 1962. Nor has the scholarship of these three men proved inaccurate. Therefore, Lin'an will be discussed here briefly, only for the purpose of providing enough information to examine its plan during the century and a half when it was an imperial city.

Although never before an imperial city, Lin'an, like every previous Chinese capital, had an urban history that could be traced to the Warring States period. By about 600, when the first city wall at Lin'an was constructed, the artificial West Lake had already been dug. *Lin'an zhi* (Record of Lin'an) says that the early-seventh-century wall was 36 *li* and 90 *bu*.[18] In the eighth century the city extended west to include six wells that supplied the residents with saline-free water. In 893 an additional eastern rampart, closer to the Zhe River, was added. Two hundred thousand workers plus the armies of thirteen districts labored during this period of wall extension, which resulted in almost 30 kilometers of defensive perimeter. Both the seventh and ninth-century walls are shown in Figure 23.

The next building period at Hangzhou took place following the establishment of Song rule, thereafter known as the Southern Song. The Song got off to a slow start due to their resistance to accepting the new site as the capital of their shrunken regime. Since they were also slow to incur expenses for palace hall improvement or wall reinforcement and extension, it is ironic that this second Song imperial city came to rival Bianliang in wealth and luxury, to have well over a million residents, and to surpass the former Song primary capital in beauty. This most casually adopted imperial city became the wealthiest and most populous in the world in the late twelfth and thirteenth centuries.[19]

The grandeur and sophistication of Lin'an have been immortalized in Marco Polo's description of Quinsai, the Italian name for Lin'an presumably derived from the Chinese term *jingshi* ("capital") or *xingzai* ("traveling palace").[20] To Marco Polo, late-thirteenth-century Lin'an appeared a city of hundreds of miles of wide streets and canals and twelve thousand bridges. Every imaginable food could be had in its markets. The fine houses of its friendly and thriving residents were protected from fire by watch stations and firefighting equipment placed at approximately 500-yard intervals throughout the city.[21] Hundreds of hot springs, each accommodating over one hundred bathers, were also found in the city Polo described. In his description of the palace, Marco Polo reverts to typical Chinese hyperbolic detail, relating that ten thousand men could eat there with ease.

Contrasting the urbane and sometimes exotic life

was the simplicity of the Song city plan. Essentially it consisted of a palace-city located in the south center of an outer wall.[22] The main thoroughfare and north–south axis of the imperial-city was the imperial-way, so named after Lin'an assumed imperial status. Different from every other imperial capital, the road ran southward toward the palace and then continued beyond the palace-city's south gate to the Altars of Heaven and Earth.

Like its Northern Song ancestor, much of Lin'an within the city walls was occupied by markets. As at Bianliang, both commercial activity and the population quickly poured beyond the city walls. Yet lodged between West Lake and the Zhe River the capital offered little room for urban growth, so that its population was even denser than Bianliang's.[23] Still, Lin'an was not so populated that it could not be appreciated for its scenery. The beauty of the Song city is preserved in a block-printed illustration from *Lin'an zhi* (Figure 130).

The source of Figure 130 is *Xianshun Lin'an zhi* (Record of Lin'an of the *xianshun* period [1265–1274]), reissued in 1867. The original source of the drawing was a manuscript version of the text based on an original printed during the final years of Song control of the region.[24] Two other drawings from

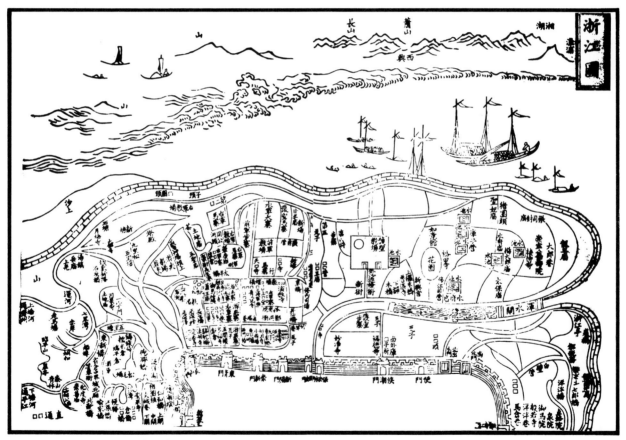

Figure 130. *The Zhe River*, Lin'an (Hangzhou), Zhejiang. [*Xianshun Lin'an zhi*, 1867 rev. ed.]

the surviving set of four (Figures 131 and 132) show notable places in the capital. More important, they provide evidence about the Chinese perception of an imperial city.

Figure 131 shows the outer wall and gates, bridges across major waterways, and most prominently the imperial-way—projecting from the city moat across the right leaf of the drawing to the left leaf, where the thoroughfare bends before the approach to the palace-city. The inner walled enclosure is a long, narrow rectangle located in the lower left of this scheme, whose fourth wall, bounded by mountains, is not indicated. Also illustrated are monasteries, ward and district names, government offices, temples, and notable mansions and scenic spots.

The scheme showing the rectangular palace-city within the perfectly rectangular outer city may seem surprising when one knows the true shape of the city (see Figure 23). Surprising too is the third thirteenth-century illustration (Figure 132). Its palace-city is a nearly perfect square, the focus of the outer city, just somewhat off-center.

The presentation of Lin'an and its palace-city in Figures 131 and 132 offers more examples of the phenomenon we have observed in plans of other Chi-

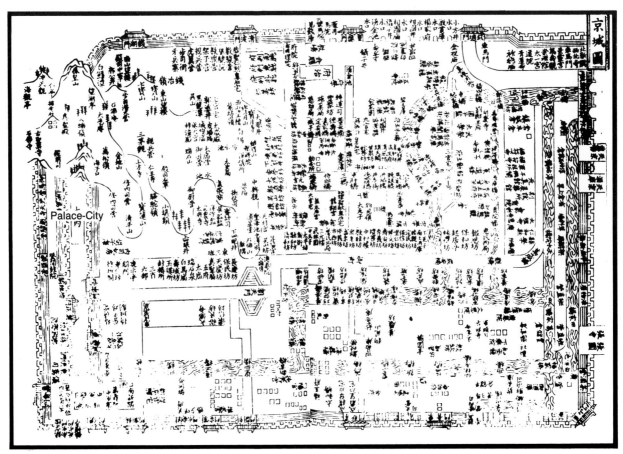

Figure 131. *The Capital City*, Lin'an. [*Xianshun Lin'an zhi*, 1867 rev. ed.]

nese imperial cities: The city's actual scheme may be considered irrelevant to the historical record. The Chinese imperial city is supposed to be geometrically perfect. In a case such as Lin'an, in which it was not, illustrations like those from *Xianshun Lin'an zhi* amend fact so that the capital will appear perfect for posterity. Thus the heavenly approved and classically sanctioned plan could transcend transitory earthen timbers and mud-brick walls joined by man. The prepared drawings for *Lin'an zhi* assured that when the material remains of Song Lin'an could no longer be found, the city plan, although fictitious, would ever after be recorded, perceived, and certified as an ideal Chinese imperial city. This legacy was a particular concern for China under Mongolian rule.

IMPERIAL CITIES OF THE MONGOLS

By the time Lin'an fell to the Mongols in the late 1270s the rest of China had been subject to non-Chinese rule by the descendants of Chinggis Khan (ca. 1162–1227) for more than a decade. In a sense, the Mongols themselves were simply next in a line of non-Chinese rulers who conquered China and controlled portions of it for a century or more. Yet

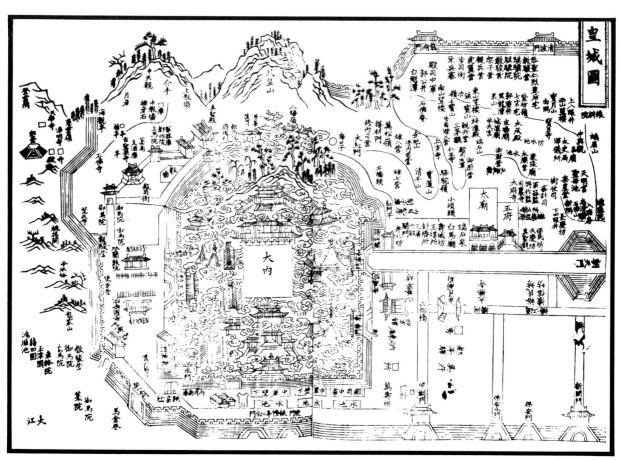

Figure 132. *The Imperial City,* Lin'an. [*Xianshun Lin'an zhi,* 1867 rev. ed.]

Mongolian rule of China was distinct from all instances of non-Chinese rule that had preceded it: The years of Mongolian rule were the first period in Chinese history when not even a part of China remained in Chinese hands; what is more, China was part of a much vaster empire which at its zenith spanned Asia from the Qipchak Steppe and Persian Gulf to the East China Sea.

The Mongols had begun their attack on Chinese cities in the first decades of the thirteenth century while Chinggis Khan was still alive. Although the Mongols razed the Jin capital Zhongdu after several years of siege in 1214, the focus of Mongolian conquest during the first three decades of the thirteenth century was Central and West Asia. Only in the 1230s did the Mongolian armies return to North China, this time under the leadership of Chinggis's third son and successor Ögödei (r. 1229–1241). In February 1234 the Jin emperor committed suicide, an act which marked the collapse of his dynasty. A year later the Mongols attacked Song-controlled Sichuan, Hebei, and Anhui. The southeastern territories of the Song managed to resist the Mongolian onslaught longer, finally falling in 1279.

It was perhaps contact with Chinese-style cities that brought some of the Mongolian leaders to the realization, even in the generation of Chinggis, that certain accommodations to sedentary ways could accelerate their grand plan of a universal empire. Many years before the 1250s, when there is evidence of Mongolian designs on China as a center of their rule, the Mongols established a power base at a city. Located today in the Mongolian People's Republic, the city Khara-Khorum is considered the first Mongolian imperial city. The second, at a site called Kaiping Fu in the present Inner Mongolian Autonomous Region, was established by Chinggis's grandson Khubilai in 1256. Third and most important of the Mongols' imperial cities was the

great capital, Dadu, also built by Khubilai Khan. Each of these three examples of the Mongolian achievement in imperial architecture was distinct in its own right, and each served a different purpose.

Khara-Khorum

The location of Khara-Khorum was still uncertain at the beginning of the nineteenth century.[25] At the end of the century two Russian teams excavated the site which had by then been identified.[26] Russian and Chinese discussion of the city at that time agreed that it had been built by Ögödei, and excavation seemed to confirm this idea. Only in 1925 was it suggested that the Khara-Khorum used by Ögödei as a military and administrative center had a history during Chinggis Khan's rule.[27] Soviet excavation at Khara-Khorum in 1949 under the directorship of Sergei Kiselev yielded proof of its earlier history. Kiselev found that the city had thrived even at the time of the Tang dynasty, when inhabitants were followers of the Buddhist faith. During the time of Chinggis Khan, Khara-Khorum had been both a military camp and a commercial and handicraft center. Its permanent halls, however, and the notion of a capital city for a Mongolian empire, probably came into existence under Ögödei.

The Khara-Khorum of Ögödei's nephew Möngke Khaghan was visited in 1254 by Friar William of Rubruck, a Christian missionary and envoy of King Louis of France. Friar William's account of his travels in search of the Khan was a most important source of information for early and later Russian excavators. According to the friar, Khara-Khorum was smaller than the French village of St. Denis, and the monastery of St. Denis was ten times greater than the palace. He wrote:

There are two quarters in it; one of the Saracens in which are the markets, and where a great many

Tartars gather on account of the court, which is always near this (city), and on account of the great number of ambassadors; the other is the quarter of the Cathayans, all of whom are artisans. Besides these quarters there are great palaces, which are for the secretaries of the court. There are there twelve idol temples of different nations, two mahummeries in which is cried the law of Machomet, and one church of Christians in the extreme end of the city. The city is surrounded by a mud wall and has four gates. At the eastern is sold millet and other kinds of grain, which, however, is rarely brought there; at the western one, sheep and goats are sold; at the southern, oxen and carts are sold; at the northern, horses are sold.[28]

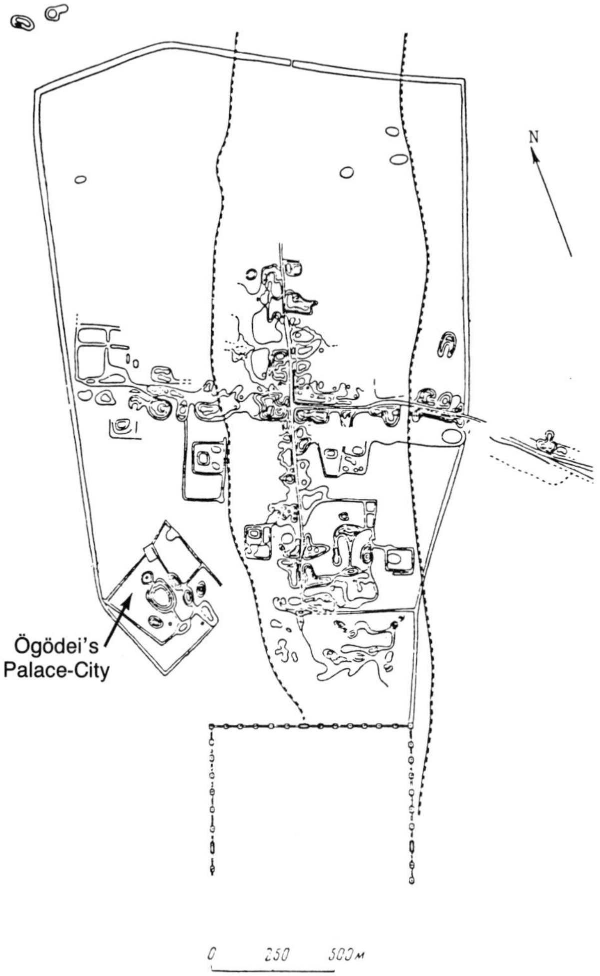

According to Soviet excavators, Khara-Khorum stood on an artificial hill composed of alternate layers of sand and clay.[29] An earthen wall some 1,000 meters on the north side, approximately one-and-a-half times that distance on the west, and 2 kilometers on the east surrounded the city (Figure 133). Along the southern portion of the western wall was Ögödei's palace area, itself a walled compound (Figure 134). That wall was only about a meter

Ögödei's
Palace-City

0   250   500 м

Figure 133. Khara-Khorum, Mongolian People's Republic (ca. 1229–1241). [Kiselev, *Drevnemongol'skie goroda*, p. 128]

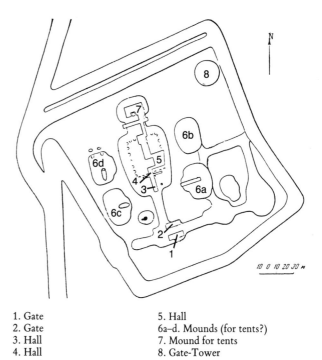

1. Gate
2. Gate
3. Hall
4. Hall
5. Hall
6a–d. Mounds (for tents?)
7. Mound for tents
8. Gate-Tower

Figure 134. Ögödei's palace-city at Khara-Khorum. [Kiselev, *Drevnemongol'skie goroda*, p. 162]

high and 15 to 18 meters thick. Most noticeable in the scheme is the orientation of the city on an axis roughly 45 degrees off due north. A peculiarity of the wall itself was the double wall along the northwest side.

The inner walled area may be thought of as a palace-city. Its dimensions along diagonals from northeast to southwest, and northwest to southeast, respectively, were 255 by 225 meters. It was, in other words, a roughly square-shaped wall of unusual orientation. Turning the plan 45 degrees would have placed the main imperial construction on a strict north–south axis. West of the palace area near the south was a pond filled by a canal from the Orkhon River more than 5 kilometers away.

Like the rectangular shape of the outer walls and the axis of orientation, the arrangement of halls along that axis corresponded to a Chinese scheme. At the south end of the palace-city were two gates, one in front of the other. The southern gate was 36 by 17 meters. Northeast of the gates were two larger halls (Figure 134, nos. 3 and 4), which Kiselev believed to be official halls for audiences, banquets, and the reception of guests. The first was 40 by 11 meters and stood on a platform three-quarters of a meter high. The second was more than twice the size of the first, 80 by 55 meters; its foundation platform was over 3 meters high. This hall may be the palace described by Friar William of Rubruck.[30] A third platform (Figure 134, no. 5), 38 by 25 meters and over 2.5 meters high, stood northeast of the other two. Behind was a low, circular mound (Figure 134, no. 7)—the location of residential tents for the now imperial Mongols. Although the relatives of Chinggis and Ögödei lived in native comfort at Khara-Khorum and other Mongolian cities, the placement of their residential area behind the public or audience halls of timber was in accord with the classical Chinese "court in front, private chambers in back" dictum. The erection of tents

on a mound further evidences an accommodation of Mongolian comforts to the Chinese system of elevated, permanent halls. Kiselev also uncovered the remains of a gate-tower about 35 meters inside the inner wall in the north-northeast corner of the city (Figure 134, no. 8). The excavator has suggested that this gate-tower was the sole survivor of an original group of four, all constructed in imitation of the corner wall towers of a Chinese city. The symmetrically positioned mounds, two on either side of the main imperial axis (Figure 134, nos. 6a–6d), may have had tents on top of them.[31]

Architectural fragments found at Khara-Khorum further attest to the pervasive Chinese character of the first Mongolian imperial city. The main halls were supported by regularly spaced implanted pillars. Tortoise bases from imperial stelae were found. So too were ceramic roof pieces, including Chinese dragons. In fact, Kiselev suggests that every timber structure at Khara-Khorum had a Chinese-style roof.[32]

Several cities outside of China, including capitals of the Liao, Jin, and Western Liao, might suggest possible architectural models for Mongolian city building. Yet the plan and spread of buildings symmetrical to a north–south main axis (compared to the single axial arrangement of Bohai, Liao, and early Jin imperial city architecture) indicate a decisive choice in favor of Chinese tradition. When it came to imperial city building, it must have been clear to the Mongols, who had seen so much of Asia in their campaign of conquest, that China's architecture offered the most splendid models of imperial rule. More obvious imitation of Chinese imperial architecture and its associated symbolism would occur at subsequent Mongolian capitals.

Shangdu

In 1256, Möngke Khaghan (r. 1251–1258), fourth in the line of Mongolian rulers that began with

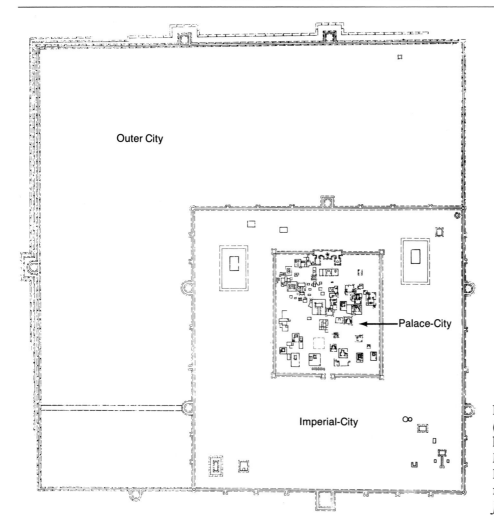

Outer City

Palace-City

Imperial-City

Figure 135. Shangdu (Kaiping Fu), the Mongolian upper capital, Inner Mongolian Autonomous Region, after 1256 to 1370. [Harada and Komai, *Jōto,* pl. 1]

Chinggis, ordered his younger brother Khubilai (1215–1294), who at the time was leading military expeditions in China, to found a city at a site in Northeast Asia, located today in the Inner Mongolian Autonomous Region. For the design of the new city Kaiping Fu, Khubilai called upon his trusted Chinese adviser Liu Bingzhong (1216–1274).

The city that Liu designed had three walls and was oriented only 7 degrees west of due north (Figure 135). The walls enclosed the palace-city, impe-

rial-city, and outer city, typical by the mid-thirteenth century of Chinese imperial urban plans. The outer wall measured nearly 2.5 kilometers on each side and was made of pounded earth.[33] Rising 4 to 6 meters high, it had one west gate and two gates at each of its other faces. The eastern and southeastern gates provided direct access to the second city, all of whose walls housed Kaiping Fu's administrative offices and some monasteries. North of the imperial-city's center, but included within it,

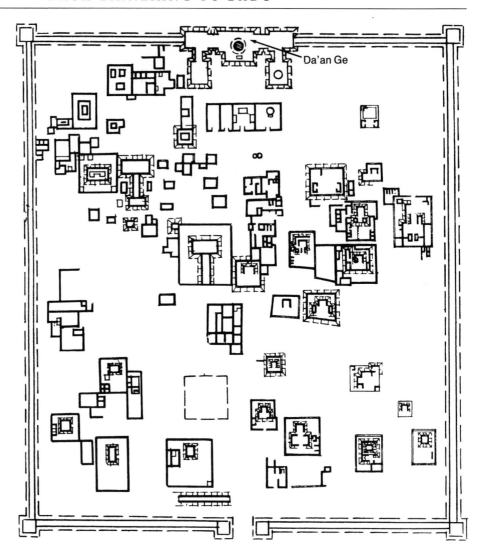

Da'an Ge

Figure 136. Plan of the palace-city of Shangdu. [Harada and Komai, *Jōto,* pl. 2]

was the palace-city. Roughly square, its walls measured about 600 meters east to west and 675 meters north to south.

The palace-city was the portion of Kaiping Fu where the influence of Chinese planning was most strongly felt (Figure 136). Its main structural compound, Da'an Ge, stood along the north wall of the palace-city, facing south. Consisting of five parts, the main central hall was largest. Adjoining

it were east and west wing halls, themselves joined by front rooms to the south. Together, the structure resembled an inverted U, similar in plan to Hanyuan Hall of the Tang Daming palace complex (see Figure 86, no. 1). Literary evidence states that Da'an Ge was built under the supervision of Chinese craftsmen and painters, including painter Wang Zhenpeng, who was employed at the court of Khubilai Khan.[34]

The collected writings of Yuan court poet Zhou Boqi provide fascinating, if unsubstantiable, details about this main hall complex of Khubilai's first permanent capital.[35] According to Zhou, Da'an Ge was moved to the Kaiping Fu site from the Northern Song capital Bianliang, where the building complex had been called Xichun Ge.[36] Buildings from the earlier non-Chinese capital of the Jin, Zhongdu, were said to have reused pieces from Bianliang also. Thus the association of imperial Song architecture with later non-Chinese rulers' imperial capitals continued another century. The literary evidence—like city plans published in the thirteenth and fourteenth centuries—attests to the perception of an imperially sponsored program of legitimation of Mongolian building projects according to models of a native Chinese dynasty. Other architectural complexes of the Shangdu palace-city named in Zhou Boqi's writings are Shuijing (Crystal) Hall and Kuizhang Ge, the latter also the name of an imperial study and painting gallery at Khubilai's great capital Dadu.

Besides Da'an Ge, the only building groups that have been located among the ruins of Kaiping Fu are monastic.[37] The remains of the monasteries Huayan Si and Qianyuan Si are among the buildings shown in Figure 136. They are the keys to confirmation that Khubilai's Chinese adviser Liu Bingzhong implemented a preconceived and profoundly Chinese scheme for this city's architecture.

According to records of the time, Liu Bingzhong called for the establishment of eight major monasteries in the "eight corners" of the city.[38] The "eight corners" were the four cardinal directions and the four corners midway between them (the true corners of the city). The same eight positions corresponded to the eight deities of certain Tantric Buddhist mandalas in use by the Liao and Jin and sometimes shown on the eight faces of their masonry pagodas.[39] The Buddhist association probably had appeal to the Mongols, many of whom practiced Tantric Buddhism of the Nepal–Tibet region. Yet for Liu Bingzhong the number eight had a second association—namely, eight fundamental trigrams of the *Yi jing* (Book of changes). The monasteries Huayan and Qianyuan, in the northeast and northwest quadrants, were associated with the trigrams *gen* and *qian,* respectively, and the symbolic layout of the city could thus trace its roots to the classic Chinese text of the Zhou dynasty.

In 1264 Kaiping Fu was elevated to capital status and became known as Shangdu (upper capital). Post-1264 literary descriptions do not describe a city of great imperial halls and monastery buildings such as Da'an Ge or Huayan Si might suggest. Rather, it seems that after Khubilai moved his primary base of power south to Dadu in 1267 little new building occurred at the northern capital.

Marco Polo's description of the outer walled area of Shangdu after 1275 as a huge game reserve is corroborated by the fact that no permanent architecture has been excavated there. Polo writes that within the wall were

fountains and rivers of running water and very beautiful lawns and groves enough. And the great Kaan keeps all sorts of not fierce wild beasts which can be named there, and in very great numbers, that is harts and bucks and roe-deer, to give to the gerfalcons to eat and to the falcons, which he keeps in mew in that place. . . . And he always goes himself to see them in mew at least once every week. And the great Kaan often goes riding through this park which is surrounded with a wall and takes with him one tame leopard or more on the crupper of his horse, and when he wishes he lets it go and takes one of the aforesaid animals. . . . And he does that often for his pleasure and for amusement. And certainly this place is so well kept and adorned that it is a most noble thing of great delight. And . . . in the middle place of that park thus surrounded with a wall, where there is a most beautiful grove, the great Kaan has made for his dwelling a great palace or loggia which is all of canes, upon beautiful pillars gilded and varnished, and on top of each pillar is a great dragon all gilded which winds the tail round the pillar and holds up the ceiling with the head, and stretches out the arms, that is one to the right hand for the support of the ceiling and the other in the same way to the left. . . . The roof of this palace is also all of canes gilded and varnished so well and so thickly that no water can hurt it. . . . Moreover the great Kaan had made it so arranged that he might have it easily taken away and easily set up, . . . for when it is raised and put together more than two hundred ropes of silk held it up in the manner of tents all round about.[40]

The "cane palace" is the only edifice Marco Polo describes. Wang Shidian's *Jin bian* (Notes on forbidden cities), probably written in the fourteenth century, lists five halls *(dian)* at Shangdu.[41] Ishida Mikinosuke, however, believes each was an "impermanent" structure.[42] Persian physician-historian Rashīd al-Dīn (1247–1318) also made reference to the function of Shangdu as a hunting park: "There are three roads to that place from the winter residence. The first, reserved for hunting matches, is allowed to be used only by ambassadors."[43]

Shangdu was thus a city with two different primary functions, each corresponding to its role in Khubilai Khan's grand plan of Chinese imperialism. During its first decade, Khubilai intended Kaiping Fu and then Shangdu to be a Chinese-style imperial city—a showcase of Mongolian designs according to the Chinese pattern. Da'an Ge, the eight great monasteries, and an Ancestral Temple were erected between 1256 and 1267. Having secured his position in China by the time Marco Polo visited Shangdu, Khubilai allowed the old buildings to remain, but the primary function of

Shangdu was changed to a hunting park, where the environment of the steppe was available for summer enjoyment of the imperial family. In its post-1267 phase the northern pleasure capital was still used by the Mongols as many as six months of the year.[44] Shangdu was burned by native Chinese resistance in 1358 and again by the new Ming government in 1370.

Dadu

In 1267 Khubilai Khan broke ground for the outer walls of his great capital Dadu. By this time the grandson of Chinggis Khan was nominally, at least, the unchallenged ruler of the entire Mongolian empire. For the design of his second and grander imperial city Khubilai once again sought the advice of his closest Chinese adviser Liu Bingzhong.[45]

From its inception Dadu was purely Chinese. It was most noticeably a triple-walled city whose concentric boundaries each had a perfect or nearly perfect geometric form (Figure 137). Begun from scratch, and restricted by the desire to maintain the water supply channeled into the site by the Jin for their capital Zhongdu, construction commenced with the 28,600-meter outer wall. Its perfect shape was marred only by a slight bend near the western part of the south gate (Figure 137, no. 65) necessitated by monastery pagodas that were there before the outer wall was entirely joined.[46] The outer wall had three gates at each face but the northern one, which had only two. From the gates emerged major north–south and east–west city avenues, each approximately 37 meters wide. The thoroughfares served as boundaries for what became—by the addition of subsidiary streets which averaged 18 meters in width—approximately fifty wards. Streets crossed the Dadu wards primarily in the east–west direction. The small alleys were about 9 meters wide.[47] Only the flow of water and one diagonal street—which ran southeast along the lake from the main western north wall gate thoroughfare to near the Drum Tower (Figure 137, no. 5)—impeded the regular division of the city outside the second walled enclosure.

Although Marco Polo may never have walked the outermost circuit of Dadu,[48] he vividly described its walls and streets:

It is twenty-four miles round, that is that on every quarter it has a face of six miles, and is exactly square by line, so that it is no more or no longer on the one side of the square than on the other. It is all walled with walls of earth which are about ten paces thick below, and more than twenty high. But I tell you that they are not so thick above as below, because all the way from the foundations upward they come tapering so that at top they are only about three paces thick. They are all entirely embattled and the battlements white. There are moreover twelve principal gates, and above each gate is a very large palace and fair, so that on each side of the walls are three principal gates and five palaces, because there is yet another palace very fair and large for each corner of the city. In all these palaces are many very great and wide halls in which the armies of those who guard the city dwell. Moreover I tell you that the whole city is set out by line; for the main streets from one side to the other of the town are drawn out straight as a thread, and are so straight and so broad that if anyone mount on the wall at one gate and look straight one sees from the one side to the other the gate of the other side, opposite to that, and they are so planned that each gate is seen as the others along the town, by the roads. And everywhere along the sides of each main street are stalls and shops of every kind. And there are about the city many palaces beautiful and great, and many beautiful inns, and many beautiful houses in great abundance. And all the pieces of land on which the dwellings are built throughout the city are square and set out by line, and on every piece

there are spacious and great palaces with corresponding courts and gardens. . . . And in this way all the city inside is laid out by square, as a chessboard is. . . . And in the middle of the city there is a very large and high palace in which is a great town clock, that is a very great bell, which sounds three times a night.[49]

Excavation at Dadu has yielded some measurements and different kinds of details than Marco Polo's writing about the city.[50] The second wall, *huangcheng,* incorporated the administrative buildings of Dadu, the wall-enclosed palace-city, and the two main residential palaces west of Taiye Pond (Figure 137, nos. 23 and 33). The latter two building complexes, begun in 1294 and 1308, were the residences of the empress dowager and crown prince, respectively. Constructed beyond the palace-city confines, their existence suggests that the imperial relations quickly surpassed the number anticipated at the time of Khubilai.

To a certain extent the size of the Dadu palace-city was predetermined by geographical features. Necessarily within the administrative-city, the palace-city was further bounded to the west by Taiye Pond, an artificial waterway adjoining other directed watercourses that flowed from beyond the outer city walls, through Dadu, and out again. The man-made island Wanshou Shan, which stood in Taiye Pond and was connected to the administrative-city east and west of the pond, was the only architectural remnant of Jin Zhongdu that the Mongols spared. The unusual and no doubt symbolic building configuration on the artificial landmass may have contributed to Khubilai's decision to save it, but a constant flow of water to his palaces may have been an even more significant factor in his decision. In any case, the presence of the island and water meant that his imperial-city had to be divided into two, with the 3,480-meter palace-city walls to the east and the residential palaces to the west. Within the three building complexes of the palace-city, Khubilai and later Mongolian emperors of China gave audiences, conducted other court ceremonies, and occasionally held more private affairs. Khubilai died in a hall of the smallest of the three, Yude Hall complex, in 1294.[51]

Franciscan Friar Odoric of Pordenone, who stayed at Dadu between 1325 and 1328, described the artificial island and palaces in his travel account. Of Wanshou Shan he wrote:

> And within the enclosure of the great palace there hath been a hill thrown up on which another palace is built, the most beautiful in the whole world. And this whole hill is planted over with trees, wherefrom it hath the name of the *Green Mount.* And at the side of this hill hath been formed a lake [more than a mile round], and a most beautiful bridge built across it. And on this lake there be such multitudes of wild-geese and ducks and swans, that it is something to wonder at.[52]

The best description of individual halls from Dadu is provided by the Ming dynasty official Xiao Xun. Charged with the destruction of the Mongo-

lian capital at the end of the fourteenth century in preparation for rebuilding the city by the new Chinese dynasty, Xiao made a record of what he saw in its final days.[53] Of Khubilai's main audience hall, Daming Dian, Xiao wrote:

> Daming Hall is raised on a base about five *chi* [about 170 centimeters] high. In front [at the south side] is the stairway, of three steps. Surrounding the hall is a marble balustrade carved with figures of dragons and phoenixes. Each vertical post of the balustrade rests upon a sea dragon, whose head protrudes beyond the edge of the terrace. Every outside pillar of the hall is square in shape, about five to six *chi* in width, and decorated with raised flowers, golden dragons, and clouds, on top of which are carved decorations three or four *chi* high. . . . In the center of the ceiling is a pair of coiling dragons. On all four sides of the hall are golden and red mullioned windows with gold leaf attached to the intervening spaces.[54]

The desire of Khubilai and his successors to maintain Mongolian rule of China, and the use of architecture as a means of legitimating their power,

---

1. Jiande Storehouse
2. Guangxi Storehouse
3. North Secretariat
4. Bell Tower
5. Drum Tower
6. Center Pavilion
7. Center Marker
8. Datianshou Wanning Monastery
9. Daochao Storehouse
10. Second Surveillance Precinct (Office)
11. District Manager of Dadu (Office)
12. Confucian Temple
13. Bolin Monastery
14. Chongren Storehouse
15. Secretariat
16. Chongguo Monastery
17. Heyi Storehouse
18. Wanning Bridge
19. Houzai Back Gate
20. Imperial Garden
21. Houzai Gate
22. Xingsheng Palace Back Garden
23. Xingsheng Palace Complex
24. Dayongfu Monastery
25. Altars of Soil and Grain
26. Scenic Spot
27. Hongren Monastery
28. Qionghua Island
29. Ying Island
30. Wansong Laoren Pagoda
31. Prince's Palace
32. West Front Garden
33. Longfu Palace Complex
34. Longfu Palace Front Garden
35. Yude Hall
36. Yanchun Pavilion Complex
37. Xihua Gate
38. Donghua Gate
39. Daming Hall
40. Chongtian Gate
41. Chishan Platform
42. Workers' Supervision Office
43. Gongchen Hall
44. Chongzhen Wanshou Palace
45. Sheep Pen
46. Grass and Sand
47. Bureau of Academicians
48. Raw Provisions Storehouse
49. Fuel Storage Field
50. Saddle and Reins Storehouse
51. Military Equipment Storehouse
52. Kitchen Workers' Chamber(s)
53. Magistrates' Chamber(s)
54. Military Guard Chamber(s)
55. Ancestral Temple
56. Dashengshou Wan'an Monastery
57. Storehouse
58. Yunxian Altar
59. Taiyishen Altar
60. Xingguo Monastery
61. Southern Secretariat
62. City-God Temple
63. Bureau of Punishments
64. Shuncheng Storehouse
65. Haiyun and Ke'an Twin Pagodas
66. Daqingshou Monastery
67. Office of Grand Historian
68. Wenming Storehouse
69. Bureau of Ritual
70. Bureau of the Military

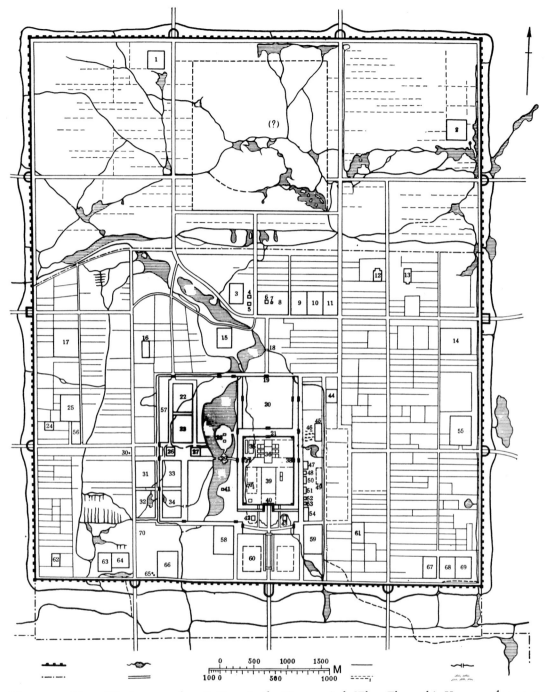

Figure 137. Plan of Dadu, at modern Beijing, in the Yuan period. [Zhao Zhengzhi, *Kaogu xuebao* no. 1 (1966), p. 141]

have already been noted. The architecture of the Chinese city of walls worked in another way for the Mongols, as well. Behind the walls it was possible for the ruler and princes of the blood to reside in tents and to engage in age-old shamanistic rituals of the steppe in the manner of their ruling predecessors at Khara-Khorum in total privacy.[55] From the outside, however, the image of Dadu would be perceived as any past Chinese imperial city, even seventh to ninth-century Chang'an—as an awe-inspiring walled compound whose ceramic tile roofs projected imperial power. On a smaller scale, the timber frame and plaster walls of an individual palace building could be easily transformed overnight. In the case of Dadu, silk wall paintings that decorated the palaces of former Chinese emperors were rapidly replaced by animal skins.[56]

Still, evidence of the Mongolian use of China's architecture and city planning for purposes of legitimation is overwhelming. From groundbreaking onward the planning and construction of Dadu followed the dictates of the *Kaogong ji* specifications for Wangcheng. In fact, it can be argued that formally Dadu was more a part of the classical tradition of Chinese urban planning than any city that had come before it.[57]

Already at the site when Khubilai designated it as his primary capital was Wanshou Shan, whose stone was believed in Mongolian times to have been transported north by the Jin from Northern Song Bianliang.[58] Similarly the approach to the imperial sectors of the city followed Song–Jin precedent: a T-shaped imperial-way/palace-place combination was designed due south of the imperial-city (Figure 138). (At the two earlier capitals the approach was south of the palace-city; see Figures 127 and 129.) Furthermore, it can be argued that the three walls of Dadu followed the concentric arrangement of Bianliang. Dadu also had its Ancestral Temple on the east and Altars of Soil and Grain on the west of the city; the construction of the Ancestral Temple took place while Khubilai was still reigning from Shangdu.[59] Nevertheless, the plan and planning of Dadu are distinct from those of all earlier imperial cities of China.

During the excavation of Dadu a stone engraved with the phrase *zhongxin zhi tai* ("center marker") was found (Figure 137, no. 7). It stood slightly east of *zhongxin ge* (Center Pavilion; Figure 137, no. 6). Archaeologists have determined that the center marker was intended to be equidistant from the midpoints of the north and south walls and the east and west walls. In theory, then, it should have been possible to construct the outer Dadu wall from the

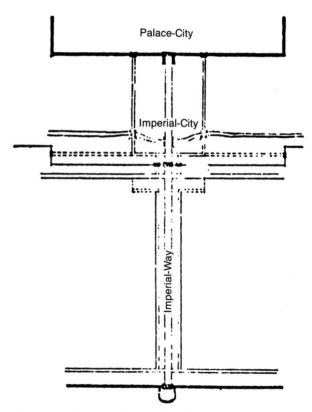

Figure 138. Plan of the T-shaped approach to Dadu's imperial-city. [Hou and Wu, *Wenwu* no. 9 (1977), p. 5]

single center point. Not only is Khubilai's Dadu the only known city for which a center marker has been found, but we further know, in contrast to the seemingly similarly planned city Bianliang, that construction of the Dadu outer wall preceded any building within the city. Even though the decision was made not to place the palaces in the exact center of the outer city,[60] the planning and initial building were conducted in strict adherence to *Kaogong ji* dictates. Thus intent further distinguishes this city from others with similar plans. As noted earlier, the plan of Daxing–Chang'an follows a different lineage of imperial city building in China, but it is worth saying again that even though the Sui–Tang capital was built anew like Dadu, its building order was the reverse of that stipulated in the *Kaogong ji*. At the sixth through

ninth-century capital, the palaces were constructed first and the outer wall last.

The use of the city plan to legitimate Mongolian rule did not stop with Khubilai or Dadu. During the reign of Qutuqtu (1330–1333) the encyclopedia *Shilin guangji* was published. In it appeared the plan of Bianliang shown in Figure 126. Although the Northern Song city itself was lost by this time, the restored image of the idealized city was very much alive and similarities between it and Wangcheng have already been noted. Furthermore, the fictitious plan of the destroyed Jiankang (see Figure 67) was published sometime after 1341 during the last decades of Yuan rule. Thus the plan of the imperial city Dadu was associated with the idealized Wangcheng scheme not only when the city was built during the time of Liu Bingzhong's influence at

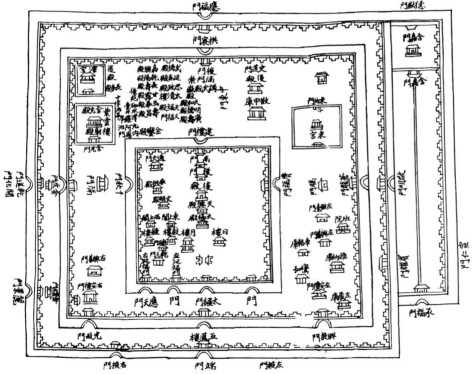

Figure 139. Plan of the Western Capital, Luoyang, in the Northern Song period. [*Henan zhi,* as preserved in *Yongle dadian, juan* 9561; Taipei repr., 1974, 5th plan]

court but also three-quarters of a century later through court sponsorship of publications in which the idealized plans of Bianliang and Jiankang, fictitiously based on the Wangcheng design, appeared. The late Yuan court-sponsored publications made it possible for historians of the Chinese city to see a continuous chain of imperial planning from Wangcheng through the fourteenth century.

The publication of fictitious plans in the thirteenth century was not limited to the Mongols, however. The plans of Lin'an in official gazetteers from the years during and after the fall of the Song (see Figures 131 and 132) had the same purpose as the *Shilin guangji* publication of Bianliang or the *zhizheng*-period gazetteer plan of Jiankang—but for a different reason. For the Southern Song, the city that in its time could never be ideally designed because of topographical constraints could, after its timber buildings had long been destroyed, be recorded as one that had conformed to the norms of Chinese imperial planning.

The profound impact of Wangcheng on the Chinese conception of imperial city planning is nowhere more obvious than in Figure 139, an illustration from the Yuan-period record of Henan province *(Henan zhi)*. It is hard to believe that the highly geometrized scheme is Luoyang, western capital of the Northern Song dynasty. Seeing this and the other plans published during Mongolian rule, one can understand how the overidealized plan of Pingcheng (see Figure 68) came to be published for a city whose actual design in all likelihood resembled Ye or Northern Wei Luoyang.

To the list of ironies of Chinese history, then, one must add the city plan at the time of Mongolian rule. It was Khubilai Khan who resurrected classical sources for new imperial city designs and rekindled interest in them. The pedigree of the Dadu scheme was such that even after the Mongols were chased back to their homeland, the city that they built and others before it, all of which lay in ruins, survived in idealized and even fictitious drawings. The published plans of the thirteenth and fourteenth centuries of former Chinese capitals like Bianliang, Lin'an, Jiankang, and Luoyang would assure the continuation of a single imperial city scheme—the idealized city of Wangcheng—as the model for all subsequent capital cities in China.

MING, QING, AND BEYOND

ZHU Yuanzhang, leader of the strongest faction of southern Chinese rebels, overthrew the Dadu government in 1368. Thereupon he returned to his homeland and power base in South China where two years earlier he had begun the construction of a city at Yingtian. On that site near the ruins of former capitals of the Six Dynasties, Zhu founded an imperial city for the new Ming dynasty. This southern capital, Nanjing, was the first city south of the Yangzi River from which an emperor ruled a unified China.

NANJING

Like all Chinese capitals that had preceded it, the site of Nanjing had a long urban history. The second and first millennia B.C. settlements Jinling and Moling were followed by Jianye and Jiankang. When the Chen capital Jiankang fell in 589 to Sui Wendi, he ordered its total destruction. It was not until the eighth century that a city again began to flourish on the site. After the fall of the Tang at the beginning of the tenth century, Nanjing was again, briefly, an imperial city of the Southern Tang dynasty (937–975). The predominant architectural remains from this period, as from the previous imperial years during the Six Dynasties, are royal tombs. Nanjing was also a temporary capital during the first few years of the Southern Song dynasty.

Plans of the tenth through thirteenth century cities at Nanjing that survive in local records reveal little. They uniformly show a rectangular or square walled city with the palace-city roughly in its center (Figures 140 and 141)—a plan which by now can be labeled "idealized" at best and possibly "of questionable accuracy." Plans of Zhu Yuanzhang's capital are quite different. The Ming founder's huge and sprawling city incorporated portions of Nanjing's imperial ruins inside a wall that curved in

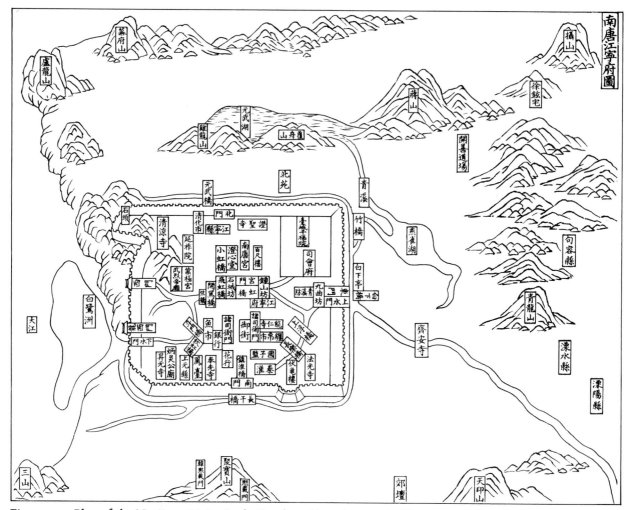

Figure 140. Plan of the Nanjing vicinity in the Southern Tang (937–975). [*Jiangning Fu zhi;* photograph taken from Gaillard, *Nankin,* between pp. 120 and 121]

response to both topography and new construction (Figure 142). The irregularities of the late-four-teenth-century plan are clear even in the same local record from which Figures 140 and 141 have been taken (Figure 143).

Nanjing's new outer wall was huge. Its length has been recorded as 96 *li* (about 50 kilometers),[1] although in fact it was only about three-quarters of

that length.[2] Heavily fortified with *wengcheng,* the space inside the wall can be thought of as three units. From east to west they were a roughly rectangular area that included the new walled palace-city, the old tenth-century capital and Six Dynasties capitals in the center, and an extension for the population and a military installation in the northwest (see Figure 21).

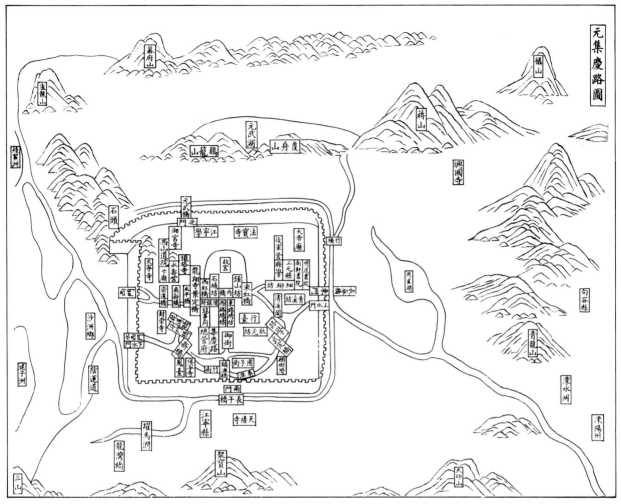

Figure 141. Plan of the Nanjing vicinity in the Yuan period. [*Jiangning Fu zhi;* photograph taken from Gaillard, *Nankin,* between pp. 152 and 153]

The imperial-city and palace-city of the Hongwu emperor (Zhu Yuanzhang) constituted a sharp contrast to the rest of the city, for they were built in strict adherence to Chinese convention (Figure 144). The imperial-city was square-shaped and enclosed by a wall that had a gate at each face. It was approached by an imperial-way (Figure 144, no. 1) and palace-place (Figure 144, no. 2) from the south, in the same position as the T-shaped space of Dadu. (One recalls that the approach was due south of the palace-cities at Bianliang and Zhongdu.) East and west of the imperial-way were official bureaus. Southeast and southwest of the water-enclosed palace-city, known by the Ming as Zijin Cheng (Purple Forbidden City, or Polar Forbidden City), in their age-old positions, were the Ancestral Temple

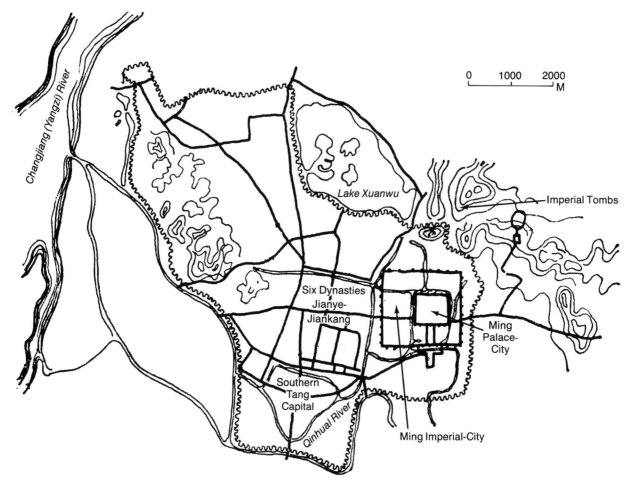

Figure 142. Plan of Nanjing in the Ming dynasty. [Dong, *Zhongguo chengshi,* p. 72]

and Altars of Soil and Grain, respectively (Figure 144, nos. 3 and 4). The palace-city, with Wu (Noon, or Meridian) Gate at its south center (Figure 144, no. 5), was a rectangular space entered by four gates, approached by its own imperial-way (Figure 144, no. 6) along an axis that included the main halls and south and north gates of the imperial-city and outer city. The principal halls of the palace-city formed two groups: three at the front, or south, and three behind. The halls of the south-ern group (Figure 144, no. 7) were larger than their northern counterparts (Figure 144, no. 8), but both groups consisted of broad front and back halls and a square-shaped or shorter hall between them. The formations were manifestations of the *gong* plan. Reflecting long-standing Chinese tradition, the three front halls were "public," used for imperial audiences or proclamations, and the three back halls were more private in function.

Buildings throughout the city were beacons of

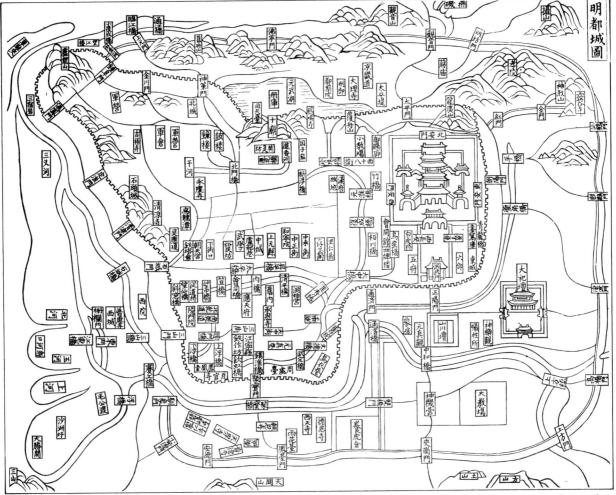

Figure 143. Plan of Nanjing in the Ming dynasty. [*Jiangning Fu zhi;* photograph taken from Gaillard, *Nankin*, between pp. 234 and 235]

Nanjing's imperial status. From 1366 to 1367, even before the ultimate victory over the Mongols, old palaces were restored and the Soil and Grain altars had been erected.[3] During the same period the Hanlin Academy for scholar-officials was opened and Circular and Square Mounds for imperial sacrifices were constructed. The temple to Zhu Yuanzhang's ancestors was completed during the ninth

moon of 1367. Upon the official founding of the Ming dynasty at the end of the following year, the Hongwu emperor performed sacrifices at the Circular Mound for the first time. He also designated an imperial tomb area at the southern foot of Mount Zijin, northeast of the city. His own tomb was begun in 1381 and completed two years later, by which time his empress, Ma, had already been

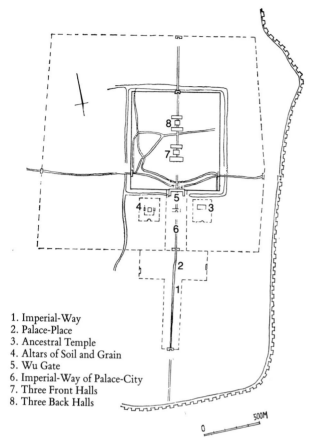

1. Imperial-Way
2. Palace-Place
3. Ancestral Temple
4. Altars of Soil and Grain
5. Wu Gate
6. Imperial-Way of Palace-City
7. Three Front Halls
8. Three Back Halls

Figure 144. Plan of the palace-city and imperial-city of Ming Nanjing. [Dong, *Zhongguo chengshi*, p. 73]

been estimated at one million.[4] Even if it were only half that number in 1391,[5] a million people certainly lived in the city by the end of the fifteenth century. A century later Father Matteo Ricci described Nanjing as the "first city of China."[6] By that time, however, masses of its population had been resettled northward in anticipation of what was to be China's last great imperial city.

FENGYANG

Before turning to the ultimate achievement in Chinese imperial city planning, Beijing, it is worth looking at what has been called a Ming "quasi-capital,"[7] Fengyang. It was a city which, in spite of imperial intentions, never achieved true capital status.

Just a year into his reign, in the ninth moon of 1369, the Hongwu emperor initiated a "three-capital system" *(san jingdu tizhi)* in which Yingtian, Bianliang, and Linhao, the site of his birth, presently in Fengyang Xian, were designated the southern, northern, and central capitals, respectively. Ming historical records relate that the emperor considered all the main capitals of former times, rejecting each but Bianliang, for the following reasons:

> Previously the emperor had asked his old followers about the site for a capital. Some said "Kuanchung (Guanzhong [Chang'an]) is secure, impregnable, and well supplied." Some said "Loyang [Luoyang] is in the center of the empire, equidistant for tribute coming from all directions. Pienliang [Bianliang] was also the old capital of the Sung (Song)." Still others said that the Yuan palaces are still there in Pei-p'ing [Beiping (the former Dadu)]. Going there could save the people effort. The emperor said: "All that has been said is fine but times change. Ch'ang-an [Chang'an], Luoyang, and Pien-liang sufficed for the Chou

interred there. Meanwhile, in 1375 Hongwu had dedicated a temple to one hundred eight meritorious generals. Two years later he built a Dasi (Great Sacrifice) Hall in the southern suburbs for offerings to the heavens. A Confucian Temple was built at the southern capital in 1382, some eight years after the erection of the great Confucian Temple at the sage's birthplace Qufu. The construction of outerwall gates for the city, eventually numbering twelve, continued through Hongwu's reign.

The population of Nanjing in the mid-1370s has

[Zhou], Ch'in [Qin], Han, Wei, T'ang [Tang], and Sung. But in pacification the people have had no rest. If I were to establish a capital in those places the supplies and labor would have to be provided by Chiang-nan [Jiangnan (the lower Yangzi region)]. It would be a heavy burden on the people. Even if I were to go to Pei-p'ing the palaces would still require changes. That would not be easy either. Now Chien-yeh [Jianye] has a natural moat in the Yangtze [Yangzi] River and is protected by surrounding hills. It is the dominant position in Chiang-nan. It is truly adequate for establishing a state. Lin-hao [Linhao] has the Yangtze before it and the Huai behind it. This is protection upon which it can depend. It can be supplied with grain by water. I intend to make it the Middle Capital. What do you think?'' The officials all answered ''Excellent!''[8]

In September 1368, the same month in which Yingtian was established as the southern capital Nanjing, the old Song capital was renamed Kaifeng and given the status of northern capital in a dual-capital system. Hongwu intended to divide his time between the two capitals, but by the next year the importance of Kaifeng was only nominal.

In that same year, 1369, Hongwu declared a central capital Zhongdu at his birthplace in Anhui province. One-hundred-forty thousand people were transferred to Linhao (Fengyang). Building continued until the fourth moon of 1375, when it was somewhat abruptly abandoned. According to *Ming shi lu* (Record of Ming history), construction had too greatly exhausted the strength of the people.[9] Fengyang maintained auxiliary status during the Hongwu reign, but after 1375 imperial building was concentrated at Nanjing.

Linhao of 1369–1375 was a triple-walled city built west of an earlier city near the site of present-day Fengyang Xian (Figure 145). The earthen outer wall of the Ming central capital was 3 *zhang* high

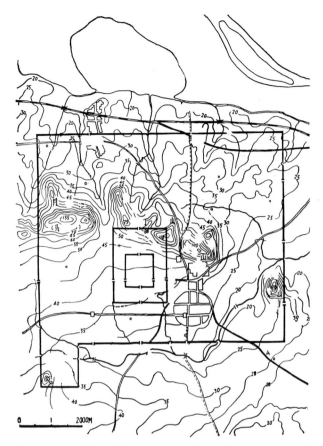

Figure 145. Plan of Fengyang, Anhui, the Ming central capital (1369–1375). [Dong, *Zhongguo chengshi,* p. 76]

and measured 50 *li* 443 *bu.* Perhaps because mountains formed a natural city boundary, the wall was not further fortified by a moat. In addition to the nine entry portals, battlements were built into the wall. The one peculiar feature of the otherwise nearly perfectly square Zhongdu of the Ming was its southwest corner. There, according to men of the time, the wall was transformed into the beak of a phoenix *(fenghuang),* the mythical being whose name's first character, *feng,* was shared by the name of the city. Due south of the phoenix beak was an imperial tomb site.[10]

Just south and west of the center were the walled imperial-city and palace-city of Fengyang. The former was 13.5 *li* in perimeter with a 2-*zhang*-high brick wall enclosing it; the latter's wall measured 6 *li* in circumference. Each wall had one gate, and straight lines were formed by corresponding directional gates of all three walls.

What survives of the city—as well as complete records of it—suggests that initially a full-fledged imperial city was anticipated. In 1370 over four thousand households were transferred to Linhao. The same year an Ancestral Temple and Soil Altar were built southeast and southwest of Wu Gate, the main southern entrance to the palace-city. During the first moon of 1371 the emperor built a Circular Mound, a Square Mound, and Altars to the Sun, Moon, Mountains, and Rivers. Prefectures and districts subject to the administration of Fengyang increased yearly. Still, by 1376 the official move back to Nanjing was under way.

The plan of the imperial districts of Ming Zhongdu bore obvious resemblance to the Mongolian capital at Dadu, to Nanjing in Ming times, and to the final Ming capital Beijing. To enter the capital one would cross Fengyang Bridge (Figure 146, no. 1) south of the outer wall and directly proceed to the main south city gate (Figure 146, no. 2), named Hongwu after the city's founder. Continuing directly north on Hongwu Boulevard along the tri-lane *qianbulang* (thousand-pace corridor) (Figure 146, no. 3), one came to a T-shaped palace-place (Figure 146, no. 4) which terminated at Chengtian Gate (Figure 146, no. 5), south gate of the administrative-city. It had the same name as the equivalent gate at Ming Nanjing. To either side of the continuation of the main south–north axis through the city were government offices. They terminated at the inverted-U-shaped Wu Gate (Figure 146, no. 6), named as the entrance to the palace-cities of the earlier and later Ming capitals. East and west in the outer city of Ming Zhongdu were Bell and Drum towers (Figure 146, nos. 7 and 8). There were also temples to former emperors, to the city-god, and to meritorious officials. Built anew, the Ming central capital at Fengyang is the latest example of a Chinese imperial city whose only constraints in planning were topographical.

A far grander city, however, was to stand on the man-made ruins that survived from the Mongols' imperial city in North China. Renamed Beiping (Northern Peace) shortly after the fall of the Mongols, the city did not reclaim its role until the first years of the fifteenth century when Zhu Yuanzhang's son, soon to become the Yongle emperor, set out from his station at the former Yuan imperial capital to launch a campaign against his nephew, successor to the throne at Nanjing.

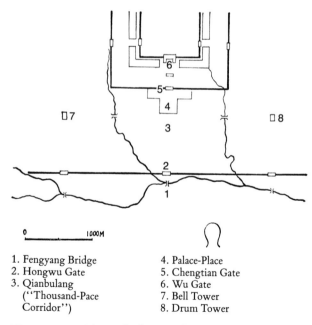

1. Fengyang Bridge
2. Hongwu Gate
3. Qianbulang ("Thousand-Pace Corridor")
4. Palace-Place
5. Chengtian Gate
6. Wu Gate
7. Bell Tower
8. Drum Tower

Figure 146. Plan of the southern approach to the imperial-city and palace-city of the Ming central capital. [Dong, *Zhongguo chengshi*, p. 77]

Solidifying his power in 1403, the new ruler Yongle renamed the northern city Beijing (Northern Capital) and began construction of his imperial city there in 1407. The new city was completed by 1420 and the capital of China was officially moved the following year to the site where it would remain through the duration of imperial rule.

BEIJING IN MING TIMES

Since the days of Khubilai Khan and Marco Polo, the site of Beijing has been the most famous Chinese city. Indeed, during the last several hundred years Beijing has been recognized as one of the world's great capitals. Certainly it has been the focus of more popular and scholarly attention than any other Chinese city.[11] Here Beijing is discussed particularly as it relates to earlier Chinese imperial cities.

Among the paramount concerns of Zhu Di (to become the Yongle emperor) for his capital in the north was one shared by all other north-minded rulers of China: how to protect his city from attack by northern peoples. Thus, long before the Ming decision to return the primary capital there, the walls of the former Mongolian imperial city had been rebuilt or reinforced. Work had begun on the outer wall in 1370, at which time the northern face was moved 2.9 kilometers southward to protect the smaller population, gathered primarily in the old city's south.

The planning of Ming Beijing has been explained by legend, as well. It is told that the body of eight-armed Nezha, the mythical boy who had killed the son of the Dragon King, is the basis for the city's design. The specific association between Nezha and the city was revealed independently to both the chief and deputy imperial advisers. The story was still told in the twentieth century.[12]

Meanwhile, the northern water supply had become polluted,[13] so for the duration of the Ming dynasty and during Qing rule by the Manchus (1644–1911) the capital remained south of its thirteenth- and fourteenth-century location (see Figure 114). Between 1419 and 1421 the southern boundary of the city was extended about a kilometer southward in order to accommodate new government offices, but the perimeter of the Ming outer wall was still smaller than it had been under the former dynasty. Even so, fully two percent of the Chinese population was involved in the construction of Beijing at the end of the second decade of the fifteenth century.[14]

More than a century later, a southern extension to the city known as the "outer city" was built. The new wall, which included 6.7 kilometers of the southern edge of the old city's outer wall, was 22.5 kilometers in perimeter. After the completion of the southern sector, from the mid-sixteenth century onward, the northern great-walled enclosure was known as the inner city and the southern walled enclosure became the outer city. The northern inner-city wall was 23.5 kilometers in perimeter and together the inner and outer cities occupied an area of 62 square kilometers.

The imperial city Beijing as it is known today was essentially complete when the outer city was walled in 1553.[15] The Qing dynasty, begun in 1644, did some rebuilding, especially during the sixty-year reigns of Kangxi (1662–1722) and Qianlong (1736–1796), but these emendations were primarily repair work on existing palatial or other imperial structures or additional housing for imperial relatives inside the Forbidden City. In other words, the architectural transition between imperial mid-Ming and imperial Qing Beijing was less than that at the points between earlier dynasties. Not only did the site of the capital remain the same, but the old city was not ravaged and former walls, buildings, and monuments were reused. Changes were often as

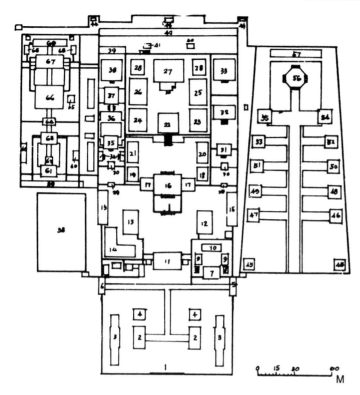

1. Screen Wall	34. Side Halls
2. Anterooms to the Throne Rooms	35. Huiguang Hall
	36. Baojiu Palace
3. Side Rooms	37. Jiansi Studio
4. Music Pavilions	38. Chonghu Pavilion
5. Civil Officials' Rooms	39. Seven Bay Hall
6. Military Officials' Rooms	40. Zhan Chamber
7. Ancestral Temple Gate	41. Tang District
8. Shunshan Rooms	42. Twenty-eight Bay Granary
9. Offering Halls	43. Palace Inspection Room
10. Ancestral Temple	44. Inspection Rooms
11. Da Qing Gate	45. Pavilions
12. Xiangfeng Tower	46–53. Pavilions of the Eight Manchu Banners
13. Feilong Pavilion (Storehouse for Imperial Treasures)	54. Pavilion of the Left Wing Commander
14. Southern Tower	55. Pavilion of the Right Wing Commander
15. Seven Bays of Rooms	56. Dazheng Hall (of Administration)
16. Chongzheng Hall	
17. Side Gates	57. Storehouse for Imperial Chariots
18. Rihua Tower	58. Imperial Storehouse
19. Xiaji Tower	59. Tuanfang Chamber
20. Shishan Studio	60. Side Halls
21. Xiezhong Studio	61. Miao Tower
22. Fenghuang Tower	62. Platform
23. Hengqing Palace	63. Jiaying Hall
24. Fuyong Palace	64. Gate
25. Guansui Palace	65. Stele Pavilion
26. Linzhi Palace	66. Wensu Pavilion (Imperial Library)
27. Qingning Palace	
28. Side Halls	67. Yangxi Studio
29. Gate	68. Side Halls
30. Gate	69. Nine Bay Hall
31. Shunhe Hall	
32. Jiezhi Palace	
33. Jingdian Hall	

Figure 147. Plan of the palace-city of Shenjing, Shenyang, Liaoning (1625–1644). [Ye Dasong, *Zhong-guo jianzhu shi*, vol. 2, p. 840]

simple as the renaming of a gate—for instance, Da Ming (Great Ming) Gate was renamed Da Qing. When speaking of imperial Beijing, therefore, it is usually appropriate to refer to the Ming–Qing city. While the Ming still ruled China, one imperial city was built by the Manchus, the non-Chinese group who would later establish the headquarters of their dynasty, the Qing, at Beijing. That city will be discussed briefly here before we consider Beijing from the sixteenth through the nineteenth centuries.

SHENYANG

In 1616 Nurhachi—the man who would be known as the dynastic founder, Qing Taizu—attacked the Ming and established himself at a city called Chetuala. Two years later he transferred his capital to Jiefan, in present Liaoning province. The Manchu capital was again transferred in 1620 to a site southeast of Jiefan, known as Sa'erhu. The following year Nurhachi moved his capital to Liaoyang, where it remained for four years, until Shenyang (Mukden), the most important Manchu capital prior to Beijing, was selected for his imperial city.[16]

Shenyang, today in Liaoning province, had a history as a walled city that began during Liao rule. Those walls were destroyed late in the Jin period. The city was rebuilt under the Yuan, at which time it was called Shenyang. A 25-*chi* wall was built around Shenyang by the Ming in 1388.

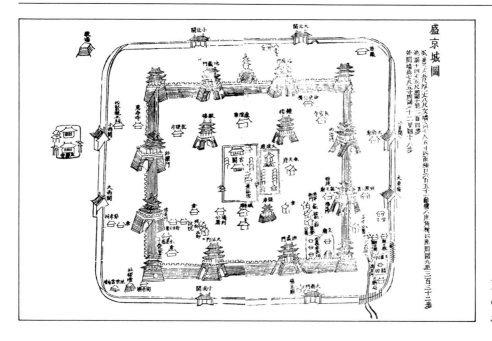

Figure 148. Idealized plan of Shenjing. [*Shenjing tong zhi*, ill. 1]

In the twenty years that Nurhachi and his successor, Huang Taiji, employed Shenyang as their capital (1625–1644) the layout of imperial buildings within the 9-*li* inner-walled enclosure came to resemble its counterparts in the Ming capitals Nanjing and Beijing (Figure 147). A gate led to three main halls along a north–south imperial axis. Right and left of the two back halls were residential palaces. An imperial study complex stood east (as one faced south) of the axis, and rows of pleasure pavilions were constructed south of an octagonal hall to the west. Shenyang also had an Ancestral Temple (Figure 147, no. 10) on the same side of the city. The outer city wall, shown in an idealized scheme in Figure 148, was lengthened to 32 *li* (about 16 kilometers) in 1680.

MING–QING BEIJING

Some of the most dramatic images of Beijing are provided by the city walls. Photographs published by Swedish art historian Osvald Siren in the 1920s are known worldwide,[17] but the walls of Beijing made a similarly vivid impression on a European as he approached the city two hundred years earlier. Such descriptions were used in 1736 by J. B. Du Halde, who described and mapped Chinese cities he had never seen. Du Halde may be following the impressions of Matteo Ricci when he compares the walls of Beijing and Nanjing:

The circumference of the walls of the two cities [of Beijing] together, minus the suburbs, has been measured and does not exceed 52 Chinese *li*. Thus it is smaller than Nanjing. Yet the true difference between the two cities lies in the width, height, and beauty of the walls. Those of Beijing are superb, worthy of the capital of the greatest empire in the world. Nanjing's walls are straight, appearing never to have been better than those of the ancient Beijing, which are no improvement over the walls of ordinary provincial cities.

One can ride a horse a great distance on the walls of the new Beijing via a ramp. Along the way numerous guard stations can be found. The towers are within the range of a bowshot. After passing a certain number of them one finds many grander ones, where a few reserve troops can be stationed.

The portals of the wall are high and vaulted, with large pavilions of up to nine stories, each of which is pierced with windows or cannon holes. The ground story is a large room in which there are soldiers and officers on duty, or those who will relieve them.

In front of each portal is a space of more than 360 feet which functions as an armory enclosed by a semicircular wall whose height and width are the same as those of the rest of the wall. . . . Each of the portals with a nine-story tower has a double pavilion.[18]

Du Halde also published a map of Beijing (Figure 149), one of more than twenty in his study.

Post-1553 Beijing is best described from the inside outward and then from south to north (see Figure 2). Innermost was the walled compound Zijin Cheng (Purple Forbidden City)—which derived its name from the "Purple Bright Constellation with Polaris in the center"—whose name in English is usually shortened to Forbidden City. Its walls measured 960 meters north to south and 760 meters east to west. Surrounding the Forbidden City was Beijing's administrative-city, essentially a rectangle minus the southwestern corner that bent around Taiye Pond. During China's last imperial age, Taiye Pond was divided into three parts: Bei (north), Zhong (middle), and Nan (south) Hai (lakes). In Ming times the water that flowed from Taiye Pond was channeled to encompass both the inner and outer cities.

The focus of Beijing's architecture was unquestionably south to north. Countless maps like Figure 150 illustrate the buildings that stood along this axis, many of which survive, even if in restored states, today. With no building higher than two stories, the grandeur and magnitude of the several-mile axis is unambiguously expressed as horizontal progression.

One began the approach to the center at Yongding Gate, southern terminus to the Ming–Qing outer city (see Figure 2). The nearly 3 kilometers from there to the south central inner-city gate, Zhengyang Gate, were flanked at the southern end by the Altar of Heaven complex on the east (Figure 2, no. 4) and the Altar of the First Crops on the west (Figure 2, no. 8). Beginning northward from Zhengyang Gate, however, a line of buildings extended almost continuously along an approximately 7-kilometer distance to the inner-city north wall.

Just north of Zhengyang Gate was Da Ming (later Da Qing) Gate (Figure 150, no. 1). There began the T-shaped combination of imperial-way, or *qianbulang,* and palace-place. Through the palace-place snaked a waterway, crossable via five marble bridges (Figure 150, no. 2), that eventually connected to the former Taiye Pond. East and west of the imperial-way were offices of the government. At the northern terminus of the palace-place was Tian'an Gate (Figure 150, no. 3). Northward from Tian'an Gate was a long, narrow space which passed through Duan (Uprightness) Gate (Figure 150, no. 4) before coming to the spectacular Meridian (Wu) Gate (Figure 150, no. 5), entrance to the Forbidden City (Figure 151). East and west between Uprightness and Meridian gates were the Ancestral Temple (Figure 150, no. 6) and twin Altars of Soil and Grain (Figure 150, no. 7).

Even the quintuple-entry, double-eaved, winged Wu Gate (shown in Figure 1 and Figure 151, no. 1) did not fully anticipate what followed within the connecting four walls, four gates, and corner towers of the Polar Forbidden City. Upon entering, one immediately came upon the second set of five marble bridges (Figure 150, no. 8; Figure 151, no. 2)

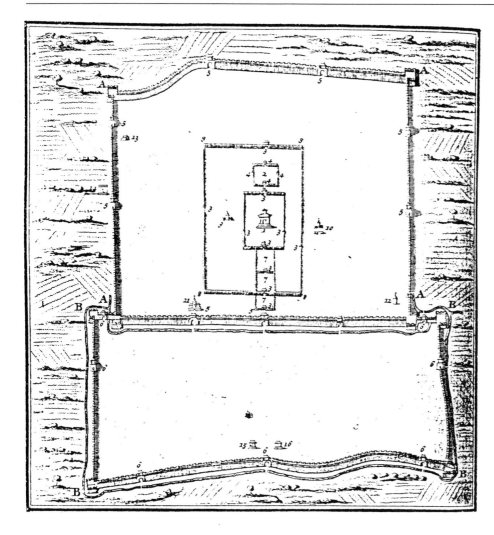

Figure 149. Plan of Beijing. [J. B. Du Halde, *Déscription de la Chine,* vol. 1, pl. 1]

that spanned the sinuous Jinshui River. Beyond was the Gate of Great Harmony (Taihe Men) (Figure 150, no. 9; Figure 151, no. 3), joined by a covered corridor that enclosed all but the north center of the Three Great Halls (Figure 150, no. 10), focal point of imperial Beijing. About 150 meters behind were the three halls themselves, raised on a triple-tier *gong*-shaped marble platform.

The first and largest, the Hall of Great Harmony (Taihe Dian), 64 meters across and 35 meters in width (Figure 151, no. 4), was the site of the New Year's ceremony, the celebration of the winter solstice, the emperor's birthday, and the announcement of successful candidates in the imperial examinations. The second, the Hall of Central Harmony (Zhonghe Dian) (Figure 151, no. 5), much smaller in size, was a square-shaped hall where the emperor would make his final preparations before entering the Hall of Great Harmony. The emperor also entered annually to examine the seeds for the new

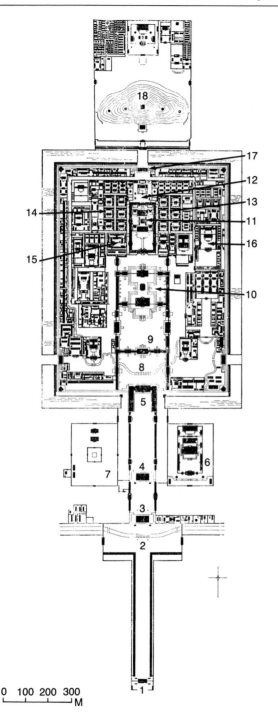

harvest. In the third hall, the Hall of Preserving Harmony (Baohe Dian) (Figure 151, no. 6), imperial examinations were given, the emperor honored successful scholars of the highest rank, certain official appointments were made, and banquets for foreign ambassadors were held during the Qing dynasty. The Hall of Central Harmony is equidistant from the other two, and the three together are a perfect manifestation of the *gong* plan. This pivot of the Forbidden City has been graphically rendered in Figure 152.

Directly behind the Three Great Halls were the Three Back Halls (Figure 150, no. 11), smaller-scale replicas of the former. They were raised on a single marble platform and surrounded by a covered corridor with gates on all four sides. From 1420, when the halls were constructed, until the beginning of the Qing dynasty they were the "back private chamber" counterparts to the more public Three Great Halls. The first was the emperor's bedroom, the place where even in the Qing dynasty a deceased emperor lay in state. The second was the empress's throne room and ceremonial hall, and the last was the empress's bedchamber. In the seventeenth century, during the reign of the Kangxi emperor, the front hall was used for audiences or for receiving ambassadors, the second as a storage

1. Da Ming (Qing) Gate
2. Five Marble Bridges
3. Chengtian (Tian'an) Gate
4. Duan Gate
5. Wu Gate
6. Ancestral Temple
7. Twin Altars of Soil and Grain
8. Five Marble Bridges
9. Taihe (Great Harmony) Gate
10. Three Great Halls
11. Three Back Halls
12. Imperial Garden
13. Six Eastern Palaces
14. Six Western Palaces
15. Yangxin Palace Complex
16. Ningshou Palace Complex
17. Shenwu Gate
18. Jing Shan (Coal Hill)

Figure 150. Plan of the Forbidden City, Beijing. [Liu Dunzhen, *Zhongguo gudai jianzhu shi*, 1st edition, between pp. 282 and 283]

place for the imperial seals, and the third for preparations for native imperial Manchu rites, including the sacrificial slaughter of hogs. Behind the Three Back Halls was the imperial garden (Figure 150, no. 12), located in the same position as royal gardens in so many former Chinese imperial cities.

Flanking the back halls were the six eastern and six western palaces (Figure 150, nos. 13 and 14), both groups arranged in two clusters of three. They were used predominantly as residential space for imperial wives and widows. Other important imperial residential complexes of the Forbidden City were Yangxin complex (Figure 150, no. 15), where the famous Empress Dowager Cixi (1835–1908) ruled behind a curtain, and Ningshou Palace complex in the northeast (Figure 150, no. 16), refurbished by the Qianlong emperor for his retirement.

Behind Shenwu Gate (Figure 150, no. 17), back gate of the Forbidden City, was Jing Shan (Figure 150, no. 18), the artificial mountain better known in the West as Coal Hill. Almost 2 kilometers further, past the north gate of the administrative-city, were the final beacons along Beijing's axis: the Drum and Bell towers (Figure 2, no. 20). Less than a kilometer separated the Bell Tower from the north outer-city wall.

The other symbols of Beijing the imperial city were its dynastic altars. Among them, the Altar of Heaven is as well known in the West as the Forbid-

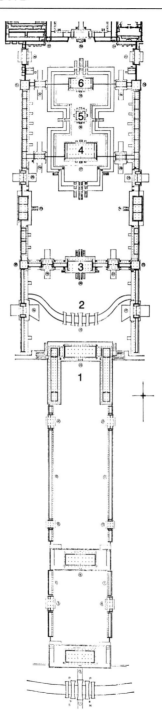

1. Wu Gate
2. Five Marble Bridges
3. Taihe (Great Harmony) Gate
4. Taihe (Great Harmony) Hall
5. Zhonghe (Central Harmony) Hall
6. Baohe (Preserving Harmony) Hall

Figure 151. Plan of the Forbidden City from the Marble Bridges to the Back Gate. [Liu Dunzhen, *Zhongguo gudai jianzhu shi,* 1st edition, between pp. 282 and 283]

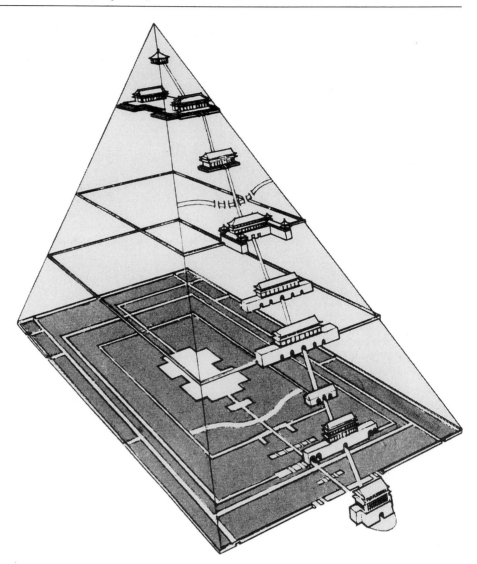

Figure 152. Plan of Beijing interpreted as volume. [Drawing by Thomas Kubota, in Wu, *Chinese and Indian Architecture*, fig. 136; published with permission of Nelson Wu]

den City. In Ming times worship of the heavens was given more attention than other focii of imperial worship. The architecture of the Altar of Heaven complex, which captures the essential symbolism of the Chinese imperial city, is unique in the universe of forms (Figure 153).

The Altar of Heaven complex was one of the two spots in Beijing that determined the southern boundary of the outer city. Originally, however, it stood beyond the Ming walls, east of the central north–south axis, contained within its own horseshoe-shaped double wall (Figure 154). The outer wall was nearly 1,700 meters east to west at the base, and the longest north–south dimension was just less than 1,600 meters. The perimeter of the second enclosure was about five-eighths that of the outer one. Two axes cut across the altar complex— one from the south side of the inner wall to its northern gate and the second from the east side of the inner wall to an outer-wall west gate. As in many imperial compounds described already, the main north–south axis contained three structures, but here each was circular in plan. The northern and southern were enclosed by squares. From south to north, along the way the emperor proceeded during his yearly rites, they were the Circular Mound, the Imperial Vault of Heaven, and the Hall for Prayer for a Prosperous Year. All three were in place by the Jiajing era (1522–1566) of the Ming dynasty.[19] The emperor made his procession through the ritual spaces during the first moon of the year to obtain heavenly confidence and to pray for a bountiful harvest and again at the time of the winter solstice to read his proclamation to heaven of the yearly occurrences.

Every aspect of the Altar of Heaven complex is symbolic. The two forms themselves, the circle and square, stand for the perfect circular shape of heaven and the square shape of earth. They are the same as those combined in the Han composite ritual hall (see Figure 15). Not surprisingly, associations between the Han and Ming ceremonial structures were suggested in the Ming dynastic history.[20] Yet because of surviving architecture as well as texts, the symbolism of the Ming buildings can be described more thoroughly. At the Circular Mound flagstones were arranged atop the altar in nine concentric circles, with nine stones in the first and multiples of nine in each successive ring up to eighty-one in the ninth tier, the number nine symbolizing the emperor and the heavens. At the Hall for Prayer for a Prosperous Year, the numbers twelve for the months, twelve for the divisions of the Chinese day, and four for the seasons combine to equal the total number of columns, twenty-eight, the same as the number of *she* (lunar lodges),

the twenty-eight star groups identified by Han astronomers.[21]

The Altar of Heaven complex was only one of the sacrificial areas of Beijing designated by the Yongle emperor and enlarged or rebuilt during later Ming or Qing reigns. The Altar of Earth (Di Tan) was constructed in a smaller enclosed area north of the Ming city (see Figure 2, no. 5). Occupying the northern quadrant, the Altar of Earth could combine with the Altar of Heaven in the south (Figure 2, no. 4), the Altar of the Sun in the east (Figure 2, no. 6), and the Altar of the Moon in the west (Figure 2, no. 7), the latter two also out-

Figure 153. The Altar of Heaven complex from the air. [Chinese Academy of Architecture, *Ancient Chinese Architecture,* p. 161]

1. Western Gate to the Altars
2. Western Heavenly Gate
3. Ritual Instruments Office
4. Sacrificial Animals Stable
5. Abstinence Palace
6. Circular Mound
7. Imperial Vault of Heaven
8. Complete Virtue Gate
9. Imperial Kitchen and Storage
10. Slaughter Pavilion
11. Precious Clothing Platform
12. Gate of Prayer for a Prosperous Year
13. Hall for Prayer for a Prosperous Year
14. Hall of the Imperial Heavens
15. Yuelu Bridge
16. Yongding Gate
17. Bell Tower
18. Altar of Agriculture (First Crops)

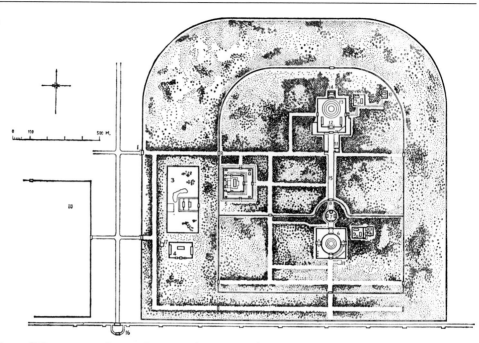

Figure 154. Plan of the Altar of Heaven complex in the Qing dynasty. [After Liu Dunzhen, *Zhongguo gudai jianzhu shi,* 1st edition, p. 348]

side the city walls, so that imperial worship could be manifest in the four quarters. In addition, a small Altar of Agriculture (First Crops) was built opposite the Altar of Heaven in a similarly horse-shoe-shaped enclosure (Figure 2, no. 8; Figure 154, no. 18) in the mid-Ming dynasty. The Ancestral Temple (Figure 2, no. 2) and twin Soil and Grain altars (Figure 2, no. 3) had been erected southeast and southwest of the Forbidden City under Emperor Yongle.

NINETEENTH-CENTURY BEIJING

The first serious challenges to imperial urban architecture in China occurred only during the final reigns of the Qing dynasty. The key issue which confronted the city was modernization. It was the same dilemna faced by the entire country in the nineteenth century, especially the second half of the century. Although Beijing would not be the only Chinese city to suffer Western attacks, and more would be modernized to greater or lesser degrees before and after the fall of imperial rule in 1911, the capital city with its nexus of forbidden and administrative quarters at the center was the one that would need the most radical alteration in order to confront the twentieth century.

The focus of change, when it finally occurred, was due south of the Forbidden City in the vicinity of Tian'an Gate, the palace-place, and *qianbulang.* Under the Qianlong emperor the area looked as it appears in Figure 155. A wall and gate were added in 1754 at either end of the T-shaped formation, together with an entrance at the south. Later, further east and west gates were added beyond the two side gates so that passage to and from the urban center

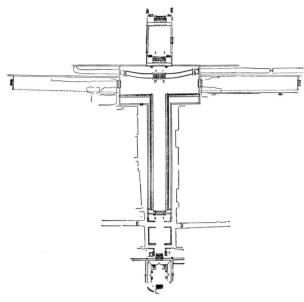

Figure 155. The Beijing palace-place at the time of the Qianlong emperor (r. 1736–1796). [Drawing after *Qianlong jingcheng quantu;* Hou and Wu, *Wenwu* no. 9 (1977), p. 9]

was possible only by way of the Forbidden City or administrative offices. During the last years of the Qing empire the area around the palace-place suffered a second attack from Western troops. A decade later, at the beginning of the Republican period, Da Qing Gate was renamed Zhonghua (China), but much more dramatic change was to take place.

TWENTIETH-CENTURY BEIJING

In 1915 the *wengcheng* at Zhengyang Gate were dismantled to allow direct passage between the Tian'an Gate area and the outer city (Figure 156). Thereupon, the former palace-place became the political focus of the republic. The May Fourth Movement (an anti-government student protest aimed at modernization) was proclaimed at what had become known as Tian'an Men Square in 1919, and six years later the May Thirtieth Movement (protesting the Versailles Treaty) was initiated. The December Ninth Movement (an anti-Japanese protest) was launched from the same spot in 1935. Finally, on 1 October 1949, Mao Zedong raised the five-star red flag from Tian'an Gate, proclaiming the People's Republic of China.

It was at this juncture, halfway into the twentieth century, that the key decisions were made about the urban and architectural future of the new capital of the People's Republic. Opinions of politicians, architects, urban planners, and historians ranged from advocacy of the destruction of all signs of China's imperial past to preservation of historically or architecturally important buildings devoid of their original associations—and everything in between. The debate about the redesign or redesignation of a vast city with a multimillennial past was, and is, ongoing. Several general policies and certain specific decisions have been made since 1950, however.

The most impressive has been the transformation of imperial space into people's space. In general, all former imperial buildings and monuments have been preserved, but now they are public museums or national monuments. Since the age-old focus, Tian'an Men Square, could not be readily turned into a monument or park, it therefore presented the greatest challenge. In the process of transformation it became a symbol of the goals of the new nation. What is more, transformation there continued from the 1950s through the late 1970s—years that spanned the waxing and waning of Soviet influence in China, the Great Leap Forward, and the Cultural Revolution.

The first post-Liberation structure erected at Tian'an Men Square was the Monument to the People's Heroes, completed by 1 May 1958 (Figure 157), in time for the tenth anniversary of the People's Republic. Exemplifying the goals and ideals of

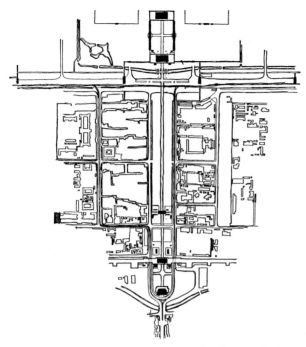

Figure 156. Tian'an Men Square in the first half of the twentieth century. [Hou and Wu, *Wenwu* no. 9 (1977), p. 10]

the new republic, the monument was a huge granite obelisk, 120 feet in height, with a marble base showing such historical scenes as Minister Lin Zixu's destruction of opium crates in Guangzhou (Canton) in 1842, the Taiping Rebellion of 1851, the May Fourth demonstration, guerrilla warfare against the Japanese between 1937 and 1945, and the Communists crossing the Yangzi in 1949. It is inscribed with calligraphy of the party leaders Mao Zedong and Zhou Enlai. Although the Ming–Qing city wall boundaries are still indicated on many current maps of Beijing, by this time the old city walls and most of the gates had been torn down to make way for urban expansion. Moreover, Chang'an Street, extending from either side of the old palace-place, was further lengthened on the east and west

to form a counteraxis, finally obliterating the traditional single north–south focus of the imperial city. Ring roads for car travel and an underground rapid transit system had also been constructed. By the end of the 1980s a fourth ring road was under way (Figure 158).

Through the decade, proposals and plans were submitted for the transformation of the urban core. A survey of some submitted in 1954 (Figure 159), 1956 (Figure 160), and 1958 (Figure 161) indicates that the one certainty of the planning was that Tian'an Men Square would become a huge open space accommodating between four-hundred and five-hundred thousand people assembled for political rallies or ceremonies. In order to create the new public area, both sides of the imperial-way plus several structures of the T-shaped area that remained intact in 1949 had to be torn down.

By 1958 there was also agreement about three other buildings that were to stand in Tian'an Men Square. One would be the Great Hall of the People (Renmin Dahui Tang), planned as part of a 561,786-square-foot building complex that would occupy more space than the original halls of the Forbidden City. Rising 30 to 40 meters on the western side of Tian'an Men Square, the Great Hall of the People was taller than the former imperial Tian'an Gate. East of the square between Tian'an Gate and the Monument to the People's Heroes were to be two museums—one containing objects relevant to the Cultural Revolution and the second, the Museum of Chinese History, the major museum of China today. Again many proposals for the arrangement were offered, six of which have been published by Wu Liangyong.[22] Figure 4 shows the scheme that was adopted.

Between 1960 and 1964 debate about Beijing raged again—this time over the issue of *shou* ("preserve") versus *fang* ("release") old monuments. Questions that had been asked about the Great Hall

Figure 157. Tian'an Men Square today showing the Monument to the People's Heroes and the Mausoleum of Chairman Mao. [Steinhardt photograph]

of the People and the two museums were directed to the city as a whole: Did the people want to tear down more ceramic-tile-roofed, wide-eaved buildings in favor of the new Western flat-roofed structures like the Great Hall of the People? Should skyscrapers be erected? If so, how could they and other Western architectural types fit into the surrounding courtyard-style neighborhoods? Did Beijing want stone to replace timber as at Tian'an Men Square? Should the grid system of ancient capitals maintained in the lanes and alleys of Beijing give way to more large open spaces like Tian'an Men Square, or did the capital want to retain a single focus? Some of the issues remain unresolved today, but certain policy guidelines have been established. Specific imperial buildings and premodern neighborhoods, including several shopping districts, are subject to restrictive building codes. Surrounding architecture, even if new, within a certain radius of these buildings must be lower than the buildings to be preserved.[23] For instance, new buildings in the vicinity of Miaoying Monastery, Guangji Monastery, Huguo Monastery, Bolin Monastery, Yonghe Lamasery, the Confucian Temple, the National Academy, and the East Mosque can be no taller than 9 meters. Other buildings in Beijing may rise as high as 45 meters, and a few skyscrapers of about 100 meters can also be built.

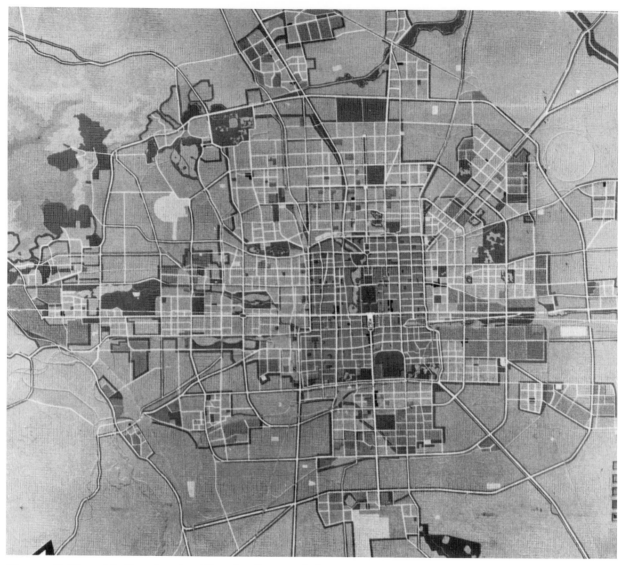

Figure 158. Plan of Beijing showing Chang'an Street and the ring roads. [Courtesy of Liu Kaiji, Beijing Municipal Architecture and Building Bureau]

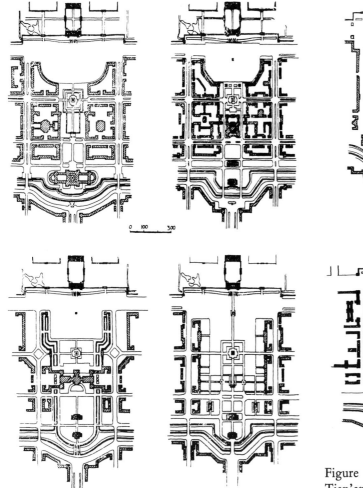

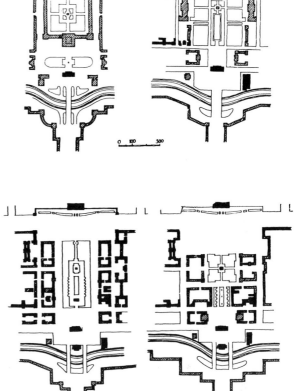

Figure 159. 1954 proposals for the transformation of Tian'an Men Square, Beijing. [Wu Liangyong, *Jianzhu shi lunwen ji* 2 (1979), p. 20]

Figure 160. 1956 proposals for the transformation of Tian'an Men Square, Beijing. [Wu Liangyong, *Jianzhu shi lunwen ji* 2 (1979), p. 21]

The death of Mao Zedong in 1976 turned the ongoing debate over Beijing's architecture to another monument: his mausoleum. Should it be a *ling,* or royal tomb, in accordance with ancient funerary standards; should it be a building complex such as those constructed in the north, east, and west of Beijing for Ming and Qing rulers; or should it perhaps resemble the more recent mausoleum of Sun Yatsen (Zhongshan) in Nanjing, built in traditional style? Or should it be a revolutionary monument, and if so, what architectural criteria would satisfy that label? Should it in some way be Chinese in style? On 6 November of that year the decision was made to put the mausoleum in

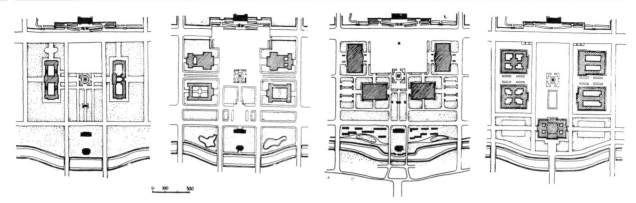

Figure 161. 1958 proposals for the transformation of Tian'an Men Square, Beijing. [Wu Liangyong, *Jianzhu shi lunwen ji* 2 (1979), p. 27]

Tian'an Men Square, but questions of its size, height, and relation to other buildings remained. Placing the mausoleum in the center of the square might make it symbolically more important than the Great Hall of the People, which did not stand on the main north–south axis of the city.

Figure 4 shows the focus of Beijing as it still appeared in 1987. Chairman Mao's Mausoleum is in the center, rising above the Monument to the People's Heroes, between the monument and Zhengyang (or Qian) Gate. When the mausoleum was built, the square was again enlarged so that it could accommodate six hundred thousand people. As Beijing approaches the twenty-first century it may be called the archetypal Chinese imperial city—one that has gracefully weathered every governmental and political change while maintaining the imperial landmarks of a four-thousand-year urban history.

NOTES

Only the briefest identifiable references are provided here. All titles are cited fully in the References.

CHAPTER 1

1. Many discussions of the emperor's role in society and his relation to heaven and the cosmos are available. A recommended study is Marcel Granet, *La Pensée chinoise*.

2. On these ideas see William Theodore De Bary, et al., *Sources of Chinese Tradition*, vol. 1, pp. 198–204. On the four-sided worldview and its relation to Chinese architecture see Nelson Wu, *Chinese and Indian Architecture*, and Paul Wheatley, *The Pivot of the Four Quarters*, especially pp. 411–476.

3. The Chinese term for this bird is *que* or *qiao* (sparrow). It is often illustrated as a phoenix, more suitable than a sparrow as the representative of the south because of its auspicious connotations. Throughout the text *zhuque* is translated as "vermilion bird."

4. Recently published population figures for China's premodern cities are available in Dong, *Zhongguo chengshi jianshe shi*. G. William Skinner assesses some of the sources of population figures in his introduction to *The City in Late Imperial China*, pp. 3–31.

5. An extensive bibliography is available for the subject of Chinese geomancy. Suggested introductory reading is Steven Bennett, "Patterns of the Sky and Earth," and Andrew March, "An Appreciation of Chinese Geomancy." More extensive treatment of the subject is available in Sophie Clément et al., *Architecture du paysage en Asie orientale,* and an interesting discussion of the lore of *fengshui* is found in J. J. M. De Groot, *The Religious System of China*, vol. 3.

6. The *gong* arrangement is reserved for high-ranking imperial and Buddhist buildings. The *gong* scheme and other patterns of spatial enclosure are discussed in Liu, *Zhongguo gudai jianzhu shi,* 2d ed., pp. 8–13.

7. Howard Wechsler argues that the role of heaven and the importance of heaven worship superseded ancestor worship even in the seventh century. See *Offerings of Jade and Silk*, pp. 107–122. On the role of heaven and heaven worship in Ming China see Jeffrey Meyer, *Peking as a Sacred City*. The Altar of Heaven is discussed in Nancy S. Steinhardt, *Chinese Traditional Architecture*, pp. 140–149; Shan, "Mingdai yingzao shiliao: Tian Tan"; and Ishibashi, *Ten-dan*.

8. The city-god and other folk temples of the Chinese city are discussed in Stephen Feuchtwang, "School-Temple and City God," in G. W. Skinner, ed., *The City in Late Imperial*

China, pp. 581–608, and David Johnson, "The City-God Cults of Tang and Sung China."

9. For Wang Shiren's reconstruction of the composite ritual hall see his "Han Chang'an Cheng nanjiao lizhi jianzhu." On this structure see also Yang Hongxun, *Jianzhu kaoguxue lunwen ji*, pp. 169–200.

10. On locations and functions of bell and drum towers see Tanaka Tan, "Jujiro ni tatsu hoji rokaku." Professor Tanaka has provided me with an unpublished manuscript on the subject as well.

11. The relation between commerce and the city is not discussed here. For studies dealing with wards or guilds and trade within them see Denis Twitchett, "The T'ang Market System"; Twitchett, "Merchant, Trade and Government in Late T'ang"; Shiba Yoshinobu, *Commerce and Society in Sung China;* and Sidney Gamble, *Peking: A Social Survey.*

12. For a general discussion of Chinese imperial tombs see Yang, *Zhongguo gudai lingqin zhidu shi yanjiu.*

13. It is interesting that in a study of contemporary Chinese cities Xi'an and Beijing are still the two main subjects. See C. P. Lo, "Shaping Socialist Chinese Cities: A Model of Form and Land Use," in C. K. Leung and N. Ginsburg, eds., *China: Urbanization and National Development,* pp. 130–155.

14. James Legge, *The Chinese Classics,* vol. 5: *The Ch'un Ts'ew with the Tso Chuen,* p. 115.

15. This definition is used by John R. Watt in "The Yamen and Urban Administration," in Skinner, *The City in Late Imperial China,* p. 353.

16. *Han-Ying cidian* (The Pinyin Chinese–English Dictionary), Beijing, 1979, p. 88.

17. The source of this interpretation is an often quoted passage of *Guanzi* which says that *nei* is *cheng* and *chengwai* is *guo.* The passage is discussed in Komai, *Chūgoku tojō,* p. 3; Guo Husheng, "Zicheng zhidu," esp. pp. 665–671; and Matsumoto, "Mindai Chūto kensetsu shimatsu," esp. pp. 66–67. Neither premodern nor contemporary Chinese mapmakers and scholars have been consistent in their references to walled enclosures of Chinese imperial cities. The names discussed in these paragraphs are based on my own readings of texts and recent scholarship. Other names for city enclosures may be found.

18. Legge, *The Chinese Classics,* vol. 5, p. 115. The same passage is quoted by Matsumoto.

19. According to Farmer, *Early Ming Government,* p. 176, in Ming times *jing* was used only for the northern and southern capitals, whereas *du* referred to capitals of other directions or

the center. Matsumoto reiterates this point in "Mindai Chūto kensetsu shimatsu."

20. At certain times the designation of five capitals may have been desirable because of the correspondence between the number five and the Five Elements. Most of the auxiliary capitals of Chinese dynasties are listed in Li Jiafu, *Zhongguo gudai jianzhu yishu.* For a good discussion of the multiple-capital system of the Ming dynasty see Edward L. Farmer, *Early Ming Government.*

CHAPTER 2

1. David Knechtges, trans., "Eastern Metropolis Rhapsody" (Dongjing fu), *Wen xuan,* p. 301.

2. Most of the classical texts are available in at least partial translation, many of them in several versions. Since the Han dynasty there has been debate about the dates of certain texts; modern literature disputing the dates is available in Chinese, Japanese, and Western languages. Paul Wheatley discusses important literary sources for the history of the Shang and Zhou cities in *Pivot of the Four Quarters,* pp. 13–20 and 150–160, respectively. Suggested translations of texts used in this chapter are: Arthur Waley, trans., *The Book of Songs (Shi jing);* Bernhard Karlgren, trans., *The Book of Odes (Shi jing);* James Legge, trans., *The Chinese Classics,* vol. 5, for the *Zuo zhuan* (Commentary of Zuo) and *Chun Qiu* (Spring and Autumn annals); Burton Watson, trans., *Records of the Grand Historian,* for the *Shi ji;* Clae Waltham, translator and modernizer of the Legge version, *The Book of Documents (Shu jing);* and Bernhard Karlgren, "The Book of Documents" and "Glosses on the Book of Documents," pts. 1 and 2, for the same text; Chai and Chai's updated version of James Legge, *The Book of Rites (Li ji),* 2 vols.; Edouard Biot, trans., *Le Tcheou-li (Zhou li),* 2 vols.; J. I. Crump, *Chan-kuo Ts'e* (Discourses of the Warring States); and W. Allyn Rickett, *Guanzi.*

3. Dates of the legendary emperors have been determined by classical Chinese scholars from the texts. They have not been validated by other evidence.

4. These events are summarized in Gu Yanwu, *Lidai diwang zhaijing ji,* pp. 87–90.

5. As many as ten different dates for the duration of Shang have been derived from reading texts. For a summary of the dates of Shang see Chang Kwang-chih, *Archeology of Ancient China,* 3d ed., p. 297. On the lineage of Shang kings see Chang, *Shang Civilization,* pp. 4–19. It is generally accepted that the Shang used seven different capital city sites from

approximately the middle of the eighteenth century B.C. until about the third quarter of the twelfth century B.C.

6. These two passages are also quoted in Wheatley, *Pivot of the Four Quarters,* p. 430.

7. On the transfer of capitals see Chang Kwang-chih, "Xia, Shang, Zhou Sandai duzhi."

8. This is a reference to the practice of divination through the use of tortoise shells. On scapulimancy and other forms of Shang divination see David Keightley, *Sources of Shang History,* esp. pp. 3–27.

9. Waltham, *Book of Documents,* pp. 85–86.

10. Waley, *Book of Songs,* p. 281.

11. Chang, *Shang Civilization,* pp. 159–160.

12. Karlgren, *Book of Odes,* pp. 198–199.

13. On the date of the *Zhou li* see Bernhard Karlgren, "The Early History of the *Chou li* and *Tso chuan* Texts."

14. In the Zhou dynasty *jiangren* was an official title. Later it referred to a designer or planner of at least minor official rank. The title is sometimes translated as "architect," but since there is no premodern Chinese counterpart for our architect it is best to think of *jiangren* as a man in the emperor's service who works on construction projects in a capacity ranging from builder to craftsman.

15. *Kaogong ji,* juan 2/11a–12b. For a French translation see Biot, *Le Tcheou-li,* vol. 2, pp. 553–559. Wheatley's translation is somewhat different in *Pivot of the Four Quarters,* pp. 426 and 411.

16. Paul Wheatley calls the passage the *locus classicus* for the layout of Chinese capitals. Other authors who consider the city plan lineage from the *Kaogong ji* to be so important include Clément, Dong, He, Komai, and Murata.

17. For the *Li ji* discussion of the Ming Tang see Wang Mengba, *Li ji jinzhu jince,* vol. 1, pp. 421–429. The Ming Tang is also described in *juan* 55 of *Yi Zhou shu,* pp. 162–164.

18. *Xi'an Banpo,* caption to pl. 12. For more on Banpo and the Neolithic period in China see Jessica Rawson, *Ancient China,* pp. 13–40, and Chang, *Archeology of Ancient China,* 3d ed., pp. 80–184.

19. On Chengziyai see Li Chi, *Ch'eng-tzu-yai.*

20. Erlitou is one of a cluster of early Shang or pre-Shang sites in the vicinity of modern Luoyang and Yanshi. At present it is one of the most extensively excavated.

21. Xu Xunsheng investigated Erlitou with the hope of identifying the site of Bo, the earliest Shang capital. The theory is still unconfirmed. Xu published his findings in "Yijiuwushijiu-nian Yuxi diaocha."

22. Articles of particular relevance to Erlitou are "Henan Yanshi Erlitou yizhi"; "Henan Yanshi Erlitou Zao-Shang gongdian"; Qi Yingtao, "Zhongguo zaoqi mujiegou jianzhu"; and R. Thorp, "Origins of Chinese Architectural Style."

23. On the second Erlitou palace compound see "Henan Yanshi Erlitou erhao gongdian"; Yin Weizhang, "Erlitou wenhua zai tantao"; "Yanshi Shang cheng de chubu"; and "Yijiubashisan-nian qiuji Henan Yanshi Shang cheng fajue baogao."

24. On this Shang site at Yanshi see "Yijiubashisi-nian chun Yanshi Shixianggou Shang cheng gongdian."

25. On Zhengzhou see An Zhimin, "Yijiuwu'er-nian qiuji Zhengzhou Erligang fajue ji"; An Jinhuai, "Zhengzhou diqu de gudai yicun"; and Chang, *Shang Civilization,* esp. pp. 263–288.

26. On Panlongcheng see Yang Hongxun, "Cong Panlong Cheng," and Robert Bagley, "P'an-lung-ch'eng."

27. An immense bibliography can be compiled for Yin (Anyang). Here the city is considered solely from the point of view of its plan. For more information see Li Chi, *Anyang,* and Chang, *Shang Civilization,* esp. pp. 69–135.

28. Chang, *Archeology of Ancient China,* p. 321.

29. Chang, "Towns and Cities in Ancient China," in *Early Chinese Civilization,* esp. pp. 67–68.

30. Miao Changyan, "Sanfu yange," *Sanfuhuang tu,* p. 5.

31. Wang Shimin, "Zhoudu Feng, Hao weizhi shangjue," and Hu Qianying, "Feng-Hao diqu." Hu's suggested locations are shown in Figure 18. His article convincingly refutes Wang's proposals for the location of the two capitals.

32. On Fengchu see "Shaanxi Qishan Fengchu Cun," and Robert Thorp, "Origins of Chinese Architectural Style."

33. See, for example, Miyazaki, "Sengoku jidai no toshi." Miyazaki points out that in the Warring States period cities came to be known as *xian* or *jun* according to the number of troops quartered in them.

34. The three lineages of imperial city planning in China are the thesis of my article "Why Were Chang'an and Beijing So Different?"

35. On the actual Wangcheng see "Luoyang Jianbin Dong Zhou chengzhi" and "Zhongguo Kexue Yuan Kaogu Yanjiu Suo yijiuliushi-nian tianye gongzuo." The history and locations of Wangcheng and Chengzhou are explained in Li Xueqin, *Eastern Zhou and Qin Civilizations,* pp. 16–22.

36. The results of the Japanese excavation of Lüdu were published by Komai Kazuchika. See especially *Kyoku-fu Rojō*

no iseki and a summary of those findings in *Chūgoku tojō*, pp. 21–49. Qufu is also discussed by Murata in *Chūgoku no teito*, pp. 29–31, and Sekino in *Chūgoku kōkogaku kenkyū*, pp. 327–339, which focuses on Lingguang Hall. More recent Chinese investigation of Lüdu has been published as *Qufu Lü Guo gucheng* and Tian, "Qufu Lücheng kantan." For a summary of the findings see He Yeju, *Zhongguo gudai chengshi*, pp. 35–53. For a summary and translation of some of the Chinese material see David Buck, "Archeological Explorations at the Ancient Capital of Lu."

37. See Tao and Ye, "Gu Wei Cheng he Yu Wang Cheng," p. 61. On Anyi see also "Shanxi Xia Xian Yu Wang Cheng diaocha."

38. The plan of this city, Wuguo, is published in "Houma Dong Zhou xunren mu," p. 15.

39. On Jiang see Chang Wenzhai, "Shanxi Xiangfen Zhaokang fujin gudai chengzhi."

40. On Yan Xiadu see "Hebei Yi Xian Yan Xiadu gucheng kancha"; "Hebei Yi Xian Yan Xiadu dishiliu-hao mu"; "Yan Xiadu di'ershi'er-hao yizhi"; "Yijiuliushisi-yijiuliushiwu-nian Yan Xiadu muzang baogao"; "Hebei Yi Xian Yan Xiadu sishisi-hao mu"; and Ou Yan, "Shilun Yan Xiadu chengzhi."

41. Handan was excavated by Komai and Sekino in 1939, and their findings were published in *Han-tan* (1954). For the later Chinese survey of Handan see "Hebei Handan shiqu gu yizhi."

42. Of the long bibliography on Houma, "Shanxi Houma Shangma Cun" is a good introduction to the city and its architectural remains. Findings at the site are summarized in Li, *Eastern Zhou and Qin Civilizations*, pp. 40–58.

43. On Linzi see Sekino, *Chūgoku kōkogaku kenkyū*, pp. 241–294; "Shandong Linzi Qi gucheng"; Qun Li, "Linzi Qi Guo gucheng"; and Liu Dunyuan, "Chun Qiu shiqi Qi Guo gucheng."

44. Plans of cities of this type may be found in Chang, *Archeology of Ancient China*, 3d ed., pp. 321–350.

45. The bronze plate and other material from the Zhongshan kings are discussed in "Hebei Sheng Pingshan Xian Zhan Guo Shiqi Zhongshan Guo muzang"; Fu Xinian, "Zhan Guo Zhongshan Wang Cuo mu"; Yang Hongxun, "Zhan Guo Zhongshan Wang ling"; *Chūzan ōkoku bunbutsu ten;* and Li, *Eastern Zhou and Qin Civilizations*, pp. 93–107.

46. On the first emperor's tomb and terracotta army see Maxwell Hearn, "The Terracotta Army of the First Emperor of Qin," in Wen Fong, ed., *The Great Bronze Age of China*, pp. 353–373, and Robert Thorp, "The Lishan Necropolis," in

G. Kuwayama, ed., *The Great Bronze Age of China: A Symposium*, pp. 72–83.

47. Wang Zhongshu convincingly reiterates the continuation of Zhou–Qin city patterns in "Zhongguo gudai ducheng," p. 505.

48. On the excavation of Qin Xianyang see "Qindu Xianyang gucheng" and "Qindu Xianyang diyihao gongdian jianzhu."

49. The *Shi ji*, an earlier text, gives somewhat different dimensions. See Miao Changyan, "Sanfu yange," *Sanfuhuang tu*, p. 6.

50. Palace 1 from Xianyang has been theoretically reconstructed as a bilevel structure raised on a 3,100-meter-square *hangtu* foundation. The architectural complex was to have been surrounded by a covered arcade, supported by pillars, from which stairs led to the upper story. Individual rectangular rooms were situated around a central courtyard. Subterranean drainpipes provided water for all parts of the compound, and food was stored in underground pits. On this reconstruction see Tao Fu, "Qin Xianyang Gong diyi-hao yizhi fayuan."

51. Alexander Soper, *The Evolution of Buddhist Architecture in Japan*, p. 11.

52. Miao Changyan, "Sanfu yange," *Sanfuhuang tu*, p. 5.

CHAPTER 3

1. David Knechtges, "Western (Han) Metropolis Rhapsody" (Xijing fu), *Wen xuan*, pp. 201–207.

2. They are mentioned in "Western (Han) Capital Rhapsody" (Xidu fu). See Knechtges, *Wen xuan*, p. 103.

3. The maps of Chang'an originally published with *Sanfuhuang tu* are no longer extant. Mapmaking was a common practice in the Han dynasty; several Han maps are published and discussed in Annelise G. Bulling, "Ancient Chinese Maps."

4. These works are listed in the References.

5. The principal archaeologist of the Han capitals in the last two decades has been Wang Zhongshu.

6. Wang Zhongshu, *Han Civilization*, p. 4.

7. C. W. Bishop, "An Ancient Chinese Capital," pp. 76–77.

8. Ye Dasong, *Zhongguo jianzhu shi*, pp. 399–407.

9. Wang, *Han Civilization*, p. 1.

10. Wang, *Han Civilization*, p. 2, and Wang Zhongshu, "Zhongguo gudai ducheng," p. 505.

11. Stephen Hotaling has deduced somewhat different mea-

surements for the walls of Chang'an by using what he calls a "grid system." See Hotaling, "The City Walls of Han Chang'an."

12. Wheatley, *Pivot of the Four Quarters,* p. 443.

13. Wang, "Zhongguo gudai ducheng," p. 505.

14. Knechtges, "Western Capital Rhapsody," *Wen xuan,* pp. 103–107.

15. Miyazaki, "Les villes en Chine," esp. pp. 390–392.

16. Ibid., p. 389.

17. Wang, "Zhongguo gudai ducheng," p. 507.

18. Ibid.

19. Miyazaki, "Les villes en Chine," p. 387.

20. Ibid., p. 382.

21. Wang, "Zhongguo gudai ducheng," p. 506.

22. On the history of the Ming Tang and related structures see William Soothill, *The Hall of Light;* Cai Zhi (133–192), *Ming Tang yueling lun;* Jonny Hefter, "Ming-t'ang-miao-ch'in-t'ung-k'ao"; Hui Dong, *Ming Tang dadao lu;* "Ming Tang wei," *juan* 14 of the *Li ji;* Henri Maspero, "Le Ming-t'ang et la Crise Religieuse chinoise avant les Han"; Sun Xingyan (1753–1818), *Ming Tang kao;* Ruan Yuan (1764–1849), *Ming Tang lun;* Wang Guowei (Qing), *Ming Tang qinmiao tongkao;* and "Ming Tang," *juan* 55 of *Yi Zhou shu.*

23. Knechtges, "Eastern Metropolis Rhapsody," *Wen xuan,* pp. 245–247.

24. Citing *Kuodi zhi,* Xiong Cunrui takes issue with the belief that the Luoyang used by the Eastern Han began under the Western Han; he suggests instead Qin origins for the city. See Xiong, "Re-evaluation of the Naba-Chen Theory," pp. 138–139. That Qin palaces were reused by the Western Han is also stated in the opening line from *Wen xuan* quoted above.

25. Hans Bielenstein, "Lo-yang in Later Han Times," p. 12. Professor Bielenstein's is the most extensive Western-language study of the Eastern Han capital.

26. Wang, "Zhongguo gudai ducheng," p. 507, whose source is *Henan zhi.*

27. He Yeju, "Guanyu woguo gudai chengshi," p. 65.

28. This connective causeway is emphatically portrayed in Bielenstein's plan of Han Luoyang published in "Lo-yang in Later Han Times," p. 124. Bielenstein's map places the two palace complexes adjacent to the north and south city outer walls, positions which Wang Zhongshu has not been able to confirm by excavation.

29. Cai Zhi (Eastern Han), "Han guandian zhi yishi xuan-yong," p. 9. Bielenstein, p. 35, is puzzled by the statement, noting that 37 by 7 *zhang* (283 by 53 feet), the dimensions of the hall, would have allowed only 14 square centimeters per person. The hall is smaller than the main hall of Weiyang Gong from Western Han Chang'an. Still, the main hall of every Chinese palace complex was grand, and one should expect exaggerated descriptions, such as that for Epang Palace of the Qin, for all of them.

30. Bielenstein, "Lo-yang in Later Han Times," pp. 40–41.

31. On the locations of Eastern Han tombs with respect to the capital see Bielenstein, "Lo-yang in Later Han Times," pp. 83–85.

32. Photographs of its remains are published in Wang, *Han Civilization,* figs. 49–52.

33. Halls and gates are labeled in the Shijie Press, 1974, reprint of *Henan zhi.* The gates of the eastern, northern, and western walls of the 1974 reprint and Figure 60 correspond in name and position. On the south wall, only two gates are shown in the *Henan zhi* plan, and only the eastern of them shares a name with the east gate of the south wall in Figure 60. Pingcheng Gate of Figure 60 is indicated by name in the *Henan zhi* plan, but it is not shown as part of the outer wall.

34. For a study of the plans of Luoyang published in *Yongle dadian,* see Zuo Ming, "*Yongle dadian juan* 9561."

CHAPTER 4

1. The capitals of certain states and kingdoms are not discussed here because no plans of them survive: They are the capitals of the Former Zhao at Pingyang, the Later Zhao at Rangguo, the Former Yan at Longcheng, the Former Shu at Chengdu, the Former Liang at Guzang, the Western Qin at Yuanchuan, the Later Yan at Zhongshan (later Longcheng), the Later Liang at Guzang, the Southern Liang at Yuedu, the Western Liang at Dunhuang, the Northern Liang at Zhangye, the Southern Yan at Guangyuan, the Northern Yan at Long-cheng, and the Xia Guo at Tongwan, plus Former Zhao, Former Qin, and Later Qin at Chang'an, Later Zhao and Former Yan at Ye, and Northern Zhou at Jinyang.

2. It would not be surprising if the simple single-walled city, a possible fourth type mentioned for Eastern Zhou cities, were built for some of the capitals listed in note 1.

3. The best information about Six Dynasties capitals Jianye and Jiankang is found in Zhu Xie, *Jinling guji tukao,* pp. 95–127; Louis Gaillard, *Nankin,* pp. 35–117; and Murata Jiro, *Chūgoku no teito,* pp. 88–95. There is some discrepancy in the Jianye measurements provided by Zhu Xie. He writes that each wall of the palace-city was 120 *zhang,* but that its perimeter was 500 *zhang.* For the outer wall Zhu gives 20 *li* 19 *bu* as the perimeter, with the eastern and western walls slightly

longer than the northern and southern ones. These figures are quite different from those in "Wu Capital Rhapsody" (Wudu fu), which are 47 *li*, 210 *bu*, 2 *chi* for the outer wall. See Knechtges, *Wen xuan*, p. 394.

4. Knechtges, "Wu Capital Rhapsody," *Wen xuan*, p. 401.

5. I have not found any discrepancies between Zhu's measurements for the Jiankang walls and those in other sources, but there are some differences in plans. Only eight outer wall gates are indicated on Zhu Xie's map (Figure 64), whereas twelve are shown in the plan from *Jiangning Fu zhi* (Figure 65). Similar inconsistencies are found in a comparison of the plans of Eastern Jin–Song Jiankang from the same two sources. Zhu Xie lists the gate names for the five capitals at Jiankang on pp. 106–107 and pp. 114–115 of his book. His sources predate *Jiangning Fu zhi* and include official histories of the dynasties that ruled at Jiankang, the Tang dynasty text *Jiankang yi lu* (Record of remains at Jiankang), and *Zhizheng Jinling xinzhi* (New record of Jinling from the *zhizheng* reign) from the fourteenth century.

6. Zhu Xie's plan of Song Jiankang is published in *Jinling guji tukao* between pp. 104 and 105.

7. From 552 to 554 the Liang had a capital at Jiangling in modern Hubei. This capital is mentioned in *Bei Qi shu* (History of the Northern Qi), *juan* 45, which has been translated by Albert Dien as *Pei Ch'i Shu 45: Biography of Yen Chih-t'ui;* see esp. pp. 8–9.

8. The most important source for Pingcheng is *Wei shu*. Archaeological data for Pingcheng are listed in note 10 and the References.

9. These events are summarized in Murata, *Chūgoku no teito,* p. 72.

10. The results of Japanese excavation at Datong are published in Mizuno, "Daitō tsushin," pts. 1 and 2. More Chinese studies based on archaeology, including the excavation of the Northern Wei period tomb of Sima Jinlong, are "Datong nanjiao Bei Wei yizhi"; "Shanxi Datong Shijia Zhan Bei Wei Sima Jinlong mu"; Su Bai, "Shengle, Pingcheng yidai de Tuoba Xianbi-Bei Wei yiji"; and "Shanxi Datong nanjiao chutu."

11. Murata, *Chūgoku no teito,* pp. 71–76.

12. Knechtges, "Ye Capital Rhapsody," *Wen xuan,* pp. 451–453.

13. Figure 70 is also published in Dong, *Zhongguo chengshi,* p. 21, and Yu Weichao, "Zhongguo gudai ducheng guihua," p. 57.

14. Knechtges, "Ye Capital Rhapsody," *Wen xuan,* pp. 449–451.

15. On Luoyang see Yan Wenru, "Luoyang Han, Wei, Sui, Tang chengzhi kancha"; "Han–Wei Luoyang Cheng"; and Su Bai, "Bei Wei Luoyang Cheng."

16. The tendency of *Henan zhi* to idealize city plans has already been noted. Similarly contrived schemes of Wei and Jin Luoyang are found in the illustrations to the text.

17. There are discrepancies between the recorded names of gates in *Luoyang qielan ji* and *Jin shu*.

18. Ideas about Northern Wei Luoyang's plan have been presented by Naba Toshisada, Chen Yinke, Komai Kazuchika, Mori Shikazō, and most recently Tonami Mamoru (in Ueda, *Tojō*). Their works are listed in the References. Each author has been concerned with the contradiction explained in this paragraph and has given an opinion about the influence of the Northern Wei Luoyang plan on later Tang and Japanese city plans. Aspects of the scholarly debate not resolved by the 1978 plan are discussed in Chapter 5. Murata Jiro summarizes some of the Japanese research in *Chūgoku no teito,* pp. 85–86.

19. For these reports see note 15.

20. Fan, *Luoyang qielan ji jiaozhu, juan* 5, p. 349. This translation appears in Ho Ping-ti, "Lo-yang," p. 66.

21. Ho Ping-ti's study, "Lo-yang," proves that 220 wards, the number specified in *Luoyang qielan ji,* is correct. See esp. pp. 66–70.

22. Su Bai's plan is published in "Bei Wei Luoyang Cheng," colorplate 4. He Yeju's slightly clearer version has been used as Figure 73.

23. W. J. F. Jenner, *Memories of Lo-yang,* p. 271; see also pp. 117–118.

24. Wards are shown only in the outer city of Northern Wei Luoyang in plans published by Wang ("Zhongguo gudai gucheng," p. 511) and Dong (*Zhongguo chengshi jianshe shi,* p. 23). Wu Liangyong, "A Brief History of Ancient Chinese City Planning," p. 26, indicates no wards.

25. The number of temples, forty-two, is clearly stated at the beginning of Yang Xuanzhi's text. (See Yang Yi-t'ung, *Record of Buddhist Monasteries,* p. 5, and Jenner, *Memories of Lo-yang,* p. 141.) The total number of monasteries was 1,367, although the number seems to be misprinted as 1,376 in Jenner, *Memories,* p. 116.

26. Jenner, *Memories,* pp. 116–118.

27. On Yongning Si see "Han–Wei Luoyang Cheng"; see p. 205 for a plan of what remains today. On Baima Si see Xu Jinxing, *Baima Si,* and Xin, *Luoyang Baima Si.*

28. This process is discussed in many publications concerning Buddhist cave-temples of the fifth to sixth centuries. See, for example, Akiyama Terukazu, *The Arts of China;* Annette

Juliano, *Art of the Six Dynasties;* L. Sickman and A. Soper, *The Art and Architecture of China;* and A. Soper, *Literary Evidence for Early Buddhist Art in China.*

29. When the last Northern Wei emperor at Luoyang was taken to Ye, another member of the Northern Wei imperial family led followers to Chang'an. From 535 to 557, Chang'an was the Western Wei capital. Ruins from the time of the Han were used for the imperial buildings. The Eastern Wei capital at Ye endured only from 534 to 550, at which point a pro-Chinese faction established a capital of the Northern Qi dynasty there. It survived until 577.

30. Murata Jiro excavated at Ye in the first half of this century. His findings are published in *Chūgoku no teito,* pp. 181–260; pp. 187 and 199–260 are especially relevant to Eastern Wei Ye.

31. Murata, *Chūgoku no teito,* pp. 228–235.

32. Knechtges, "Shu Capital Rhapsody," *Wen xuan,* pp. 356–358.

33. Wang Wencai's three articles on Chengdu in *Sichuan shiyuan xuebao* are the only recent studies known to me. I would like to thank Tanaka Tan for sending me copies of these articles. This use of *zicheng* is unusual.

34. A. C. Moule and P. Pelliot, *Marco Polo,* p. 266.

35. Knechtges, "Shu Capital Rhapsody," *Wen xuan,* p. 358.

36. Shengle is discussed in Murata, *Chūgoku no teito,* pp. 69–70; Komai, *Chūgoku no tojō,* p. 72; and Su, "Shengle, Pingcheng yidai de Tuoba Xianbi."

37. Luoyang conforms to this pattern only when the pre-501 city is considered.

38. Wang Zhongshu, "Zhongguo gudai ducheng," p. 511, suggests six points of change in imperial planning from the Han through the period of Northern and Southern dynasties; his points 1, 2, 4, and 6 coincide with those cited here. His third point concerns what he describes as a movement northward of the palaces; his sixth point is a shift in the positions of markets from north to south. The first of his additional two points is invalidated by the plan of Eastern Zhou Jiang. As for markets, it seems premature to make a generalization about them when their locations at Shengle, Pingcheng, Jianye, Jiankang, Ye, and Chengdu are not confirmed by excavation.

CHAPTER 5

1. A discussion of the foreign exotica in the Chinese capital is found in Edward Schafer, *The Golden Peaches of Samarkand.* For a general discussion of the Tang, see A. Wright and D. Twitchett, *Perspectives on the T'ang.*

2. Edward Schafer makes this point in "The Last Years of Chang'an."

3. These incidents are told in *Sui shu* (Sui history) and are summarized in Xiong, "Re-evaluation of the Naba-Chen Theory," p. 148. Suggested reasons for the move south and east of the old Han city include the decay of old buildings, some of which had been used during the period of Northern and Southern Dynasties, and an intolerable salt content in the water. See also Tanaka Tan, "Zuicho kenchikusha sekkei to kōshō."

4. The dimensions of the city and streets are even more staggering when one considers Xiong Cunrui's comparison of its area to Byzantine Constantinople (which was one-sixth the area of Daxing) or Edward Schafer's comparison of street width to Fifth Avenue in New York City (which is only 100 feet, or about 30 meters). See Xiong, "Re-evaluation of the Naba-Chen Theory," p. 152, and Schafer, "The Last Years of Chang'an," p. 137.

5. The most useful bibliography for Daxing–Chang'an is Wei Shu, *Liangjing xinji;* Xu Pingfang, "Tangdai liangjing de zhengzhi"; Su Bai, "Sui–Tang Chang'an cheng"; Satō's article in Ueda, *Tojō;* the numerous articles by Ma Dezhi; and Hang Dezhou et al., "Tang Chang'an Cheng."

6. For sources of the association between the hexagram *qian* from the *Yi jing* (Book of changes) and Daxing see Xiong, "Re-evaluation of the Naba-Chen Theory," p. 149. Debate about the relevance of these passages and the strength of association between Chinese geomancy and the city persists. The famous dissenting opinion was published by Naba Toshisada in his "Shina shuto keikaku" and was later discussed by Chen Yinke in *Sui-Tang zhidu.*

7. On the Tang market system see Denis Twitchett, "Merchant, Trade and Government in Late T'ang" and "The T'ang Market System."

8. Few names of Chinese builders or planners survive. For those of Sui–Tang see Tanaka, "Zuicho kenchikusha." A few others are found in the general works Li Fang, *Zhongguo yishujia zhenglie,* and the six-part study by Liang Qixiong et al., "Zhejiang lu." On Yuwen Kai see Xiong, "Re-evaluation of the Naba-Chen Theory," esp. pp. 147–158.

9. This distance is given in *Henan zhi, juan* 3, p. 13. The move from the Han–Wei site has also been attributed to salt content in the water. See Tonami in Ueda, *Tojō,* pp. 322–323.

10. *Henan zhi, juan* 3, p. 13. There seems to be a misprint in the dimension of the north wall, which is given as 70 plus, instead of what should be 10 plus, *li.* On archaeology at Sui–Tang Luoyang, see the article by Su Bai.

11. In the plans from *Yongle dadian* different offices are indicated in the administrative-city sectors in the Sui and the Tang plans of Luoyang.

12. Plans from *Henan zhi* published in Zuo Ming's *"Yongle dadian"* provide hall names not printed in the original *Yongle dadian*.

13. Details of the excavation of Daming Gong are published in Ma Dezhi, *Tang Chang'an Daming Gong,* and Ma Dezhi, "Yijiuwushijiu- yijiuliushi-nian Tang Daming Gong fajue." On specific buildings of Daming Gong see Liu and Fu, "Linde Dian"; Guo Yifu, "Hanyuan Dian"; Fu Xinian, "Tang Chang'an Daming Gong Hanyuan Dian"; Fu Xinian, "Tang Chang'an Daming Gong Xuanwu Men"; and Yang Hongxun, *Jianzhu kaoguxue lunwen ji,* pp. 234–252.

14. These are the numbers given by Fukuyama Toshio in Hiraoka and Komai, *Chōan to Rakuyō,* vol. 7, p. 43.

15. On Mizong Hall of Qinglong Si see "Tang Qinglong Si yizhi"; "Tang Qinglong Si yizhi tacha jilue"; Yang Hongxun, "Tang Chang'an Qinglong Si"; Ma Dezhi in *Zhongguo kaoguxue yanjiu,* pp. 277–285; and Yang Hongxun, *Jianzhu kaoguxue lunwen ji,* pp. 210–233.

16. See Fu Xinian in *Wenwu yu kaogu lunji,* pp. 322–343.

17. For a discussion of some of these capitals see Paul Wheatley and Thomas See, *From Court to Capital,* esp. pp. 103–109.

18. On the theoretical reconstruction of Naniwa see Nakao Yoshiharu in Ueda, *Tojō,* pp. 55–97.

19. On this point see Kishi in Ueda, *Tojō,* pp. 99–139.

20. Takeda Yūkichi, ed., *Nihon shoki,* vol. 6, bk. 29, no. 63, p. 85, and no. 109, p. 116. For a translation of the relevant passages see W. G. Aston, *Nihongi,* vol. 2, pp. 344 and 362. Sixteen years earlier, in 667, a capital had been built at Ōtsu.

21. Ueda, *Tojō,* p. 88, has a reconstruction of Naniwa showing the combined work of six scholars.

22. Wooden tallies excavated near the northern city boundary say that Fujiwara-kyō had a back garden. See Kishi in Ueda, *Tojō,* p. 109.

23. In addition to articles by Kishi and Satō in *Tojō,* see Tsuboi, *Heizei-kyū seki* for more information about the Heijō capital.

24. See Tsuboi, *Heizei-kyū seki,* pp. 29–31; for a model of the gate see the first plate in the book.

25. On the Nagaoka and Kuni capitals see articles by Ashikaga and Nakayama in Ueda, *Tojō.* Emperor Shōmu also had a detached palace at Shigaraki from which he governed, but the place was never designated a capital *(kyō).*

26. These dimensions have been calculated from the presumed positions of the Kamo and other rivers. Justification for the figures is presented by Ashikaga in Ueda, *Tojō,* pp. 205–225. On the Heian capital see also Nakayama in Ueda, *Tojō,* pp. 227–253.

27. Saichō, Kūkai, and Ennin were several of the famous monks who traveled in China during the Tang period. On Kūkai see Yoshito Hakeda, *Kūkai: Major Works.* On Ennin's travel account see Edwin Reischauer, *Ennin's Travels in T'ang China.*

28. Su Bai proposes approximately the same eight points in "Sui–Tang Chang'an Cheng he Luoyang Cheng," p. 421.

29. Kishi Toshio in Ueda, *Tojō,* pp. 99–139.

30. Wang, "Guanyu Riben guducheng," gives strong support to the theory of Tang origins for the Japanese capitals discussed in this chapter and sharply attacks Kishi Toshio's argument for Northern Wei Luoyang as the source of the Japanese city plans.

31. This feature is shown on the map published by Wang Zhongshu in "Guanyu Riben guducheng," p. 354.

32. On the Bohai capital see Chen Xianchang, "Tangdai Bohai Shangjing," and Harada and Komai, *Tung-ching-ch'eng.* The title of Harada and Komai's work reflects the fact that when the capital was "rediscovered" during the Qing dynasty it was referred to by the city's name in the tenth to twelfth centuries under Liao rule: Dongjing Cheng, or eastern capital.

33. These dimensions are published in Chen, "Tangdai Bohai Shangjing," p. 87. Dong Jianhong gives the figures 4,500 by 3,300 meters in *Zhongguo chengshi,* p. 36.

34. On Pyongyang and its palace-city see Nagashima, "Kokuri no tojō."

35. On Yingcheng Lu see Li Yiyou, "Yuan Yingchang Lu gucheng diaocha ji."

36. Naba Toshisada, "Shina shuto keikaku shijō yori kōsatsu shitaru Tō no Chōanjō." Chen Yinke's idea about Pingcheng appears in *Sui-Tang zhidu,* p. 64.

37. Mori, "Hoku Ki Rakuyō."

38. Komai has published this idea in several places. One of the most accessible is *Chūgoku no tojō,* pp. 9–10 and 15.

39. These ideas are summarized in Tanaka, "Zuicho kenchikusha," pp. 227–229. I have also mentioned them in "The Plan of Khubilai Khan's Imperial City," p. 150.

CHAPTER 6

1. On the names and locations of the Bohai capitals see Komai, *Chūgoku no tojō,* pp. 203–211, and Wei Zuncheng, "Bohai chengzhi." In addition to Chang'an and Luoyang, the cities of Taiyuan, Chengdu, Tingfu Zhou, Fengxiang, and Xingzhou served as capitals during the Tang dynasty.

2. The most extensive Western-language study of Liao history and culture is Karl Wittfogel and Feng Chia-sheng, *History of Chinese Society: Liao*. A good Chinese source is Shu, *Qidan shehui jingji shigao*. Information on each of the five capitals is found in both, as well as in works by Murata, Takeshima, Tamura, and Zhu Qiqian listed in the References.

3. Probably because of the shape of the southeastern and southwestern portions of the southern city of Shangjing, each author has given slightly different dimensions for the lengths of its walls. The figures used here are taken from Japanese excavation reports. The most recent Chinese publication, however, Dong's *Zhongguo chengshi*, p. 58, uses the much longer lengths of 2,000 by 2,200 meters for the north city and 2,200 by 1,400 meters for the south city.

4. On the implications of Hancheng see Yao, *Dongbeishi luncong,* pp. 193–216. Among the non-Khitan population of Hancheng at Shangjing were Uygurs and Bohai. Uygur merchants were clustered east of the south wall gates, according to the *Liao shi*. On this point see Murata, *Chūgoku no teito,* p. 132.

5. The city was aligned 30 degrees east of due north, and the main halls should have had the same alignment.

6. Chen, *Qidan shehui jingji shigao,* pp. 92–93, whose source is *Liao shi, Dili zhi,* and Murata, *Chūgoku no teito,* p. 139.

7. Tamura, *Chūgoku seifuku ōchō,* vol. 1, pp. 342–345.

8. Important information on the Liao southern capital was published in Zhu Qiqian, "Liao-Jin Yanjing." In certain instances more recent research has contradicted Zhu's work. Concerning the outer wall perimeter of the city, for instance, Chen Lu, in "Liao Yuzhou shi," believes the 36 *li* figure given in *Liao shi, Dili zhi,* and used by Zhu, is inaccurate; following the account of a Song official, he uses the dimension 25 *li*. More recently the figure has been amended to 27 *li*. See Chen Gaohua, *Yuan Dadu,* p. 5.

9. The Liao capital was built on the ruins of a Tang city which had itself suffered attack during the period of the Five Dynasties. It is uncertain which old halls used by the Liao had been damaged during the post-Tang conflagration.

10. For more about it see Sekino and Takeshima, *Ryō-Kin jidai no kenchiku to sono Butsuzō,* pp. 303–307, and Tokiwa and Sekino, *Shina Bukkyō shiseki,* p. 226.

11. Both Murata, *Chūgoku no teito,* pp. 140–141, and Chen, *Qidan shehui,* p. 89, make this point about Zhongjing.

12. These dimensions are published in Tamura, *Chūgoku seifuku ōchō,* vol. 1, p. 336. Different figures are published in a brief note on the city in *Wenwu* no. 2 (1960), p. 77. The Chinese measurements are the ones used by Chen in *Qidan shehui,* p. 90. Since no plan accompanies Chen's report, Tamura's plan is used together with his dimensions here. Zhongjing is one of several cities discussed in this book which has been excavated by teams of different nationalities at different times. Often the more recent Chinese reports, which may or may not be the results of further excavation, do not recognize earlier material published during the Japanese occupation. The Liao and Jin cities north or northeast of Beijing are the most problematic in this regard; in this book, a studied decision has been made city by city as to which scholarship, combined with excavation, is most accurate.

13. Tamura, *Chūgoku seifuku ōchō,* vol. 1, p. 333.

14. For general information on the Liao western capital see Chen, *Qidan shehui,* pp. 95–96. On the architecture of Xijing see Liang Sicheng, "Datong gujianzhu."

15. On the rise of the Jurchen see A. P. Okladinov, *The Soviet Far East in Antiquity,* and Tao Jing-shen, *The Jurchen.*

16. The excavation reports for Jin Shangjing are listed in the References. Susan Bush discusses the Soviet and Japanese findings and the debate over wall construction order at the Jin upper capital in "Archeological Remains of the Chin Dynasty." A later study is Sun Zhanwen, "Bai Cheng kaogu," based on a report in *Heilongjiang ribao,* 14 October 1962.

17. Torii Ryūzo believes the building order to have been the reverse.

18. Tao Jing-shen, *The Jurchen,* p. 31.

19. Dong Jianhong, *Zhongguo chengshi,* p. 68, whose source is *Da Jin Guo zhi*. In the recorded history of Liao and Jin, the Song capital Bianliang is the most often mentioned model for imperial urbanism. This fact is evidence that the Chinese imperial city functioned as a symbol and means of legitimation for conquest dynasties.

20. On the names and building dates of the hall see Sonoda, "Kin no Jō-kyō shi"; dimensions are provided on pp. 428–429.

21. They are listed in discussions of the Jin eastern capital—including Murata, *Chūgoku no teito,* p. 150; Li Jiafu, *Zhongguo jianzhu,* p. 145; and Tamura, *Chūgoku seifuku ōchō,* vol. 2, pp. 327–330.

22. These are discussed in Sekino and Takeshima, *Ryō-Kin jidai no kenchiku.*

23. Murata, *Chūgoku no teito,* pp. 150–151. Li Jiafu, *Zhongguo jianzhu,* p. 145, says no new structures were built, but he does not give the source of his information.

24. Zhu Qiqian, "Liao–Jin Yanjing." For a recent study of Zhongdu see Yan Wenru, "Jin Zhongdu" and *Beijing Shi,* pp. 82–96.

25. The sources available on Jin Zhongdu do not clearly state whether the palace-city was enclosed by a wall or by

what we might think of as a covered corridor. As a result of ambiguous sources, plans for both types of cities can be found. Hou and Wu, "Tian'an Men," p. 4, published the plan of the city with three walls used here. Dong, *Zhongguo chengshi,* p. 61, shows the city with two walls but on p. 62 uses a tri-walled city plan. Chen Gaohua, *Yuan Dadu,* p. 15; He, *Kaogong ji,* p. 6; Yan, "Jin Zhongdu," p. 8; and Hou, "The Transformation of the Old City of Beijing, China," p. 221, all publish plans with two walls. In the following paragraph I refer to the second enclosure from the outside as the imperial-city.

26. Several dimensions have been proposed for the perimeter of Jin Zhongdu. In 1933 Zhu Qiqian used the figure 36 *li* in "Liao–Jin Nanjing," pp. 65–66. A critique of the article, published by Liang Sicheng, "Review of Zhu Qiqian," presented textual evidence for measurements of both 25 *li* and 36 *li* but believed 25 *li* to be more accurate. That dimension was published by Zhu in "Jin Zhongdu," p. 69. Most recently, in "Tian'an Men," p. 4, Hou and Wu used the dimension 36 *li* 7 *bu,* based on a measurement published in Yan, "Jin Zhongdu," p. 9. The dimension generally used for the Zhongdu imperial-city is 9 *li* 30 *bu.* The source of this measurement is *Jinlu tu jing,* a section of *Lanben lu.*

27. Zhu published an updated version of Figure 116 in his "Jin Zhongdu." The details of the map are almost illegible in the article.

28. Fu Xinian, "Shanxi Sheng Fanshi Xian Yanshan Si."

29. Zhu Qiqian, "Liao–Jin Yanjing," pp. 65–66 and 72–73.

30. At the time of repair under Jin Emperor Shizong (r. 1161–1190) a new rectangular walled area called Xiao Chengzi (Little City) was built east of Shangjing. Xiao Chengzi is discussed in Sonoda, "Kin no Jō-kyō shi," pp. 439–441, where a plan with its main buildings is included, and in Sun Zhanwen, "Bai Cheng kaogu," p. 86.

31. The Tangut city Khara-Khoto was excavated in 1908–1909 and published by P. K. Kozlov in *Mongoliia i Amdo i mert'i gorod Khara-khoto* (German trans., *Mongolei, Amdo und die tote Staat Chara-Choto*). The city was visited several times by Sir Aurel Stein, whose findings are published in *Innermost Asia,* vol. 1, pp. 429–506. Other references to Khara-Khoto are Chen Bingying, "Xi Xia xiujian"; E. I. Lubo-Lesnichenko, "Istoriko-Arkheologicheskoe izuchenie g. Khara-Khoto"; and Guo and Li, "Nei Menggu Heicheng."

32. Guo and Li, "Nei Menggu Heicheng," p. 3. Dong, *Zhongguo chengshi,* gives the dimensions as approximately 500 by 364.4 meters.

33. For a plan of Bukhara in the ninth to tenth centuries see

A. M. Belenitskii, I. B. Bentovich, and O. G. Bol'shakov, *Srednevekovyi gorod Srednei Azii,* p. 243.

CHAPTER 7

1. In Song times, the primary capital Bianzhou, or Bianliang, was the eastern one. The Song western capital was Luoyang, the southern capital Yingtian Fu, and the northern capital Daming Fu.

2. Meng Yuanlao, *Dongjing menghua lu,* p. 26.

3. E. Reischauer and J. K. Fairbank, *East Asia: The Great Tradition,* p. 220.

4. Denis Twitchett, "Merchant, Trade and Government in Late T'ang" and "The T'ang Market System."

5. On the Song commercial system and resulting social changes see Shiba Yoshinobu, *Commerce and Society in Sung China.*

6. Dong Jianhong, *Zhongguo chengshi,* p. 53. Robert Hartwell has estimated the population of Bianliang in the year 1078 as between seven hundred fifty thousand and one million. See Hartwell, "A Cycle of Economic Change," pp. 125–126.

7. Edward Kracke, "Sung K'ai-feng."

8. Xu Song, ed., *Song huiyao jigao, juan* 188/8a.

9. He Yeju published the plan with three concentric walls in *Kaogong ji,* p. 8. This plan is especially questionable, for he cites *Song huiyao jigao* as one of his sources.

10. This plan is published in Skinner, *The City in Late Imperial China,* p. 61.

11. On this monastery see Alexander Soper, "Hsiang-kuo ssu," whose discussion relies heavily on Meng, *Dongjing menghua lu;* see also Xu Pingfang, "Bei Song Kaifeng Da Xiangguo Si pingmian fuyuan tushuo."

12. James T. C. Liu, "The Sung Emperors and the *ming-t'ang* or Hall of Enlightenment."

13. Numerous versions of the painting exist. On "Qingming shanghe tu" see Roderick Whitfield, "Chang Tse-tuan's *Ch'ing-ming shang-ho t'u,*" and his dissertation of the same title.

14. This event is recorded in Wang Mingqing, *Huizhu lu,* pp. 300–301.

15. Zhu Qiqian, "Liao-Jin Yanjing," pp. 56–66 and 72–73.

16. Hou and Wu, "Tian'an Men," p. 4.

17. Works by these scholars about Hangzhou during the Southern Song are listed in the References.

18. Zhou Cong, ed., *Qiandao Lin'an zhi, juan* 2, pp. 21–22.

19. Jacques Gernet, *Daily Life in China on the Eve of the Mongol Invasion,* p. 25.

20. A. C. Moule, *Quinsai*, pp. 3–11.

21. Every writer on Lin'an has been impressed with its fire prevention program. Marco Polo's description is found in Moule and Pelliot, *Marco Polo*, p. 332. Gernet writes about it in *Daily Life*, pp. 34–38. The rest of Marco Polo's description of the city can be found in Moule and Pelliot, *Marco Polo*, pp. 326–345.

22. Moule points out that by the time Marco Polo visited Lin'an, after the fall of the Song to the Mongols, the outer wall was gone. He emphasizes the Mongolian policy of settlement, even of cities, without walls, symbolizing the vast unboundedness of the Mongolian empire. Many cities used and built by the Mongols did have walls, however; three of these cities are discussed below.

23. Dong, *Zhongguo chengshi*, p. 56.

24. *Lin'an zhi* was issued three times during the Southern Song dynasty: during the Qiandao (1165–1173), Shunyou (1249–1252), and Xianshun (1265–1274) reigns. The drawings published in the nineteenth century reissue of the last Song version of the local record are believed to be based on manuscript plans stored in the library of Ding Bing at Hangzhou. In the mid-twentieth century the plans were thought to be in Nanjing and may have been transferred from there to Taiwan. On this point see Moule, "Marco Polo's Description of Quinsai," p. 108, and Moule, *Quinsai*, p. 12.

25. In 1817 Jean-Pièrre Abel-Rémusat suggested a possible location for Khara-Khorum in a paper entitled, "Recherches sur la ville de Kara-Korum." It was published seven years later in *Histoire et mémoires de l'Institut Royal de France*, vol. 7.

26. Their findings are published in A. M. Pozdniev, *Mongolia i Mongoliĭ*, and V. V. Radlov, *Atlas der Alterthümer der Mongolei*. The identification of the site was in part due to careful reading of the travel account of Friar William of Rubruck, from which a passage is quoted below, and the Persian *Jamī 'al-Tavārīkh* of Rashīd al-Dīn, relevant sections of which are available in English in John A. Boyle, *The Successors of Genghis Khan*, pp. 61–62. On the accuracy of the early excavations see Sergei Kiselev, *Drevnemongol'skie goroda*, p. 132.

27. Paul Pelliot, "Note sur Karakorum." Francis Cleaves found more evidence for the Chinggisid history of Khara-Khorum in a Sino-Mongolian stele of 1346, the translation of which he published in "The Sino-Mongolian Inscription of 1346."

28. W. W. Rockhill, trans., *The Journey of William of Rubruck*, pp. 221–222.

29. Kiselev's *Drevnemongol'skie goroda* is still the latest Soviet word on Khara-Khorum, esp. pp. 132–184. Most of the material in the following paragraph is taken from it. For more on Khara-Khorum and other cities built by the Mongols in the thirteenth and fourteenth centuries see my "Imperial Architecture Along the Mongolian Road to Dadu."

30. Rockhill, *William of Rubruck*, pp. 209–210.

31. Kiselev, *Drevnemongol'skie goroda*, p. 142.

32. Ibid., p. 164.

33. Details about Shangdu are taken from Harada and Komai, *Jōto*; Impey, "Shang-tu"; Ishida, "Gen no Jōto"; and Jia, "Yuan Shangdu."

34. Liang Qixiong et al., "Zhejiang Lu" (1930), p. 158. On the painting of Wang Zhenpeng see Marsha Smith Weidner, "Painting and Patronage at the Mongol Court of China: 1260–1368," pp. 132–176.

35. Zhou Boqi's writings are found in *Shangjingyi congshu.*

36. Ishida, "Gen no Jōto," p. 291.

37. Jia, "Yuan Shangdu."

38. Hok-lam Chan, "Liu Ping-chung," p. 107, and Nogami Shunsei, "Gen no Jōto no Bukkyō."

39. One example of this type of pagoda is the Great Pagoda of Daming Cheng, published in Takeshima and Sekino, *Ryō-Kin jidai*, vol. 2, pp. 22–29.

40. Moule and Pelliot, *Marco Polo*, pp. 185–186.

41. Wang Shidian, *Jin bian, juan* 1/17b.

42. Ishida, "Gen no Jōto," p. 290.

43. Yule and Cordier, *Cathay and the Way Thither*, vol. 3, p. 116. Rashīd's source of information about Khara-Khorum and Shangdu is Juvaynī's thirteenth-century *History of the World Conqueror* (in Persian), translated by J. A. Boyle.

44. Marco Polo wrote that Khubilai spent only June, July, and August in Shangdu, but according to Paul Ratchnevsky, "Über den mongolischen Kult," p. 426 and n. 48, the Khan spent as many as six months at the northern capital.

45. I have discussed Liu's role in the planning of Dadu in "The Plan of Khubilai Khan's Imperial City."

46. The jut in the southern outer wall of Dadu is much more apparent in the plan of the city published in Hou and Wu, "Tian'an Men," p. 5.

47. On the streets and wards of Dadu see Xu Pingfang, "Gudai Beijing de chengshi guihua," pp. 118–119, and Wang Biwen, "Yuan Dadu chengfang kao."

48. Polo wrote that the city had twelve outer-wall gates, a number presumably based on his firsthand experience at the east, south, or west face. (See Moule and Pelliot, *Marco Polo*, p. 212.) Friar Odoric of Pordenone, who was in Dadu in the fourteenth century, wrote the same thing. (See Yule and Cordier, *Cathay and the Way Thither*, vol. 2, p. 217.) The latter account may be based on Odoric's knowledge of Marco Polo's text.

49. Moule and Pelliot, *Marco Polo*, pp. 212–213. The "palaces" which Polo mentions in the first part of the description are gate-towers with palatial-style roofs.

50. The most important studies of Dadu based on excavation are "Yuan Dadu de kancha"; Zhao Zhengzhi (posthumous), "Yuan Dadu"; Hou and Wu, "Tian'an Men"; Hou, "Yuan Dadu Cheng"; and Chen Gaohua, *Yuan Dadu*.

51. Khubilai died in Zitan (Purple Sandalwood) Hall of the Yude palace complex on 18 February 1294, according to Song Lian, ed., *Yuan shi, juan* 17, p. 376.

52. Yule and Cordier, *Cathay and the Way Thither*, vol. 2, pp. 218–219.

53. Xiao Xun's text, *Gugong yi lu*, is one of two essential primary sources for a study of the Dadu imperial buildings and their decoration. The second is *juan* 21 of Tao Zongyi's (1346–1415) *Zhuogeng lu*, published in 1366.

54. Xiao Xun, *Gugong yi lu*, p. 1. I have used this paragraph and others in an attempt to reconstruct Yuan halls in "Toward the Definition of a Yuan Dynasty Hall."

55. Paul Ratchnevsky discusses some of the steppe practices maintained by the imperial Mongols in "Über den mongolischen Kult." The more sinified Manchu government of China, beginning in the seventeenth century, also retained some native rites.

56. Tao Zongyi, *Zhuogeng lu, juan* 21, pp. 251 and 253, writes that yellow skins of a feline were hung at Daming Hall and ermine skins were suspended from the wall of a small hall behind it.

57. This is the position presented in my "Plan of Khubilai Khan's Imperial City" and "Why Were Chang'an and Beijing So Different?"

58. Tao Zongyi, *Zhuogeng lu, juan* 1, pp. 15–16.

59. The first Ancestral Temple at Dadu was ordered to be built in 1263 and begun in 1264. Sacrifices at the Altars of Soil and Grain were ordered in 1271 but were not enacted until 1293. See Song Lian, ed., *Yuan Shi, juan* 76, pp. 1879–1880.

60. Hou Renzhi's writings explain that an adequate water supply channeled from the west and flowing around the imperial-city was probably the prime motivation for the location of the Dadu imperial-city.

CHAPTER 8

1. Zhu Xie, *Jinling guji tukao*, p. 191.

2. F. W. Mote, "The Transformation of Nanking," p. 136. Mote's figure, about 37 kilometers, is based on a U.S. Army survey.

3. Information for this paragraph is drawn primarily from Zhu Xie, *Jinling guji tukao*, pp. 191–195, and L. Gaillard, *Nankin*, pp. 156–188. Zhu's bibliography, found on pp. 2–10 of his book, contains a number of items not available to me.

4. Mote, "The Transformation of Nanking," pp. 132 and 138.

5. The population given in Dong, *Zhongguo chengshi*, p. 74, is over 473,000.

6. L. J. Gallagher, *China in the Sixteenth Century*, p. 269.

7. E. Farmer, *Early Ming Government*, p. 178.

8. Ibid., pp. 45–46.

9. Ibid., pp. 49–51.

10. On Fengyang see Matsumoto, "Mindai Chūto."

11. Since it is nearly impossible to give any sort of complete reference list for Beijing, only recent and general books, or those especially helpful to this author, are provided in the References.

12. Jin Shoushen, "The Eight Armed Nezha," *Beijing Legends*, pp. 7–17. This legend was also the subject of a lecture by Chan Hok-lam at the Princeton East Asia Colloquium in April 1986. I would like to thank Professor Chan for sending me a forthcoming article on the subject.

13. On this point—and the general issue of water and its relation to planning in Beijing—see Hou, "Beijing dushi fazhan."

14. Yang Boda and Weng Wen-go, *Peking*, p. 78.

15. The original intent of the sixteenth-century enlargement of Beijing was to extend the outer wall northeast and northwest of its present position, once again forming a rectangular outer enclosure. The city today has an inverted T-shape because the government ran out of funds before the planned wall could be completed.

16. A general discussion and illustrations of Shenyang are available in Ye, *Zhongguo jianzhu shi*, vol. 2, pp. 839–845.

17. Many of them are published in Osvald Siren, *The Walls and Gates of Peking*.

18. J. B. Du Halde, *Description . . . de la Chine*, pp. 135–136.

19. For Ming-period illustrations of these halls see Shan Shiyuan, "Mingdai yingzao shiliao: Tian Tan."

20. On this point see Jeffrey Meyer, *Peking as a Sacred City*, pp. 98–107.

21. On the lunar lodges see Edward Schafer, *Pacing the Void*.

22. Wu, "Tian'an Men guangchang." Other articles especially pertinent to the planning of Beijing after 1949 are Hou and Wu, "Tian'an Men"; Hou, "Beijing Cheng lishi fazhan"; Zhang, "Cong Beijing Cheng de lishi"; and Wu, "Beijing Shi guihua."

23. The monuments and neighborhoods are discussed in Zhang, "Cong Beijing Cheng de lishi."

GLOSSARY

The following list of Chinese, Japanese, and Korean terms does not include names of dynasties or rulers. Only the names of authors or titles that appear in the text are included; other authors and titles are listed in the References. If the same romanized term is used for two different characters, the term is listed in the order that it appears in the text.

An 安
Anhag 安鶴
Anji 安濟
Anle 安樂
Anyang 安陽
Anyi 安邑
Asuka 飛鳥

Baicheng 白城
Baima Si 白馬寺
Ban Gu 班固
Banpo 半坡
bao 保
Baohe 保和
Bei 北
Bei Qi shu 北齊書
Beidu 北都
Beijing 北京
Beiping 北平
Bencheng 本城
Bi Yong 辟雍
Bi Yuan 畢沅
Bianjing 汴京
Bianliang 汴梁
Bianzhou 汴州
Biao 彪
Bo 亳
bō 坊
Bohai 渤海
Bolin Si 柏林寺
bu 步

Cao Cao 曹操
Cao Pi 曹丕
Chang'an 長安
Chang'an Xian zhi 長安縣志
Chang'an zhi (tu) 長安志(圖)
Changle 長樂
Changsha 長沙

chao 朝
Chen 陳
Chen Yinke 陳寅恪
cheng 城
Cheng Wang 成王
Chengdu 成都
Chenghuang Miao 城隍廟
Chengtian 承天
chengwai 城外
Chengzhou 成周
Chengziyai 城子崖
Chetuala 赫圖阿拉
chi 尺
chi 池
Chōdō-in 朝堂院
Chōshū-den 朝集殿
Chu 楚
Chun Qiu 春秋

Da 大
Da Jin guo zhi 大金國志
Da Ming 大明
Da Qing 大清
Da'an (Ge) 大安(閣)
Dacheng 大成
dacheng 大城
Dading Fu 大定府
Dadu 大都
Daigoku-den 大極殿
dairi 大裏
Daming (Fu) 大明(府)
Daming Gong 大明宮
danei 大內
Danyang 丹陽
Dasi 大祀
Datong 大同
Deyang 德陽
Di Tan 地壇
Ding 丁
Ding Bing 丁丙

diqu 地區
Dong Jianhong 董鑒泓
Dongjing (Cheng)
　東京(城)
Dongjing menghua lu
　東京夢華錄
du 都
Duan 端
Dunhuang 敦煌

Ennin 圓仁
Epang 阿房
Erlitou 二里頭

Fan Chengda 范成大
Fan Ye 范曄
fang 坊
fang 放
Feng 豐
Fengchu 鳳雛
fenghuang 鳳凰
fengshui 風水
Fengyang 鳳陽
fu 府
fu 賦
Fujiwara 藤原
Fuzhou 福州

Gao Jiong 高熲
Gao Longcha 高隆叉
Geng 耿
Geng Jicai 庚秀才
genyue 艮嶽
gong 宮
gong 工
gongcheng 宮城
Gu Yanwu 顧炎武
Guai 拐
guan 觀
Guandi 關帝
Guangji Si 廣濟寺
Guangyang 廣陽
Guangyuan 廣園
Guangzhou 廣州
Guanzhong 關中
Guanzhong tengji tukao
　關中勝蹟圖考

Gui 桂
guicheng 龜城
gulou 鼓樓
guo 郭
Guozi Jian 國子監

Han jiu yi 漢舊儀
Hancheng 漢城
Handan 邯鄲
hangtu 奮土
Hangzhou 杭州
Hanlin 翰林
Hanyuan 今元
Hao (capital) 鎬
Hao (pond) 滈
Hao (river) 鄗
Harbin 哈尔滨
He Chou 何稠
Heian-kyō 平安京
Heicheng 黑城
Heijō-kyō 平城京
Helong Zigan 賀龍子幹
Henan zhi 河南志
hou gong 後宮
Hou Han shu 後漢書
Houma 候馬
Hu Qianying 胡謙盈
Huai 淮
huangcheng 皇城
Huangji 黃集
Huayan Si 華嚴寺
Huguo Si 護國寺
hutong 胡同

Ikaruga 斑鳩
Ishida Mikinosuke
　石田幹之助

Ji 薊
Ji Tan 稷壇
jian 間
Jian 鉄
Jiang 姜
Jiang 江
Jiangling 江陵
Jiangnan 江南
Jiangning Fu zhi 江寧府志

jiangren 匠人
Jiankang 建廉
Jiankang yi lu 建廉遺錄
Jianye 建業
Jianzhang 建章
Jiefan 界凡
Jin 晉
Jin 金
Jin bian 禁扁
Jin shi 金史
Jin shu 晉書
jing 京
Jing Shan 景山
jingshi 京市
Jinling 金陵
Jinling guji tukao
　金陵古蹟圖考
Jinling xin zhi 金陵新志
Jinshui 金水
Jinyang 晉陽
Jinyong Cheng 金鏞城
jō 條
jō 条
jō 坊
jun 郡

Kaifeng 開風
Kaiping Fu 開平府
Kamo 鴨
kanyu 堪輿
Kaogong ji 考工記
Kishi Toshio 岸俊男
Koguryŏ 高句麗
Komai Kazuchika
　駒井和愛
Kong Yanzhou 孔彥舟
Kuizhang Ge 奎章閣
Kūkai 空海
Kuni-kyō 恭仁京
Kunming 昆明
Kyōto 京都

li 里
li 闤
Li Daoyuan 酈道元
Li Haowen 李好文
Li ji 禮記

Liang 梁
Liang Hanchen 梁漢臣
Liao shi 遼史
Liaoyang 遼陽
licheng 裏城
Lin Zixu 林則徐
Lin'an 臨安
Lin'an zhi 臨安志
Linde 麟德
ling 陵
Ling Tai 靈台
Lingbi 靈璧
Lingguang 靈光
Linhao 臨濠
Linhuang 臨潢
Linzi 臨淄
Lishan 驪山
Liu Bang 劉邦
Liu Bingzhong 劉秉忠
Liu Jingyang 劉敬陽
Liu Long 劉龍
Longcheng 龍城
Longquan Fu 龍泉府
Longshou 龍首
lu 路
(*lü*) *li* 閭閭
Lü 魯
Lü Dafang 呂大防
Lu Yanlun 盧彥倫
Luo 洛
luocheng 羅城
Luoyang 洛陽
Luoyang qielan ji
　洛陽伽藍記
Luoyi 洛邑
Lüshi Chun Qiu 呂氏春秋

mamian 馬面
Mang 邙
Mao Zedong 毛澤東
miao 廟
Miao Changyan 廟昌言
Miaoying 妙應
Ming Tang 明堂
Minghuang Gong 明廣宮
Mingjiao 明教
Mingshi lu 明史錄

Miyazaki Ichisada 宮崎市定
Mizong 密宗
Moling 秣陵
Mori Shikazō 森鹿三
Mudan 牡丹

Naba Toshisada 那波利貞
Nagaoka 長岡
Naniwa 難波
Nanjing 南京
nei 內
neicheng 內城
Nihon shoki 日本書紀
Nihongi 日本紀
Ningshou 寧壽
Niucun 牛村
Nongye Tan 農業壇
Nüzhen 女真

Panlongcheng 盘龍城
Pingcheng 平城
Pingquan 平泉
Pingshan 平山
Pingyang 平陽
Pyongyang 平壤

Qi 齊
qian 乾
Qian Han shu 前漢書
qianbulang 千步廊
qianchao, houqin 前朝後寢
Qianling 乾陵
Qianyuan Si 乾元寺
qin 寢
Qin 秦
Qinglong Si 青龍寺
Qingming 清明
Qingyuan 慶元
Qionghua 瓊花
Qufu 曲阜
Qujiang 曲江

Rangguo 襄國
Renmin Dahui Tang
  人民大會堂
Renzheng 仁政
Ri Tan 日壇

Sa'erhu 撒爾滸
Saichō 最澄
san jingdu tizhi 三京都體制
San Tai 三台
Sancai tuhui 三才圖會
Sanfuhuang tu 三輔廣圖
Sanli tu 三禮圖
Shangdu 上都
Shangjing 上京
Shanglin Yuan 上林苑
Shanhua Si 善化寺
shaocheng 少城
She Tan 社壇
shendao 神道
sheng 省
Shengle 盛樂
Shenlong 神龍
Shenwu 神武
Shenyang 盛陽
Shenyang tongzhi 盛陽通志
shi 市
Shi Huangdi 始皇帝
Shi ji 史記
Shi jing 詩經
Shigaraki 滋賀
Shilin guangji 事林廣記
shou 收
Shoukang 壽康
Shu 蜀
Shu jing 書經
Shu jing tu shuo 書經圖說
Shudu fu 蜀都賦
Shui jing zhu tu 水經注圖
Shuijing 水晶
si 寺
si'he yuan 四合院
sishen 四神
Song 宋
Song huiyao jigao
  宋會要輯稿
Song Minqiu 宋敏求
Sonoda Kazuki 園田一龜
Su Bai 宿白
Su Wei 蘇威
Sun Yat-sen (Zhongshan)
  孫中山
Suzaku 朱雀

Ta Zurong 大祚榮
Tai Miao 太廟
taicheng 太城
Taichu Gong 太初宮
Taihe 太和
Taiji 太極
Taishen 台神
Taiye Chi 太液池
Tang liangjing chengfang kao
  唐兩京城坊考
Tian Tan 天壇
Tian'an 天安
Tianwen 天文
Tongtai 同泰
Tongtian 通天
Tongwan 統萬
Tongyue 銅樂
Tuoba 拓跋

waicheng 外城
Wang Shidian 王士點
Wang Shimin 王世民
Wang Wencai 王文才
Wang Zhenpeng 王振鵬
Wang Zhongshu 王仲殊
wangcheng 王城
Wanshou Shan 萬壽山
Wei 渭
Wei 魏
Wei shu 魏書
Weiyang Gong 未央宮
wen 文
Wen xuan 文選
Wenchang 文昌
wengcheng 甕城
Wu 吳
wu 武
Wu 午
Wudu fu 吳都賦
Wujing zongyao 武經總要

Xi Xia 西夏
Xia Guo 夏國
Xiadu 下都
xian 縣
Xi'an 西安
Xianbi 鮮卑

Xiancan Tan 先蠶壇
xiang 巷
xiang 鄉
Xiannong Tan 先農壇
Xianshun Lin'an zhi
  咸淳臨安志
Xianyang 咸陽
xiaocheng 小城
Xiao Xun 蕭洵
Xiaotun 小屯
Xibeigang 西北岡
Xichun 熙春
Xijing fu 西京賦
Xinchang 新昌
xinggong 行宮
Xingle Gong 興樂宮
Xingqing Gong 興慶宮
xingzai 行在
Xintian 新田
Xiongnu 匈奴
Xu Han shu 續漢書
Xu Song 徐松

Yamada 山田
Yan 燕
Yang Shoujing 楊守敬
Yang Suo 楊素
Yang Xuanzhi 楊衒之
Yangcheng 陽城
yangma 羊馬
Yangxin 陽新
Yangzhou 楊州
Yanjing 燕京
Yanpi 閻毗
Yanshan 岩山
Yanshi 偃師
Yao Jiazao 樂嘉藻
Ye 業
Ye Dasong 葉大松
Yedu fu 業都賦
Yezhong ji 業中記
yi 邑
Yi 易
Yi jing 易經
Yi Zhou shu 逸周書
Yide 懿德
Yin 殷

Yingchang Lu 應昌路
Yingtian 應天
Yiting 掖庭
Yong'an 永安
Yongding 永定
Yonghe 雍和
Yongle dadian 永樂大典
Yongning 永寧
Yuan 袁
Yuanhe 元和
Yuanzhou 苑州
yudao 御道
Yude 玉德
Yue Tan 月壇
Yuedu 樂都

Yun'gang 雲崗
Yuwen Kai 宇文愷
Yuzhou 渝州

Zao 漕
Zhan Guo ce 戰國策
zhang 丈
Zhang 漳
Zhang Yi 張儀
Zhang Zeduan 張擇端
Zhangye 張掖
Zhao 趙
Zhaoming Gong 昭明宮
Zhe 浙
zhen 鎮

Zhengtian 正天
Zhengyang 正陽
Zhengzhou 鄭州
zhizheng 至正
Zhizheng Jinling xinji
    至正金陵新記
Zhonghe 中和
Zhonghua 中華
Zhongjing 中京
zhonglou 鐘樓
zhongmen 中門
Zhongshan 中山
zhongxin ge 中心閣
zhongxin zhi tai 中心之台
Zhou 周

zhou 州
Zhou Boqi 周伯琦
Zhou Enlai 周恩來
Zhou li 周禮
Zhu Xie 朱偰
Zhu Yuanzhang 朱元章
Zhuque (qiao) 朱雀
zicheng 子城
Zijin Cheng 紫禁城
Zitan 紫壇
Zong Miao 宗廟
Zuo Si (Taichong)
    左思(太沖)
Zuo zhuan 左傳

REFERENCES

ASIAN LANGUAGES

All Chinese names and titles are rendered in *pinyin* with the exception of widely known authors who have published under alternative spellings in the West. In those cases, *pinyin* is provided in brackets. Japanese names and titles are rendered according to the modified Hepburn system. Specific editions or reprints are provided for sources quoted in the text or used for illustrations. For more general references such as dynastic histories, for which many editions are available, only author and title are provided.

Adachi Kiroku 足立喜六. *Chōan shiseki no kenkyū* [Research on the remains of Chang'an] 長安史跡の研究. 2 vols. Tokyo: Tōyō bunko ronshū, 1933.

An Jinhuai 安金槐. "Shilun Zhengzhou Shangdai chengzhi—Aodu" [Discussion of the Shang city Zhengzhou—the Ao capital] 試論鄭州商代城址—隞都. *Wenwu* no. 4/5 (1961): 73–80.

———. "Zhengzhou dichu de gudai yizun jieshao" [Introducing the ancient remains in Zhengzhou] 鄭州地區的古代遺存介紹. *Wenwu* no. 8 (1957): 16–20.

An Zhimin 安志敏. "Yijiuwu'er-nian qiuji Zhengzhou Erligang fajue ji" [Record of the excavation in the spring of 1952 of Erligang material from Zhengzhou] 一九五二年秋季鄭州二里岡發掘記. *Kaogu xuebao* no. 8 (1954): 65–107.

Aoki Tomitaro 青木富太郎. "Gen Daito" [Yuan Dadu] 元大都. *Rekishi kyōiku* 5, no. 7 (1957): 35–41.

Atago Matsuo 愛宕松男. "Gen no Daito" [Yuan Dadu] 元の大都. *Rekishi kyōiku* 14, no. 12 (1966): 59–65.

Ban Gu [32–92] 班固. *Han shu* [History of the Han dynasty] 漢書.

———. "Liangdu fu" [Two capitals rhapsody] 兩都賦. *Wen xuan.*

———. *Qian Han shu* [History of the Former Han dynasty] 前漢書.

Beijing shi [History of Beijing] 北京市. Beijing: Beijing Daxue, 1985.

Bi Yuan [1730–1797] 畢沅. *Guanzhong tengji tukao* [Illustrated research on famous ruins in the Guanzhong area] 關中勝蹟圖考. 1776.

Bukkyō geijutsu [Ars Buddhica] 51 (May 1963), entire issue.

Cai Fan 蔡蕃. *Beijing guyunhe yu chengshi gongshui yanjiu* [Research on ancient canals and waterways of Beijing] 北京古运河舉城市供水研究. Beijing: Beijing Press, 1987.

Cai Zhi [133–192] 蔡質. "Han guandian zhi yishi xuanyong" [Selected official regulations and ceremonies of the Han] 漢官典職儀式選用. *Chengji congshu,* vol. 875.

————. *Ming Tang yueling lun* [Discourses on the monthly advances of the Ming Tang] 明堂月令論.

Chang Kwang-chih [Zhang Guangzhi] 張光直. "Xia, Shang, Zhou Sandai duzhi yu Sandai wenhua yitong" [The system of multiple capitals in the Three Dynasties—with a discussion of the cultural similarities and differences of the Three Dynasties] 夏商周三代都制與三代文化異同. *Guoli Zhongyang Yanjiu Yuan lishi yuyan yanjiu* 56 (1984): 51–71.

Chang Wenzhai 暢文齋. "Shanxi Xiangfen Zhaokang fujin gudai chengzhi diaocha" [Excavation of an ancient city in the vicinity of Zhaokang, Xiangfen, Shanxi] 山西襄汾趙康附近古代城址調查. *Kaogu* no. 10 (1963): 544–546.

Chang'an Xian zhi [Record of Chang'an district] 長安縣志. Reprint. Taipei: Shangwu Press, 1935.

Chen Bingying 陳炳應. "Xi Xia xiujian de chengzhen baozhai" [Cities and fortresses built by the Xi Xia] 西夏修建的城鎮堡塞. In *Xi Xia wenwu yanjiu*, pp. 81–104. Yinchuan: Ningxua People's Press, 1985.

Chen Cheng-siang [Zhengxiang] 陳正祥. *Zhongguo wenhua dili* [Chinese cultural geography] 中國文化地理. Hong Kong: Joint Publishers, 1981.

Chen Gaohua 陳高華. *Yuan Dadu* [Yuan Dadu] 元大都. Beijing: Beijing Press, 1982.

Chen Hongnian 陳鴻年. *Gudu fengwu* [Scenery of the ancient capitals] 古都風物. Taipei: Zhengzhong Publishing Company, 1970.

Chen Jiuheng 陳久恒. "Sui-Tang Dongdu chengzhi de kancha he fajue" [Investigation and excavation of the Sui–Tang eastern capital] 隋唐東都城址的勘查和發掘. *Kaogu* no. 3 (1961): 127–135.

————. "'Sui-Tang Dongdu chengzhi de kancha he fajue' xuji" ["Investigation and excavation of the Sui–Tang eastern capital" continued] 隋唐東都城址的勘查和發掘續記. *Kaogu* no. 6 (1978): 361–378.

Chen Lu 陳籙. "Liao Yuzhou Shi rong yu lie" [The appearance of Liao Yuzhou] 遼幽州市容與例. *Zhonghe ribao* 2, no. 9 (1941): 38–48.

Chen Shou [233–297] 陳壽. *Sanguo zhi* [Record of the Three Kingdoms] 三國志.

Chen Shu 陳述. *Qidan shehui jingji shigao* [Khitan society and economics] 契丹社會經濟史稿. Beijing: Sanlian Publishing Company, 1963.

Chen Xiangchang 陳顯昌. "Tangdai Bohai Shangjing Longquan Fu yizhi" [Remains of Longquan Fu, the Bohai upper capital during the Tang period] 唐代渤海上京龍泉府遺址. *Wenwu* no. 9 (1980): 85–89.

Chen Yinke 陳寅恪. *Sui-Tang zhidu yuanyuan luelun gao* [Investigation into the origins of the Sui–Tang system] 隋唐制度淵源略論稿. Reprint. Taipei: Sanlian Publishing Company, 1963; 1st ed., Shanghai, 1944.

Chen Yuanjing, editor 陳元靚. *Shilin guangji* [Compendium of a forest of affairs] 事林廣記. 1333.

Chen Zongfan, editor 陳宗蕃. *Yandu congkao* [Collected studies of Beijing] 燕都叢考. Reprint. Beijing: Xinxue Press, 1969.

Cheng Dachang [1123–1195] 程大昌. *Yonglu* [Harmony record] 雍錄.

Chūzan ōkoku bunbutsu ten [Exhibition of cultural relics from the Zhongshan kingdom] 中山王国文物展. Tokyo: Tokyo National Museum, 1981.

Da Jin Guo zhi [Record of the great Jin state] 大金國志.

"Datong nanjiao Bei Wei yizhi" [Remains of the Northern Wei in the southern suburbs of Datong] 大同南郊北魏遺址. *Wenwu* no. 1 (1972): 83–84.

"Dengfeng wangchenggang yizhi de fajue" [Excavation of the remains of a royal city hillock at Dengfeng] 登封王城崗遺址的發掘. *Wenwu* no. 3 (1983): 8–20.

Dong Jianhong 董鑒泓, et al. *Zhongguo chengshi jianshe shi* [History of Chinese city construction] 中國城市建設史. Beijing: Zhongguo Jianzhu Gonye Press, 1982. 2d printing, 1985.

Du Yu and Zhu Lingling, editors 杜瑜 朱玲玲. *Zhongguo lishi dilixue lunzhu suoyin* [Index of writings and commentaries on Chinese historical geography] 中國歷史地理學論注索引. Beijing: Shumu Wenxian Press, 1986.

Duan Pengqi 段鵬琦. "Han–Wei Luoyang cheng de jige wenti" [Some problems regarding Han–Wei Luoyang] 漢魏洛陽城的幾個文題. *Zhongguo kaoguxue yanjiu*, pp. 244–253. Beijing: Wenwu Press, 1986.

Fan Chengda [1126–1193] 范成大. *Lanpei lu* [Record of grasping the reins] 攬轡錄. *Zhibuzu Zhai congshu*. Vol. 215. Reprint. Taipei, 1966.

Fan Xiangyong 范祥雍. *Luoyang qielan ji jiaozhu* [Collated commentaries on *Luoyang qielan ji* (Record of Buddhist monasteries of Luoyang)] 洛陽伽藍記校注. Shanghai: Gudian Wenxue Press, 1958.

Fan Ye [398–445] 范曄. *Hou Han shu* [History of the Later Han] 後漢書.

Fang Hao 方豪. *Song shi* [History of the Song] 宋史. 2 vols. Taipei: Zhonghua Wenhua Press, 1954.

————. "Songdai chengshi zhi yanjiu" [Research on Song cities] 宋代城市之研究. In *Fang Hao liushi zishu gao*, 2 vols., vol. 2, pp. 1335–1360. Taipei: Xuesheng Book Company, 1969.

Fang Xuanling [578–648] 房玄齡. *Jin shu* [History of the Jin] 晉書.

Feng Kuan 奉寬. "Yanjing gucheng kao" [Research on the old city of Yanjing] 燕京故城考. *Yanjing xuebao* bo. 5 (June 1940): 833–911.

Fu Xinian 傅喜年. "Shaanxi Qishan Fengchu Xi Zhou jianzhu yizhi chutan" [Preliminary discussion of the Western Zhou architectural remains at Fengchu, Qishan, Shaanxi] 陝山岐山鳳雛西周建築遺址初談. *Wenwu* no. 1 (1981): 65–74.

———. "Shanxi Sheng Fanshi Xian Yanshan Si nandian Jindai bihuazhong suohui jianzhu de chubu fenxi" [Early stages of analysis of Jin period wall paintings of architecture in the south hall of Yanshan Monastery, Fanshi county, Shanxi] 山西省繁峙縣岩山寺南殿金代壁畫中所繪建築的初步分析. *Jianzhu lishi yanjiu* 1 (1982): 119–151.

———. "Tang Chang'an Daming Gong Hanyuan Dian yuan-zhuang de tantao" [Research on the original appearance of the Hanyuan Hall of Daming Gong at Tang Chang'an] 唐長安大明宮含元殿原狀的探討. *Wenwu* no. 7 (1973): 30–48.

———. "Tang Chang'an Daming Gong Xuanwu Men ji Zhongxuan Men fuyuan yanjiu" [Research on the recon-struction of Xuanwu Gate and Zhongxuan Gate of Daming Gong from Tang Chang'an] 唐長安大明宮玄武門及重玄門復原研究. *Kaogu xuebao* no. 2 (1977): 131–158.

———. "Tangdai suidao xingmu de xingzhi gouzao he suo-fanying de dishang gongshi" [Aboveground palace archi-tecture as reflected on the walls of Tang tomb paths] 唐代隧道型墓的形制構造和所反映的地上宮室. In *Wenwu yu kaogu lunji*, pp. 322–343. Beijing: Wenwu Press, 1986.

———. "Zhan Guo Zhongshan Wang Cuo mu chutu de zhaoyu tu ji qi lingyuan guizhi de yanjiu" [Research on the plan of the tomb of King Cuo of the Zhongshan kingdom of the Warring States period and the arrange-ment of the surrounding tombs] 戰國中山王響墓出土的兆域圖及其陵園規制的研究. *Kaogu xuebao* no. 1 (1980): 97–118.

Fukuyama Toshio 福山敏男. "Kōchō *Ryūkyō shinki* kan daisan" [Notes on *juan* 3 of *Liangjing xinji*] 校注兩京新記卷第三. *Bijutsu kenkyū* 1, no. 170 (1953): 31–66.

Ge Hong, editor 葛洪. *Xijing zaji* [Miscellanies of the western capital] 西京雜記. Shanghai: Shangwu Press, 1929.

Goi Naoku 坪井清足. "Kan no Chōan-jō" [Han Chang'an]

漢の長安城. *Nihon to Chūgoku ni okeru toshi no hikaku-shi no kenkyū* 1 (1988): 2–46.

Gu Yanwu [1613–1682] 顧炎武. *Lidai diwang zhaijing ji* [Re-cord of imperial residences and capitals through history] 歷代帝王宅京記. Reprint. Taipei: Guangwen Press, 1960.

Guanzhong congshu [Collected writings about Guanzhong] 關中叢書.

Guo Baojun 郭寶鈞. "Luoyang gucheng kancha jianbao" [Brief investigation of Luoyang] 洛陽古城勘察簡報. *Kaogu tongxun* no. 1 (1955): 9–21.

Guo Husheng 郭湖生. "*Tai, cheng* kao" [Investigation of *tai* and *cheng*] 台城考. *Liu Dunzhen Xiansheng jiushi danchen jinian lunwen*. Nanjing: Nanjing Gongye Yuan Jianzhu Yanjiu Suo, 1987.

———. "Wei–Jin Nan Bei chao zhi Sui–Tang gongshi zhidu yange" [Evolution of the palace system from Wei–Jin through the Northern and Southern Dynasties and the Sui–Tang] 魏晋南北朝至隋唐宮室制度沿革. *Liu Dun-zhen Xiansheng jiushi danchen jinian lunwen*. Nanjing: Nan-jing Gongye Yuan Jianzhu Yanjiu Suo, 1987.

———. "Zicheng zhidu" [The *zicheng* system] 子城制度. *Tōhō gakuhō* 57, no. 3 (1985): 665–683.

Guo Yifu 郭義孚. "Hanyuan Dian waiguan fuyuan" [Recon-struction of the exterior appearance of Hanyuan Hall] 含元殿外觀復原. *Kaogu* no. 10 (1963): 567–572.

Guo Zhizhong and Li Yiyou 郭治中 李逸友. "Nei Menggu Heicheng kaogu fajue jiyao" [Notes on the excavation of Heicheng in Inner Mongolia] 內蒙古黑城考古發掘紀要. *Wenwu* no. 7 (1987): 1–23.

Han-Tang bihua [Wall painting Han to Tang] 漢唐壁畫. Bei-jing: Waiwen Press, 1974.

Han tuo [Han rubbings] 漢拓. Taipei: Xiongshi Book Com-pany, 1976.

"Han–Wei Luoyang Cheng Bei Wei Jianchun Men yizhi de fajue" [Excavation of remains of Jianchun Gate of the Northern Wei dynasty from Han–Wei Luoyang] 漢魏洛陽城北魏建春門遺址的發掘. *Kaogu* no. 9 (1988): 814–818.

"Han–Wei Luoyang Cheng chubu kancha" [Early stages in the excavation of Han–Wei Luoyang] 漢魏洛陽城初步勘查. *Kaogu* no. 4 (1973): 198–208.

Han–Wei Luoyang gucheng [The Han–Wei city of Luoyang] 漢魏洛陽古城. Luoyang: Han–Wei Gucheng Wenwu Baoguan Suo, 1985.

Hang Dezhou 杭德州, et al. "Tang Chang'an Cheng diqi chubu tance" [Early survey of excavated remains of Tang

Chang'an] 唐長安城地基初步探測. *Kaogu xuebao* no. 3 (1958): 79–94.

Harada Yoshi and Komai Kazuchika 原田淑 駒井和愛. *Jōto: Manko Doron-nōru ni okeru Gendai toshi no chōsa* [Shangdu: Summer capital of the Yuan dynasty in Dolon-nor, Mongolia] 上都・蒙古ドロンノールに於ける元代都市の調査. Tokyo: Tō'a kōko gakkai, 1941.

—————. *Tung-ching-ch'eng* [Dongjing Cheng] [The Bohai capital Shangjing] 東京城. Tokyo: Tō'a kōko gakkai, 1939.

Hattori Katsuhiko 服部克彦. "Hoku Ki no Rakuyō" [Northern Wei Luoyang] 北魏の洛陽. *Rekishi kyōiku* 14, no. 12 (1966): 37–43.

He Guanbao 賀官保. *Luoyang wenwu yu guyi* [Cultural relics and ancient remains in Luoyang] 洛陽文物與古遺. Beijing: Wenwu Press, 1987.

He Yeju 賀鄴鉅. "Guanyu woguo gudai chengshi guihua tixi zhi xingcheng ji qi chuantong fazhan de ruogan wenti" [Concerning the formation of China's ancient city planning system and some questions concerning its development] 關于我國古代城市規畫体系之形成及其傳統發展的若干問題. *Jianzhu lishi yu lilun* 3–4 (1982–1983): 53–74.

—————. "*Kaogong ji*" yingguo zhidu yanjiu [Research on the building system via the *Kaogong ji*] 考工記營國制度研究. Beijing: Zhongguo Jianzhu Gongye Press, 1985.

—————. *Zhongguo gudai chengshi guihua shi luncong* [Discussion of the history of ancient Chinese city planning] 中國古代城市規畫史論從. Beijing: Zhongguo Jianzhu Gongye Press, 1986.

—————. "*Zhou Guan*" wangji guihua chutan [Initial investigation of the imperial city plan in *Zhou Guan*] 「周官」王畿規劃初探. *Jianzhu lishi yanjiu* 1 (1982): 96–118.

"Hebei Gaocheng Taixi Cun de Shangdai yizhi" [Shang remains at Taixi village, Gaocheng, Hebei] 河北藁城台西村的商代遺址. *Kaogu* no. 5 (1973): 266–271.

"Hebei Gaocheng Xian Shangdai yizhi he muzang de diaocha" [Excavation of Shang remains and tombs in Gaocheng, Hebei] 河北藁城縣商代遺址和墓葬的調查. *Kaogu* no. 1 (1973): 25–29.

"Hebei Gaocheng Xian Taixi Cun Shangdai yizhi yijiuqishisannian de zhongyao faxian" [Important excavation in 1973 of Shang remains at Taixi village, Gaocheng, Hebei] 河北藁城縣台西村商代遺址一九七三年的重要發現. *Wenwu* no. 8 (1974): 42–49.

"Hebei Handan shiqu gu yizhi diaocha jianbao" [Brief report on ancient excavated remains in Handan city district, He-

bei] 河北邯鄲市區古遺址調查簡報. *Kaogu* no. 2 (1980): 142–146.

"Hebei Sheng Pingshan Xian Zhan Guo shiqi Zhongshan Guo muzang fajue jianbao" [Brief report on the digging at the necropolis of the Zhongshan kingdom from the Warring States period in Pingshan, Hebei] 河北省平山縣戰國時期中山國墓葬發掘簡報. *Wenwu* no. 1 (1979): 1–31.

"Hebei Yi Xian Yan Xiadu dishiliu hao mu fajue" [Excavation of Tomb 16 at Yan Xiadu, Yi Xian, Hebei] 河北易縣燕下都第十六號墓發掘. *Kaogu xuebao* no. 2 (1965): 79–102.

"Hebei Yi Xian Yan Xiadu gucheng kancha he shijue" [Investigation and digging at the old city of Yan Xiadu, Yi Xian, Hebei] 河北易縣燕下都古城勘查和試掘. *Kaogu xuebao* no. 1 (1965): 83–106.

"Hebei Yi Xian Yan Xiadu sishisi hao mu fajue baogao" [Report on digging at Tomb 44 at Yan Xiadu, Yi Xian, Hebei] 河北易縣燕下都四十四號墓發掘報告. *Kaogu* no. 4 (1975): 228–240.

"Henan Yanshi Erlitou erhao gongdian yizhi" [Remains of Palace 2 at Erlitou, Yanshi, Henan] 河南偃師二里頭二號宮殿遺址. *Kaogu* no. 3 (1983): 206–216.

"Henan Yanshi Erlitou yizhi fajue jianbao" [Brief report on the excavated remains at Erlitou, Yanshi, Henan] 河南偃師二里頭遺址發掘簡報. *Kaogu* no. 5 (1965): 215–224.

"Henan Yanshi Erlitou yizhi san-, ba-qu fajue jianbao" [Brief report on the excavation of Areas 3 and 8 at Erlitou, Yanshi, Henan] 河南偃師二里頭遺址三、八區發掘簡報. *Kaogu* no. 5 (1975): 302–309.

"Henan Yanshi Erlitou Zao Shang gongdian yizhi fajue jianbao" [Brief report on excavated remains of an early Shang palace hall at Erlitou, Yanshi, Henan] 河南偃師二里頭早商宮殿遺址發掘簡報. *Kaogu* no. 4 (1974): 234–248.

Henan zhi [Record of Henan province] 河南志. Yuan. Reprint. Taipei: Shijie Press, 1974.

Hiraoka Takeo 平岡武夫. "Tō Chōan-jō no tōnanbu" [The southeastern part of Tang Chang'an] 唐長安城の東南部. *Tōyōshi kenkyū* 9, no. 4 (1952): 37–53.

—————. "Tō no Chōan" [Tang Chang'an] 唐の長安. *Rekishi kyōiku* 14, no. 12 (1966): 44–51.

Hiraoka Takeo and Imai Kiyoshi 平岡武夫 今井清. *Tōdai no Chōan to Rakuyō* [Tang Chang'an and Luoyang] 唐代の長安と洛陽. 7 vols. Kyoto: Jimbunkagaku kenkyū-sho, 1956.

Ho Ping-ti [He Bingdi] 何炳棣. "Bei-Wei Luoyang chengguo guihua" [The walls and plan of Northern Wei Luoyang] 北魏洛陽城郭規劃. In *Guangju Li Ji Xiansheng qishisui lunwen ji*, pp. 219–244. Pt. 1. Taipei: Qinghua Xuebao, 1965.

Hou Renzhi 候仁之. "Beihai Gongyuan yu Beijing Cheng" [Beihai Park and Beijing] 北海公園與北京城. *Wenwu* no. 4 (1980): 10–12.

———. "Beijing Cheng: lishi fazhan de tedian ji qigaizao" [Beijing: Special features of its historical development and transformation] 北京城:歷史發展的特點及其改造. *Lishi dili* 2 (1982): 12–20.

———. "Beijing Cheng de yange" [The evolution of Beijing] 北京城的沿革. In *Bufang ji*, pp. 1–12. Beijing: Beijing Press, 1984.

———. "Beijing dushi fazhan guochengzhong de shuiyuan wenti" [On the question of water sources for the development of the city of Beijing] 北京都市發展過程中的水源問題. *Beijing Daxue xuebao* 1 (1955): 47–73.

———. "Beijing Jinshui He kao" [Study of Jinshui River, Beijing] 北京金水河考. *Yanjing xuebao* 30 (1946): 107–134.

———. "Beijing jiucheng pingmian sheji de gaizao" [Restructuring the plan of the old city of Beijing] 北京舊城平面設計的改造. *Wenwu* no. 5 (1973): 1–13 and 29.

———. "Guanyu gudai Beijing de jige wenti" [Several questions concerning Beijing in former times] 關於古代北京的幾個問題. *Wenwu* no. 9 (1959): 1–7.

———. *Lishi dilixue de lilun yu shijian* [Theory and practice of historical geography] 歷史地理學的理論與實踐. Shanghai: Shanghai Renmin Press, 1979.

———. *Lishishang de Beijing Cheng* [Beijing through history] 歷史上的北京城. Beijing: Zhongguo Qingnian Press, 1962.

———. "Yuan Dadu Cheng yu Ming–Qing Beijing Cheng" [Yuan Dadu and Ming–Qing Beijing] 元大都城與明清北京城. *Gugong Bowu Yuan yuankan* no. 3 (1979): 3–21 and 38.

Hou Renzhi, editor 候仁之. *Beijing lishi ditu ji* [Historical maps of Beijing] 北京歷史地圖集. Beijing: Beijing Press, 1986.

Hou Renzhi and Wu Liangyong 候仁之 吳良鏞. "Tian'an Men guangchang lizan" [In praise of Tian'an Men Square] 天安門廣場禮贊. *Wenwu* no. 9 (1977): 1–15.

"Houma Dong Zhou xunren mu" [Eastern Zhou tombs with sacrificial burials at Houma] 候馬東周殉人墓. *Wenwu* nos. 8–9 (1960): 15–18.

"Houma Niu Cun guchengnan Dong Zhou yizhi fajue jianbao" [Brief report on the Eastern Zhou remains south of the old city of Niu Cun, Houma] 候馬牛村古城南東周遺址發掘簡報. *Kaogu* no. 2 (1962): 55–62.

Hu Qianying 胡謙盈. "Feng-Hao diqu zhu shuidao de tacha" [Looking into the various waterways in the Feng-Hao area] 豐鎬地區諸水道的踏察. *Kaogu* no. 4 (1963): 188–197.

Hui Dong, editor [Qing] 惠棟. *Ming Tang dadao lu* [Record of the great way of the Ming Tang] 明堂大道路. *Jingxun Tang congshu. juan* 37–40.

Imanishi Haruaki, editor 今西春秋. "*Genryūkyō-jō zenzu*" *kaisetsu oyobi sakuin* [Explanation and index of *Qianlong jingcheng quantu* [Complete maps of the capital in the Qianlong period] 「乾隆京城全圖」解説及索引. Beijing: Beiping Yinyin Press, 1940.

Iriya Yoshitaka 入矢義高. "Sōdai shimin seikatsu no ichi sokumen" [A sidelight on city life in the Song dynasty] 宋代市民生活の一側面. *Tōyōshi kenkyū* 11, no. 4 (1952): 54–76.

Ishibashi Ushio 石橋丑雄. *Ten-dan* [Altar of Heaven] 天壇. Tokyo: Yamamoto Book Company, 1957.

Ishida Mikinosuke 石田幹之助. "Gen no Jōto ni tsuite" [Concerning Yuan Shangdu] 元の上都に就いて. *Nihon Daigaku sōritsu shichijushū kinen shū* 1 (October 1960): 271–319.

Itō Michiharu 伊藤道治. "In-Shu jidai no toshi" [Yin–Zhou cities] 殷周時代の都市. *Rekishi kyōiku* 14, no. 12 (1966): 22–28.

Jia Zhoujie 賈洲杰. "Yuan Shangdu diaocha baogao" [Excavation report of Yuan Shangdu] 元上都調查報告. *Wenwu* no. 5 (1977): 65–74.

Jiang Weishui 姜渭水. *Zhongguo jiandu shi* [History of city building in China] 中國建都市. Taipei: Heping Press, 1957.

Jiangning Fu zhi [Record of Jiangning prefecture] 江寧府志. Qing.

Kaogong ji [Record of trades] 考工記. In *Guanzhong congshu*, vol. 6, *juan* 1–2.

Katō Shigeshi 加藤繁. "Sōdai ni okeru toshi no hattatsu ni tsuite" [The development of cities during the Song dynasty] 宋代における都市の發達について. In *Shina keizaishi kōshō*, pp. 93–140. Tokyo: Kōbundō, 1952–1953.

Kobayashi Chisei [?] 小林知生. "Tō-a Kōkogakkai Hoki Ki Heijō-seki chōsa gaihyō" [Summary of excavation at Northern Wei Pingcheng by the East Asia Archaeology Society] 東亞考古学会北魏平城址調査概評. *Kōkogaku zasshi* 29, no. 10 (1939): 74–75.

Koga Noboru 古賀登. "Kandai Chōan no kenchiku puran"

[Architectural plan of Han Chang'an] 漢代長安の建築 プラン. *Tōyōshi kenkyū* 31, no. 2 (1972): 182–215.

Komai Kazuchika 駒井和愛. *Chūgoku kōkogaku ronshū* [Collection of treatises on Chinese archaeology] 中國考古学 論叢. Tokyo: Keiyū Press, 1974.

———. *Chūgoku tojō, Bokkai kenkyū* [Chinese cities, Bohai researches] 中國都城・渤海研究. Tokyo: Yūzan-kaku Press, 1977.

———. "Gen Jōto shi no chōsa" [Excavation of the remains of Yuan Shangdu] 元上都市の調査. *Kōkogaku zasshi* 28, no. 9 (1937): 80–81.

———. "Gen no Jōto narabi ni Daito no heimen ni tsuite" [Concerning the plans of Shangdu and Dadu of the Yuan] 元の上都並に大都の平面に就いて. *Tōa ronshū* 3 (1940): 129–140.

———. *Kyoku-fu Rojō no iseki* [Remains of the Lü capital Qufu] 曲阜魯城の遺蹟. Tokyo: Tokyo Daigaku Kōkogaku kenkyū-sho, 1950.

Lao Gan 勞榦. "Bei Wei Luoyang Cheng tu de fuyuan" [Reconstruction of the plan of Northern Wei Luoyang] 北魏 洛陽城圖復原. *Guoli Zhongyang Yanjiu Yuan lishi yuyan yanjiu* 20, pt. 1 (1948): 299–312.

Li Chi [Ji] 李濟. *Chengziyai* [Chengziyai] 城子崖. Nanjing: Guoli Zhongyang Yanjiuyuan Lishi Yuyan Yanjiu Suo, 1934.

Li Daoyuan [d. 527] 酈道元. *Shui jing zhu* [Commentary to the *Water Classic*] 水經注.

Li Delin [530–590] and Li Baiyao [565–648] 李德林 李百藥. *Bei Qi shu* [History of the Northern Qi] 北齊書.

Li Fang 李放. *Zhongguo yishujia zhenglie* [Collected material on Chinese artisans] 中國藝術家徵略. n.p., 1912.

Li Haowen [Yuan] 李好文. *Chang'an zhi tu* [Illustrated record of Chang'an]. 長安志圖. Bi Yuan, ed. Reprint. *Jingdiao Tang congshu*, no. 24. Reprint. *Siku quanshu*, ser. 9, vol. 162. Taipei: Shangwu Press, 1978.

Li Jiafu 李甲孚. *Zhongguo gudai jianzhu yishu* [Ancient Chinese architecture and art] 中國古代建築藝術. Taipei: Beiya Press, 1977.

Li Jiancai 李健才. "Ji, Hei liangsheng xibu diqu sizuo Liao-Jin gucheng kao" [Investigation of four ancient Liao-Jin cities in the western area of Jilin and Heilongjiang] 吉黑兩省西 部地區四座遼金古城考. *Lishi dili* 2 (1982): 94–103.

———. "Jilin Tahu Cheng diaocha jianbao" [Brief report on excavation at Tahu, Jilin] 吉林他虎城調查簡報. *Kaogu* no. 1 (1964): 46–48.

Li Lian 李濂. *Bianjing yiji zhi* [Record of historical remains of Bianliang] 汴京遺蹟志.

Li Xueqin 李學勤. "Kaogu faxian yu Dong Zhou wangdu" [Excavation at the Eastern Zhou royal city] 考古發現與 東周王都. *Ou-Hua xuebao* no. 1 (May 1983): 93–104.

Li Yiyou 李逸友. "Nei Menggu Yuandai chengzhi gaishuo" [Discussion of Yuan city sites in Inner Mongolia] 內蒙古 元代城址概說. *Nei Menggu wenwu kaogu* 4 (1986): 87–107.

———. "Yuan Yingchang Lu gucheng diaocha ji" [Excavation report on the old city Yingchang Lu from the Yuan period] 元應昌路古城調查記. *Kaogu* no. 10 (1961): 531–533.

Li Yunhe 李允鉌. *Huaxia yijiang* [Artistic conception of Chinese design] 華夏意匠. Hong Kong: Wideance Press, 1982.

Liang Qixiong 梁啓雄, et al. "Zhejiang lu" [Recorded biographies of craftsmen] 哲匠錄. *Zhongguo yingzao xueshe huikan* 1, no. 2 (1930): 126–159; 3, no. 3 (1932): 91–120; 4, no. 2 (1933): 60–85; 4, nos. 3–4 (1934): 219–257; 5, no. 2 (1934): 75–105; 6, no. 2 (1935): 116–156.

Liang Sicheng 梁思成. "Datong gujianzhu diaocha baogao" [Report on ancient architecture in Datong] 大同古建築 調查報告. *Zhongguo yingzao xueshe huikan* 4, nos. 3–4 (1934): 1–168.

———. Review of "Zhu Qiqian. 'Liao-Jin Yanjing chengguo gongyuan tukao'" 朱啓鈐・遼金燕京城郭宮園圖考. *Zhongguo yingzao xueshe huikan* 6, no. 4 (1936): 165–168.

———. *Zhongguo jianzhu* [Chinese architecture] 中國建築. Reprint. Taipei, n.d.

———. *Zhongguo jianzhu shi* [History of Chinese architecture] 中國建築史. Reprint. Taipei, 1980.

Liang Sicheng and Lin Huiyin 梁思成 林徽音. "Pingjiao jianzhu zalu" [Miscellaneous notes on architecture in suburban Beijing] 平郊建築雜錄. *Zhongguo yingzao xueshe huikan* 3, no. 4 (1932): 98–110.

Lin Xiuzhen 林秀貞. "Dongbei diqu Jindai chengshi de leixing" [Types of cities in the northeastern provinces during the Jin period] 東北地區金代城市的類型. In *Zhongguo kaoguxue yanjiu*, pp. 301–308. Vol. 1, Beijing: Wenwu Press, 1986.

Liu Dunyuan 劉敦原. "Chun Qiu shiqi Qi Guo gucheng de fuyuan yu chengshi buju" [Reconstruction and layout of the old city of the Qi capital in the Spring and Autumn period] 春秋時期齊國故城的復原與城市布局. *Lishi dili* 1 (1981): 148–159.

Liu Dunzhen 劉敦楨. "Handai Chang'an Cheng ji Weiyang Gong" [Han Chang'an and Weiyang Gong] 漢代長安城 及未央宮. *Zhongguo yingzao xueshe huikan* 3, no. 3 (1932): 147–169.

———. "Qing huangcheng gongdian yamen tu niandai kao" [Research on the date of the drawings of palaces and *yamen* of the Qing imperial-city] 清皇城宫殿衙署圖年代考. *Zhongguo yingzao xueshe huikan* 6, no. 2 (1935): 106–115.

———. *Zhongguo gudai jianzhu shi* [History of traditional Chinese architecture] 中國古代建築史. Beijing: Zhongguo Jianzhu Gongye Press, 1st ed., 1980; 2d ed., 1984.

Liu Ruoyu [Ming] 劉若愚. *Ming gong shi* [History of the Ming palaces] 明宫史.

Liu Tong and Yu Yizheng 劉侗 于奕正. *Dijing jingwu lue* [Brief account of the scenery of the imperial city] 帝京景物略. 1635. Reprint. Taipei: Shijie Press, 1963.

Liu Xu [887–946] 劉煦. *Jiu Tang shu* [Old Tang history] 舊唐書.

Liu Yunyong 劉运勇. *Xi Han Chang'an* [Western Han Chang'an] 西漢長安. Beijing: Wenwu Press, 1982.

Liu Zhiping 劉致平. "Xi'an xijiao gudai jianzhu yizhi kancha chuji" [Preliminary report on excavated remains of ancient architecture from the western suburbs of Xi'an] 西安西郊古代建築遺址勘察初記. *Wenwu cankao ziliao* no. 3 (1957): 5–10.

———. *Zhongguo jianzhu leixing ji jiegou* [Types and structures of Chinese architecture] 中國建築類型及結構. Beijing: Zhongguo Jianzhu Gongye Press, 1957.

Liu Zhiping and Fu Xinian 劉致平 傅熹年. "Linde Dian fuyuan de chubu yanjiu" [Preliminary research on the reconstruction of Linde Hall] 麟德殿復原的初步研究. *Kaogu* no. 7 (1963): 385–402.

Lu Hui 陸翽. *Yezhong ji* [Record of Ye] 鄴中記. *Congshu jicheng* 3804.

Lu Zhaoyin 盧兆蔭. "Tang Qinglong Si yizhi tacha jilue" [Notes on the process of examination of the remains of Qinglong Monastery of the Tang dynasty] 唐青龍寺遺址踏察記略. *Kaogu* no. 7 (1964): 346–354.

"Luoyang faxian Sui–Tang Cheng jiacheng chengqiang" [The side walls excavated at Sui–Tang Luoyang] 洛陽發現隋唐城夾城城墙. *Kaogu* no. 11 (1983): 1000–1003.

"Luoyang Han–Wei gucheng beiyuan yihao mamian de fajue" [Excavation of bastion 1 from the north wall of Han–Wei Luoyang] 洛陽漢魏古城北垣一號馬面的發掘. *Kaogu* no. 8 (1986): 726–730 and 760.

"Luoyang Jianbin Dong Zhou chengzhi fajue baogao" [Excavation report on the Eastern Zhou city at the Jian riverbank, Luoyang] 洛陽澗濱東周城址發掘報告. *Kaogu xuebao* no. 2 (1959): 15–36.

"Luoyang Sui–Tang Hanjia Cang de fajue" [Excavation of Hanjia Storehouse from Sui–Tang Luoyang] 洛陽隋唐含嘉倉的發掘. *Wenwu* no. 3 (1973): 49–62.

Ma Dezhi 馬德志. "Tang Chang'an Cheng kaogu jilue" [Brief notes on Chang'an of the Tang] 唐長安城考古記略. *Kaogu* no. 11 (1963): 595–611.

———. *Tang Chang'an Daming Gong* [Daming palace complex of Tang Chang'an] 唐長安大明宫. Beijing: Kexue Press, 1959.

———. "Tang Chang'an huangcheng Hanguang Men yizhi fajue jianbao" [Brief report on the excavation of Hanguang Gate of the imperial-city at Tang Chang'an] 唐長安皇城含光門遺址發掘簡報. *Kaogu* no. 5 (1987): 441–448 and 480.

———. "Tang Chang'an Xingqing Gong fajue" [Excavation of Xingqing palace complex from Tang Chang'an] 唐長安興慶宫發掘. *Kaogu* no. 10 (1959): 549–558.

———. "Tang Chang'an yu Luoyang" [Tang Chang'an and Luoyang] 唐長安與洛陽. *Kaogu* no. 6 (1982): 640–646.

———. "Tang Daming Gong fajue jianbao" [Brief report on the excavation of Tang Daming Gong] 唐大明宫發掘簡報. *Kaogu* no. 6 (1959): 296–301.

———. "Yijiuwushijiu-yijiuliushi-nian Tang Daming Gong fajue jianbao" [Brief excavation report on the 1959–1960 season at Tang Daming Gong] 一九五九-一九六〇年唐大明宫發掘簡報. *Kaogu* no. 7 (1961): 341–344.

Ma Dezhi and Yang Hongxun 馬德志 楊鴻勛. "Guanyu Tang Chang'an Dong Gong fanwei wenti de yantao" [Concerning the problems of the scope of the Eastern Palace at Tang Chang'an] 關於唐長安東宫範圍問題的研討. *Kaogu* no. 1 (1978): 60–64.

Ma Xianxing 馬先醒. "Handai zhi Chang'an yu Luoyang" [Han Chang'an and Luoyang] 漢代之長安與洛陽. Ph.D. dissertation, Zhongguo Wenhua Xueyuan, 1970.

Maeda Masana 前田正名. *Heijō no rekishi-shirigakuteki kenkyū* [Research on the historical studies of Pingcheng] 平城の歷史地理学的研究. Tokyo: Kazama Book Company, 1979.

Matsumoto Takaharu 松木隆晴. "Mindai Chūto kensetsu shimatsu" [The establishment of the Ming central capital] 明代中都建設始末. *Tōhōgaku* no. 67 (1984): 62–75.

Meng Yuanlao [Song] 孟元老. *Dongjing menghua lu* [Record of dreaming of *hua* in the eastern capital] 東京夢華錄. Reprint. Taipei: Shijie Press, 1972.

Miao Changyan 苗昌言. *Sanfu huangtu* [Illustrated description of the three districts of the metropolitan area] 三輔黄圖. Late third century. Reprint. Taipei: Shijie Press, 1974.

Ming shi lu [Record of Ming history] 明史錄.

Miyakawa Hisayuki 宮川尚志. *Rokuchō shi kenkyū* [Research into Six Dynasties history] 六朝史研究. Tokyo: Nihon Gakujutsu Shinkō Kai, 1956.

Miyazaki Ichisada 宮崎市定. "Chūgoku jōdai wa hōkensetsu ka toshi kokka ka?" [Was early China a feudal system or city-states?] 中国上代は封建制か都市國家か. *Shirin* 33, no. 1 (1950): 144–163.

———. "Chūgoku jōkaku no kigen isetsu" [Differing opinions on the origins of Chinese cities] 中国城郭の起源異説. *Ajia-shi kenkyū* 1 (1957): 57–65.

———. "Kandai no risei to Tōdai no jōsei" [The Han *li* system and the Tang *jō* system] 漢代の里制と唐代の坊制. *Tōyōshi kenkyū* 21, no. 3 (1962): 271–294.

———. "Sengoku jidai no toshi" [Warring States period cities] 戰國時代の都市. In *Tōhō gakkai soritsu gojū shūnen kinen*, pp. 342–357. Tokyo: Tōhō gakkai, 1962.

Mizuno Seiichi 水野清一. "Daitō tsushin" [Communications from Datong] 大同通信. *Kōkogaku*, pt. 1, 9, no. 8 (1938): 410–415; pt. 2, 9, no. 9 (1938): 434–437.

Mori Shikazō 森鹿三. "Hoku Ki Rakuyō-jō no kibo ni tsuite" [Concerning the plan of Northern Wei Luoyang] 北魏洛陽城の規模について. *Tōyōshi kenkyū* 9 (1952): 317–330.

———. "Lao Gan-shi no 'Hoku Ki Rakuyō-jō zuteki fukugen' o hyōsu" [A criticism of Lao Gan's 'Reconstruction of the Plan of Northern Wei Luoyang'] 勞幹氏の「北魏洛陽城圖的復原」を評す. *Tōhō gakuhō* 20 (March 1951): 185–194.

Murata Jiro 村田治郎. *Chūgoku no teito* [Chinese imperial cities] 中国の帝都. Kyoto: Sōgeisha, 1981.

———. "Daito ni okeru heimen zukei no mondai" [The problem of the Dadu plan] 大都における平面圖型の問題. In *Chūgoku no teito*, pp. 309–338.

———. "Gen no Daito no toshi keikaku ni tsuite" [Concerning the plan of Yuan Dadu] 元の大都の都市計畫について. *Kenchiku gakkai taikai ronbunshū* 8 (1938): 238–242.

———. "Gyōto kōryaku" [Brief consideration of Yedu] 鄴都考略. In *Kuwabara Hakushi kanreki kinen Tōyōshi ronshū*, pp. 41–92. Tokyo: Kōbun-dō, 1934.

———. "Kin Jōkyō ishi no ichi mondai" [A question about the remains of the Jin upper capital] 金上京遺址の一問題. *Mammō* 17, no. 1 (1936): 114–129.

———. "Kin Jōkyō ishi tsūkō" [Investigation of the remains of the Jin upper capital] 金上京遺址通考. *Mammō* 18, no. 9 (1937): 110–114.

———. "Kin no Jōkyō Kainei Fujō no iseki" [Remains of the upper capital of the Jin at Huining Fu] 金の上京会寧府城の遺跡. In *Chūgoku no teito*, pp. 261–307.

Naba Toshisada 那波利貞. "Ryō-Kin Nan-kyō, En-kyō kojō kyōiki kō" [Research on the city regions of Liao–Jin Nanjing and Yanjing] 遼金南京燕京故城疆域考. In *Takase Hakushi kanreki kinen Shina gaku ronshū*, pp. 455–515. Tokyo: Kōbun-dō, 1928.

———. "Shina shuto keikaku shijō yori kōsatsu shitaru Tō no Chōanjō" [An inquiry into Tang Chang'an in light of the history of Chinese city planning] 支那首都計畫史上より考察したる唐の長安城. In *Kuwabara Hakushi kanreki kinen Tōyōshi ronshū*, pp. 1203–1269. Tokyo: Kōbun-dō, 1934.

Nagashima Kimichika 永島暉臣愼. "Kokuri no tojō to kenchiku" [Koguryŏ's capital and its architecture] 高句麗の都城と建築. *Naniwa-kyū seki no kenkyū* 7 (1981): 247–260.

Naideweng [Xi Hu Laoren] 耐德翁 [西湖老人]. *Ducheng jiteng* [Record of the splendors of the capital] 都城記勝. 1247.

Nakamura Haruhisa 中村春壽. *Ni-Kan kodai toshi keikaku* [Plans of early Japanese and Korean cities] 日韓古代都市計画. Tokyo: Rokkō, 1978.

Nalan Chengde, ed. 納蘭成德. *Sanli tu* [Illustrated three ritual classics] 三禮圖. 1676.

Nogami Shunsei 野上俊靜. "Gen no Jōto no Bukkyō" [Buddhism at Yuan Shangdu] 元の上都の佛教. *Bukkyō shigaku* 1, no. 2 (1950): 1–15.

Okazaki Fumio 岡崎文夫. "Rokudai teiyū kōryaku" [Brief consideration of Six Dynasties imperial cities] 六代帝邑攷略. In *Kuwabara Hakushi kanreki kinen Tōyōshi ronshū*, pp. 41–92. Tokyo: Kōbun-dō, 1934.

———. "Tōdai ni okeru Chōan to Rakuyō" [Tang Chang'an and Luoyang] 唐代における長安と洛陽. *Tōyōshi kenkyū* 16, no. 3 (1957): 280–310.

Okazaki Kei 岡崎敬. "Zui Daikyo Tō Chōan to Tōto Rakuyō-jō—kinen no chōsa seika o chūshin toshite" [Central ideas of the excavation in recent years at Sui Daxing–Tang Chang'an and Sui–Tang Luoyang] 隋大興唐長安と東都洛陽城―近年の調査成果を中心として. *Bukkyō geijutsu* 51 (May 1963): 86–108.

Ono Katsutoshi 小野勝年. "Chōan no Daimei-kyū" [Chang'an Daming Gong] 長安の大明宮. *Bukkyō geijutsu* 51 (May 1963): 109–120.

Ou Yan 甌燕. "Shilun Yan Xiadu chengzhi de niandai" [Discussion of the date of Yan Xiadu] 試論燕下都城址的年代. *Kaogu* no. 7 (1988): 645–649.

Ouyang Xiu [1007–1072] 歐陽修. *Xin Tang shu* [New Tang history] 新唐書.

Qi Yingtao 祁英濤. "Zhongguo zaoqi mujiegou jianzhu de

shidai tezheng" [Notes on the epochal features of early Chinese timber frame architecture] 中國早期木結构建築的時代特征. *Wenwu* no. 4 (1983): 60–74.

"Qindu Xianyang diyihao gongdian jianzhu yizhi jianbao" [Brief report on architectural remains of Palace 1 at the Qin capital Xianyang] 秦都咸陽第一號宮殿建築遺址簡報. *Wenwu* no. 11 (1976): 12–24.

"Qindu Xianyang gucheng yizhi de diaocha he shijue" [Excavation and investigation of the remains of the ancient Qin capital Xianyang] 秦都咸陽故城遺址的調查和試掘. *Kaogu* no. 6 (1962): 281–289.

Qingming shanghe tu [The painting *Qingming shanghe tu* (Springtime festival on the river)] 清明上河圖. Beijing: Xinhua Book Company, 1979.

Qufu Lü Guo gucheng [Qufu, old city of the Lü state] 曲阜魯國古城. Jinan: Shandong Sheng Wenwu Kaogu Yanjiu Suo, 1982.

Qun Li 群力. "Linzi Qi gucheng kantan jiyao" [Notes on the exploration of the old city Linzi of Qi] 臨淄齊故城勘探紀要. *Wenwu* no. 5 (1972): 45–54.

Rekishi kyōiku 歷史教育. 14, no. 12 (1966), entire issue.

Ruan Yuan [1764–1849] 阮元 *Ming Tang lun* [Discourses on the Ming Tang] 明堂論.

Satō Taketoshi 佐藤武敏. *Chōan* [Chang'an] 長安. Tokyo: Kondō Publishing Company, 1971.

————. "Kandai no toshi" [Han cities] 漢代の都市. *Rekishi kyōiku* 14, no. 12 (1966): 29–35.

————. "Tōdai no shisei to oko—tokuni Chōano chūshin toshite" [The Tang city system and *hang*—with special attention to Chang'an] 唐代の市制と行—とくに長安を中心として. *Tōyōshi kenkyū* 25, no. 3 (1966): 32–59.

Sekino Takeshi 關野雄. *Chūgoku kōkogaku kenkyū* [Research in Chinese archaeology] 中國考古学研究. Tokyo: Tokyo University Press, 1963.

Sekino Takeshi and Komai Kazuchika 關野雄 駒井和愛. *Hantan* [Handan] 邯鄲. Tokyo and Kyoto: Tōa kōko gakkai, 1954.

"Shaanxi Qishan Fengchu Cun Xi Zhou jianzhu fajue jianbao" [Brief report on the excavation of the architectural foundation at Fengchu, Qishan, Shaanxi] 陝西岐山鳳雛村西周建築發掘簡報. *Wenwu* no. 10 (1979): 27–37.

Shaanxi tongzhi [Local record of Shaanxi province] 陝西通志. 1735. Reprint. Taipei: Huawen Book Company, n.d.

Shan Shiyuan 單士元. "Mingdai yingzao shiliao: Tian Tan" [Historical materials on Ming construction: the Altar of Heaven] 明代營造史料:天壇. *Zhongguo yingzao xueshe huikan* 5, no. 3 (1935): 111–138.

"Shandong Linzi Qi gucheng shijue jianbao" [Brief report on the investigation of the old Qi city of Linzi in Shandong] 山東臨淄齊故城試掘簡報. *Kaogu* no. 6 (1961): 289–297.

"Shanxi Datong nanjiao chutu Bei Wei jin tong ji" [Gold and bronze objects from the Northern Wei period unearthed in the southern suburbs of Datong] 山西大同南郊出土北魏金銅器. *Kaogu* no. 11 (1983): 997–999.

"Shanxi Datong Shijia Zhan Bei Wei Sima Jinlong mu" [The tomb of Sima Jinlong of the Northern Wei from Shijia Zhan, Datong, Shanxi] 山西大同石家寨北魏司馬金龍墓. *Wenwu* no. 3 (1972): 20–33.

"Shanxi Houma Shangma Cun Dong Zhou muzang" [Eastern Zhou tombs in Shangma, Houma, Shanxi] 山西候馬上馬村東周墓葬. *Kaogu* no. 5 (1963): 229–245.

"Shanxi Xia Xian Yu Wang Cheng diaocha" [Excavation of Yu Wang's city in Xia county, Shanxi] 山西夏縣禹王城調查. *Kaogu* no. 9 (1963): 474–479.

Shi Zhangru 石璋如. "Yindai dishang jianzhu fuyuan zhi yi lie" [An example of reconstruction of aboveground Yin period architecture] 殷代地上建築復原之一例. *Guoli Zhongyang Yanjiu Yuan lishi yuyan yanjiu* 1 (1954): 269–280.

————. "Yindai dishang jianzhu fuyuan de di'er lie" [A second example of the reconstruction of aboveground Yin period architecture] 殷代地上建築復原的第二例. *Guoli Zhongyang Yanjiu Yuan lishi yuyan yanjiu* 29 (1970): 321–341.

Shimada Masao 島田正郎. "Ryō-Kin no Chōjō" [The Liao-Jin Great Wall] 遼金の長城. *Sundai shigaku* no. 4 (1954): 46–64.

Sima Guang 司馬光. *Zizhi tongjian* [Comprehensive mirror for aid in government] 資治通鑑. 1084.

Sima Tan and Sima Qian 司馬談 司馬遷. *Shi ji* [Record of the grand historian] 史記. Second to first centuries B.C.

Sogabe Shizuo 曾我部靜雄. *Kaihō to Kōshū* [Kaifeng and Hangzhou] 開封と杭州. Tokyo: Fuzanbō, 1940.

————. "Nan-Sō no toshi" [Southern Song cities] 南宋の都市. *Rekishi kyōiku* 5, no. 7 (1957): 29–34.

Song Lian [1310–1381], editor 宋濂. *Yuan shi* [History of the Yuan] 元史. Reprint. Beijing: Zhonghua Press, 1976.

Song Minqiu 宋敏求. *Chang'an zhi* [Record of Chang'an] 長安志. 1075. Reprint. *Siku quanshu*, ser. 9, vol. 162. Taipei: Shangwu Press, n.d.

Sonoda Ikki 園田一龜. "Kin no Jō-kyō shi・Hakujō ni tsuite" [On the ruins of the Jin upper capital, the White City] 金の上京址白城に就いて. *Kōkogaku zasshi* 29, no. 27 (1939): 411–443.

Su Bai 宿白. "Bei Wei Luoyang Cheng he Bei Mang lingmu"

[Northern Wei Luoyang and tombs at the North Mang Mountains] 北魏洛陽城和北邙陵墓. *Wenwu* no. 7 (1978): 42–52.

———. "Shengle, Pingcheng yidai de Tuoba Xianbi—Bei Wei yiji" [Tuoba and Xianbi in the area of Shengle and Pingcheng—Northern Wei remains] 盛樂平城一帶的拓跋鮮卑—北魏遺迹. *Wenwu* no. 11 (1977): 38–46.

———. "Sui–Tang Chang'an Cheng he Luoyang Cheng" [Sui–Tang Chang'an and Luoyang] 隋唐長安城和洛陽城. *Kaogu* no. 6 (1978): 409–425.

Sun Chengze [1593–1675] 孫承澤. *Chunming mengyu lu* [Record of dreams in the spring] 春明夢餘錄.

Sun Jianai [Qing] 孫家鼐 et al. *Shu jing tu shuo* [Illustrations and notes to the *Shu jing*] 書經圖說.

Sun Kekuan 孫克寬. "Yuandai Shangdu kaolue" [Research on Yuan Shangdu] 元代上都考略. In *Menggu Hanjun yu Hanwenhua yanjiu*, pp. 191–198. Taipei: Wenxing Book Company, 1959.

Sun Xingyan [Qing] 孫星衍. *Ming Tang kao* [Research on the Ming Tang] 明堂考. *Wenjing Tang congshu*. Vol. 8. Reprint. Taipei, 1968.

Sun Xiuren and Zhu Guochen 孫秀仁 朱國忱. "Heilongjiang Lalin He you'an kaogu diaocha" [Excavation on the right bank of the Lalin River in Heilongjiang] 黑龍江拉林河右岸考古調查. *Kaogu* no. 12 (1964): 603–606.

Sun Zhanwen 孫占文. "Bai Cheng kaogu lueshu" [Notes on archaeology at the White City] 白城考古略述. In *Heilongjiang Sheng shi tansuo*, pp. 84–87. Harbin: Heilongjiang Renmin Press, 1983.

Takeda Yūkichi, editor 武田祐吉. *Nihon shoki* [Record of Japan] 日本書記. Tokyo: Asahi Shimbun Press, 1969–1973.

Takeshima Takuichi and Sekino Tadashi 竹島卓一 關野貞. *Ryō-Kin jidai no kenchiku to sono Butsuzō* (Liao–Jin Buddhist architecture and its sculpture] 遼金時代の建築と其佛像. Tokyo: Tōhō bunka gakuin Tōkyō kenkyū-sho, 1925 (plates); Ryōbun Book Company, 1944 (text).

Tamura Jitsuzō 田村實造. *Chūgoku seifuku ōchō no kenkyū* [Research on the Chinese conquest dynasties] 中国征服王朝の研究. 3 vols. Kyoto: Tōyōshi kenkyū kai, 1964–1986.

Tanaka Tan 田中淡. "Jujiro ni tatsu hoji rokaku" [Towers for keeping time at the crossroads] 十字路に立つ報時楼閣. *Chyamus* no. 5 (1983): 20–22.

———. "Sen Shin jidai kyūshitsu kenchiku josetsu" [Introduction to residential architecture of the pre-Qin period] 先秦時代宮室建築序說. *Tōhō gakuhō* 52, no. 3 (1980): 123–197.

———. "Shūgen kenchiku ishi no kaishaku" [Interpretation

of architectural remains on the Zhou plain] 周原建築遺址の解釋. In *Kin Hakken Chūgoku kagakushi shiryō no kenkyū*, ed. Yamada Keiji, pp. 265–346. Kyoto: Jimbun Kagaku Kenkyū-sho, 1985.

———. "Zuichō kenchikusha no sekkei to kōshō" [Investigation and proof of Sui dynasty architects] 隋朝建築の設計と考證. In *Chūgoku no kagaku to kagakusha*, ed. Yamada Keiji, pp. 209–306. Kyoto: Jimbun Kagaku Kenkyū-sho, 1978.

"Tang Chang'an Cheng Xinghua Fang yizhi zuantan jianbao" [Brief report on drilling at the remains of Xinghua Ward of Tang Chang'an] 唐長安城興化坊遺址鑽探簡報. *Wenwu* no. 1 (1972): 43–46.

Tang Jinyu 唐金裕. "Xi'an Xijiao Handai jianzhu yizhi fajue baogao" [Excavation report of Han dynasty architectural sites in the western suburbs of Xi'an] 西安西郊漢代建築遺址發掘報告. *Kaogu xuebao* no. 2 (1959): 45–54.

"Tang Qinglong Si yizhi" [Remains of Tang Qinglong Monastery] 唐青龍寺遺址. *Kaogu* no. 5 (1974): 322–327 and 321.

Tao Fu 陶复. "Jianzhu kaogu sanshi nian zongshu" [Summary of thirty years of architecture and archeology] 建築考古三十年綜述. *Jianzhu lishi yu lilun* 3–4 (1982–1983): 13–52.

———. "Qin Xianyang Gong diyihao yizhi fuyuan wenti de chubu tantao" [Early stages in the discussion of the reconstruction of the remains of Palace 1 at Qin Xianyang] 秦咸陽宮第一號遺址復原問題的初步探討. *Wenwu* no. 11 (1976): 31–41.

Tao Zhenggang and Ye Xueming 陶正剛 葉學明. "Gu Wei Cheng he Yu Wang Cheng diaocha jianbao" [Excavation report on the ancient Wei city and Yu Wang's city] 古魏城和禹王城調查簡報. *Wenwu* no. 4/5 (1962): 59–65.

Tao Zongyi 陶宗儀. *Zhuogeng lu* [Record upon resting from the plow] 輟耕錄. 1368. Reprint. Shanghai: Zhonghua Press, 1959.

Tian An 田岸. "Qufu Lücheng kantan" [Excavation at the Lü city Qufu] 曲阜魯城勘探. *Wenwu* no. 12 (1982): 1–12.

Tian'an Men [Tian'an Men Square] 天安門. Beijing: Beijing Press, 1957.

Tokiwa Daijō and Sekino Tadashi 常盤大定 關野貞. *Shina Bukkyō shiseki* [Historical remains of Buddhism in China] 支那佛教史蹟. 5 vols. Tokyo: Bukkyō Shiseki Kenkyū-kai, 1926–1929.

Torii Ryūzō 鳥居龍藏. "Jin Shangjing Cheng Fosi kao" [Research on Buddhist monasteries at Jin Shangjing] 金上京城佛寺考. *Yanjing xuebao* 1–2 (1925): 19–30.

———. "Jin Shangjing Cheng ji qiwenhua" [Jin Shangjing

and its culture] 金上京城及其文化. *Yanjing xuebao* 25 (1948): 194–204.

———. *Ryō no bunka* [Liao culture] 遼の文化. 4 vols. Tokyo: Tōhō Bunka Gakuin Tōkyō Kenkyū-sho, 1937.

Toriyama Kiichi 鳥山喜一. "Kin no Jō-kyō shi" [Remains of the Jin upper capital] 金の上京址. *Mammō* 16, no. 9 (1935): 192–201.

———. "Kin no Jō-kyō shi no shutsudohin ni tsuite" [On object excavated at the Jin upper capital] 金の上京址の出土品に就いて. *Seikyū gakusō* 29 (1935): 148–156.

Tōyōshi kenkyū 東洋史研究. 11, no. 4 (1952), entire issue.

Tsuboi Kiyotari 坪井清足. *Heizei-kyū seki* [Remains of Heijō palace] 平城宮蹟. Tokyo: Shibundō, 1975.

Tuo Tuo [1313–1355], attributed 托托. *Jin shi* [History of the Jin] 金史.

———. *Liao shi* [History of the Liao] 遼史.

———. *Song shi* [History of the Song] 宋史.

Ueda Masaaki 上田正昭. *Tojō* [Cities] 都城. Tokyo: Shakai Shisōsha, 1976.

Umehara Kaoru 梅原郁. "Sōdai no chihō toshi" [Song cities] 宋代の地方都市. *Rekishi kyōiku* 14, no. 12 (1966): 52–58.

Utsunomiya Kiyoyoshi 宇都宮清吉. "Sai Kan no shuto Chōan ni tsuite" [On the Western Han capital Chang'an] 西漢の首都長安について. *Tōyōshi kenkyū* 11, no. 2 (1952): 296–316.

Wang Beichen 王北辰. "Yuan Dadu xingjianqian dangdi de hehushui xi" [The hydrographic network of lakes and rivers in the Yuan before the construction of Beijing] 元大都興建前當地的河湖水系. In *Huanjing bianqian yanjiu*, ed. Hou Renzhi, pp. 147–155. Beijing: Haiyang Press, 1984.

Wang Biwen [Puzi] 王璧文 [璞子]. "Liao–Jin Yanjing chengfang gongdian shulue" [Brief description of city blocks and palaces of Liao–Jin Yanjing] 遼金燕京城坊宮殿述略. *Kejishe wenji* 11 (1984): 20–43.

———. Review of Zhu Xie, "Yuan Dadu gongdian tukao" 朱偰 · 元大都宮殿圖考. *Zhongguo yingzao xueshe huikan* 6, no. 4 (1937): 168–177.

———. "Yan Wang Fu yu Zijin Cheng" [The King of Yan District and the Purple Forbidden City] 燕王府與紫禁城. *Gugong Bowu Yuan yuankan* no. 1 (1979): 70–77.

———. "Yuan Dadu chengfang kao" [Research on the city districts of Yuan Dadu] 元大都城坊考. *Zhongguo yingzao xueshe huikan* 6, no. 3 (1936): 69–120.

———. "Yuan Dadu pingmian guihua shulue" [Discussion of the plan of Yuan Dadu] 元大都平面規劃述略. *Gugong Bowu Yuan yuankan* 2 (1960): 61–82.

———. "Yuan Dadu siguanmiaoyu jianzhi yange biao" [A tabulated chronology of the building of temples and monasteries at Yuan Dadu] 元大都寺觀廟宇建置沿革表. *Zhongguo yingzao xueshe huikan* 6, no. 4 (1937): 130–161.

Wang Chongren 王崇人. *Gudu Xi'an* [The old city of Xi'an] 古都西安. Beijing: Wenwu Press, 1982.

Wang Guowei [1877–1927] 王國維. *Ming Tang miaoqin tongkao* [Research on the Ming Tang and the private temple] 明堂廟寢通考. *Xuetang congshu*, vol. 11.

Wang Jianying 王劍英. "Mingchu yingjian Zhongdu ji qidui gaijian Nanjing he yingjian Beijing de yingxiang" [Early Ming building of the central capital and the influence of its plan on the rebuilding of Beijing] 明初營建中都及其對改建南京和營建北京的影響. *Lishi dili* 3 (1985): 8–97.

Wang Mengba, annotator, and Wang Yunwu, commentator 王夢鷗 王雲五. *Li ji jinzhu jince* [Modern commentary and annotation for the *Li ji*] 禮記今註今譯. 2 vols. Taipei: Shangwu Press, 1973.

Wang Mingqing [1127–ca. 1215] 王明清. *Huizhu lu* [Record of writings and conversations] 揮麈錄. Reprint. Beijing: Zhonghua Press, 1964.

Wang Shidian 王士點. *Jin bian* [Notes on forbidden cities] 禁扁. Fourteenth century.

Wang Shimin 王世民. "Zhoudu Feng, Hao weizhi shangjue" [Positions of the Zhou capitals Feng and Hao] 周都豐鎬位置商榷. *Lishi yanjiu* no. 2 (1958): 63–70.

Wang Shiren 王世仁. "Han Chang'an Cheng nanjiao lizhi jianzhu yuanchuang de tuice" [Conjectures on the original appearance of the architectural remains of the ritual structures in the southern suburbs of Han Chang'an] 漢長安城南郊禮制建築原狀的推測. *Kaogu* no. 9 (1963): 501–515.

Wang Wencai 王文才. "Chengdu chengfang kao" [Research on Chengdu] 成都城坊考. *Sichuan shiyuan xuebao*, pt. 1: no. 1 (1981): 58–66 and 29; pt. 2: no. 4 (1981): 73–75; and pt. 3: no. 1 (1982): 70–78.

Wang Zhongshu 王仲殊. "Guanyu Riben guduoheng zhidu de yuanliu" [Sources of the ancient Japanese city system] 關于日本古都城制度的源流. *Kaogu* no. 4 (1982): 354–370.

———. "Han Chang'an Cheng kaogu gongzuo de chubu shouhuo" [Early results in excavation at Han Chang'an] 漢長安城考古工作的初步收获. *Kaogu tongxun* no. 5 (1957): 102–104.

———. "Han Chang'an Cheng kaogu gongzuo shouhuo xuji" [Further notes on excavation at Han Chang'an] 漢長安城考古工作收获續記. *Kaogu tongxun* no. 4 (1958): 23–32.

———. "Zhongguo gudai ducheng gaishuo" [General discussion of ancient Chinese cities] 中國古代都城概說. *Kaogu* no. 5 (1982): 505–515.

Wei Hong [Han] and Sun Xingyan [Qing], compiler 衛宏 孫星衍. *Han jiuyi* [Ancient ceremonies of the Han] 漢舊儀. *Zhibuzu Zhai congshu*. Vol. 3. Reprint. Changsha: Shangwu Press, 1939.

Wei Shou [506–572] 魏收. *Wei shu* [History of the Wei] 魏書.

Wei Shu [Tang] 韋述. *Liangjing xinji* [New record of the two (Tang) capitals] 兩京新記.

Wei Songshan 魏嵩山. "Hangzhou chengshi de xingqi ji qichengqu de fazhan" [The rise of Hangzhou and the development of its city districts] 杭州城市的興起及其城區的發展. *Lishi dili* 1 (1981): 160–168.

Wei Wangqi 魏王基. *Kuodi zhi* [Record of drawing together the land] 括地志.

Wei Zheng [580–643] 魏徵. *Sui shu* [History of the Sui] 隋書.

Wei Zuncheng 魏存成. "Bohai chengzhi de faxian yu fenqi" [Excavation and stages of Bohai city remains] 渤海城址的發現與分期. *Dongbei kaogu yu lishi* no. 1 (1982): 89–94.

Wu Liangyong 吳良鏞. "Beijing Shi guihua chuyi" [My opinion about the design of Beijing] 北京市規劃芻議. *Jianzhu shi lunwen ji* 3 (1979): 167–176.

———. "Tian'an Men guangchang de guihua" [The plan and construction of Tian'an Men Square] 天安門廣場的規劃. *Jianzhu shi lunwen ji* 2 (1979): 14–50.

Wu Yongjiang 吳永江. "Tang Daming Gong yizhi" [Remains of Tang Daming Gong] 唐大明宮遺址. *Wenwu* no. 7 (1981): 90–92.

Wu Zimu 吳自牧. *Mengliang lu* [Dreaming of the capital while rice is cooking] 夢粱錄. 1274 or 1334.

Xi'an Banpo [Banpo at Xi'an] 西安半坡. Beijing: Wenwu Press, 1982.

Xi'an wenwu yu guyi [Cultural relics and ancient remains at Xi'an] 西安文物與古遺. Beijing: Wenwu Press, 1983.

Xiang Qiuhua 項秋華. "Qian Han gongdian jianzhu dui zhengju de yingxiang" [The influence of politics on Early Han palace architecture] 前漢宮殿建築對政局的影響. Ph.D. dissertation, Zhonghua Wenhua Xueyuan, 1981.

Xianshun Lin'an zhi [Record of Lin'an written during the *xianshun* reign [1265–1275] 咸淳臨安志.

Xiao Tong [501–531] 蕭統. *Wen xuan* [Literary collection] 文選.

Xiao Xun 蕭洵. *Gugong yi lu* [Record of the remains of imperial palaces] 故宮遺錄. 1398. Reprint. Taipei: Shijie Press, 1963.

Xu Jiarui 徐嘉瑞. "Bei Song shoudu de minzhong shenghuo ji qiyishu" [People's life and their art in the Northern Song capital] 北宋首都的民眾生活及其藝術. *Yuyan wenxue zhuankan* 1 (1936): 89–100.

Xu Jinxing 徐金星. *Luoyang Baima Si* [Baima Monastery at Luoyang] 洛陽白馬寺. Beijing: Wenwu Press, 1985.

Xu Pingfang 徐苹芳. "Bei Song Kaifeng Da Xiangguo Si pingmian fuyuan tushuo" [Illustrations and discussion of the plan of Xiangguo Monastery at Kaifeng from the Northern Song] 北宋開封大相國寺平面復原圖說. In *Wenwu yu kaogu lunji*, pp. 357–369. Beijing: Wenwu Press, 1987.

———. "Gudai Beijing de chengshi guihua" [The city plan of old Beijing] 古代北京的城市規劃. In *Huanjing bianqian yanjiu*, ed. Hou Renzhi, pp. 115–121. Beijing: Haiyang Press, 1984.

———. "Tangdai liangjing de zhengzhi, jingji, he wenhua shenghuo" [Government, economics, and cultural life in the two Tang capitals] 唐代兩京的政治經濟和文化生活. *Kaogu* no. 6 (1982): 647–656.

———. "Yuan Dadu Yelikewen shizisi kao" [Research on Christian churches at Yuan Dadu] 元大都也里可溫十字寺考. In *Zhongguo kaoguxue yanjiu*, pp. 309–316. Beijing: Wenwu Press, 1986.

Xu Song [1741–1848], compiler 徐松. *Song huiyao jigao* [Rules and regulations of the Song] 宋會要輯稿. Reprint. Beijing: Guoli Beijing Tushuguan, 1936.

———. *Tang liangjing chengfang kao* [Research on the city districts of the two Tang capitals] 唐兩京城坊考. 1848. Reprint. Taipei: Shijie Press, 1974.

Xu Xunsheng 徐旭生. "Yijiuwushijiu-nian Yuxi diaocha 'Xiaxu' de chubu baogao" [Early report of the 1959 excavation of the remains of Xia west of Yu] 一九五九年豫西調查「夏墟」的初步報告. *Kaogu* no. 11 (1959): 592–600.

Yan Chongnian 閻崇年. *Zhongguo lidai ducheng gongyuan* [Cities and palaces of China through history] 中國歷代都城宮苑. Beijing: Zijin Cheng Press, 1987.

Yan Wenru 閻文儒. "Jin Zhongdu" [Jin Zhongdu] 金中都. *Wenwu* no. 9 (1959): 8–12.

———. "Luoyang Han, Wei, Sui, Tang chengzhi kancha ji" [Record of excavation at the Han, Wei, Sui, and Tang sites of Luoyang] 洛陽漢魏隋唐城址勘查記. *Kaogu xuebao* no. 9 (1955): 117–136.

———. "Sui–Tang Dongdu Cheng he jianzhu ji qixingzhi" [Sui–Tang eastern capital architecture and its system] 隋唐東都城和建築及其形制. *Beijing Daxue xuebao* 4 (1956): 81–100.

"Yan Xiadu di'ershi'er hao yizhi fajue baogao" [Excavation report of Site 22 at Yan Xiadu] 燕下都第二十二號遺址發掘報告. *Kaogu* no. 11 (1965): 562–570.

Yang Hongxun 楊鴻勛. "Cong Panlong Cheng Shangdai

gongdian yizhi tan Zhongguo gongdian jianzhu fazhan de jige wenti" [Several questions concerning the development of Chinese palatial architecture in the light of Shang palace remains from Panlong Cheng] 從盤龍城商代宮殿遺址談中國宮殿建築發展的幾個問題. *Wenwu* no. 2 (1976): 16–25.

——. "Fengxiang chutu Chun Qiu Qingong tonggou—jingong" [Excavation at Fengxiang of copper beams and golden hangers from Qin palaces of the Spring and Autumn period] 鳳翔出土春秋秦宮銅构—金釭. *Kaogu* no. 2 (1976): 103–108.

——. *Jianzhu kaoguxue lunwen ji* [Collected essays on architectural archaeology] 建築考古學論文記. Beijing: Wenwu Press, 1987.

——. "Tang Chang'an Cheng Qinglong Si Mizong Diantang (yizhi si) fuyuan yanjiu" [Research on the reconstruction of the Esoteric Hall (remains no. 4) at Qinglong Monastery from Tang Chang'an] 唐長安城青龍寺密宗殿堂(遺址四)復原研究. *Kaogu xuebao* no. 3 (1984): 383–401.

——. "Xi Zhou qiyi jianzhu yizhi chubu kaocha" (Preliminary investigation of the architectural remains from the Western Zhou at Qishan] 西周岐邑建築遺址初步考察. *Wenwu* no. 3 (1981): 23–33.

——. "Zhan Guo Zhongshan wang ling ji zhaoyu tu yanjiu" [Research on the tomb and plan of the Zhongshan kings of the Warring States period] 戰國中山王陵及兆域圖研究. *Kaogu xuebao* no. 1 (1980): 119–138.

Yang Kuan 楊寬. *Zhongguo gudai lingqin zhidu shi yanjiu* [Research into the history of the ancient Chinese tomb system] 中國古代陵寢制度史研究. Shanghai: Guji Press, 1985.

Yang Naiji 楊乃濟. "*Qianlong jingcheng quantu* kaolue" [Summary of research on *Qianlong jingcheng quantu*] 「乾隆京城金圖」考略. *Gugong Bowu Yuan yuankan* no. 4 (1984): 8–24.

Yang Shoujing [1839–1915] 楊守敬. *Shui jing zhu tu* [Illustrated commentary on the *Shui jing*] 水經注圖. Reprint. Taipei: Wenhai Press, 1966.

Yang Xuanzhi [d. 555?] 楊衒之. *Luoyang qielan ji* [Record of Buddhist monasteries of Luoyang] 洛陽伽藍記.

"Yanshi Shang cheng de chubu shentan he fajue" [Preliminary stages of excavation and investigation of the Shang city at Yanshi] 偃師商城的初步勘探和發掘. *Kaogu* no. 6 (1984): 488–504.

Yao Congwu 姚從吾. *Dongbei shi luncong* [Essays on the history of the northeastern provinces] 東北史論叢. Taipei: Zhengzhong Book Company, 1959.

Yao Jiazao 樂嘉藻. *Zhongguo jianzhu shi* [History of Chinese architecture] 中國建築史. 1933. Reprint. Taipei: Huashi Press, 1977.

Ye Dasong 葉大松. *Zhongguo jianzhu shi* [History of Chinese architecture] 中國建築史. Pt. 1. Taipei: Xinming Press, 1971. Pt. 2. Taipei: Zhongguo Dianji Jishu Press, 1976.

Ye Longli [Song] 葉隆禮. *Qidan Guo zhi* [Record of the Khitan state] 契丹國志.

Ye Ziqi 葉子奇. *Caomu zi* [Grass and wood] 草木子. 1875.

"Yecheng diaocha ji" [Record of excavation at Ye] 鄴城調查記. *Kaogu* no. 1 (1963): 15–24.

Yi Jiasheng 易家胜. *Nanjing wenwu yu guyi* [Cultural relics and ancient remains in Nanjing] 南京文物與古遺. Beijing: Wenwu Press, 1982.

Yi Zhou shu [Lost history of the Zhou] 逸周書.

"Yijiubashisan-nian qiuqi Henan Yanshi Shang cheng fajue jianbao" [Brief report on the excavation of a palace at the Shang city at Yanshi, Henan, in autumn 1983] 一九八三年秋期河南偃師商城發掘簡報. *Kaogu* no. 10 (1984): 872–879.

"Yijiubashisi-nian chun Yanshi Shixianggou Shang cheng gongdian fajue baogao" [Brief report on the excavation of a palace at the Shang city Shixianggou at Yanshi in spring 1984] 一九八四年春偃師尸乡沟商城宮殿發掘報告. *Kaogu* no. 4 (1985): 322–335.

"Yijiuliushisi-yijiuliushiwu-nian Yan Xiadu muzang baogao" [Excavation report on the tombs from Yan Xiadu uncovered from 1964 to 1965] 一九六四--一九六五年燕下都墓葬報告. *Kaogu* no. 11 (1965): 548–561.

Yin Weizhang 殷瑋璋. "Erlitou wenhua zai tantao" [Another discussion of Erlitou culture] 二里頭文化再探討. *Kaogu* no. 4 (1984): 352–356.

Yongle dadian [Encyclopedia of the Yongle reign] 永樂大典. *Juan* 9561. 1408.

Yoshida Mitsukuni 吉田光邦. "Kandai no toshi" [Han cities] 漢代の都市. *Tōhō gakuhō* 67, no. 11 (1974): 217–242.

Yu Fuwei 余扶危. *Sui–Tang Dongdu Hanjia Cang* [Hanjia Storehouse from the Sui–Tang eastern capital] 隋唐東都含嘉倉. Beijing: Wenwu Press, 1982.

Yu Ji [Yuan] 虞集. "Dadu Chenghuang Miao bei" [Stele of the City-God Temple at Dadu] 大都城隍廟碑. *Daoyuan xuegu lu. Juan* 23.

Yu Minzhong 于敏中. *Rexia jiuwen kao* [Research on *Rexia jiuwen*] 日下舊文考. 1774.

Yu Weichao 俞偉超. "Han Chang'an Cheng xibeibu kancha ji" [Record of the investigation in the northwestern suburbs of Han Chang'an] 漢長安城西北部勘查記. *Kaogu tongxun* no. 5 (1966): 20–26.

———. "Zhongguo gudai ducheng guihua de fazhan jieduan xing" [Stages in the development of ancient Chinese city planning] 中國古代都城規劃的發展阶段性. *Wenwu* no. 2 (1985): 52–60.

Yu Zhuoyun 于倬雲. *Zijin Cheng gongdian* [Palaces of the Forbidden City] 紫禁城宮殿. Hong Kong: Shangwu Press, 1982.

"Yuan Dadu de kancha he fajue" [Excavation and investigation at Yuan Dadu] 元大都的勘查和發掘. *Kaogu* no. 1 (1972): 19–28.

Zeng Gongliang, editor 曾公亮. *Wujing zongyao* [Collection of important military techniques] 武經總要. ca. 1040. Reprint. *Siku quanshu zhenben chuji* nos. 167–171. Taipei: Shangwu Press, n.d.

Zhang Anzhi 張安治. *Qingming shanghe tu* [The painting *Qingming shanghe tu* (Springtime festival on the river)] 清明上河圖. Beijing: Renmin Meishu Press, 1979.

Zhang Congxian and Dong Zengzhen [Qing] 張聰賢 董曾臣. *Chang'an Xian zhi* [Record of Chang'an district] 長安縣志.

Zhang Longhai and Zhu Yude 張龍海 朱玉德. "Linzi Qi Guo gucheng de paishui xitong" [The drainage system at Linzi of the Qi state] 臨淄齊國故城的排水系統. *Kaogu* no. 9 (1988): 784–787.

Zhang Ning 張寧. "Ji Yuan Dadu chutu wenwu" [Notes on objects excavated at Yuan Dadu] 記元大都出土文物. *Kaogu* no. 6 (1972): 25–31 and 58.

Zhang Pingzi [Heng] (78–139) 張平子(衡). "Dongjing fu" [Eastern metropolis rhapsody] 東京賦. *Wen xuan.*

———. "Xijing fu" [Western metropolis rhapsody] 西京賦. *Wen xuan.*

Zhang Yuhuan 張馭寰. *Zhongguo gudai jianzhu jishu shi* [History of Chinese architecture and technology] 中國古代建築技術史. Beijing: Kexue Press, 1985.

Zhang Zugang 張祖剛. "Cong Beijing Cheng de lishi lai yanjiu Beijing jiucheng de baohu guihua" [Preservation planning of the old city of Beijing based on the history of Beijing] 從北京城的歷史來研究北京舊城的保護規劃. *Zhongguo lishi yu lilun* 3–4 (1982–1983): 75–89.

Zhao Zhengzhi 趙正之. "Yuan Dadu pingmian guihua fuyuan de yanjiu" [Research on the plan of Yuan Dadu and its reconstruction] 元大都平面規劃復原的研究. *Kaogu xuebao* no. 1 (1966): 125–141. Written posthumously by Xu Pingfang.

Zhao Zhiquan and Liu Zhongfu 趙芝荃 劉忠伏. "Henan

Yanshi Shixianggou Shang cheng diwuhao gongdian qizhi fajue jianbao" [Brief report on the excavation of Palace Foundation 5 at the Shang city Shixianggou, Yanshi, Henan] 河南偃師尸乡沟商城第五號宮殿基址發掘簡報. *Kaogu* no. 2 (1988): 128–140.

Zhongguo gudu yanjiu [Research ancient Chinese cities] 中國古都研究. Hangzhou: Zhejiang Renmin Press, 1986.

Zhongguo jianzhu jianshi [Short history of Chinese architecture] 中國建築簡史. 2 vols. Beijing: Zhongguo Gongye Press, 1957.

Zhongguo kaoguxue yanjiu [Research on Chinese archaeology] 中國考古學研究. Beijing: Wenwu Press, 1986.

"Zhongguo Kexue Yuan Kaogu Yanjiu Suo yijiuliushi-nian tianye gongzuo de zhuyao shouhuo" [Important gains in fieldwork of the Archaeology Research Institute of the Chinese Academy of Sciences in 1960] 中國科學院考古研究所一九六〇年田野工作的主要收获. *Kaogu* no. 4 (1961): 214–218.

Zhou Boqi [Yuan] 周伯琦. *Shangjingyi congzhu* [Collected writings on Shangdu] 上京邑叢書. Reprint. *Siku quanshu*, no. 108. Taipei: Shangwu Press, 1971.

Zhou Cong, editor [Song] 周淙. *Qiandao Lin'an zhi* [*Lin'an zhi* written in the *qiandao* reign (1165–1174)] 乾道臨安志. Reprint. Shanghai: Shangwu Press, 1936.

Zhou Mi 周密. *Wulin jiushi* [Old affairs of the military grove] 武林舊事. ca. 1280–1290.

Zhu Qiqian [1871–1962] 朱啓鈐. "Jin Zhongdu gongdian tukao" [Plans and research on the halls of Jin Zhongdu] 金中都宮殿圖考. *Wenwu cankao ziliao* no. 7 (1955): 69–75.

———. "Liao–Jin Yanjing chengguo gongyuan tukao" [Plans and research on the halls and gardens of Liao–Jin Yanjing] 遼金燕京城郭宮苑圖考. *Wenzhe jikan* 6, no. 1 (1939): 49–81.

Zhu Qiqian and Gan Duo 朱啓鈐 闞鐸. "Yuan Dadu gongyuan tukao" [Plans and research on the halls and gardens of Yuan Dadu] 元大都宮苑圖考. *Zhongguo yingzao xueshe huikan* 1, no. 3 (1930): 1–118.

Zhu Xie 朱偰. *Jinling guji mingteng yingji* [Collection of notable spots that remain in Jinling (Nanjing)] 金陵古蹟名勝影集. Shanghai: Shangwu Press, 1936.

———. *Jinling guji tukao* [Pictures and research on ancient remains in Jinling] 金陵古蹟圖考. Shanghai: Shangwu Press, 1936.

Zhu Yizun 朱彝尊. *Rexia jiuwen* [Record of life day by day] 日下舊聞. 1688.

Zhu Youzeng, editor [Qing] 朱右曾. *Yi Zhou shu jixun jiaoce*

[Collected and collated commentaries on *Yi Zhou shu*] 逸周書集訓校釋. Taipei: Shijie Press, 1956.

Zhuang Jinqing 庄錦清. "Tang Chang'an Cheng xishi yizhi fajue" [Excavated remains of the west market from Tang Chang'an] 唐長安城西市遺址發掘. *Kaogu* no. 5 (1961): 248–250.

Zuo Ming [Xia Nai] 作銘 [夏鼐]. "*Yongle dadian juan* 9561 yin *Yuan Henan zhi* de gudai Luoyang tu shisi fu" [Fourteen illustrations of Luoyang from *Yuan Henan zhi* according to *juan* 9561 of the *Yongle dadian*] 「永樂大典」卷9561引元河南志的古代洛陽圖十四幅. *Kaogu xuebao* no. 2 (1959): 37–55.

Zuo Si [ca. 250–ca. 305] 左思. "Shudu fu" [Shu capital rhapsody] 蜀都賦. *Wen xuan*.

———. "Weidu fu" [Wei capital rhapsody] 魏都賦. *Wen xuan*.

———. "Wudu fu" [Wu capital rhapsody] 吳都賦. *Wen xuan*.

WESTERN LANGUAGES

Abe Takeo. "Where Was the Capital of the West Uighurs?" Translated by Leon Hurwitz. In *Silver Jubilee Volume of the Jimbun Kagaku Kenkyū-sho*, pp. 435–450. Kyoto: Kyoto University, 1954.

Abel-Rémusat, Jean-Pièrre. "Recherches sur la ville de Kara-Korum." *Histoire et mémoires de l'Institut Royal de France* 7 (1824): 234–291.

Akiyama Terukazu. *The Arts of China*. Vol. 2. Alexander Soper, translator. Tokyo and Palo Alto: Kodansha International, 1969.

Arlington, L. C. *The Story of the Peking Hutongs*. Beiping: Henri Vetch, 1931.

Arlington, L. C., and Lewisohn, William. *In Search of Old Peking*. Beiping: Henri Vetch, 1935.

Aston, W. G., translator. *Nihongi*. Rutland: Charles A. Tuttle Company, 1972.

Ayscough, Florence. "Notes on the Symbolism of the Purple Forbidden City." *Journal of the North China Branch of the Royal Asiatic Society* 52 (1921): 51–78.

Bagley, Robert. "P'an-long-ch'eng: A Shang City in Hupei." *Artibus Asiae* 39, nos. 3/4 (1977): 165–219.

Bart'old, Vasilii V. *Turkestan Down to the Mongol Invasions*. London: Luzac, 1958.

Belenitskii, A. M., Bentovich, I. B., and Bol'shakov, O. G. *Srednevekovyi gorod Srednei Azii*. Leningrad: Nauka, 1973.

Bennett, Steven. "Patterns of the Sky and Earth: A Chinese Science of Applied Cosmology." *Chinese Science* 3 (1978): 27–38.

Bichurin, Iakinf. *Zapiski o Mongolii*. 2 vols. St. Petersburg: Kapla Kraija, 1828.

Bielenstein, Hans. "Lo-yang in Later Han Times." *Bulletin of the Museum of Far Eastern Antiquities* 48 (1976): 1–142.

———. "The Restoration of the Han Dynasty." *Bulletin of the Museum of Far Eastern Antiquities* 26 (1954): 1–209.

Biot, Edouard, translator. *Le Tcheou-li*. 2 vols. Paris: Imprimerie nationale, 1851.

Bishop, Carl Whiting. "An Ancient Chinese Capital, Earthworks at old Ch'ang-an." *Antiquity* 13 (1938): 68–78.

Bouillard, G. "Note Succinct sur l'Histoire de Peking et sur les Diverses Encientes de cette Ville." *Bulletin of the Museum of Far Eastern Antiquities* 1 (1929): 39–60.

Boyd, Andrew. *Chinese Architecture and Town Planning*. London: Tiranti Press, 1962.

Boyle, John A. *History of the World Conqueror*. 2 vols. Cambridge: Harvard University Press, 1958.

———. *The Mongol World Empire*. London: Variorum Reprints, 1977.

———. *The Successors of Genghis Khan*. New York: Columbia University Press, 1971.

Bredon, Juliet. *Peking*. Shanghai: Kelly & Walsh, 1922.

Bretschneider, Emil. *Archeological and Historical Researches on Peking and Its Environs*. Shanghai: American Presbyterian Mission Press, 1876.

Buck, David. "Directions in Chinese Urban Planning." *Urbanism Past and Present* 1 (1975–1976): 24–35.

Buck, David, editor and translator. "Archeological Explorations at the Ancient Capital of Lu at Qufu in Shandong Province." *Chinese Sociology and Anthropology* 19, no. 1 (1986): 1–76.

Bulling, Annelise Gutkind. "Ancient Chinese Maps." *Expeditions* 20, no. 2 (1978): 16–25.

Bush, Susan. "Archeological Remains of the Chin Dynasty (1115–1234)." *Bulletin of Sung-Yuan Studies* 17 (1981): 6–31.

Cameron, Nigel. *Barbarians and Mandarins*. New York and Tokyo: John Weatherhill, 1970.

Cameron, Nigel, and Brake, Brian. *Peking: A Tale of Three Cities*. New York: Harper & Row, 1965.

Chan Hok-lam. *The Historiography of the Chin Dynasty: Three Studies*. Wiesbaden: Steiner, 1970.

———. "Liu Ping-chung (1216–74): A Buddhist-Taoist Statesman at the Court of Khubilai Khan." *T'oung Pao* 53 (1967): 98–146.

Chang Chun-shu. *Premodern China: A Bibliographical Introduction*. Ann Arbor: University of Michigan Center for Chinese Studies, 1971.

Chang Kwang-chih. *The Archeology of Ancient China.* 4th ed. New Haven and London: Yale University Press, 1986. (Notes are cited from 3d ed., 1977.)

———. *Early Chinese Civilization: Anthropological Perspectives.* Cambridge: Harvard University Press, 1976.

———. *Shang Civilization.* New Haven and London: Yale University Press, 1980.

Chang Sen-dou. "The Historical Trend of Chinese Urbanization." *Annals of the American Association of Geographers* 53, no. 2 (1963): 109–143.

———. "The Morphology of Walled Capitals." In *The City in Late Imperial China,* ed. G. William Skinner, pp. 75–100. Stanford: Stanford University Press, 1977.

———. "Peking: The Growing Metropolis of Communist China." *Geographical Review* 55, no. 3 (July 1965): 313–327.

———. "Some Aspects of the Urban Geography of the Chinese Hsien Capital." *Annals of the American Association of Geographers* 51 (1961): 23–45.

Chen, C. Z. "Some Ancient Chinese Concepts of Town and Country." *Town and Planning Review* 19 (1943): 160–163.

Chen Cheng-siang. "The Growth of Peiching." *Ekistics* no. 253 (December 1976): 377–383.

———. "The Urban Development of Peking." *Journal of the Institute of Chinese Studies of the Chinese University of Hong Kong* 7, no. 1 (December 1974): 41–94.

Cheng Te-k'un [Zheng Dekun]. "Chin-Han Architectural Remains." *Zhongguo wenhua yanjiusuo xuebao* 9 (1978): 503–584.

Chinese Academy of Architecture. *Ancient Chinese Architecture.* Beijing and Hong Kong: China Building Industry Press and Joint Publishing Company, 1982.

Cleaves, Francis. "The Sino-Mongolian Inscription of 1346." *Harvard Journal of Asiatic Studies* 15, nos. 1–2 (1952): 1–123.

Cleaves, Francis, translator. *The Secret History of the Mongols.* Cambridge: Harvard University Press, 1982.

Clément, Pierre. *Les Capitales chinoises, leur modèle et leur site.* Paris: L'institut Français d'Architecture, 1983.

Clément, Sophie, et al. *Architecture du paysage en Asie orientale.* Paris: L'institut Français d'Architecture, 1982.

Crump, J. I. *Chan-kuo Ts'e.* Oxford: Oxford University Press, 1970.

Dawson, Christopher. *The Mongol Mission.* London: Sheed & Ward, 1955.

De Bary, William Theodore, and Embree, A. T., editors. *A Guide to Oriental Classics.* New York: Columbia University Press, 1964.

De Bary, William Theodore, et al. *Sources of Chinese Tradition.* Vol. 1. New York: Columbia University Press, 1960.

De Crespigny, R. *The Records of the Three Kingdoms: A Study in the Historiography of the San Kuo Chi.* Canberra: Australian National University Centre of Oriental Studies, 1970.

De Groot, J.J.M. *The Religious System of China.* 6 vols. Leyden: E. J. Brill, 1892–1910.

De Guignes, Joseph. *Voyages à Peking, Manille et l'Île de France faits dans l'intervalle des années 1784 à 1801.* Paris: Imprimerie Impériale, 1808.

De Rachewiltz, Igor. *Papal Envoys to the Great Khan.* Stanford: Stanford University Press, 1971.

Dien, Albert. *Pei Ch'i Shu 45: Biography of Yen Chih-t'ui.* Bern: Herbert Lang, 1976.

Du Halde, J. B. *Déscription geographique, historique, chronologique, politique, et physique de l'empire de la Chine et de la Tartarie chinoise.* Paris: Henri Scheurleer, 1736.

Dubs, Homer, translator. *The History of the Former Han Dynasty.* 3 vols. Baltimore: Waverly Press, 1938–1955.

Eberhard, Wolfram. "The Structure of the Pre-Industrial Chinese City." *Settlement and Social Change in Asia.* Hong Kong: Hong Kong University Press, 1967.

Edkins, Joseph. *Description of Peking.* Shanghai: Shanghai Mercury Office, 1898.

Eisenstadt, Shmuel. *The Political Systems of Empires.* New York: Free Press of Glencoe, 1963.

Elvin, Mark. "Chinese Cities Since the Sung Dynasty." In *Towns in Societies,* Essays in Economic History and Historical Sociology, ed. Philip Abrams and E. A. Wrigley, pp. 79–89. Cambridge: Cambridge University Press, 1978.

Elvin, Mark, and Skinner, G. William, editors. *The Chinese City Between Two Worlds.* Stanford: Stanford University Press, 1974.

Farmer, Edward L. *Early Ming Government: The Evolution of Dual Capitals.* Cambridge: Harvard University Press, 1976.

Favier, Alphonse. *Peking: histoire et déscription.* Paris: Imprimerie des Lazaristes au Pé-t'ang, 1897.

Fei Hsiao-t'ung [Xiaotong]. "New Peking—The People's Capital." *People's China* 1, no. 3 (February 1950): 9–11.

Feuchtwang, Stephan. "School-Temple and City God." In *The City in Late Imperial China,* ed. G. William Skinner, pp. 581–608. Stanford: Stanford University Press, 1977.

Fong, Wen, editor. *The Great Bronze Age of China.* New York: Metropolitan Museum of Art, 1980.

Freedman, Maurice. "Geomancy." *Proceedings of the Royal Anthropological Institute of Great Britain and Ireland* 98 (1968): 5–15.

Gaillard, Louis. *Nankin d'alors et d'aujourd'hui*. Shanghai: Catholic Mission, 1903.

Gallagher, Louis J., S. J., translator. *China in the Sixteenth Century: The Journals of Matthew Ricci: 1583–1610*. New York: Random House, 1942.

Gamble, Sidney. *Peking: A Social Survey*. New York: George H. Doran Company, 1921.

Geil, William E. *The Eighteen Capitals of China*. London: Constable, 1911.

Geiss, James. "Peking Under the Ming." Ph.D. dissertation, Princeton University, 1979.

Gernet, Jacques. *Daily Life in China on the Eve of the Mongol Invasion, 1250–1275*. Stanford: Stanford University Press, 1970.

———. "Note sur les villes chinoises au moment de l'apogée islamique." In *The Islamic City*, ed. A. M. Hourani and S. M. Stern, pp. 77–85. Philadelphia: University of Pennsylvania Press, 1970.

Granet, Marcel. *La pensée chinoise*. Paris: La Renaissance du livre, 1934.

Haeger, John W., editor. *Crisis and Prosperity in Sung China*. Tucson: University of Arizona Press, 1975.

Hakeda, Yoshito. *Kūkai: Major Works*. New York: Columbia University Press, 1972.

Handlin, Oscar. *The Historian and the City*. Cambridge: Harvard University Press, 1963.

Harper, A. P. "A Visit to Peking." *China Recorder* no. 10 (1879): 23–27.

Hartwell, Robert. "A Cycle of Economic Change in Imperial China: Coal and Iron in Northeast China, 750–1350." *Journal of the Economic and Social History of the Orient* 10, no. 2 (1967): 102–159.

Hefter, Jonny. "Ming-t'ang-miao-ch'in-t'ung-k'ao." *Ostasiatische Zeitschrift* 17 (1931): 70–86.

Hermann, Albert. *An Historical Atlas of China*. Chicago: Aldine Publishing Company, 1966.

Ho Ping-ti. "Lo-yang, A.D. 495–534." *Harvard Journal of Asiatic Studies* 26 (1966): 52–101.

Hotaling, Stephen. "The City Walls of Han Chang'an." *T'oung Pao* 64, nos. 1–3 (1978): 1–46.

Hou Renzhi. "The Transformation of the Old City of Beijing, China." In *World Patterns of Modern Urban Change*, ed. M. Conzen, pp. 217–239. Chicago: University of Chicago Department of Geography, 1986.

Hucker, Charles O. *China: A Critical Bibliography*. Tucson: University of Arizona Press, 1962.

Hwang Ming-chorng [Huang Mingchong]. "A Study of Urban Form in Eighteenth Century Beijing." M.A. thesis, M.I.T., 1986.

Ignatius, Father Ying Ch'ien-li. "Hsiao's Record of the Imperial Palaces of Khanbaliq." *Bulletin of the Catholic University of Peking* 8 (1934): 27–46.

Impey, L. "Shang-tu, Summer Capital of Khubilai Khan." *Geographical Review* 20 (1925): 584–604.

Jagchid, Sechin. "The Kitans and Their Cities." *Central Asiatic Journal* 25, nos. 1–2 (1981): 70–88.

Jahn, Karl. "Rashīd al-Dīn and Chinese Culture." *Central Asiatic Journal* 15 (1970): 134–147.

Jenner, W.J.F. *Memories of Lo-yang, 495–534*. New York and Oxford: Oxford University Press, 1981.

Jin Shoushen. *Beijing Legends*. Beijing: Panda Books, 1982.

Johnson, David. "The City-God Cults of T'ang and Sung China." *Harvard Journal of Asiatic Studies* 45, no. 2 (1985): 363–457.

Juliano, Annette. *Art of the Six Dynasties*. New York: China Institute, 1973.

Karlgren, Bernhard. "The Book of Documents." *Bulletin of the Museum of Far Eastern Antiquities* 22 (1950): 1–82.

———. *The Book of Odes*. Stockholm: Museum of Far Eastern Antiquities, 1950.

———. "The Early History of the *Chou li* and *Tso chuan* texts." *Bulletin of the Museum of Far Eastern Antiquities* 3 (1931): 1–59.

———. "Glosses on the Book of Documents." *Bulletin of the Museum of Far Eastern Antiquities* 20 (1948): 39–315.

———. "Glosses on the Book of Documents II." *Bulletin of the Museum of Far Eastern Antiquities* 21 (1949): 63–206.

Kates, George. "A New Date for the Origins of the Forbidden City." *Harvard Journal of Asiatic Studies* 7 (1942–1943): 180–202.

Keightley, David. *Sources of Shang History*. Berkeley and Los Angeles: University of California Press, 1978.

Kiselev, Sergei. "Drevnie goroda Mongolii." *Sovetskaia Arkheologiia* 2 (1957): 91–101.

———. *Drevnemongol'skie goroda*. Moscow: Nauka, 1965.

Knechtges, David. *The Han Rhapsody*. Cambridge: Cambridge University Press, 1976.

Knechtges, David, translator and annotator. *Wen xuan*. Princeton: Princeton University Press, 1982.

Kozlov, P. K. *Mongolei, Amdo und die tote Staat Chara-Choto*. Berlin: Neufeld & Henius, 1925.

Kracke, Edward. "Sung K'ai-feng: Pragmatic Metropolis and Formalistic Capital." In *Crisis and Prosperity in Sung China*, ed. John Haeger, pp. 49–77. Tucson: University of Arizona Press, 1975.

Kwanten, Luc. *Imperial Nomads*. Philadelphia: University of Pennsylvania Press, 1979.

L'architecture d'aujourd'hui 201 (February 1979).

Legge, James. *The Ch'un Ts'ew with the Tso Chuen*. Vol. 5 of *The Chinese Classics*. Oxford: Oxford University Press, 1872.

Legge, James, Chai, and Chai. *Li Chi: Book of Rites*. 2 vols. New Hyde Park: University Books, 1967.

Leung. C. K., and Ginsburg, Norton. *China: Urbanization and National Development*. Chicago: University of Chicago Press, 1980.

Lewis, John W., editor. *The City in Communist China*. Stanford: Stanford University Press, 1971.

Li Chi [Ji]. *Anyang*. Seattle: University of Washington Press, 1977.

Li Xueqin. *Eastern Zhou and Qin Civilizations*. New Haven: Yale University Press, 1985.

Lin Yu-tang. *Imperial Peking*. London: Elek Books, 1961.

Liu, James T. C. "The Sung Emperors and the *ming-t'ang* or Hall of Enlightenment." *Études Song i Memoriam Étienne Balazs*, ed. Françoise Aubin, pp. 45–58. Ser. 2, no. 1. Paris: Mouton, 1973.

Loewe, Michael. *Everyday Life in Early Imperial China*. New York: Harper & Row, 1968.

———. "The Growth of Cities." In *Imperial China*, ed. Michael Loewe, pp. 221–246. London: Allen & Unwin, 1966.

Lu Yu-tsun. "Re-evaluation of Ancient Chinese City Planning." *Chinese Culture* 2, no. 4 (1960): 17–31.

Lubo-Lesnichenko, E. I. "Istoriko-Arkheologicheskoe izuchenie g. Khara-Khoto." *Strany i narody Vostoka* 6 (1968): 115–124.

Ma, Laurence. "The Chinese Approach to City Planning." *Asian Survey* 19 (September 1979): 838–855.

———. *Commercial Development and Urban Change in Sung China*. Geographical Publication no. 6. Ann Arbor: University of Michigan, 1971.

March, Andrew. "An Appreciation of Chinese Geomancy." *Journal of Asian Studies* 27, no. 2 (February 1968): 253–267.

Maspero, Henri. "Le Ming-t'ang et la Crise Religieuse chinoise avant les Han." *Mélanges chinoises et bouddhiques* 9 (1948–1951): 1–71.

Meyer, Jeffrey. *Peking as a Sacred City*. Taipei: Orient Cultural Service, 1976.

Miyazaki Ichisada. "Les villes en Chine a l'Époque des Han." *T'oung Pao* 48, nos. 4–5 (1960): 376–392.

Moscato, Michael, compiler. *Imperial Cities: The Capitals of Japan from the Oldest Times Until 1229*. Writings of Richard A. Ponsonby-Fane. Frederick, Md.: University Publications of America, 1979.

Mote, Frederick. "Cities in North and South China." In *Symposium on Historical, Archaeological and Linguistic Studies on Southern China, Southeast Asia and the Hong Kong Region*, ed. F. S. Drake, pp. 153–155. Hong Kong: University of Hong Kong Press, 1967.

———. "The City in Traditional Chinese Civilization." In *Traditional China*, ed. James T. C. Liu and Wei-ming Tu, pp. 42–49. New York: Prentice-Hall, 1970.

———. *Intellectual Foundations of China*. New York: Alfred A. Knopf, 1971.

———. "A Millennium of Chinese Urban History: Form, Time, and Space Concepts in Soochow." *Rice University Studies* 59, no. 4 (1974): 35–65.

———. "The Transformation of Nanking." In *The City in Late Imperial China*, ed. G. William Skinner, pp. 101–153. Stanford: Stanford University Press, 1977.

Moule, Arthur C. "Hang-chou to Shang-tu A.D. 1276." *T'oung Pao* 16 (1915): 393–419.

———. "Marco Polo's Description of Quinsai." *T'oung Pao* 33 (1937): 105–128.

———. *Quinsai with Other Notes on Marco Polo*. Cambridge: Cambridge University Press, 1957.

———. "The Wonder of the Capital." *New China Review* 3 (1921): 1–17 and 356–357.

Moule, Arthur C., and Pelliot, Paul. *Marco Polo: The Description of the World*. London: George Routledge & Sons, 1938.

Mullie, Joseph. "Les anciennes villes de l'empire des grands Leao au royaume Mongol de Bārin." *T'oung Pao* 21 (1922): 105–231.

Murphey, Rhoads. "The City as a Center of Change: Western Europe and China." *Annals of the American Association of Geographers* 64 (December 1954): 349–362.

Needham, Joseph. *Science and Civilization in China*. 7 vols. Cambridge: Cambridge University Press, 1954–1983.

Okladinov, A. P. *The Soviet Far East in Antiquity*. Translations from Russian Sources no. 6. Toronto: University of Toronto Press, 1965.

Pannell, Clifton. "Past and Present City Structure in China." *Town Planning Review* 48 (1977): 157–172.

Pelliot, Paul. "Note sur Karakorum." *Journal Asiatique*, ser. 12, no. 5 (1925): 372–375.

———. *Notes on Marco Polo*. 2 vols. Paris: Imprimerie Nationale, 1959–1963.

Peng, George T. "The Philosophy of the City Design of Peking." *Ekistics* no. 33 (February 1972): 124–129.

Pirazzoli-T'Serstevens, Michèle. *Living Architecture: Chinese.* Robert Allen, translator. New York: Grosset & Dunlap, 1971.

"Planning for the Capital." *China Reconstructs* 21 (October 1972): 3–6.

Playfair, G.M.H. *The Cities and Towns of China.* Reprint. Taipei: Chengwen Publishing Company, 1968.

Ponsonby-Fane, R.A.B. "The Capital and Palace of Heian." *Transactions of the Japan Society of London* 22 (1925): 107–229.

———. *Kyoto, the Old Capital of Japan.* Kamikamo: Ponsonby Memorial Society, 1956.

Pozdniev, A. *Mongolia i Mongoliĭ.* 2 vols. St. Petersburg: Imperial Academy of Science, 1896–1898.

Radlov, V. V. *Atlas der Alterthümer der Mongolei.* St. Petersburg: Akademie der Wissenschaften, 1892.

Ratchnevsky, Paul. "Über den mongolischen Kult am Hofe der Grosskhane in China." In *Mongolian Studies,* ed. Louis Ligeti, pp. 417–443. Amsterdam: B. R. Grüner, 1970.

Rawson, Jessica. *Ancient China: Art and Archeology.* New York: Harper & Row, 1980.

Recent Archaeological Discoveries in the People's Republic of China. Paris: UNESCO, 1984.

Recent Discoveries in Chinese Archeology. Beijing: Foreign Language Press, 1984.

Reischauer, Edwin O. *Ennin's Travels in T'ang China.* New York: Ronald Press, 1955.

Reischauer, Edwin, and Fairbank, John K. *East Asia: The Great Tradition.* Boston: Houghton Mifflin, 1960.

Rickett, W. Allyn. *Guanzi.* Princeton: Princeton University Press, 1985.

Rockhill, William W., translator. *The Journey of William of Rubruck.* London: Hakluyt Society, 1900.

Schafer, Edward. *The Golden Peaches of Samarkand.* Berkeley and Los Angeles: University of California Press, 1963.

———. "The Last Years of Ch'ang-an." *Oriens Extremis,* pt. 2, 10 (1963): 133–179.

———. *Pacing the Void.* Berkeley and Los Angeles: University of California Press, 1977.

Serruys, Henry. "Ta-tu, Tai-tu, Dayidu." *Chinese Culture* 2, no. 4 (1960): 73–96.

Shiba Yoshinobu. *Commerce and Society in Sung China.* Mark Elvin, translator. Ann Arbor: University of Michigan Center for Chinese Studies, 1970.

———. "Urbanization and Development of Markets in the Lower Yangtze Valley." In *Crisis and Prosperity in Sung China,* ed. John Haeger, pp. 13–48. Tucson: University of Arizona Press, 1975.

Sickman, Laurence, and Soper, Alexander. *The Art and Architecture of China.* 3d ed. Harmondsworth: Penguin Books, 1971.

Siren, Osvald. *A History of Chinese Art.* Vol. 4: *Architecture.* London: Ernest Benn, 1930.

———. *The Imperial Palaces of Peking.* 3 vols. Paris: Van Oest, 1926.

———. "Tch'ang-ngan au temps des Souei et des T'ang." *Revue des Arts Asiatiques* 4 (1927): 40–46 and 89–104.

———. *The Walls and Gates of Peking.* 3 vols. London: John Lane, 1924.

Sjoberg, Gideon. *The Pre-industrial City, Past and Present.* Glencoe, Ill.: Free Press, 1960.

Skinner, G. William, editor. *The City in Late Imperial China.* Stanford: Stanford University Press, 1977.

Skinner, R.T.F. "Peking 1953." *Architectural Review* 114, no. 10 (1953): 255–258.

Soothill, William. *The Hall of Light.* London: Lutterworth Press, 1951.

Soper, Alexander. *The Evolution of Buddhist Architecture in Japan.* Princeton: Princeton University Press, 1942.

———. "Hsiang-kuo ssu, an Imperial Temple of the Northern Sung." *Journal of the American Oriental Society* 68, no. 1 (1948): 19–45.

———. *Literary Evidence for Early Buddhist Art in China.* Ascona: Artibus Asiae, 1959.

Spence, Jonathan. *To Change China.* Boston: Little, Brown, 1969.

———. *The Memory Palace of Matteo Ricci.* New York: Viking Penguin, 1984.

Stein, M. Aurel. *Innermost Asia.* 2 vols. Oxford: Clarendon Press, 1928.

Steinhardt, Nancy S. *Chinese Traditional Architecture.* New York: China Institute, 1984.

———. "Imperial Architecture Along the Mongolian Road to Dadu." *Ars Orientalis* 18 (1989): in press.

———. "Imperial Architecture Under Mongolian Patronage: Khubilai's City of Daidu." Ph.D. dissertation, Harvard University, 1981.

———. "The Plan of Khubilai Khan's Imperial City." *Artibus Asiae* 44, nos. 2/3 (1983): 137–158.

———. "Toward the Definition of a Yuan Dynasty Hall." *Journal of the Society of Architectural Historians* 47, no. 1 (1988): 57–73.

———. "Why Were Chang'an and Beijing So Different?"

Journal of the Society of Architectural Historians 45, no. 4 (1986): 339–357.

Stouzhina, Emilie P. *Kitaĭskĭ gorod, XI–XIII vv.* Moscow: Nauka, 1979.

Suzuki Kakichi. *Early Buddhist Architecture in Japan.* Tokyo, New York, and San Francisco: Kodansha International, 1980.

Tao Jing-shen. *The Jurchen in Twelfth Century China.* Seattle: University of Washington Press, 1976.

Thorp, Robert. "An Archeological Reconstruction of the Lishan Necropolis." In *The Great Bronze Age of China: A Symposium,* ed. George Kuwayama, pp. 72–83. Los Angeles County Museum Symposium. Seattle: University of Washington Press, 1983.

———. "Origins of Chinese Architectural Style: The Earliest Plans and Building Types." *Archives of Asian Art* 36 (1983): 22–39.

Till, Barry. *In Search of Old Nanking.* Hong Kong: Joint Publishing Company, 1982.

Toby, Ronald. "Why Leave Nara?" *Monumenta Nipponica* 40, no. 3 (1985): 331–347.

Towers, G. "City Planning in China." *Journal of the Royal Town Planning Institute* 59 (1973): 127–137.

Trewartha, Glenn. "Chinese Cities: Origins and Functions." *Annals of the American Association of Geographers* 42 (March 1952): 69–93.

Tuan Yi-fu. "A Preface to Chinese Cities." In *China,* pp. 218–253. Chicago: Aldine, 1969.

Twitchett, Denis. "Merchant, Trade and Government in Late T'ang." *Asia Major,* n.s. 14, no. 1 (1968): 63–95.

———. "The T'ang Market System." *Asia Major,* n.s. 12, no. 2 (1966): 202–243.

Tyrwhitt, Jacqueline. "The City of Chang'an." *Town Planning Review* 39, no. 1 (1968): 21–27.

Waley, Arthur. *The Book of Songs.* New York: Grove Press, 1937.

Wallacker, Benjamin, et al. *Chinese Walled Cities.* Hong Kong: Chinese University Press, 1979.

Waltham, Clae, translator and modernizer [of Legge]. *The Book of Documents.* Chicago: Henry Regnery, 1971.

Wang Yi-t'ung, translator. Yang Xuanzhi. *A Record of Buddhist Monasteries of Lo-yang.* Princeton: Princeton University Press, 1984.

Wang Zhongshu. *Han Civilization.* New Haven and London: Yale University Press, 1982.

Watson, Burton. *Records of the Grand Historian.* New York and London: Columbia University Press, 1969.

Weber, Max. *The City.* Don Martindale and G. Neuwirth, translators. New York: Free Press, 1966.

Wechsler, Howard. *Offerings of Jade and Silk.* New Haven: Yale University Press, 1985.

Weidner, Marsha Smith. "Painting and Patronage at the Mongol Court of China, 1260–1368." Ph.D. dissertation, University of California, Berkeley, 1982.

West, Stephen. "The Interpretation of a Dream: The Sources, Evaluation, and Influence of the *Dongjing Meng Hua Lu.*" *T'oung Pao* 71 (1985): 63–108.

Wheatley, Paul. "The Ancient Chinese City as a Cosmological Symbol." *Ekistics* no. 39 (March 1975): 147–158.

———. "Archeology and the Chinese City." *World Archeology* 2, no. 2 (1970): 159–185.

———. *The Pivot of the Four Quarters.* Chicago: Aldine, 1972.

Wheatley, Paul, and See, Thomas. *From Court to Capital: A Tentative Interpretation of the Origins of the Japanese Urban Tradition.* Chicago and London: University of Chicago Press, 1978.

Whitfield, Roderick. "Chang Tse-tuan's *Ch'ing-ming shang-ho t'u.*" Ph.D. dissertation, Princeton University, 1965.

———. "Chang Tse-tuan's *Ch'ing-ming shang-ho t'u.*" *Proceedings of the International Symposium on Chinese Painting.* Taipei: National Palace Museum, 1972.

Wittfogel, Karl, and Feng Chia-sheng. *History of Chinese Society: Liao.* Philadelphia: American Philosophical Society, 1949.

Wright, Arthur. "The Cosmology of the Chinese City." In *The City in Late Imperial China,* ed. G. William Skinner, pp. 33–73. Stanford: Stanford University Press, 1977.

———. "Symbolism and Function, Reflections on Ch'ang-an and Other Great Cities." *Journal of Asian Studies* 24, no. 4 (1965): 667–679.

———. *The Sui Dynasty.* New York: Alfred A. Knopf, 1979.

———. "Viewpoints on a City." *Ventures* 5, no. 1 (1965): 15–23.

Wright, Arthur, and Twitchett, Denis, editors. *Perspectives on the T'ang.* New Haven: Yale University Press, 1973.

Wu Liangyong. "A Brief History of Ancient Chinese City Planning." *Urbs et Regio,* vol. 38. Kassel: Gesamthochschulbibliothek, 1986.

Wu, Nelson. *Chinese and Indian Architecture.* New York: George Braziller, 1963.

Xiong Cunrui. "Re-evaluation of the Naba-Chen Theory on

the Exoticism of Daxingcheng, the First Sui Capital." *Papers on Far Eastern History* 35 (March 1987): 135–166.

Yang Boda and Weng Wan-go. *The Palace Museum: Peking.* New York: Abrams, 1982.

Ying Hsu [Xu]. "The Transformation of a City." *People's China* 1, no. 3 (February 1950): 11–16.

Yule, Sir Henry, and Cordier, Henri. *Cathay and the Way Thither.* 4 vols. London: Hakluyt Society, 1913–1916.

About the Author

Nancy Shatzman Steinhardt received her Ph.D. from Harvard University, where she was a Junior Fellow. She is co-translator of *Early Buddhist Architecture in Japan* and author of *Chinese Traditional Architecture* and numerous scholarly articles on Chinese architecture, city planning, wall painting, and Sino-Islamic painting. She is currently assistant professor of art history at the University of Pennsylvania.